VISION
West Nottinghamshire

...nal Studies

Relationship marketing

Visit the *Relationship Marketing, fourth edition* Companion Website at
www.pearsoned.co.uk/egan to find valuable **student** learning material
including

- An online glossary to explain key terms
- Annotated links to relevant sites on the web

Relationship marketing

Exploring relational strategies in marketing

FOURTH EDITION

JOHN EGAN
London South Bank University

Financial Times
Prentice Hall
is an imprint of

Harlow, England • London • New York • Boston • San Francisco • Toronto • Sydney • Singapore • Hong Kong
Tokyo • Seoul • Taipei • New Delhi • Cape Town • Madrid • Mexico City • Amsterdam • Munich • Paris • Milan

Pearson Education Limited

Edinburgh Gate
Harlow
Essex CM20 2JE
England

and Associated Companies throughout the world

Visit us on the World Wide Web at:
www.pearsoned.co.uk

First published 2001
Second edition published 2004
Third edition published 2008
Fourth edition published 2011

ISBN: 978-0-273-73778-0

British Library Cataloguing-in-Publication Data
A catalogue record for this book is available from the British Library

Library of Congress Cataloging-in-Publication Data
Egan, John, 1952–
    Relationship marketing : exploring relational strategies in marketing / John Egan. – 4th ed.
        p. cm.
    Includes bibliographical references and index.
    ISBN 978-0-273-73778-0 (pbk.)
    1. Relationship marketing.   I. Title.
    HF5415.55.E34   2011
    658.8′12–dc22

                                                                                    2011001765

10 9 8 7 6 5 4 3 2
15   14   13   12   11

Typeset in 9/12pt Stone Serif by 35
Printed and bound in Great Britain by Ashford Colour Press Ltd, Gosport, Hampshire

For Alison, Tom and Alice

Contents

Part III Managing and controlling the relationship

11 Relationship management   227

12 Relationship technology   250

13 Conceptual developments   264

Supporting resources

Visit **www.pearsoned.co.uk/egan** to find valuable online resources

Companion Website for students
■ An online glossary to explain key terms
■ Annotated links to relevant sites on the web

For instructors
■ Complete, downloadable Instructor's Manual
■ PowerPoint slides that can be downloaded and used for presentations

For more information please contact your local Pearson Education sales representative or visit
www.pearsoned.co.uk/egan

Preface

As I noted in the first edition, although the main title *Relationship Marketing* sets out the parameters of this text, it is the subtitle that may prove more enlightening. Exploring relational strategies in marketing continues to acknowledge the role that relationship marketing (RM) plays in modern management and establishes the contexts in which RM is most beneficially exercised. This is not, however, a 'how-to' text on relationship marketing, customer relationship management or any of the various relational business subject areas (complete with prescriptive solutions). Rather, this book seeks to generate questions and debate and encourage individual responses to particular marketing situations.

The book is not without bias. It is most definitely written from the viewpoint of marketing as an art rather than a science, and my concerns regarding the mathematical manipulation of sometimes spurious data no doubt resonate in the text. I concur with that body of opinion that views marketing as a 'messy set of rules, tools and guidelines that produce (results) according to the expertise and sensitivity of the craftsman (or craftswoman), not the empirical accuracy of the rules, tools and guidelines' (Damarest, 1997, p. 375). This may understandably annoy some of my more mathematically and statistically minded colleagues.

Despite this one fundamental bias, I have attempted to be objective. This does not negate, however, the responsibility of the reader to make up his or her own mind as to whether to accept or refute any of the positions taken in the text. While reading this book, maintain a healthy scepticism and question conclusions and research findings in whatever way you see fit.

Although not strictly necessary, I have continued the tradition of past editions and fully referenced each author or authors as several research colleagues have indicated that it is useful to them.

Book structure

The book is divided into three parts. Part I discusses ideas surrounding relational strategies in general and, in particular, relationship marketing. Part II analyses over several chapters the central RM tenet of the 'core firm and its relationships'. Part III explores the management process, the place of technology in relational strategy management and the conceptual developments associated with relationship marketing.

New to this edition!

As RM is an evolving discipline, this latest edition references the latest developments in the field. In particular it examines three concepts that are associated with RM: notably customer relationship management (CRM), social marketing and service-dominant logic. The book also examines in greater depth the influence of technological developments such as social media. There are a number of new case studies referencing and highlighting issues discussed in the text. The Glossary has been updated for this edition.

Comprehensive web resources

A complete package of supplements is available to assist students and instructors in using this book. Visit <www.booksites.net/Egan> to find an Instructor's manual, PowerPoint slides and links to other useful sites.

Acknowledgements

The first edition would never have seen the light of day without the help of a number of people whose input I gratefully acknowledge. In particular I would also like to thank the following reviewers for their pre-revision review comments:

Roger Baty, University of Central England
David Gilbert, University of Surrey
Caroline Tynan, Nottingham University Business School
Cleopatra Veloutsou, University of Glasgow
Peter Verhoef, Erasmus University

I am grateful to the publishers, and in particular to David Cox, Andrew Harrison and Chris Shaw, for their support on this latest edition of *Relationship Marketing.*

Last, but very definitely not least, I continue to be grateful to my family for putting up with me locking myself away and to whom this book is dedicated.

I welcome any comments or suggestions regarding this fourth edition. I take this opportunity to thank those readers (students and lecturers in the main) who have made comments and suggestions in the past some of which I have incorporated in this latest edition. As Brown (2002) notes, the ongoing debate over definitions, domains and the nature of the discipline itself is a sign of a healthy and imaginative marketing environment. So let's get healthy!

John Egan
September 2010
eganj@lsbu.ac.uk

References

Brown, S. (2002) 'Vote, vote, vote for Philip Kotler', *European Journal of Marketing*, 36 (3), 313–24.
Damerest, M. (1997) 'Understanding knowledge management', *Long Range Planning* 30 (3), 374–84.

Publisher's acknowledgements

We are grateful to the following for permission to reproduce copyright material:

Figures

Figures 2.1, 2.6, 7.1 and 8.1 adapted from *Relationship Marketing*, London: Butterworth-Heinemann (Christopher, M., Payne, A. and Ballantyne, D. 1991); Figure 2.3 after Towards a paradigm shift in marketing: an examination of current marketing practices, *Journal of Marketing Management*, 13 (5), pp. 383–406 (Brodie, R.J., Coviello, N.E., Brookes, R.W. and Little, V. 1997), © Westburn Publishers Ltd., www.westburn.co.uk, reproduced with permission; Figure 2.4 from The concept of the marketing mix, *Journal of Advertising Research*, 4 (June), pp. 2–7 (Borden, N. 1964), Copyright Warc www.journalofadvertisingresearch.com, reproduced with permission; Figure 2.4 from *Basic Marketing: A Managerial Approach*, 6th ed., Homewood, IL: Richard D. Irwin (McCarthy, E.J. 1978) p. 39, Copyright 1978 by McGraw-Hill Companies, Inc. – Books, reproduced with permission of McGraw-Hill Companies, Inc. – Books in the format Textbook via Copyright Clearance Center; Figures 3.1, 4.3 and 7.3 adapted from Developing buyer-seller relationships, *Journal of Marketing*, 51, pp. 11–27 (Dwyer, F.R., Schurr, P.H. and Oh, S. 1987), American Marketing Association, reprinted with permission; Figures 3.3 and 6.3 adapted from Customer loyalty: toward an integrated conceptual framework, *Journal of the Academy of Marketing Science*, 22 (2), pp. 99–113 (Dick, A.S. and Basu, K. 1994), Sage Publications, with kind permission from Springer Science + Business Media B.V. and American Marketing Association; Figure 4.3 adapted from *Relationship Marketing for Competitive Advantage: Winning and Keeping Customers*, Oxford: Butterworth Heinemann (Payne, A., Christopher, M. and Peck, H. 1995); Figure 4.4 adapted from *Principles of Direct and Database Marketing*, Pearson Education (Tapp, A. 1998) p. 150, © Alan Tapp; Figure 4.5 adapted from *The Loyalty Effect: The Hidden Force Behind Growth, Profits and Lasting Values*, Harvard Business School Press, Boston, MA (Reichheld, F.F. 1996) Copyright © 1996 Harvard Business School Publishing Corporation, all rights reserved, reprinted by permission of Harvard Business School Press; Figure 4.6 adapted from Adopting share of wallet as a basis for communications and customer relationship management, *Journal of Direct Data and Digital Marketing (Interactive Marketing)*, 2 (1), pp. 29–40 (Pompa, N., Berry, J., Reid, J. and Webber, R. 2000), Copyright © 2000,

Macmillan Publishers Ltd., reprinted by permission from Macmillan Publishers Ltd.; Figure 5.3 from The IMP perspective: assets and liabilities of business relationships in Sheth, J.N. and Parvatiyar, A. (eds), *Handbook of Relationship Marketing*, pp. 69–93 (Hakansson, H. and Snehota, I.J. 2000), Thousand Oaks, CA: Sage, Copyright 2000 by Sage Publications Inc. Books. Reproduced with permission of Sage Publications Inc. Books in the format Textbook via Copyright Clearance Center; Figure 7.4 after Service failure and loyalty: an exploratory empirical study of airline customers, *Journal of Services Marketing*, 12 (1), pp. 7–22 (Bejou, D. and Palmer, A. 1998), © Emerald Group Publishing Limited, all rights reserved; Figure 7.6 from *Total Relationship Marketing: Rethinking Marketing Management From 4Ps to 30Rs*, Oxford: Butterworth-Heinemann (Gummesson, E. 1999) p. 184; Figure 7.7 adapted from Managing customer relations for profit: the dynamics of relationship quality, *International Journal of Service Industry Management*, 5, pp. 21–38 (Storbacka, K., Strandvik, T. and Grönroos, C. 1994); Figure 10.2 adapted from Knowledge and relationship marketing: where, what and how? in 2nd www Conference on Relationship Marketing 15/11/99-15/02/00 paper 4, p. 8 (www.mcb.co.uk/services/conferen/nov99/rm) (Tzokas, N. and Saren, M. 2000); Figure 11.2 adapted from *The Principles of Marketing*, 4th ed., London: Pitman (Brassington, F. and Pettitt, S. 2006) p. 1000; Figure 12.1 adapted from In one-to-one marketing, which one comes first?, *Interactive Marketing*, 1 (4), pp. 354–367 (Mitchell, A. 2000), reproduced with permission of the author.

Text

Box 2.2 adapted from *Relationship Marketing for Competitive Advantage: Winning and Keeping Customers*, Oxford: Butterworth Heinemann (Payne, A., Christopher, M. and Peck, H. 1995); Extracts on pages 59, 155 and Box 7.5 from Managing customer relations for profit: the dynamics of relationship quality, *International Journal of Service Industry Management*, 5, pp. 21–38 (Storbacka, K., Strandvik, T. and Grönroos, C. 1994), © Emerald Group Publishing Limited, all rights reserved; Case Study on page 67 from The art of the soft sell, *Business Week* (Quittner, J.), 9 October 2009, Bloomberg L.P.; Box 3.2 from No room for loyalty at United, *Daily Telegraph* (White, J.), 16 June 2007, © Telegraph Media Group Limited 2007; Case Study on page 95 from Get fat on chat, *The Marketer* (Gray, R.), March 2009; Box 7.2 adapted from *Principles of Services Marketing*, 2nd revised ed., London: McGraw-Hill (Palmer, A.J. 1998) p. 11, reproduced with the kind permission of The McGraw-Hill Companies, all rights reserved; Extracts on pages 173, 180 and 182 from Marketing in the new millennium, *European Journal of Marketing*, 29 (12), pp. 23–41 (Doyle, P. 1995), © Emerald Group Publishing Limited, all rights reserved; Case Study on page 184 from Resetting the sun, *The Marketer* (Barda, T.), December/January 2009; Extract on page 191 and Box 9.1 from Buyer/supplier partnering in British industry: the automative and telecommunications sectors, *Journal of Marketing Management*, 13 (8), pp. 758–76 (Brennan, R. 1997), © Westburn Publishers Ltd., www.westburn.co.uk, reproduced with permission; Case Study on page 200 from How to . . . choose the perfect partner, *The Marketer* (Murphy, C.), November 2008 (modified 11 May 2010); Case Study on page 220 from Mumsnet's the word, *Management Today* (Garrett, A.), 1 May 2010, reproduced from MT magazine with the permission of the copyright owner,

Haymarket Business Publications Limited; Case Study on page 243 from A decisive edge, *Management Today* (Alexander, R.), May 2007, reproduced from MT magazine with the permission of the copyright owner, Haymarket Business Publications Limited; Box 11.2 from MPs quiz Tesco and Nectar card executives on data privacy: Commons committee continues investigation of 'surveillance society', *Computerworld* (Shifrin, T.), www.computerworlduk.com, 7 June 2007; Case Study on page 261 from Social networking; cash cow or corporate headache?, *The Marketer* (Rowles, D.), April 2010; Box 12.1 from Unto This Last – Local craftmanship at mass production prices, Matt Sinclair, 26 February 2010, http://no-retro.com/home/category/mass-customisation/; Case Study on page 276 from The perfect touch, *The Marketer* (Orton-Jones, C.), February 2009.

The Financial Times

Case Study on page 40 from What the Willy Wonka of BSkyB knows about customers, *Financial Times*, *FT.com* (Stern, S.), 16 April 2007; Case Study on page 138 from Find a way into the hearts of customers, *Financial Times* (Delves Broughton, P.), 8 November 2010.

In some instances we have been unable to trace the owners of copyright material, and we would appreciate any information that would enable us to do so.

List of figures

List of abbreviations

AMA	American Marketing Association
ARPU	average revenue per user
B2B	business-to-business/industrial marketing
B2C	business-to-consumer marketing or consumer marketing
CIM	Chartered Institute of Marketing
CPT	cost-per-thousand (media audience measurement)
CRM	customer relationship management
CSR	corporate soail responsibility
DbM	database marketing
DgM	digital marketing
DM	direct marketing
DMA	Direct Marketing Association
EDI	electronic data interchange
ERP	enterprise resource planning
FMCG	fast-moving consumer goods
HRM	human resource management
IDM	Institute of Direct Marketing
IM	internal marketing
IMP	Industrial Marketing and Purchasing Group
ISP	Institute of Sales Promotion
IT	information technology
LV	lifetime value
NPD	new product development
NPV	net present value
PIMS	profit impact of marketing strategy
PLC	product life cycle
PMP	process management perspective
PTM	part-time marketers
R&D	research and development
RFV	recency, frequency, monetary value model
RM	relationship marketing
ROI	return on investment
ROR	return on relationships

S-DL	service-dominant logic
SEO	search engine optimisation
SME	small/medium-sized enterprises
SRC	supplier/retailer collaboration
TM	transactional (or transaction-based) marketing
TQM	total quality management
WOM	word of mouth
WWW	World Wide Web
ZOT	zone of tolerance

Part I
Relationships

This first part describes and analyses the market phenomenon that has become generally known as **relationship marketing (RM)**. RM is itself 'shorthand' for quite a wide range of 'relationship-type' strategies that have developed over the past few decades in product as well as service markets and in consumer as well as business-to-business sectors although not necessarily with the same intensity or success.

In the last edition a 'prequel' was added (Chapter 1) detailing the progression of marketing to the point where writers began to question the validity of the traditional marketing paradigm. This has been reviewed and refreshed for this edition. Chapter 2 continues the development of relationship marketing itself from this point. As Chapter 2 develops it may become apparent that agreement on a definition of RM is far from generally accepted. The chapter does, however, build up (or construct) a working definition that may be a starting point for analysis. Those readers who prefer to 'deconstruct' are invited to jump ahead to page 38 where they will find the definition upon which the second half of this chapter is based.

Chapter 3 investigates the concept of relationships, both actual and metaphoric. It examines whether relationships with constructs as nebulous as 'organisations' and/or as intangible as 'brands' are possible and whether they are a result, a prelude to and/or a mediating factor in the establishment of interpersonal and non-personal relationships. It examines various forms and types of relationship (including so-called customer loyalty) and examines these from the perspective of the RM debate.

Chapter 4 looks at the economic arguments that are seen to underpin RM. In a commercial world RM strategies must be based on the perceived profitability of relationship retention and longevity. The question of whether relational strategies are necessarily right in every instance is, however, questioned.

Chapter 5 discusses the concept of a 'marketing strategy continuum'. This suggests the need to develop a portfolio of strategies not only across industries but within individual organisations.

Chapter 6 looks at drivers to the adoption of relational strategies over traditional marketing techniques.

1 100 years of marketing

Key issues

- Historical development of marketing during the twentieth century
- Development and progression of marketing theory

Introduction

Although we see **marketing** as a twentieth-century phenomenon, much of what we would today recognise as marketing practice existed long before its formal beginnings as a field of study. From the time of the ancient Greeks through the great economists of the 1700s and 1800s (including Smith, Malthus, Jevons, Ricardo, Mill and Marshall), concepts such as markets, marginal analysis, value, production, humans as social and economic entities, competition and the role of governments had already been raised and extensively debated (Wilkie and Moore, 2003). Ambler (2004), for example, traces marketing thought to the Middle Ages with the first formal analysis of buyer motivation by St Thomas Aquinas (1225–74) and St Bernardino of Siena's (1380–1444) recognition of function, **market price** (i.e. economic benefit) and **psychological benefits**. In the nearer term it is also possible to track marketing's direct economic origins back through to the 'Physiocrats' of the eighteenth century and the 'Austrian School of Economics' at the end of the nineteenth century (Broeckelmann, 2004) and its mercantile origins to eighteenth-century English entrepreneurs such as Josiah Wedgwood (1730–95). Marketing, therefore, is as old as commerce and has been practised for centuries. What the twentieth century brought that was new was a recognition of marketing as an independent discipline and what might be called the specialist marketer (Ambler, 2004).

One undisputed fact about the birth of modern marketing and its formative years is that it was largely North America-dominated. Unlike its precursor, economics, which was largely of European origin and was to retain its internationalism, modern marketing began, developed and flourished in the USA. Not that recognisable concepts did not exist internationally, but it was in the USA that marketing was recognised early on as a subject worthy of academic endeavour. This young discipline benefited from that country's powerful sense of individualism and entrepreneurship, its exuberance and fierce competition (Witkowski, 2005). That the USA subsequently became the world's largest economy strengthened and consolidated its prime position. This heritage is the reason why, even in the current global commercial and academic marketplace, American marketing journals, and indeed American academics, still, rightly or wrongly, dominate the discipline.

The early days

It was commercial pressures that brought the marketing debate to the fore in the USA. By the end of the nineteenth century the Industrial Revolution had created such quantities of products (at substantially lower prices) as to completely change the nature of US consumer markets from sellers' markets where choice was limited (and expensive) to buyers' markets where competitors vied for the patronage of the consumer. In Europe, and notably the UK, somewhat different dynamics existed early in the century. 'Job and batch' production continued here long after North American manufacturers adopted 'flow production' methods. One reason for this was that the UK was a very unequal society with much of the country's wealth in a very few hands, the majority of the population poor and few in between these two extremes. A large market for consumer indulgences simply did not yet exist. In the USA, meanwhile, there was a growing middle class at whom moderately priced consumer goods could be targeted. Under these conditions, for example, the cost of buying a motor vehicle fell 60 per cent with the advent of production line techniques enabling a growing number of people to afford them. By 1923 Ford Motor Company had sold over two million Model Ts largely to an aspiring middle class.

Modern marketing in the eyes of many observers (e.g. Bartels, 1976) began at the turn of the twentieth century, when more structured academic attention started to be given to the area of market distribution, a topic that was evolving and assuming great prominence in the marketplace (Wilkie and Moore, 2003). Although it is acknowledged that marketing grew out of the field of economics, modern marketing owes much of its independence to its challenge of accepted economic tenets. Economic theorists had long held the view that value was created by production. Say's Law (Jean-Baptiste Say, 1767–1832) stated that there could be no demand without supply and that no sooner was a product produced than it afforded a market for other products to the full extent of its value (Say, 1803). However, mass production capabilities required mass consumption which in turn required more complex and varied distribution systems and a more sophisticated understanding of tools to influence mass consumer demand (Wilkie and Moore, 2003). By 1900 marketers were proposing that demand consisted of more than just the ability to purchase and that it also required desire on the part of the consumer. The suggestion was that desire could be increased and manipulated by factors (e.g. distribution, advertising) other than the mere existence of supply (Bartels, 1976) and value added beyond that of production (Wilkie and Moore, 1999).

The earliest writings on marketing concentrated on the agricultural industry where the added-value of the distribution process was evident. Other discussions were in the field of advertising covering such topics as advertising copy, layout, campaigns, principles and practice, economics and psychology (Bartels, 1976) and in 1908 Scott wrote *The Theory of Advertising*. Concepts such as **elasticity of demand** (developed by Alfred Marshall 1842–1924) were being used by marketing writers as a theoretical basis for developments in selling, advertising and promotions as well as marketing in general. **Value theory** was another area of economic (and philosophical) thought built upon by early marketers. Value theorists investigated how people value things (positively or negatively), the reasons why they make such evaluations and use consumer choice as evidence of intrinsic value. By 1910 literature relating to marketing research began to appear. The emergence of marketing research was itself the result of growing pressure to produce and apply accurate knowledge to the field and to bring the methods of science to the field of marketing (Bartels, 1976).

The decade between 1910 and 1920 has been called the 'period of conceptualization' for marketing (Bartels, 1976). In this phase marketing authors built upon distribution theory to develop their understanding of marketing. Weld (1916, p. 6) wrote 'At each step an increment of value is added by those who handle or transform the product' emphasising further that value was no longer regarded as wholly created in the production process. It was also around this time that the term 'marketing' itself was added to the commercial lexicon. Although the concept of marketing had always existed it was at this time that the word was first used as a noun as opposed to its earlier use as a verb (Petrof, 1997). Until this time what the word 'marketing' described had always been referred to as 'trade', 'distribution' or 'commerce'. Among highly influential writers of the period Ralph Starr Butler and Arch W. Shaw are considered important to the development of the new marketing discipline. Ralph Starr Butler (1882–1971), believed marketing was all about coordination, planning and the management of complex relationships. Shaw (1876–1962) distinguished three basic business operations: production, distribution and facilitating functions or administration. Given the changing forms involved between production and distribution, the latter conceived marketing as 'matter in motion' (Bartels, 1976). It was Shaw (1912, p. 708) who also first proposed the centrality of the customer when he wrote that 'the more progressive business man is searching out the unconscious needs of the consumer, and is then producing the goods to gratify them'. It was also in this period that concepts developed that were later to become known as the **commodity approach** (focusing on all marketing actions involved in a particular product category), the **institutional approach** (focusing on describing the operations of a specialised type of marketing agency, such as a wholesaler or a broker) and the **functional approach** (focusing on the purposes served by various marketing activities) (Wilkie and Moore, 2003). The functional approach in particular was to gain wide acceptance among marketing thinkers and was valued as a means of defining and rationalising the field of marketing and its numerous activities and for its usefulness in analysing marketing problems (Fullbrook, 1940). The marketing field also began to take on its own distinct academic identity when a number of US universities independently began to develop new courses in various aspects of marketing. Academic programmes including 'distributive and regulative industries', 'the marketing of products', 'methods of marketing farm products' and 'mercantile institutions' were early examples (Bartels, 1951a, 1988; Wilkie and Moore, 2003).

By the third decade of the twentieth century ideas were starting to coalesce around a number of tentative generalisations. In 1923 Fred Emerson Clark (1890–1948) produced *Principles of Marketing* (Clark, 1923) in which he defined marketing as 'those efforts which effect transfer in the ownership of goods'. Paul Dulaney Converse (1889–1968) in his book *Marketing Methods and Policies* (Converse, 1922) distinguished between the functions of middlemen and the marketing functions. Cherington (1920) added an important basis for future thought by asking whether marketing performance and societal welfare might be enhanced by focusing on the underlying functions of marketing; probably the first mention of social marketing. The ubiquitous AIDA (attention, interest, desire, action) model appeared in a publication by Strong (1925), albeit based on an idea of St Elmo Lewis writing towards the end of the previous century. The first doubts about the dangers of consumerism were also being discussed at this time largely in terms of moral degeneration (Fitchett, 2005). There was debate too about whether non-essential services could be eliminated and whether there were too many middlemen adding to costs (Wilkie and Moore, 2003). Advertising was particularly singled out for criticism regarding its '**economic value**' (e.g., Moriarty 1923; Vaughan, 1928) and whether it essentially caused prices to rise. There were also certain 'unorthodox' studies going on that were to become the bases for the further evolution of marketing such as White's (1927) very managerial proposal of a '**scientific marketing management**', offering guidance to the companies who wish to understand marketing (Skålén *et al.*, 2005).

The period 1930–40 was characterised more by the development of existing concepts rather than the production of new ideas. Exceptions included Charles F. Phillips whose book *Marketing* (Phillips, 1938) was published towards the end of the decade. His text showed an interest in the consumer that went well beyond the study of buying motives to consider the consumer as the driving force of the economy. There were also developments in theory designed to embrace what was called oligopolistic competition (Chamberlain, 1933; Sheth *et al.*, 1988; Waterschoot and Van den Bulte, 1992). In an **oligopoly**, firms operate under imperfect conditions and with a kinked demand curve. Following the fierce price competitiveness created by the **sticky** (i.e. inelastic) **demand curve** firms utilise **non-price competition** in order to achieve greater revenue and market share. This theoretical insight later led marketing theoreticians (e.g. McGarry, 1950; McKitterick, 1957; Alderson, 1957) to create 'lists' of marketing variables deduced from econometric, profit optimising equations. In 1936 the *Journal of Marketing* was launched and began to attract articles that had previously found limited favour in economic journals. Interest in marketing was also starting to develop in Europe, albeit tentatively. In September 1931 the magazine *Marketing* first appeared in the UK but it took another 37 years for the magazine's publisher, the Incorporated Sales Managers' Association, to change its name to the Institute of Marketing, the predecessor of today's Chartered Institute of Marketing.

In the 1940s an increasing number of different approaches were being considered. New emphasis was given to the management of marketing and more attention paid to the consumer viewpoint. Whereas early marketing had frequently centred on rural agriculture (e.g. Weld, 1916), after 1945 topics such as the growth of the mass market, employment, consumer savings and industrial development (e.g. Hahn, 1946; Vance, 1947; Grether, 1948) started to be discussed. The field of modern demographics developed around the explosion of births and migration patterns after the Second World War. William Lloyd Warner, an anthropologist, for example, researched American society and its class system. He divided social classes by three distinct groups, which he labelled lower, middle and upper, with each class sub-divided further into two parts. This was to become the basis of **demographic profiling**. The role of marketing theory as a science began to be seriously discussed. Leading articles such as Converse's (1945) 'The development of the science of marketing', Alderson and Cox's (1948) 'Towards a theory of marketing' and, slightly later, Bartels' (1951b) 'Can marketing be a science?' exemplified the call from scholars for more theoretical frameworks and began to explore new parameters for this body of thought (Wilkie and Moore, 2003).

An important economic distinction should once again, however, be made between what was happening in the USA and Europe at this time. While in the USA consumerism was buoyant, Europeans were still suffering from shortages that would last into the 1950s. In the UK, for example, rationing did not end until 3 July 1954. European marketing at this time was less directed at stimulating wants than restricting needs.

Modern marketing

The 1950s represented a watershed for marketing thought as the mainstream debate became steeped in science. This science-led revolution reflected a conscious movement in US business thinking. In the early 1950s the Ford Foundation started an initiative to infuse scientific theory into US business systems and marketers were quick to get involved. US business schools responded by raising admission standards and including more mathematics, statistics, economics and other sciences to the curriculum (Mentzer and Schumann, 2006). But not everyone agreed that this was the right way forward. Hutchinson (1952, p. 290) noted that the forebears of marketers were merchants not scientists and that it was a 'travesty to relate the scientist's search for knowledge to the market research man's seeking after customers'. Marketing textbooks continued to disseminate new ideas. In *Theory in Marketing*, Cox and Alderson (1950) contributed ideas such as heterogeneous markets, the uniqueness of organisational positioning and competition based on differential advantage. In the early 1950s, Borden (1954) introduced the concept of the marketing mix, a list of 12 variables (product, price, branding, distribution, personal selling, advertising, promotions, packaging, display, servicing, physical handling, fact finding and analysis) from which the marketer could blend the ingredients or variables of the mix into an integrated marketing programme.

From the mid-1950s, interest in the topic of marketing management grew rapidly effectively replacing the functionalist school of thought. From the marketing management perspective, academic marketers were viewing the discipline from the

applied to ideas, places and people in addition to products and services. **Not-for-profit** and **societal marketing** came to the fore. Some of the topics which developed at this time were in the areas of '**demarketing**' (i.e. marketing designed to change behaviour) and '**network marketing**'. While marketing boundaries continued to expand so apparently did the gap between academics and practitioners. In 1977 the American Marketing Association and the Marketing Science Institute convened a commission to evaluate the effect of research on marketing practice (Mentzer and Schumann, 2006). The conclusion of the Commission was that academic marketing had very little impact on improving marketing management practice (Myers *et al.*, 1980). The academic/practitioner divide debate was to continue into the next decade with very little evidence of a satisfactory outcome (see Brennan and Ankers, 2004).

Despite the apparent supremacy of marketing in the period doubts were starting to be raised about the all-embracing nature of the traditional marketing paradigm. These doubts largely originated from those operating within businesses and socio-political environments very different from those of the United States, for example Europe (Hammarkvist *et al.*, 1982; Elg and Johansson, 1996) and from marketers working within the industrial (business-to-business) and service sectors. Marketing had always had an uncomfortable relationship with those sectors which appeared not to fit comfortably with mainstream consumer goods.

Some attempts were made to accommodate the evident anomalies. However, rather than start again by challenging the conceptual basis of transactional marketing, the quickest and most convenient 'solution' to the problem was to paper over the cracks. The standard method of 'overcoming' deficiencies in the 4P 'tablet of faith' (Grönroos, 1994b) was to expand on the same approach – abstracting the market relationship into a list of decision-making variables (Grönroos, 1994b; Brodie *et al.*, 1997). An unintentional legacy of McCarthy's 4P model was that most of these lists used words beginning with the same letter (e.g. Lipson and Darling, 1971; Kelly and Lazer, 1973: see Grönroos, 1994b), often the letter P. From the late 1970s, this pedantry became more extreme: 'after the four Ps were definitely canonised . . . new items to the list [were] almost exclusively put in the form of Ps' (Grönroos, 1994a, p. 5). The guilty were many, Kotler (1986), public relations and politics; Booms and Bitner (1981), people, physical evidence and process; Judd (1987), people; Le Doux (1991), preservation.

The perceived orthodoxy did not, however, go wholly unchallenged. The Fall 1983 edition of the *Journal of Marketing* provided a platform with articles by Arndt (1983), Day and Wensley (1983), Deshpande (1983), Howard (1983) and Hunt (1983) much of which suggested that the traditional microeconomic view of marketing was increasingly inadequate (Ambler, 2004). The issue contained several articles which attacked the perception of marketing as a science and raised concerns about marketing's reliance on the logical positivism/empiricism perspective that now dominated research. Criticisms of transactional marketing were also generated based on the difficulties in applying it outside its original context.

Many weaknesses of the transactional paradigm were initially hidden by the rate of increase of consumer spending generated by the buoyant, post-Second World War, US economy. These defects were revealed as the competitive environment in which firms operated evolved beyond recognition in the 1980s (Turnbull and Wilson, 1989;

Blattberg and Deighton, 1991; Aijo, 1996). In the USA intra-market competition intensified considerably as the number of firms – both local and foreign – increased (Jackson, 1985; Gummesson, 1987). This spread to most developed consumer goods markets transforming them from growth to mature markets (Hammarkvist *et al.*, 1982). Firms had to compete for a static number of customers within markets that were becoming increasingly saturated with products (Berry, 1983; Morgan and Hunt, 1994), a development which has been termed 'hyper-competition' (Ohmae, 1990; Kotler, 1991). This exposed transactional marketing as a theory developed in times of growth, not stagnation (Grönroos, 1991; Gummesson, 1991) and perhaps unfit for highly competitive markets.

New frames of reference not directly associated with the marketing mix did start to appear. Sheth *et al.* (1988) saw what they called a paradigm shift in the development of strategic marketing theory. The objective here was competitive advantage and market share became its primary indicator of performance (Ambler, 2004). Porter (1979, 1985) warned against being 'stuck in the middle' between price competitiveness and distinctiveness and suggested that competitive advantage could be evaluated through the five-forces analysis (Porter, 1979). Profit impact of marketing strategy (PIMS) research in Cambridge sought to link market share to profitability as did the Boston Consulting Group matrix and other 'big is beautiful' models of the period. Despite these developments, however, most research topics published in the period still relied heavily on the 4Ps model (Gundlach and Wilkie, 1990).

The 1990s were seen as a sea-change in the attitudes of business within the Anglo-American sphere of financial influence. Short-term profits and their impact on the share price put marketers on the defensive from which many would suggest they have not recovered. Marketers were called to account and required to measure the success of their output. That they were not necessarily measuring the right things appeared to be of secondary importance to the measurement itself. Marketers from around the world, and in particular in Scandinavia, began to recognise that the traditional marketing approach had diverted marketers away from their original customer-orientated perspective.

From this point on, our history continues through the lens of relationship marketing research. The 'rise and rise of relationship marketing' (Saren, 2007, p. 12) does not mean, however, that thinking has not developed since the first edition of this book in 2001: indeed, quite the contrary. Several authors have contributed interesting perspectives which this new edition seeks to represent. One lesson that this review of history has taught this author is that, although ideas develop, what has gone before rarely goes away. Rather, theory builds on theory. This makes for a complexity which may be uncomfortable for some but which adds to the value of the discipline.

References

Aijo, T. (1996) 'The theoretical and philosophical underpinnings of relationship marketing', *European Journal of Marketing*, **30** (2), 8–18.
Alderson, W. (1957) *Marketing Behaviour and Executive Action*, Homewood, IL: Irwin.

Alderson, W. and Cox, R. (1948) 'Towards a theory of marketing', *Journal of Marketing* **13** (Oct), 137–52.

Ambler, T. (2004) 'The new dominant logic of marketing: views of the elephant', Centre for Marketing Working Paper No. 04-903, London Business School.

Arndt, J. (1983) 'The political economy paradigm: foundation for theory building in marketing', *Journal of Marketing*, Fall, **47** (4), 44–54.

Bartels, R. (1951a) 'Influences on the development of marketing thought 1900–1923', *Journal of Marketing* **16** (July), 1–17.

Bartels, R. (1951b) 'Can marketing be a science?', *Journal of Marketing*, **16** (January), 319–28.

Bartels, R. (1976) *The History of Marketing Thought*, 2nd edn, Columbus, OH: Grid Publishing.

Bartels, R. (1988) *The History of Marketing Thought*, 3rd edn, Columbus, OH: Publishing Horizons.

Bass, F.M., Buzzel, R.D., Greene, M.R., Lazer, W., Pessimier, E.A., Shawver, D., Schuchman, A. and Wilson, G.W. (1961) *Mathematical Models and Methods in Marketing*, Homewood, IL: Richard D. Irwin.

Berry, L.L. (1983) 'Relationship marketing', in Berry, L.L., Shostack, G.L. and Upah, G.D. (eds) *Emerging Perspectives on Services Marketing*, Chicago, IL: American Marketing Association, pp. 25–8.

Blattberg, R.C. and Deighton, J. (1991) 'Interactive marketing: exploring the age of addressability', *Sloan Management Review*, Fall, 5–14.

Booms, B.H. and Bitner, M.J. (1981) 'Marketing strategies and organisational structures for service firms', in Donnelly, J. and George, W.R. (eds) *Marketing of Services*, Chicago, IL: American Marketing Association, pp. 47–51.

Borden, N.H. (1954) 'The concept of the marketing mix', *Journal of Advertising Research*, **4** (June), 2–7.

Brennan, R. and Ankers, P. (2004) 'In search of relevance: is there an academic–practitioner divide in business-to-business marketing?, *Marketing Intelligence & Planning*, **22** (5), 511–19.

Brodie, R.J., Coviello, N.E., Brookes, R.W. and Little, V. (1997) 'Towards a paradigm shift in marketing: an examination of current marketing practices', *Journal of Marketing Management*, **13** (5), July, 383–406.

Broeckelmann, P. (2004) 'Austrian economics as a basis for a general marketing theory: potentials and limitations', *Humboldt-Universität zu Berlin*, <http://edoc.hu-berlin.de/master/broeckelmann-philipp-2004-11-26/HTML/front.html> (accessed 16 November 2007).

Buzzell, R.D. (1964) *Mathematical Models and Marketing Management*, Boston, MA: Harvard Graduate School of Business.

Chamberlain, E.H. (1933) *The Theory of Monopolistic Competition*, Cambridge, MA: Harvard University Press, pp. 99–113.

Cherington, P.T. (1920) *The Elements of Marketing*, New York: Macmillan.

Clark, F.E. (1923) *Principles of Marketing*, New York: Macmillan.

Converse, P.D. (1922) *Marketing Methods and Policies*, New York: Prentice Hall.

Converse, P.D. (1945) 'The development of the science of marketing: an exploratory survey', *Journal of Marketing*, **10** (July), 14–23.

Cox, R. and Alderson, W. (eds) (1950) *Theory in Marketing*, Homewood, IL: Irwin.

Day, G.S. and Wensley, R. (1983) 'Marketing theory with strategic orientation', *Journal of Marketing*, Fall, **47** (4), 79–89.

Deshpande, R. (1983) 'Paradigms lost: on theory and method in research in marketing', *Journal of Marketing*, Fall, **47** (4), 101–10.

Dixon, D.F. and Blois, K.J. (1983) 'Some limitations of the 4Ps as a paradigm for marketing', Marketing Education Group Annual Conference, Cranfield Institute of Technology, Cranfield, UK, July.

Duncan, T. and Moriarty, S.E. (1998) 'A communication-based marketing model for managing relationships', *Journal of Marketing*, **62** (April), 11–21.

Elg, U. and Johansson, U. (1996) 'Networking when national boundaries dissolve', *European Journal of Marketing*, **30** (2), 61–74, 132–41.

Engel, J.F., Blackwell, R.D. and Kollat, D.T. (1968) *Consumer Behavior*, Hillsdale IL: The Dryden Press.

Fitchett, J. (2005) 'The twenty-first century consumer society', in Kimmel, A.J. (ed.) *Marketing Communication: New Approaches, Technologies and Styles*, Oxford: Oxford University Press, pp. 42–62.

Frank, R.E., Kuehn, A.A. and Massy, W.F. (1962) *Quantitative Techniques in Marketing Analysis*, Homewood, IL: Richard D. Irwin.

Fullbrook, E.S. (1940) 'The functional concept in marketing', *Journal of Marketing*, **4** (January), 229–37.

Gardner, B.B. and Levy, S.J. (1955) 'The product and the brand', *Harvard Business Review*, March/April, 33–9.

Green, P.E. and Rao, V. (1971) 'Conjoint measurement for quantifying judgmental data', *Journal of Marketing Research*, **8** (August), 355–63.

Grether, E.T. (1948) 'The postwar market and industrialization in California', *Journal of Marketing*, **12** (Jan), 311–16.

Grönroos, C. (1991) 'The marketing strategy continuum: towards a marketing concept for the 1990s', *Management Decision*, **29** (1), 7–13.

Grönroos, C. (1994a) 'From marketing mix to relationship marketing: towards a paradigm shift in marketing', *Management Decision*, **32** (2), 4–20.

Grönroos, C. (1994b) 'Quo vadis, marketing? toward a relationship marketing paradigm', *Journal of Marketing Management*, **10**, 347–60.

Grönroos, C. (1996) 'Relationship marketing logic', *Asia–Australia Marketing Journal*, **4** (1), 7–18.

Gummesson, E. (1987) 'The new marketing: developing long-term interactive relationships', *Long Range Planning*, **20** (4), 10–20.

Gummesson, E. (1991) 'Marketing orientation revisited: the crucial role of the part-time marketer', *European Journal of Marketing*, **25** (2), 60–75.

Gundlach, G.T. and Wilkie, W.L. (1990) 'The marketing literature in public policy: 1970–1988', in Murphy, P.E. and Wilkie, W.L. (eds) *Marketing and Advertising Regulation: The Federal Trade Commission in the 1990s*, Notre Dame, IL: University of Notre Dame Press, pp. 329–44.

Hahn, L.A. (1946) 'The effects of saving on employment and consumption', *Journal of Marketing*, **11** (July), 35–43.

Hammarkvist, K.O., Hakansson, H. and Mattsson, L. (1982) *Marketing for Competitiveness*, Lund, Sweden: Liber.

Howard, J.A. (1983) 'Marketing theory of the firm', *Journal of Marketing*, Fall, **47** (4), 90–100.

Howard, J.A. and Sheth, J.N. (1969) *The Theory of Buyer Behavior*, New York: John Wiley & Sons.

Hunt, S.D. (1983) 'General theories and the fundamental explananda of marketing', *Journal of Marketing*, Fall, **47** (4), 9–17.

Hutchinson, K.D. (1952) 'Marketing as a science: an appraisal', *Journal of Marketing*, **16** (January), 286–93.

Jackson, B.B. (1985) 'Build customer relationships that last', *Harvard Business Review*, November/December, 120–8.

Judd, V.C. (1987) 'Differentiate with the 5th P: People', *Industrial Marketing Management*, **16** (November), 241–7.

Kelly, E.J. and Lazer, W. (1973) *Managerial Marketing*, Homewood, IL: Irwin.

Kent, R.A. (1986) 'Faith in the 4Ps: an alternative', *Journal of Marketing Management*, **2** (2), 145–54.

Kotler, P. (1967) *Marketing Management: Analysis, Planning and Control*, Englewood Cliffs, NJ: Prentice Hall.

Kotler, P. (1971) *Marketing Decision Making: A Model Building Approach*, New York: Holt, Rinehart & Winston.

Kotler, P. (1972) *Marketing Management: Analysis, Planning and Control*, 2nd edn, Englewood Cliffs, NJ: Prentice Hall.

Kotler, P. (1986) 'Megamarketing', *Harvard Business Review*, March/April, 117–24.

Kotler, P. (1991) *Marketing Management: Analysis, Planning and Control*, 7th edn, Englewood Cliffs, NJ: Prentice Hall.

Kotler, P. (1992) 'Total marketing', *Business Week Advance Executive Brief No. 2*, Columbus, OH: McGraw Hill.

Le Doux, L. (1991) 'Is preservation the fifth "P" or just another microenvironmental factor?', in McKinnon, G.F. and Kelley, C.A. (eds) *Challenges of New Decade in Marketing Education*, Northridge, CA: Western Marketing Educators' Association.

Lipson, H.A. and Darling, J.R. (1971) *Introduction to Marketing: An Administration Approach*, New York: Wiley.

McCarthy, E.J. (1960) *Basic Marketing*, Homewood, IL: Irwin.

McGarry, E.D. (1950) 'Some functions of marketing reconsidered', in Cox, R. and Alderson, W. (eds) *Theory of Marketing*, Chicago, IL: Irwin.

McKitterick, J.B. (1957) 'What is the marketing management concept?', in Bass, F. (ed.) *The Frontiers of Marketing Thought in Action*, Chicago, IL: AMA.

Mentzer, J.T. and Schumann, D.W. (2006) 'The theoretical and practical implications of marketing scholarship', *Journal of Marketing Theory and Practice*, **14** (3), 179–90.

Morgan, R.M. and Hunt, S.D. (1994) 'The commitment–trust theory of relationship marketing', *Journal of Marketing*, **58**, 20–38.

Moriarty, W.D. (1923) *The Economics of Marketing and Advertising*, New York: Harper & Brothers.

Myers, J.G., Massey, W.F. and Greyster, S.A. (1980) *Marketing Research and Knowledge Development*, Englewood Cliffs, NJ: Prentice Hall.

O'Driscoll, A. and Murray, J.A. (1998) 'The changing nature of theory and practice in marketing: on the value of synchrony', *Journal of Marketing Management*, **14** (5), 391–416.

Ohmae, K. (1990) *The Borderless World*, London: Collins.

O'Malley, L. and Patterson, M. (1998) 'Vanishing point: the mix management paradigm re-viewed', *Journal of Marketing Management*, **14**, 829–51.

Packard, V. (1957) *The Hidden Persuaders*, Harmondsworth, Middx: Penguin.

Payne, A. (ed.) (1995) *Advances in Relationship Marketing*, The Cranfield Management Series, London: Kogan Page.

Petrof, J.V. (1997) 'Relationship marketing: the wheel reinvented?', *Business Horizons*, Nov–Dec, 255–71.

Phillips, C.F. (1938) *Marketing*, New York: Houghton Mifflin.

Porter, Michael, E. (1979) 'How competitive forces shape strategy', *Harvard Business Review*, (March/April), 137.

Porter, Michael, E. (1985) *Competitive Advantage*, New York: The Free Press.

Saren, M. (2007) 'Marketing is everything: the view from the street', *Marketing Intelligence and Planning*, **25** (1), 11–16.

Say, J.-B. (1803) 'A treatise on political economy, or the production, distribution and consumption of wealth' (English translation).

Scott, W.D. (1908) *The Theory of Advertising*, Boston, MA: Small, Maynard & Company.

Shaw, A. (1912) 'Some problems in market distribution', *Quarterly Journal of Economics*, **26**, 700–60.

Sheth, J.N., Garner, D.M. and Garrett, D.E. (1988) *Marketing Theory: Evolution and Evaluation*, New York: Wiley.

Skålén, P., Fellesson, M. and Fougère, M. (2005) 'Marketing, government and governmentality', Proceedings of the CMS Conference 2005, University of Waikato <http://www.mngt.waikato.ac.nz/ejrot/criticalmarketing/Skalen.pdf> (accessed 6 May 2007).

Smith, W. (1956) 'Product differentiation and marketing segmentation as alternative marketing strategies', *Journal of Marketing*, **20** (July), 3–8.

Strong, E.K. (1925) *The Psychology of Selling*, New York: McGraw-Hill.

Takala, T. and Uusitalo, O. (1996) 'An alternative view of relationship marketing: a framework for ethical analysis', *European Journal of Marketing*, **30** (2), 45–60.

Turnbull, P.W. and Wilson, D.T. (1989) 'Developing and protecting profitable customer relationships', *Industrial Marketing Management*, **18**, 233–8.

Vance, L.L. (1947) 'The interpretation of consumer dis-saving', *Journal of Marketing*, **11** (Jan), 243–9.

Vargo, S. and Lusch, R. (2004) 'Evolving to a new dominant logic for marketing', *Journal of Marketing*, **67** (1), 1–17.

Vaughan, F.L. (1928) *Marketing and Advertising*, Princeton, NJ: Princeton University Press.

Waterschoot, W. and Van den Bulte, C. (1992) 'The 4P classification of the marketing mix revisited', *Journal of Marketing*, **56** (Oct), 83–93.

Weld, L.D.H. (1916) *The Marketing of Farm Products*, New York: The Macmillan Company.

White, P. (1927) *Scientific Marketing Management: Its Principles and Methods*, New York: Harper & Bros.

Wilkie, W.L. and Moore, E.S. (1999) 'Marketing's contribution to society', *Journal of Marketing*, **63** (Special Issue), 198–218.

Wilkie, W.L. and Moore, E.S. (2003) 'Scholarly research in marketing: exploring the "4 eras" of thought development', *Journal of Public Policy & Marketing*, Fall, **22** (2), 116–46.

Witkowski, T.H. (2005) 'Sources of immoderation and proportion in marketing thought', *Marketing Theory*, **5** (2), 221–31.

Zaltman, G. (1965) *Marketing: Contributions from the Behavioral Sciences*, New York: Harcourt, Brace & World.

At a second, broader, level Brodie *et al.* (1997) saw RM as a focus on actual or potential relationships between the business and its customer base with a concentration on customer retention. On a third (even broader) level, RM was seen as a form of 'customer partnering' with buyers cooperatively involved in the design of the product or service offered. Working relationships on this level implied true interaction between the buyer and seller. At a fourth (and broadest) level RM was seen as incorporating 'everything from databases to personalised service, loyalty programmes, brand loyalty, internal marketing, personal/social relationships and strategic alliances' (p. 385). When used in this way the term becomes a 'catch-all' phrase for a variety of relational (and perhaps some strictly non-relational) concepts.

This last, very broad, definition could be said to have helped create difficulties in establishing the parameters of RM from more traditional marketing approaches. As O'Malley and Tynan (2000, p. 809) note, with 'the diversity in operational approaches employed, and the lack of accepted definitions', it became 'impossible to delimit the [RM] domain'. The boundaries, they noted, were 'completely permeable and elastic' and this resulted in 'difficulties in identifying appropriate contexts for empirical research and exacerbated conceptual problems within the emerging discipline'.

RM development

Although RM undoubtedly emerged as a strong concept on the back of prior research, its dramatic growth has been strongly associated with the perceived crises in marketing that took place during the latter part of the twentieth century. To get a fuller picture of the drivers to relational strategy development, a brief examination of the history and perceived weaknesses of traditional marketing may be appropriate.

The golden age of marketing

As Chapter 1 illustrated, marketing as a distinct discipline was born out of economics around the beginning of the twentieth century (Sheth and Parvatiyar, 2000, p. 119). The turn of that century coincided with a period in history when, for the first time, products and services not strictly required for human survival became generally available to large numbers of consumers in Europe and North America. As a recognisable commercial activity, however, it came to prominence as the century developed.

If the twentieth century can be called the 'century of marketing' then the period between 1950 and 1970 could be said to have been its heyday. During this 'golden age' the public appetite for new goods and services appeared insatiable. In western markets consumption rose substantially as prices, in real terms, fell. The period coincided in the UK with the launch of independent commercial television, which was, ultimately, to become the marketer's most powerful mass-market communications medium. Consumer spending (conservatively) doubled during this time and much of this increase was attributed to the power and influence of marketing.

Marketing was hailed as amongst the most powerful forces for cultural stability at work in the world (Sherry, 2000, p. 328). Modern marketing, it appeared, could do no wrong.

As the contribution of marketing came to be regarded as more and more important so the demand for marketing education and research grew. It was during this period that many of the marketing concepts still taught in business schools around Europe, North America and the rest of the world today were first developed. In the 1960s Borden (1964) produced his 12 elements of a marketing programme (see Figure 2.4), which were later simplified further to what became known as the '4Ps of marketing' (see Figure 2.5) or the 'marketing mix' (McCarthy, 1978). The traditional marketing framework that developed during this period viewed marketing as a strategic and managerial matching process. This matching process sought to ensure that the marketing mix and internal policies of the company were appropriate to the market forces (opportunities and threats) operating within the company's competitive environment.

This traditional marketing framework was quickly adopted, by students, teachers and practitioners alike, as a straightforward, easy to remember and intuitively rational marketing model. In this era of high consumer trust, effective mass advertising, growing prosperity, homogeneous demand, poorly developed distribution channels and, above all, dominant manufacturing power (O'Driscoll and Murray, 1998, p. 396), the **'brand management model'** and the 'toolbox' approach (Grönroos, 1994b, p. 5) of the marketing mix appeared to be working very effectively indeed.

Market changes

In the 1960s the favourable conditions that had seen the growth of marketing began to change dramatically. During this decade the UK, the USA and other developed

Figure 2.4
Borden's 12 elements of a marketing programme and McCarthy's marketing mix

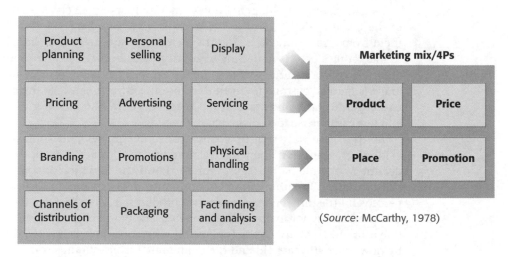

(*Source*: Borden, 1964)

Figure 2.5
Marketing mix

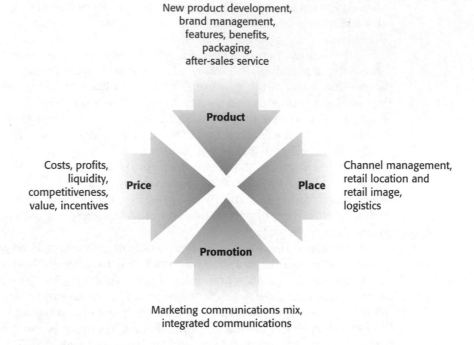

New product development,
brand management,
features, benefits,
packaging,
after-sales service

Product

Costs, profits,
liquidity,
competitiveness,
value, incentives

Price

Place

Channel management,
retail location and
retail image,
logistics

Promotion

Marketing communications mix,
integrated communications

consumer markets became saturated. Population growth, a feature and major driver behind the rise in consumer purchasing, was declining. Brands that had seen significant growth in the past plateaued and markets became dominated by oligopolies. **Branding**, originally developed to provide customers with quality assurance and little else, had, over time, evolved into a segmentation tool with different brands for each segment. As segments proliferated so did brands, contributing further to marketing's productivity problems (Sheth and Sisodia, 1999, p. 78).

As Christopher (1996, p. 55) notes, 'mature markets', such as those that developed in the UK and the USA in the 1960s, exhibit certain characteristics that differentiate them from 'growth markets' and these characteristics were to contribute significantly to marketing's perceived decline in effectiveness. In particular, consumers, faced with a surfeit of goods and services, were becoming much more demanding. In this 'buyer's market' customers began to realise the attractiveness of their spending power and began to take advantage of it. Customers were also growing more sophisticated and less easily persuaded by marketing messages.

At the same time as this greater consumer power and sophistication became evident, the perceived benefits (relative to costs) of advertising were seen to be in decline as the media market fragmented and the '**cost-per-thousand**'[5] targets rose substantially. 'Premium brand' dominance was further declining as consumers perceived little difference between rival products, leading to a decline in market share and profitability for manufacturers' brands largely in favour of retail store equivalents ('own brands'). Many of the top fast-moving consumer goods (FMCG) brands were, by now, over 40 years old and the failure rate for new brands was reaching very high levels despite often substantial marketing support. There was an erosion of margins caused by a decline in brand premiums as manufacturers' brands fought for market share. There was a subsequent increase in 'below the line' expenditure as brand owners vied for shelf space from increasingly powerful retailers. The combined effect of these changes was the downward pressure on pricing and, ultimately, profitability.

Despite the growing complexity and competitiveness of the marketplace at the end of the 1980s, marketers were still persevering with the tools and concepts of a more predictable era that had evidently now passed. According to McKenna (1991, p. viii), the homogeneity marketers continued to seek was a myth advanced by those who were still using the American market model *circa* 1950–1960. The world was changing but marketing appeared stuck in a rut.

Marketing in crisis

As marketing entered the 1990s things appeared to be going from bad to worse. Companies were beginning to question the large expenditure on marketing without a measurable return on investment that had been assumed in past decades. Accountants, looking to reduce costs and increase rates of return, asked for justi-fication of expenditure and were not pleased with the vague responses they were receiving from marketing departments. Brand-building exercises, largely based on mass advertising and with largely immeasurable outcomes, were no longer seen as justifiable.

The last decade of the twentieth century was also to see the marketing function being marginalised in many organisations (Sheth and Sisodia, 1999, p. 84). Even mar-keting pioneers such as Procter & Gamble and Unilever were abolishing the position of marketing director (Doyle, 1995, p. 23) to concentrate on other functional activi-ties. Marketing was being openly criticised for lack of innovation in the face of hostile markets and for largely adopting defensive strategies to cope. As Doyle (ibid., p. 24) noted, marketers of the period generally made the mistake of seeing marketing as a functional discipline rather than an integrated business process. This led to the belief that 'the discipline was about tactical and generally superficial segmentation and positioning rather than real innovation and the creation of sustainable competitive advantage'. This functional defensiveness was to further harden attitudes against marketers.

Marketing education

Despite the obvious problems that existed, little was changing in marketing educa-tion. Marketing theory remained mired in a futile search for laws, regularities and predictability (Brown, 1995, p. 159). The marketing mix approach was still (and arguably still is) the dominant marketing model although it was beginning to be seen as offering a too 'seductive sense of simplicity' (Christopher *et al.*, 1991, p. 8) which, despite its pedagogical virtues, was prone to misguide academic and practitioner alike (Grönroos, 1990, p. 3). The 'toolbox' approach (Grönroos, 1994b, p. 5) of science-orientated marketing was criticised as a 'neglect of process in favour of structure', leading to a consequent 'lack of study into other key variables' (Christopher *et al.*, 1991, p. 8) not suggested by the marketing mix concept. Marketers were suffering from difficulties of their own creation by applying, unmodified, the principles they had learned in past decades (Gordon, 1998, p. 1) despite the fact that the commercial world was changing all around them. Whereas the marketing mix paradigm had served a function at one time in the development of marketing theory, once it had established itself as the 'universal truth' in marketing it began to cause more harm than good (Grönroos, 1994c). It had dominated marketing for over 40 years, down-playing the relational aspects of exchange and obscuring the role of relationships in marketing (Harris *et al.*, 2003, p. 10). It seemed that the problem was no longer 'marketing myopia'[6] but the myopia of marketing (Brown, 1995, p. 179).

So it appeared that marketing, the leading department of the first three-quarters of the century, was losing its primacy to other organisational disciplines (Doyle, 1995, p. 23) and doing little to resolve the problems associated with its demise. According to Gordon (1998, p. 1), marketers were so busy attending to the practice of marketing they may not have noticed that it was, for all practical purposes, dead. If not dead, it certainly was in crisis.

Antecedents of RM

As Chapter 1 illustrated, the marketing discipline had, from its very beginning, been dominated by consumer goods marketing and in particular US consumer goods practice of the 1950s (O'Driscoll and Murray, 1998, p. 409). In most marketing texts prior to 1990, concepts, models and strategies concentrated primarily on corporate manufacturers and their consumer brands. Services and industrial (business-to-business) marketing, despite their growing recognition as important components of the overall business environment, continued to be largely treated as separate disciplines. To many marketers of the period the traditional principles of marketing did not quite 'fit' these different marketing types. Rather than question the validity of the existing model, non-consumer goods (i.e. services and business-to-business) were treated as anomalies or afterthoughts usually found in separate chapters invariably towards the end of marketing texts.

A number of marketers were, however, beginning to recognise that 'gaps' existed between marketing textbooks and analysis, on the one hand, and practical implementation, on the other (Gummesson, 1998, p. 242). They hypothesised that the disparity suggested by researchers into industrial (business-to-business) and services marketing, rather than being an argument for continued separation of the disciplines, should be considered as a basis for inclusive research. It was these researchers who were to begin the search for a more holistic view of marketing and whose radical ideas were to revolutionise marketing thought.

Industrial marketing research

Industrial marketing had always been treated as mainstream marketing's unglamorous 'poor relation', a disciplinary sub-field long overshadowed by consumer goods marketing (Brown, 1998, p. 173). The emphasis in this business seemed to be on raw materials, bulk shipments, pricing mechanisms and rational buying models where marketing played only a marginal role. What part it did play relied on extending the prevailing view of consumer marketing while acknowledging certain perceived differences (e.g. order size and frequency).

It was becoming apparent, however, largely through the work of the Industrial Marketing and Purchasing Group (IMP), that this approach did not reflect the complexities of how industrial markets operated (Naudé and Holland, 1996, p. 40). Empirical research showed that many inter-firm transactions were conducted within enduring business relationships where mutual trust and adaptation are commonplace rather than the then prevailing view of inter-firm transactions conducted largely on a contractual basis (Brennan and Turnbull, 2001, p. 1). As Baker (1999, p. 211) notes, industrial marketers had learnt that if you could not offer a 'better' product at the same price or an equivalent product at a lower price then the only way to stay in business was to foster relationships and add value through important, but usually intangible, service elements. Research suggested industrial marketing involved not just managing exchanges between companies but much more complex human interactions. This theory of **network-interaction marketing** was to be defined as all activities undertaken by the firm to build, maintain and develop customer relations (Christopher *et al.*, 1991, p. 10). The IMP literature argued that it was the ongoing nature of exchange episodes that led to the formalisation of relationships between buying and selling firms (Naudé and Holland, 1996, p. 40).

It is interesting to note that this industrial or 'business-to-business' research into interaction, relationships and networks predated RM research by at least one decade and maybe two (Mattsson, 1997a, p. 37). It stressed the importance of the understanding of the complex relationships that exist within and between industries (Naudé and Holland, 1996, p. 44) and served as a platform upon which relationship marketers were to develop their ideas.

Services marketing

If industrial (or business-to-business) marketing was the poor relation then '**services marketing**' was the black sheep. This second-class view of services *vis-à-vis* consumer goods was despite the fact that the importance of services was growing rapidly. Indeed, development in most western countries was such that they were becoming largely **service-led** as opposed to **production-led economies**. In the early 1990s, for example, the UK became the first country to export more services than physical goods and they were rapidly followed by many other economies previously distinguished as 'industrialised nations'. By the middle of that decade over 75 per cent of the working populations of the UK and the USA were employed in service industries and this movement has continued into the new millennium despite the financial downturn of the credit crunch. This rapidly changing situation both emphasised the importance of services and underlined the requirement for further research.

The intangible nature of service industries had always posed a problem to traditional marketers whose models (e.g. the **BCG matrix**, the **product life cycle**) had always proved to be an ineffectual fit. Pure service characteristics, often described as intangibility, inseparability, variability, perishability and inability to 'own' the service (Palmer, 1998, p. 11), coupled with the importance of people and processes, was providing challenges that traditional marketing concepts were having difficulty rationalising. Above all, it was in industries where the potential advantages associated with the building of relationships was recognisable, and where service differential was low, that research was most required.

Impetus for RM research

It was, therefore, to be the relationship issues surfacing in industrial and service marketing that exposed the problems of the traditional marketing model in a more explicit way than with consumer goods (Christopher *et al.*, 1991, p. 10). The stimulation for this research into industrial and service marketing was to prove key in bringing 'relationships' onto the marketing agenda.

The development of RM

With the difficulties that marketers were experiencing and the ideas emanating from industrial and service research, questions were being asked. In particular, could marketing theories and practice, designed for a bygone era, be developed to cope with the multiplicity and complexity of products and services now available, or did the whole structure require rebuilding?

The marketing mix

Research was beginning to show that the 4Ps model of marketing was evidently too restrictive for business-to-business and services marketing. Gummesson (1987) went so far as to suggest that application of the marketing mix to areas other than consumer goods could be destructive as it failed to recognise the unique features of these areas. To a growing extent the marketing mix was also becoming an outdated concept for consumer goods marketing as the importance of intangible service characteristics and customer service considerations became a prime differentiation factor between products.

The first attempts to extend beyond the restrictive nature of marketing were, however, through the adaptation of the marketing mix model. According to Grönroos (1996, p. 8) the marketing mix could still be useful but other elements, not normally regarded as part of the marketing function, needed to be added (e.g. delivering, installing, repairing, servicing and maintenance, billing, complaints, customer education). Gummesson (1994a, p. 9), too, believed that the marketing mix would always be needed, but that it had become peripheral in comparison to relationships. Other authors tried to retain the 'mix' as an easy-to-remember framework that incorporated the new marketing ideas coming through. Further Ps were added such as People, Physical evidence, Processes (Booms and Bitner, 1981), Political power and Public opinion. Other adaptations (see Gummesson, 1994a, Little and Marandi, 2003) were suggested to fill the credibility gap. Indeed, early models of RM (e.g. Christopher *et al.*, 1991, p. 13) adopted this approach by incorporating the notion of 'customer service' (and by implication an endless list of sub-functions) as additional and central to the 'updated' marketing mix (see Figure 2.6).

Kotler *et al.* (1999, p. 110) took a marginally different approach. They suggested that the marketing mix represented the seller's view of marketing and proposed that marketers should view the 4Ps from a customer-orientated perspective. Thus the 4Ps became **4Cs** (see Figure 2.7) where companies met customer needs economically, conveniently and with effective communication. Thus price became the cost to the customer, place was substituted with convenience, products and services became customer needs and wants and promotion were transformed into communication.

Valuable as these contributions were for some marketers, they were not radical enough for others. This latter group saw the attempts to update the marketing mix as failing to see the underlying problems in marketing. They suggested that the 'toolbox' approach to education had, for too long, restricted discussion of the meaning and consequences of the marketing concept. In catering for the real needs and desires of the consumers, marketing had become, in effect, the sterile management of this toolbox (Grönroos, 1994b, p. 5). To these marketers the marketing mix concept theoretically had no foundation, pedagogically no longer served a useful purpose and

Figure 2.6
Customer service and the marketing mix

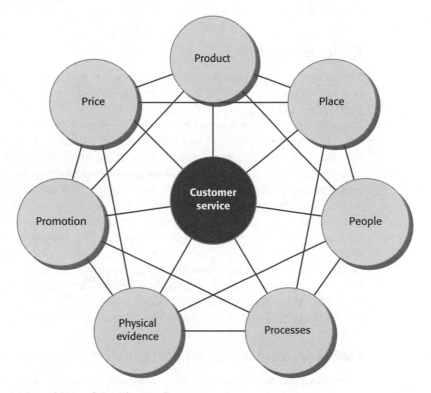

(*Source*: Adapted from Christopher *et al.*, 1991, p. 13)

Figure 2.7
From 4Ps to 4Cs

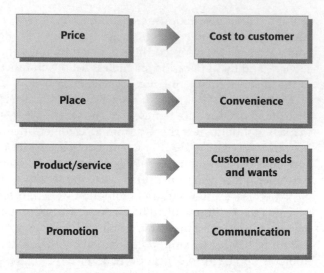

(*Source*: Based on Kotler *et al.*, 1999, p. 110)

practically was being surpassed by more dynamic approaches (O'Malley and Patterson, 1998, p. 840). Rather than tinkering with the 'mix', they believed a more fundamental change was required.

Customer supremacy

The marketing mix was not the only traditional marketing practice being challenged. It was frequently acknowledged that 'customer supremacy', the central tenet of marketing, although rational in principle was flawed in practice. What in effect was happening was that marketers attributed 'need' to individuals as a *post hoc* rationalisation to account for, and render rationality and meaning to, some recurrent behaviour observed rather than as a 'driver' (Knights *et al.*, 1994, p. 48). Despite the claims to the contrary the actual needs, wants and expectations of the customer were not perceived in reality as of paramount importance (Buttle, 1996, p. 7).

Thus, while lip-service was paid to customer supremacy, in practice marketers all too frequently ignored it. Indeed marketers appeared to view their customers in one (or both) of two ways: the first as near-passive recipients of messages and prompts from marketers, and the second as one half of a confrontational or adversarial relationship (ibid., p. 8) where the language of warfare (e.g. mission, strategy, tactics, intelligence) were regularly used (O'Malley and Tynan, 1999, p. 591). Neither perception sat comfortably with the traditional marketing doctrine of 'customer supremacy' yet they largely dictated strategy development.

Market segmentation, positioning, market share and marketing research

A number of other established marketing concepts were under attack. Market segmentation and positioning strategies were proving particularly vulnerable (Doyle,

1995, p. 27). Market segmentation, a central marketing concept, no longer appeared to be operating effectively. While markets were still being presented demographically, psychologically, attitudinally or by lifestyle, the realisation was beginning to dawn on marketers that the only category that was really meaningful was 'actual', as opposed to 'speculative', buyer behaviour (Gordon, 1998, p. 3). Rather than strategies based around real customers, traditional marketing was concerned with imaginary or illusory relationships with statistical consumers (Sisodia and Wolfe, 2000, p. 549).

Market share, widely regarded as a principal performance measure, was also under fire. It was becoming apparent that it was ambiguous and subjective (Doyle, 1995, p. 27) and largely manipulated by marketers to serve whatever arguments they sought to promote. Market (or marketing) research too was showing its limitations. It was being used by marketers to identify issues and assess customer responses to hypothetical solutions (Gordon, 1998, p. 6) based on a frequently outdated historical basis. It was also, in fast-changing markets, taking more time than marketers generally had available and was proving a barrier to swift competitive response.

The eclipse of TM

The traditional transactional marketing (TM) model was, it appeared, unsuited to complex modern marketing reality and rapidly becoming outdated. TM was seen as overly scientific, relying heavily on quantitative research, and based solely on short-term economic transactions. Vividly described by one author as 'hit and run' marketing (Buttle, 1996, p. vii), it looked to each transaction as an opportunity to 'get one over' on the gullible customer without any consideration of future contact. At the extreme it was regarded as manipulative and exploitative of the customer's ignorance (Gummesson, 1994a, p. 9).

The recognition of the problems associated with the TM model suggested a functional and theoretical 'mid-life crisis' in marketing which demanded attention. Under siege from all sides, not only were specific components of marketing being challenged but so also was the validity of the whole. It was openly debated that a 'paradigm shift' was needed if marketing was going to survive as a discipline (Grönroos, 1994b, p. 4). The apparent success of a relational approach in the service and business-to-business sectors (which were themselves beginning to receive proper recognition) began to attract the attention of other marketers, who hypothesised the emergence of a new generic marketing paradigm to possibly replace, but certainly augment, the transactional model.

The early days of RM

It was into this growing theoretical void that the concept of RM began to take shape across all areas of marketing and to excite the marketing fraternity. There are various claims as to who to invest with the 'discovery' of RM. Fred Webster in his seminal article 'The changing role of marketing' (Webster, 1992) has been credited by at least one major writer as the first to 'discover RM' (Baker, 2000), while others (e.g. Buttle, 1996) suggest that Berry (1983) was the first to publish substantive work on the subject. Saren (2007) credits academic study of the conditions and behaviours in industrial and services marketing in Europe, particularly in Sweden and Finland, in the 1970s. Evans (2002) notes that definitions of marketing in the 1950s by prominent writers such as Borch and Alderson implied the development of relationships and that the well-established 'adoption' construct within 'diffusion/adoption theory' was concerned with regular, committed purchasing. Varey (2002) credits direct marketing pioneer Lester Wunderman, who, he claims, used the term 'relationship marketing' with a client in 1949. Gummesson (1999) directs us to Dale Carnegie's 1936 book *How to Win Friends and Influence People* to find relationship marketing's bible, while Parvatiyar and Sheth (2000) would claim RM's roots were in the preindustrial age.

Whatever its heritage, RM found ready acceptance in a marketing world where it had become patently obvious that strategic competitive advantage could no longer be delivered on the basis of product characteristics alone and where corporate profitability was beginning to become associated with satisfying existing customers (Barnes, 1994, pp. 651–2). In industrial marketing, services marketing, managing distribution channels and even packaged goods marketing itself, a shift was clearly taking place from marketing to anonymous masses of customers to developing and managing relationships with more or less well-known, or at least somehow identifiable, customers (Grönroos, 1994b, p. 14).

The need for market-driven business was as strong as ever but was now perceived, more realistically, as an iterative process in which marketing strategy shapes as well as responds to buyer behaviour (Sheth and Sisodia, 1999, p. 81). It became evident that there was a need to transform marketing from a narrow set of functional skills based on the conventional marketing mix to a broader business orientation where delivery of 'superior customer value' was a key objective (Christopher, 1996, p. 64). What was needed was a form of marketing that was orientated to creating rather than controlling a market and based on developmental education, incremental improvement and ongoing process rather than simple market share tactics and raw sales data (McKenna, 1991, pp. 2–3). A clear shift would also be needed away from the adversarial mind-set implied by the bargaining power perspective towards a cooperative stance focused on mutual gain.

Towards a definition of RM

Although a clearer picture of RM may be becoming evident it may be beneficial to determine, more specifically, what is meant by the term 'relationship marketing'. One thing that will become clear very early on is that RM is not an easy concept to define in a form which is acceptable to even a majority of 'relational marketers'. Nowhere is this more evident than in the debate concerning RM and customer relationship management (CRM) (see Chapter 13).

Despite considerable academic research and practitioner interest, RM may still be regarded more as a general 'umbrella philosophy' with numerous relational variations rather than as a wholly unified concept with strongly developed objectives and strategies. Harker (1999) estimated that, at the time of writing, there were 28 substantial definitions. Dann and Dann (2001, p. 347) suggest there are nearly 50 published definitions on the subject. To confuse matters further other terms have been frequently used either as substitutes for relationship marketing, or to describe similar concepts (Buttle, 1996, p. 2). These include direct marketing, database marketing, customer relationship management, data-driven marketing, micromarketing, one-to-one marketing, loyalty (or loyalty-based) marketing, 'segment-of-one' marketing, wraparound marketing, customer partnering, symbiotic marketing, individual marketing, relevance marketing, bonding, frequency marketing, integrated marketing, dialogue marketing and interactive marketing (Vavra, 1992; Buttle, 1996; Tapp, 1998), to name but a few. Many of these relational variations describe a particular or closely associated aspect of RM philosophy rather than necessarily a holistic concept and can (arguably) rarely be said to 'stand alone' in any true sense. Others are associate concepts that may be seen to overlap with RM in some way. What is generally described as 'direct marketing' or 'database marketing', for example, while not fully mirroring RM concepts, may nevertheless include a number of recognisable relational strategies and tactics. In general, however, the major characteristics of these techniques are more transactional than relational in nature. CRM, a concept to which we will return in Chapters 11 and 13, is one 'relational approach' that has grown in popularity, particularly among many marketers. CRM's definition is as hazy as the rest but seems to relate to management of the 'lifetime relationship with the customer' usually through the use of information technology (Ryals, 2000, p. 259), and is, as such, more tactical than strategic. As the definition of RM becomes clearer these differences may become more evident (see Chapters 11 and 13).

Broad church?

RM has been used to reflect a variety of themes and perspectives. Some take a narrow functional marketing perspective, others a view that is broad and somewhat paradigmatic in approach and orientation[7] (Parvatiyar and Sheth, 2000, p. 4). As RM is used to cover a fragmented set of ideas and theoretical frameworks it has been accused of being characterised more by rhetoric than vigorous examination of what the concept actually means (Möller and Halinen, 2000, p. 30). According to Dann and Dann (2001, p. 347), asking any two relationship marketers for a definition of RM and its core principles will result in at least four definitions and five 'must have' variables. Perhaps, however, differences of emphasis are to be expected as the theory (or theories) associated with RM continue to develop. One view may be to suggest that no purist definition of RM is possible or even practical. It may be wholly valid to recognise that a term such as relationship marketing, involving as it does such a vague notion as 'relationships', is bound to generate multiple definitions. Relationships are after all 'fuzzy' entities with 'fuzzy' borders and many overlapping properties (Gummesson, 1994b, p. 18).

A potentially defendable position may be to suggest that RM should continue to remain a flexible series of concepts and ideas rather than a fixed and inflexible theory if for no other reason than its application may differ considerably from industry to industry. In effect, RM should remain a 'broad church' (see Chapter 13). It may indeed be beneficial to RM development not to become 'straight-jacketed' by one position or the other (Grönroos, 1994b, p. 10). Indeed, it may be possible, within a general relational management position, for companies to develop strategies that appear contradictory to one another yet are relevant to specific industries or even individual customer types. After all, isn't differentiation at the heart of marketing? In this way RM can make a major contribution to marketing thought and practice by challenging the embedded strategies of the past and by encouraging marketers to constantly review their business strategies in the light of changing relationships.

Common ground?

Despite the undoubted problems in coming to a consensus on the meaning and application of RM, the marketing literature on the subject can be examined to establish whether research suggests some common ground. What is clear is that the current divergence of views suggests no agreement as to a single definition of RM (one of a number of reasons[8] why its claim to 'paradigm status' may be premature). Indeed, concerns relating to the delineation of the appropriate domain have been one of the causes of a more recent criticism of RM (O'Malley and Tynan, 2000, p. 2). It is, however, equally evident that many definitions have common denominators. As such, and despite the evident difficulties, we can try to establish a 'best fit' definition from where RM can be further investigated.

RM's roots

RM, according to Gordon (1998, p. 9), is not a wholly independent philosophy but draws on traditional marketing principles. This view suggests that the basic focus upon customer needs still applies but that it is the way marketing is practised that requires changing fundamentally (Christopher, 1996, p. 55). If RM is indeed a descendant of traditional marketing then a good starting point in developing a definition of RM would be to look at how marketing has traditionally been perceived. This traditional view might be summed up succinctly using the Chartered Institute of Marketing's (CIM) (CIM, 2005) definition of marketing as:

> the management process responsible for identifying, anticipating and satisfying customer requirements profitably.[9]

This definition includes a number of assumptions that are important in the discussion of relational strategy development. 'Process' assumes that traditional marketing is a series of activities carried out as part (only) of a company's other functions. It implies a functional marketing department responsible for a fixed number of responsibilities presumably closely associated with the 'marketing mix'. It also implicitly suggests that 'identifying, anticipating and satisfying customer requirements' is the singular responsibility of the marketing department. 'Profitably' is assumed to mean that these responsibilities are carried out in a competitively superior manner (Gordon, 1998, p. 9), although there is no indication of the time scale over which this profitability should be measured.

This description of traditional marketing and others of a similar nature emphasise, above all, the functional and process nature of traditional marketing and make no explicit recognition of the long-term value of the customer (Buttle, 1996, p. 2). One particular axiom of transactional marketing is the belief that competition and self-interest are the drivers of value creation. This is challenged by the proponents of RM who believe that mutual cooperation, as opposed to competition and conflict, leads to value creation (Sheth and Parvatiyar, 1995, p. 399).

Early definition

Berry (1983, p. 25), as has been noted, was among the first to introduce the term 'relationship marketing' as a modern concept in marketing. He suggested that this 'new' approach should be defined as:

> attracting, maintaining and . . . enhancing customer relationships.

While recognising that customer acquisition was, and would remain, part of a marketer's responsibilities, this viewpoint emphasised that a 'relationship view of marketing' implied that retention and development were of equal (or perhaps even greater) importance to the company in the longer term than customer acquisition. It further implied, by differentiating between customer types, that not all customers or potential customers should be treated in the same way. The focus of traditional or mass marketing implied that whatever the status of the customer (non-customers, current customers and past customers) they were all treated in the same way and were of comparable worth and status to the organisation. RM, in contrast, saw the need to communicate in different (perhaps even contradictory) ways dependent on that customer's relationship with the organisation.

Cooperative marketing

The concept was taken a stage further by, among others, Grönroos (1996, p. 6), who challenged the traditional notion that, in order to be profitable, marketing needs to be an adversarial contest between the company and the customer. Certainly in the past markets had been frequently conceived as 'battlefields' and marketing practice dominated by combative battle metaphors (fight, competition, capture, take-over, etc.). The general view of the traditional marketing model was of businesses vying to be winners over not only their competition, but their customers as well. RM, in contrast, implied a focus on building 'value-laden relationships' and 'marketing networks' (Grönroos, 1994b, p. 9) rather than confrontation.

A change in attitude away from the traditional 'winner and loser' philosophy was also promulgated. Sheth and Sisodia (1999, p. 82) noted the clear evidence of a shift from the adversarial mind-set implied by the 'bargaining power' perspective towards a cooperative stance focused on mutual gain. Gummesson (1997, p. 56) suggested that the RM approach resulted in both parties deriving value from the transaction, and Voss and Voss (1997, p. 293) identified shared value as a key objective in the design and implementation of an RM programme. In effect 'relational marketers' were seeking strategies that produced 'win–win' situations (Gummesson, 1997, p. 56) with both parties gaining value from the buyer–seller partnership. The result was to be achieved through mutual exchange and fulfilment of promises (Grönroos, 1994b, p. 9) by *both parties* in a series of interactions over the lifetime of their relationship.

This view of marketing also implied that suppliers were not alone in creating or benefiting from the value created by the company. Rather RM was seen as an ongoing process of identifying and *creating new value* with individual customers and then *sharing the value benefits* with them over the lifetime of the association (Gordon, 1998, p. 9). A 'relationship', in these terms, was definable as the sum total of 'meaning-filled episodes' where relational partners co-produce value (Buttle, 1997, p. 148).

Relationship burdens

One important aspect of the original Berry definition required attention. The seemingly altruistic sentiments implied by RM might be seen to contradict the fact that the profit motive was still a principal business driver. The difference between RM and traditional marketing was that RM was seen to achieve this profitability through co-production and cooperation rather than through manipulation. RM would, it was suggested, potentially benefit both parties: the buyer through reduced transaction costs, and the seller through better understanding of customers' circumstances and requirements (Tynan, 1997, p. 992).

Not all relationships, however, are (or have the potential to be) profitable. Berry (2000, p. 154) notes that some customers, typically, are more profitable than others and that some are unprofitable to serve. Although, as a rule of thumb, customer retention was seen as the path to prosperity, some buyer–seller relationships were definite 'burdens' to a company (Håkansson and Snohota, 1995, p. 522). Indeed, situations can develop where a small number of highly profitable customers, in essence, subsidise a larger number of customers where the company actually loses money (Sheth and Sisodia, 1999, p. 83).

Such is the likely scale of this problem that Storbacka *et al.* (1994, pp. 31–2) suggest that it is not uncommon for 50 per cent of a retail bank's customers to be unprofitable. In later research concentrating on the Scandinavian banking system, Storbacka (1997, p. 488) reported that approximately 1 per cent of customers were responsible for the erosion of the profits from the top 25 per cent of the bank's customer base. Other researchers have made similar observations. In certain industrial markets, for example, Cooper and Kaplan (1991, p. 134) reported that 20 per cent of customers represented 225 per cent of total customer-base profitability. Around 70 per cent of these customers hovered around the break-even point while 10 per cent of the customer base represented a loss equivalent to 125 per cent of the firm's eventual profit! Allowing this situation to continue over any length of time is particularly dangerous for larger companies that may be vulnerable to entry into the market of smaller companies that systematically target their most profitable customers (Sheth and Sisodia, 1999, p. 83).

This recognition of the potential loss-making capability of some relationships suggested that marketing management from a relationship perspective must pay attention to three key objectives rather than the two areas originally suggested (Strandvik and Storbacka, 1996, p. 72):

- management of the initiation of customer relationships;
- maintenance and enhancement of existing relationships;
- handling of the termination of relationships.

This termination may be interpreted in two ways. In the first, marketing may be seen to be moving towards accepting 'customer de-selection' or 'adverse selection' (Smith, 1998, p. 4) as part of the marketing process. This might be operationalised, according to Smith, by 'dumping unprofitable customers while selectively seeking and keeping the more profitable ones' or, alternatively, by reducing the appeal of the offering such that the customer goes elsewhere of their own volition. The implication here is that cost–benefit ratios needed to be constantly monitored (Tynan, 1997, p. 992) to minimise, and where possible remove, the effect of loss-making customers. Although this perspective appears intuitively counter to a relationship philosophy, it represents a commercial realism that required incorporation into the RM definition.

A second interpretation of the requirement to manage the 'burden of relationships' (Håkansson and Snohota, 1995, p. 552) is to regard loss-making customers as part and parcel of the business. In this respect marketing needs to develop a theory of subsidisation (Sheth and Sisodia, 1999, p. 83): in effect, a strategic understanding of when and how to subsidise. This view suggests that subsidies are not always bad for business and that, if used strategically, they can turn competitive vulnerability into competitive advantage. It also challenges marketers to accept the burden of loss making in the short term in the hope of long-term profitability.

Relationships, networks and interactions

A further feature of 'older' definitions and writings on the subject of relationship marketing was that they focused wholly on the supplier–customer relationship (the **'supplier–customer dyad'**). Later contributions, however, were seen to widen RM's scope (Buttle, 1996, p. 3). The logic behind this reasoning was that you could not serve your customer well without attention to these important internal and external relationships. According to Gummesson (1999, p. 1), marketing is more than just the dyadic relationship between the buyer and the seller; rather, it represents the whole series of 'relationships, networks and interactions' which the company (or more strictly the company's employees or representatives) undertakes as part of its commercial dealings. As marketing activities are subsets or properties of society, it is suggested that these relationships, networks and interactions have been at the core of business since time immemorial.

As will become apparent in later chapters, RM thinking was developing away from the strictly 'two-way dialogue' between the supplier and the customer towards the synonymous development of other company relationships.[10] Among the relationships (the simple dyad as well as the complex networks) the parties enter into active contact with each other. This Gummesson (1999, p. 1) calls 'interaction'. Thus RM was seen to represent 'all marketing activities directed towards establishing, developing and maintaining successful relational exchanges' (Morgan and Hunt, 1994, p. 22).

RM definition

Most of the concepts, ideas and developments discussed above are present in Grönroos's (1994b, p. 9) refined definition of RM, in which he described the objectives of RM as to:

> identify and establish, maintain and enhance and, when necessary, terminate relationships with customers and other stakeholders, at a profit so that the objectives of all parties involved are met; and this is done by mutual exchange and fulfillment of promises.

No definition will ever be perfect and it may well be that other ideas and concepts may in time also require inclusion, but, as Harker (1999, p. 15) concluded, this definition seemed most elegant and succinct and represented what most researchers believed was the essence of RM. In later chapters we will investigate more closely how these concepts were translated into strategies and tactics and their perceived benefits. In particular we will look at the claims that are implicit in this definition. These include six dimensions that differ significantly from the historical definition of marketing (Gordon, 1998, p. 9):

- RM seeks to create new value for customers and then share it with these customers.
- RM recognises the key role that customers have both as purchasers *and* in defining the value they wish to achieve.
- RM businesses are seen to design and align processes, communication, technology and people in support of customer value.
- RM represents continuous cooperative effort between buyers and sellers.
- RM recognises the value of customers' purchasing lifetimes (i.e. lifetime value).
- RM seeks to build a chain of relationships within the organisation, to create the value customers want, and between the organisation and its main stakeholders, including suppliers, distribution channels, intermediaries and shareholders.

The growing interest in RM suggests a shift in the nature of marketplace transactions from discrete to relational exchanges (see Box 2.2), from exchanges between parties with no past history and no future to interactions between parties with a history and plans for future interaction (Weitz and Jap, 2000, p. 209). Interaction is an important concept in this new thinking as it had previously been assumed that buyers were passive; indeed this remains an implicit assumption of the mix-management paradigm (O'Malley, 2003, p. 127).

As Sheth and Sisodia (1999, p. 84) note, we should always bear in mind that marketing is context driven, and that the context has changed, is changing and will no doubt change in the future. Marketers need to question and challenge what these authors call the well-accepted 'law-like generalisations' (or in-bedded concepts) that have grown up around marketing. In many ways whether or not RM represents a true paradigm shift in marketing is less important than its ongoing ability to shed light on important marketing phenomena (Ambler and Styles, 2000, p. 505). Over the following chapters RM ideas, concepts, claims and perceptions will be tested as we try to establish the importance of relationship marketing. In this new edition those ideas and concepts that have grown alongside or after RM will also be examined (see Chapter 13).

Box 2.2 TM and RM compared

Transactional marketing	Relationship marketing
■ Orientation to single sales	■ Orientation to customer retention
■ Discontinuous customer contact	■ Continuous customer contact
■ Focus on product features	■ Focus on customer value
■ Short time scale	■ Long time scale
■ Little emphasis on customer service	■ High emphasis on customer service
■ Limited commitment to meeting customer expectations	■ High commitment to meeting customer expectations
■ Quality as the concern of production staff	■ Quality as the concern of all staff

(*Source*: Adapted from Payne *et al.*, 1995)

Summary

This chapter has looked at the development of relationship marketing (RM) and the considerable interest it has created among academics, consultants and practitioners alike. Although there are different perspectives evident there are also a number of common denominators beginning to develop. It looked at the roots of RM. It reviewed the perceived problems with traditional marketing in the light of fast-changing and complex markets. It examined RM's growth in popularity, acknowledging that there is no generally accepted definition. In an attempt to clarify thinking on RM, different perceptions (from simple to catch-all) were explored.

The earliest definitions of RM were analysed and found somewhat wanting. Not only was customer acquisition and retention important but ways had to be found to eliminate (or otherwise accommodate) loss-making customers. In addition RM theory was developing to include other relationships with key stakeholders. A broad definition of RM was, therefore, presented that, it is suggested, could act as a reference point from where to begin our investigation. It will not all be plain sailing, however. We should not, for example, expect anything as inherently complicated as 'relationships' to be anything other than complex and paradoxical. Indeed, marketing reality requires that we learn to live with this complexity, these paradoxes and the uncertainty, ambiguity and instability generated (Gummesson, 1997, p. 58) if we are to develop further the marketing discipline.

Discussion questions
1 What were recognised, towards the end of the twentieth century, as the perceived weaknesses of traditional marketing?
2 What were the influences that led to the development of relationship marketing?
3 What part did (a) business-to-business and (b) services marketing play in this development?
4 What are the major differences between traditional and relationship marketing?

Case study   What the Willy Wonka of BSkyB knows about customers

You might have thought that James Murdoch would have had better things to do with his time than to sit in a not particularly distinguished conference suite on London's Edgware Road, listening to 60-second 'elevator pitches' from a roomful of enthusiastic amateurs.

On a grey Wednesday afternoon last month, the 34-year-old chief executive of satellite broadcaster BSkyB gave up a few precious hours that could have been spent hammering out tactics for his battle with Sir Richard Branson's Virgin Media, or preparing for the ordeal of further scrutiny from Ofcom, the UK's media regulator.

Instead, he sat and listened carefully as BSkyB customers attempted to win his backing for various community-based or environmental initiatives, such as powering satellite dishes and digi-boxes with solar energy, or hooking up every school in the country to broadband.

The customers had been divided into teams and each had to select a brave spokesperson to make a brief submission to the chief executive. A big, blue clock projected on a screen showed how much time the speaker had left and, as the minute ran out, a loud buzz signalled that it was time to shut up. A roaming camera crew came up close to make sure every moment of each pitch was recorded.

Mr Murdoch concentrated, took notes and nodded – and very occasionally smiled. And after sitting through 20 – yes, 20 – presentations, he declared his favourite to be table 10's brain wave, 'Sky's bigger picture' – a new loyalty card for BSkyB customers that would reward green and socially responsible behaviour. The boss's verdict on the idea? 'Dynamite!'

As the energy levels in the room grew, and an atmosphere more akin to some kind of television game show developed, I was reminded of the excitement experienced by lucky holders of one of Willy Wonka's golden tickets – you know, the ones that entitled you to a once-in-a-lifetime tour of his world-famous chocolate factory. In his sober blue suit, Mr Murdoch cut a more understated and businesslike figure than Roald Dahl's extraordinary hero – who wore, you may remember, 'a black top hat on his head', 'a tail coat made of beautiful plum-coloured velvet', bottle-green trousers, pearly-grey gloves, all set off by a fine, gold-topped walking cane. The clean-cut Mr Murdoch did not, like Mr Wonka, sport 'a small, neat, pointed black beard'. While Mr Wonka's face was 'alight with fun and laughter', Mr Murdoch's emotions remained pretty firmly in check.

But what the two business leaders had in common was an understanding that there is no substitute for getting really close to your customers. Mr Murdoch wants his customers to know he cares about the same things they care about. BSkyB has been 'carbon neutral' since last year and its chief executive is a proud owner of a hybrid car – they are 'dynamite' too, apparently. At the end of the session he said, 'It is so incredibly important for us to have this dialogue with you.' He was palpably sincere. He was also exactly right.

Had the Edgware Road Hilton's conference suite been filled with hardened business leaders rather than enthusiastic amateurs, it is unlikely the same amount of energy and creativity would have been generated.

And had you been unwise enough to suggest to those business leaders that what they were engaged in was an example of '**corporate social responsibility**' (CSR), the groans would have been audible at both ends of that long and busy road.

But the idea that young Mr Murdoch is some kind of softy would clearly be misplaced. His company controls almost 70 per cent of the UK pay-TV market. Last November, BSkyB coughed up £1bn ($2bn) to grab 17.9 per cent of rival broadcaster ITV, a move that has attracted the attention of the regulator. He rarely misses an opportunity to condemn the

BBC's 'unfair' UK market position. He is now toe to toe with Virgin Media, a dispute that is heading for the High Court.

In other words, Mr Murdoch is emulating that other powerful businessman who once observed that 'monopoly is a terrible thing – until you have one' – a quotation attributed, of course, to a certain Keith Rupert Murdoch.

Smart businesses in the 21st century are going to find more and more ingenious ways of tuning in to their customers' legitimate concerns, deepening the relationship they have with them and extending their customers' appreciation of their business and their brand. You don't have to call it CSR (or even CSR 2.0) if you don't want to. But virtue is increasingly going to build competitive advantage, and inactive sneerers will be left further and further behind. Responsibility is not incompatible with aggressive competition. On the contrary, it can form a key part of a competitive strategy.

James Murdoch is a talented and hard-working young man and, if I were Virgin Media, I would be very, very worried. But, however capable he is, I'm not sure BSkyB will ever be able to match one of Willy Wonka's greatest achievements – television chocolate. This genuine technological innovation allows the broadcaster to beam real chocolate bars through the television screen into the viewers' living rooms, taking the 'customer experience' to a new level.

'Just imagine,' cried Mr Wonka, 'when I start using this across the country . . . you'll be sitting at home watching television and suddenly a commercial will flash on to the screen and a voice will say: 'EAT WONKA'S CHOCOLATES! THEY'RE THE BEST IN THE WORLD! IF YOU DON'T BELIEVE US, TRY ONE FOR YOURSELF – NOW!' And you simply reach out and take one! How about that, eh?'

From What the Willy Wonka of BSkyB knows about customers,
Financial Times, FT.com (Stern. S), 16 April 2007

Case study questions

1 Why was James Murdoch prepared to spend time considering various community-based or environmental initiatives?
2 Is this CRS or philanthropy, or are there other motives?
3 How might smart businesses tune in to their customers' legitimate concerns, deepening the relationship they have with them and extending their customers' appreciation of their business and their brand?

References

Ambler, T. and Styles, C. (2000) 'Viewpoint: the future of international research in international marketing: constructs and conduits', *International Marketing Review*, 17 (6), 492–508.

Baker, M.J. (1999) 'Editorial', *Journal of Marketing Management*, 15, 211–14.

Baker, M.J. (2000) 'Writing a literature review', *The Marketing Review*, 1, 219–47.

Barnes, J.G. (1994) 'Close to the customer: but is it really a relationship?', *Journal of Marketing Management*, 10, 561–70.

Baron, S., Conway, T. and Warnaby, G. (2010) *Relationship Marketing: A Consumer Experience Approach*, London: Sage.

Batterley, R. (2005) *Leading through Relationship Marketing*, New York, NY: McGraw-Hill.

Berry, L.L. (1983) 'Relationship marketing', in Berry, L.L., Shostack, G.L. and Upsay, G.D. (eds) *Emerging Perspectives on Service Marketing*, Chicago, IL: American Marketing Association, pp. 25–8.

Berry, L.L. (2000) 'Relationship marketing of services: growing interest, emerging perspectives', in Sheth, J.N. and Parvatiyar, A. (eds) *Handbook of Relationship Marketing*, Thousand Oaks, CA: Sage, pp. 149–70.

Booms, B.H. and Bitner, M.J. (1981) 'Marketing strategies and organisational structures for service firms', in Donnelly, J. and George, W.R. (eds) *Marketing of Services*, Chicago, IL: American Marketing Association.

Borden, N. (1964) 'The concept of the marketing mix', *Journal of Advertising Research*, **4** (June), 2–7.

Brennan, R. and Turnbull, P.W. (2001) 'Sophistry, relevance and technology transfer in management research: an IMP perspective', Middlesex University Business School, unpublished.

Brodie, R.J., Coviello, N.E., Brookes, R.W. and Little, V. (1997) 'Towards a paradigm shift in marketing: an examination of current marketing practices', *Journal of Marketing Management*, **13** (5), 383–406.

Brown, S. (1995) *Postmodern Marketing*, London: Routledge.

Brown, S. (1998) *Postmodern Marketing II*, London: International Thomson Business Press.

Buttle, F.B. (1996) *Relationship Marketing Theory and Practice*, London: Paul Chapman.

Buttle, F.B. (1997) 'Exploring relationship quality', paper presented at the Academy of Marketing Conference, Manchester, UK.

Carnegie, D. (1936) *How to Win Friends and Influence People*, New York: Simon & Schuster.

Christopher, M. (1996) 'From brand values to customer values', *Journal of Marketing Practice*, **2** (1), 55–66.

Christopher, M., Payne, A. and Ballantyne, D. (1991) *Relationship Marketing*, London: Butterworth Heinemann.

CIM (2005) *Marketing and the 7Ps*, Cookham, Berks: Chartered Institute of Marketing.

Cooper, R. and Kaplan, R.S. (1991) 'Profit priorities from activity-based costing', *Harvard Business Review*, May/June, 130–5.

Coviello, N., Brodie, R.J. and Munro, H.J. (1997) 'Understanding contemporary marketing: development of a classification scheme', *Journal of Marketing Management*, **13** (6), 501–22.

Dann, S.J. and Dann, S.M. (2001) *Strategic Internet Marketing*, Milton, Queensland: John Wiley & Sons.

De Azevedo, A. and Pomeraz, R. (2008) *Customer Obsession; How to Grow Customers in the New Age of Relationship Marketing*, Columbus, OH: McGraw-Hill.

Doyle, P. (1995) 'Marketing in the new millennium', *European Journal of Marketing*, **29** (12), 23–41.

Evans, M. (2002) 'The unreliable marketing route map and the road to hell (?)', competitive paper, Academy of Marketing Conference, Nottingham University.

Gamble, P.R., Stone, M., Woodcock, N. and Foss, B. (2006) *Up Close and Personal; Customer Relationship Marketing at Work*, London: Kogan Page.

Gordon, I.H. (1998) *Relationship Marketing*, Etobicoke, Ontario: John Wiley & Sons.

Gregutsch, M. (2004) *Relationship Marketing*, Saarbrücken: VDM.

Grönroos, C. (1990) 'Relationship approach to the marketing function in service contexts: the marketing and organization behaviour interface', *Journal of Business Research*, **20**, 3–11.

Grönroos, C. (1994a) 'From marketing mix to relationship marketing: towards a paradigm shift in marketing', *Asia–Australia Marketing Journal*, **2** (1), 9–29.

Grönroos, C. (1994b) 'From marketing mix to relationship marketing: towards a paradigm shift in marketing', *Management Decisions*, **32** (2), 4–20.

Grönroos, C. (1994c) 'Quo vadis, marketing? Towards a relationship marketing paradigm', *Journal of Marketing Management*, **10**, 347–360.

Grönroos, C. (1996) 'Relationship marketing: strategic and tactical implications', *Management Decisions*, **34** (3), 5–14.

Grönroos, C. (2000) 'Relationship marketing: the Nordic school perspective', in Sheth, J.N. and Parvatiyar, A. (eds) *Handbook of Relationship Marketing*, Thousand Oaks, CA: Sage, pp. 95–117.

Grönroos, C. and Strandvik, T. (1997) 'Editorial', *Journal of Marketing Management*, **13** (5), 342.

Gummesson, E. (1987) 'The new marketing: developing long-term interactive relationships', *Long-Range Planning*, **20** (4), 10–20.

Gummesson, E. (1994a) 'Making relationship marketing operational', *International Journal of Service Industry Management*, **5**, 5–20.

Gummesson, E. (1994b) 'Broadening and specifying relationship marketing', *Asia–Australia Marketing Journal*, **2** (1), 31–43.

Gummesson, E. (1996) 'Relationship marketing and imaginary organisations: a synthesis', *European Journal of Marketing*, **30** (2), 31–44.

Gummesson, E. (1997) 'Relationship marketing: the emperor's new clothes or a paradigm shift?', *Marketing and Research Today*, February, 53–60.

Gummesson, E. (1998) 'Implementation requires a relationship marketing paradigm', *Journal of the Academy of Marketing Science*, **26** (3), 242–9.

Gummesson, E. (1999) *Total Relationship Marketing: Rethinking Marketing Management from 4Ps to 30Rs*, Oxford: Butterworth Heinemann.

Gummesson, E. (2001) 'Are current research approaches in marketing leading us astray?', *Marketing Theory*, **1** (1), 27–48.

Håkansson, H. and Snohota, I. (1995) 'The burden of relationships or who next?', in *Proceedings of the 11th IMP International Conference,* Manchester, UK, pp. 522–36.

Harker, M.J. (1999) 'Relationship marketing defined? An examination of current relationship marketing definitions', *Marketing Intelligence and Planning*, **17** (1), 13–20.

Harris, L.C., O'Malley, L. and Patterson, M. (2003) 'Professional interaction: exploring the concept of attraction', *Marketing Theory*, **5** (1), 9–36.

Harwood, T., Garry, T. and Broderick, A. (2008) *Relationship Marketing*, Maidenhead: McGraw-Hill.

Hollensen, S. (2004) *Marketing Management; A Relationship Approach*, Harlow: FT/Prentice Hall.

Knights, D., Sturdy, A. and Morgan, R.M. (1994) 'The consumer rules? An examination of the rhetoric and "reality" of marketing in financial services', *European Journal of Marketing*, **28** (3), 42–54.

Kotler, P. (1992) 'Marketing's new paradigm: what's really happening out there?', *Planning Review*, **20** (5), 50–2.

Kotler, P., Armstrong, G., Saunders, J. and Wing, V. (1999) *Principles of Marketing*, 2nd European edn, New York: Prentice Hall.

Levitt, T. (1960) 'Marketing myopia', *Harvard Business Review*, July/August, 45–56.

Little, E. and Marandi, E. (2003) *Relationship Marketing Management*, London: International Thomson Business Press.

McCarthy, E.J. (1978) *Basic Marketing: A Managerial Approach*, 6th edn, Homewood, IL: Richard D. Irwin.

McKenna, R. (1991) *Relationship Marketing*, London: Addison Wesley.

Mattsson, L.G. (1997a) '"Relationship marketing" and the "markets as networks approach": a comparative analysis of two evolving streams of research', *Journal of Marketing Management*, **13** (5), 447–61.

Mattsson, L.G. (1997b) 'Relationships in a network perspective', in Gemünden, H.G., Rittert, T. and Walter, A. (eds) *Relationships and Networks in International Markets*, Oxford: Elsevier, pp. 37–47.

Möller, K. and Halinen, A. (2000) 'Relationship marketing theory: its roots and direction', *Journal of Marketing Management*, **16**, 29–54.

Morgan, R.M. and Hunt, S.D. (1994) 'The commitment–trust theory of relationship marketing', *Journal of Marketing*, **58** (3), 20–38.

Naudé, P. and Holland, C. (1996) 'Business-to-business marketing', in Buttle, F. (ed.) *Relationship Marketing Theory and Practice*, London: Paul Chapman.

O'Driscoll, A. and Murray, J.A. (1998) 'The changing nature of theory and practice in marketing: on the value of synchrony', *Journal of Marketing Management*, **14** (5), 391–416.

O'Malley, L. (2003) 'Relationship marketing', in Hart, S. (ed.) *Marketing Changes*, London: International Thomson Business Press, pp. 125–45.

O'Malley, L. and Patterson, M. (1998) 'Vanishing point: the mix management paradigm reviewed', *Journal of Marketing Management*, **14**, 829–51.

O'Malley, L. and Tynan, C. (1999) 'The utility of the relationship metaphor in consumer markets: a critical evaluation', *Journal of Marketing Management*, **15**, 587–602.

O'Malley, L. and Tynan, C. (2000) 'Relationship marketing in consumer markets: rhetoric or reality?', *European Journal of Marketing*, **34** (7), 797–815.

Palmer, A.J. (1996) 'Relationship marketing: a universal paradigm or management fad?', *The Learning Organisation*, **3** (3), 18–25.

Palmer, A.J. (1998) *Principles of Services Marketing*, London: Kogan Page.

Parvatiyar, A. and Sheth, J.N. (2000) 'The domain and conceptual foundations of relationship marketing', in Sheth, J.N. and Parvatiyar, A. (eds) *Handbook of Relationship Marketing*, Thousand Oaks, CA: Sage, pp. 3–38.

Payne, A., Christopher, M. and Peck, H. (eds) (1995) *Relationship Marketing for Competitive Advantage: Winning and Keeping Customers*, Oxford: Butterworth Heinemann.

Peppers, D. and Rogers, M. (2004) *Managing Customer Relationships*, Oxford: John Wiley.

Reichheld, F.F. (1996) *The Loyalty Effect: The Hidden Force behind Growth, Profits and Lasting Value*, Boston, MA: Harvard Business School Press.

Ryals, L. (2000) 'Organising for relationship marketing' in Cranfield School of Management, *Marketing Management: A Relationship Marketing Perspective*, Basingstoke: Macmillan, pp. 249–64.

Saren, M. (2007) 'Marketing is everything: the view from the street', *Marketing Intelligence and Planning*, **25** (1), 11–16.

Shajahan, S. (2006) *Relationship Marketing*, Columbus, OH: McGraw-Hill.

Sherry, J.F. Jr (2000) 'Distraction, destruction, deliverance: the presence of mindscape in marketing's new millennium', *Marketing Intelligence and Planning*, **18** (6/7), 328–36.

Sheth, J.N. and Parvatiyar, A. (1993) *Relationship Marketing: Theory, Methods and Application*, Atlanta, GA: Atlanta Centre for Relationship Marketing.

Sheth, J.N. and Parvatiyar, A. (1995) 'The evolution of relationship marketing', *International Business Review*, **4** (4), 397–418.

Sheth, J.N. and Parvatiyar, A. (2000) 'The evolution of relationship marketing', in Sheth, J.N. and Parvatiyar, A. (eds) *Handbook of Relationship Marketing*, Thousand Oaks, CA: Sage, pp. 119–45.

Sheth, J.N. and Sisodia, R.S. (1999) 'Revisiting marketing's lawlike generalizations', *Journal of the Academy of Marketing Sciences*, **17** (1), 71–87.

Sisodia, R.S. and Wolfe, D.B. (2000) 'Information technology', in Sheth, J.N. and Parvatiyar, A. (eds) *Handbook of Relationship Marketing*, Thousand Oaks, CA: Sage, pp. 525–63.

Smith, P.R. (1998) *Marketing Communications: An Integrated Approach*, 2nd edn, London: Kogan Page.

Stone, M., Woodcock, N. and Machtynger, L. (2007) *Handbook of Customer Relationship Marketing*, Northampton: Crest Publications.

Storbacka, K. (1997) 'Segmentation based on customer profitability: retrospective analysis of retail bank customer bases', *Journal of Marketing Management*, **13** (5), 479–92.

Storbacka, K., Strandvik, T. and Grönroos, C. (1994) 'Managing customer relations for profit: the dynamics of relationship quality', *International Journal of Service Industry Management*, **5**, 21–38.

Strandvik, T. and Storbacka, K. (1996) 'Managing relationship quality', in Edvardsson, B., Brown, S.W., Johnston, R. and Scheuing, E.E. (eds) *Advancing Service Quality: A Global Perspective*, New York: ISQA, 67–76.

Tapp, A. (1998) *Principles of Direct and Database Marketing*, London: Financial Times Management/Pitman Publishing.

Tuzovic, T. (2004) *Kundenorientierte Vergütungssysteme im Relationship Marketing*, Wiesbaden: Gabler.

Tynan, C. (1997) 'A review of the marriage analogy in relationship marketing', *Journal of Marketing Management*, **13** (7), 695–704.

Varey, R.J. (2002) *Relationship Marketing: Dialogue and Networks in the e-Commerce Era*, Chichester: John Wiley & Sons.

Vargo, S. and Lusch, R. (2004) 'Evolving to a new dominant logic for marketing', *Journal of Marketing*, **67** (1), 1–17.

Vavra, T.G. (1992) *Aftermarketing*, Homewood, IL: Richard D. Irwin.

Voss, G.B. and Voss, Z.G. (1997) 'Implementing a relationship marketing programme: a case study and managerial implications', *Journal of Services Marketing*, **11** (4), 278–98.

Webster Jr, F.E. (1992) 'The changing role of marketing in the corporation', *Journal of Marketing*, **56** (October), 1–17.

Weitz, B.A. and Jap, S.D. (2000) 'Relationship marketing and distribution channels', in Sheth, J.N. and Parvatiyar, A. (eds) *Handbook of Relationship Marketing*. Thousand Oaks, CA: Sage, pp. 209–44.

Whalley, S. (1999) 'ABC of relationship marketing', *SuperMarketing*, 12 March, 12–13.

Notes

1 This interest in RM texts has continued into the new millennium. Since the original 2003 edition of this book contributions have included Gregutsch (2004); Tuzovic (2004); Peppers & Rogers (2004); Hollensen (2004); Batterley (2005); Shajahan (2006); Gamble *et al.* (2006); Stone *et al.* (2007); De Azevedo & Pomeraz (2008), Harwood *et al.* (2008), Godson (2009) and Baron *et al.* (2010).

2 Reichheld uses the term 'loyalty-based management' although the term embodies what most scholars would recognise as relationship marketing concepts.
3 According to Baker (2000), Berry and Webster may have been working on RM without being aware of the Nordic school.
4 In hindsight many of the ideas emerging from the Nordic school were the basis for Vargo and Lusch's (2004) concept of a new dominant logic discussed later in this edition (see page 270).
5 Cost-per-thousand (CPT) is a frequently used comparative ratio of cost to audience or circulation.
6 A term coined by Levitt (1960) in his seminal article of the same title.
7 The narrow and broad perspectives are discussed further in Chapter 13.
8 For other reasons see Chapter 13.
9 In 2010 this still appears to be the definition preferred by the CIM. In contrast, in 2004 and again in 2007, the American Marketing Association (AMA) developed new, more relationship-friendly definitions of marketing. The 2007 version reads 'Marketing is the activity, set of institutions, and processes for creating, communicating, delivering, and exchanging offerings that have value for customers, clients, partners, and society at large'.
10 Research into business-to-business marketing RM was particularly influential in the development of these external relationship theories.

3 Relationships

Key issues

- Relationship terminology
- Organisational relationships
- Motivational investment
- Relationship loyalty
- Constrained relationship development

Introduction

This chapter looks in more depth at what is meant by the term 'relationship' and how the various definitions and concepts contribute to (and sometimes confuse) the relationship marketing debate.

Relationships

RM theory suggests that relationships add quality to marketing transactions. As Mitchell (2001, p. 33) puts it:

> Traditional markets are extremely powerful but they have huge limitations. Real human exchange is much richer than market exchange. Whenever people deal with people in 'relationships' or communities (rather than markets) they not only exchange money for goods, they share ideas, opinions, information and insights. They have a say. They also tend to form affections, bonds, ties of loyalty, feelings of obligation and so on. They begin to share and exchange values as well as value. And the people whose values are most in tune with those around them tend to form the strongest, most supportive bonds with other people.

So relationships are important. Despite this, as with so many marketing concepts, there is no definite agreement as to what is meant by the term 'relationship' within 'relationship marketing'. RM critics suggest that this lack of clarity has provided researchers with the luxury of being able to choose whatever relationship definition best suits their research agendas at any given time (O'Malley and Tynan, 1999, p. 589). A further criticism is that relationships are invariably discussed and defined from the company perspective. That consumers should be equally interested in building and sustaining relationships is often taken for granted (Carlell, 1999, p. 1). This chapter will attempt to go beyond the rhetoric and clarify what marketers mean when they talk about relationships.

Relationship terminology

The relationship metaphor dominates contemporary marketing thought and practice (Fournier, 1998, p. 343). The very word 'relationship', however, appears to many as the basis for some concern. The use of a highly emotive term to describe a commercial strategy is open to some justifiable criticism. Such language is not, however, new to marketing. Levitt (1983, p. 111) used the language of love when he declared over two decades ago that the sale merely consummated the relationship with the customer and after that the marriage began. These human relationship analogies are used frequently (see Tynan, 1997; Smith and Higgins, 2000). The RM vocabulary abounds with terms such as 'stages of a love affair', 'one night stands', 'extra marital dalliances', 'comparisons with a Mills and Boon novel' (see Brown, 1998, pp. 174–5), polygamy and seduction (Tynan, 1997, p. 987). Even the most innocent of consumers runs the risk of being described as 'flirting' with the competition or of being a 'promiscuous' shopper.

In relationship marketing, therefore, metaphors abound. The difficulties begin, however, when marketers start to believe their own rhetoric. As O'Malley and Tynan (1999, p. 593) note:

> As a conceptual tool a metaphor must be literally false whilst simultaneously offering creative possibilities. Thus in the case of RM, it is important to understand that exchange between consumers and organisations are not interpersonal relationships *per se* but that the attributes of interpersonal relationships might be usefully employed when describing or attempting to understand that exchange.

It is evident that the language of RM misleads some organisations into assuming that all customer–supplier contacts in particular are capable of closeness when many (if not most) are not much more than impersonal exchanges. Indeed, as a rhetorical device, it may have little meaning or relevance to most marketing activities (O'Malley *et al.*, 2008, p. 168). What some marketers call 'intimacy' some customers see as 'intrusion' (Smith and Higgins, 2000, p. 82) and justifiably resent it. When marketing-speak becomes hopelessly hyperbolic it is recognised, and discounted as such, by increasingly sceptical customers (Brown and Patterson, 2000, p. 658). When all types of repeat behaviour, including spurious loyalty, is seen as relationship maintenance, then the use of relationship as a metaphor in this context must be examined (Carlell, 1999, p. 8).

Two key questions must, therefore, be asked regarding relationships (Buttle, 1996, p. 11):

■ Can customer–supplier interactions ever be called 'relationships'?
■ Can customers ever develop relationships with companies and/or brands or must relationships always be interpersonal?

Needless to say, there are no straightforward answers.

Relationship forming

It would seem initially safe to assume that social relationship activity *per se* can only take place between individuals. In business-to-business markets in particular, relationships between the personnel of companies are explicitly recognised by both the buyer and the seller organisations and individuals within those organisations (Blois, 1997, p. 53). As we will see later, these bilateral and network relationships can, at times, develop into deep friendships that may even supersede an individual's loyalty to his or her own company.

In consumer markets, the premise is that building strong relationships will have a positive influence on exchange outcomes (Palmatier *et al.*, 2006, p. 140). However, many attempts to develop RM programmes give the appearance of something being 'done' to the customer (Palmer, 2000, p. 699) rather than a cooperative arrangement. It is frequently taken for granted that consumers are equally interested in building and sustaining relationships (Carlell, 1999, p. 1). In contrast, Barnes and Howlett (1998, p. 16) express the view that two characteristics must be present for an exchange situation to be described as a relationship:

■ The relationship is mutually perceived to exist and is acknowledged as such by both parties.
■ The relationship goes beyond occasional contact and is recognised as having some special status.

While acknowledging that relationships involve more than these characteristics, Barnes and Howlett suggest a 'true relationship' cannot exist if these factors are absent. The one-sided and emotionless nature of most everyday commercial (and in particular consumer goods) exchanges would suggest that they would have difficulty fulfilling such criteria. Certainly if we were to further stipulate that 'relationships' must include 'status recognition', then it is doubtful that this level of relationship could ever be developed with, for example, a local supermarket. In consumer markets, therefore, the existence of personal relationships is less obvious. Indeed as Brown (1998, p. 177) notes with some feeling: 'what consumer in their right mind would ever want to establish a relationship with a commercial organisation?'

There is empirical evidence to suggest that, regardless of what marketing strategies are implemented by the supplier, buyers frequently have no wish to enter into a relationship with a company (Palmer, 1996, p. 20). Even in service industries many customers simply do not want a relationship. In research into the US banking industry 70 per cent of consumers were unreceptive to the idea of a relationship with their bank (McAdam, 2005). It is probable that situations exist where the seller may want to develop a 'relationship' whereas the customer is happier with a transactional approach (Bund-Jackson, 1985, p. 34). This may be particularly evident in the case of certain industries (see page 62). An interesting dichotomy, it is suggested, may even be developing where, according to Sisodia and Wolfe (2000, p. 545):

> Today's customers appear to have lower expectations for a 'one and done' transaction orientated purchase (e.g. McDonald's) and higher expectations for long-term (longitudinal) purchases (e.g. from dentists). Ironically many companies offering the former tend to practice RM, whereas too many of the firms offering the latter fail to do so.

This domain extension, often under the mantle of customer relationship management (CRM), is no longer questioned, indeed as O'Malley and Tynan (1999, p. 589) note, 'researchers now treat exchange in consumer markets as though it is (or should be) relational and deliberately search for evidence of inter-personal relationship attributes'.

Despite the perceived difficulties and complications with defining the level of relationship, particularly in the consumer goods area, marketers perceive (either metaphorically or in reality) that relationships of some sort exist in commercial exchange situations.

Categorising relationships

There would appear to be a considerable number of variations in the types of relationship that are perceived to exist between a buyer and seller dependent on the industry, the company, the customer and numerous other factors. Research by Palmatier *et al.* (2006, p. 147) further suggests that customer relationships do not equally influence all exchange outcomes. Gummesson (1999) makes a valiant attempt to classify many of them in his 30Rs model. No attempt is made here to list the innumerable types (see Box II.1, p. 145 for a comprehensive list). Instead we will look at the various relationship criteria and how these impact upon relationship strategy development.

Organisational/Brand relationships

The question was raised earlier as to whether or not individual customers can have relationships with organisations and/or brands or whether relationships must always be interpersonal. Research suggests that relationships have a greater impact on customer loyalty when the target of the relationship is an individual person (Palmatier *et al.*, 2006, p. 147) and that consumers perceive greater relational benefits when engaged in a relationship with high personal contact (Kinard and Capella, 2006, p. 365). However, although social relationships are always between individuals, it is interesting to observe that customer–supplier relationships (of whatever level or closeness) frequently continue despite personnel leaving and being replaced in that relationship. This suggests that a bonding of sorts must exist, independent of company employees, between the customer (individual or company) and that organisation. Gummesson (2000, p. 6) calls this 'embedded knowledge'. He explains that if an employee leaves then 'human capital' is lost. Embedded knowledge, however, is part of the structural capital that does not disappear with the employee and is, in effect, 'owned' by the company.

From an RM perspective structural capital consists of relationships that have been made with the company, as an entity, in addition to (and perhaps parallel with) the relationship with the employees. As Gummesson (ibid.) notes, 'the more successful a company [is in tying] relationships to its structure, the less dependent it is on individual employees and the higher the value of its structural capital'. Clubs or charities may be particularly clear examples of where organisational loyalty is not necessarily directly associated with the personnel who work for it. Relationships with these organisations may last for years without, necessarily, any close bond developing with that organisation's employees. In the case of football clubs individual fans may be deeply attached to a particular player until they leave for another club!

It is also observable that reputation matters when dealing for the first time or subsequently with an organisation. The historical trustworthiness of parties in previous interactions make reputational effects possible (Rousseau *et al.*, 1998, p. 397) that may again supersede individual relationships. Thus a customer will continue to frequent a supplier for reputational reasons as well as (or even in spite of) their personal relationship with that company's employees.

Based on the recognition of embedded knowledge and reputational effects it may be suggested that organisational relationships are possible as a prelude to and/or as a mediating factor in, the establishment of interpersonal or non-personal business relationships. That relationships can exist with organisations, albeit at varying emotional levels, is supported by Blois (1997, p. 53), who suggests that, unless a counter-intuitive definition of 'relationship' is used, it is difficult, if not impossible, to suggest that firms do not have relationships. O'Malley and Tynan (1999, p. 594), too, suggest that when viewed as an association between two or more variables then it is clear a relationship exists between consumers and organisations.

Brand communities

As well as organizational relationships, where the principal relationship is with staff at the supplier–customer interface, can relationships develop with brands? According to some researchers brands can indeed be conceptualized entities with personality characteristics similar to human characteristics (Fournier and Lee, 2009). Once again the charge may be made that marketers may be taking the relationship metaphor too far. Yet there is evidence of a growing phenomenon that seems to support the contention. Variously called brand communities, brand tribes or brand sub-cultures they relate to communities who join together in allegiance to a particular brand. Although this is not a twenty-first century development (the Harley-Davidson Owners Group was set up by the company in 1983) the widespread development of the world-wide web has led to considerable growth in stand-alone and social media hosted sites. Examples include Apple, Ford, Lego, Mini-Cooper, Jaguar and Royal Enfield. Contrary to expectation, however, it is not only prestige brands that have developed a following but also some from the FMCG sector. Cadbury, for example, have 270,000[1] fans on their Wispa Facebook page making it amongst the largest brand companies in the UK.

Members of these groups are said to have a degree of awareness, and with some, a sense of obligation towards the brand community (Muniz and O'Guinn, 2001). Some brand groups are very formal and structured whereas others are much less formal with loose associations. Revisiting the question of whether these can be described as true 'relationships' this is probably best answered in respect to the motivation behind joining the community. Often they are associated with potential rewards (e.g. Coca-Cola[2]) and are, effectively, an updated loyalty scheme. Others, however, have strong bonds (see Box 3.1). One explanation is that we are tribal and like to be associated with others of a like-mind. In this case the brand is acting as the surrogate around which relationships are being formed.

Learning relationships

Relationships are part of a knowledge-generating process (Håkansson and Johanson, 2001, p. 9). Peppers and Rogers (2000, p. 244) have suggested that relationships are built on knowledge and propose that, when customers tell a company something about themselves, then it is the responsibility of the company to customise its offering to that customer. This may throw some light on the development of brand communities and why companies find them so valuable. From the point where the customer and the company first interact the relationship is seen to have started. The more the customer tells the company, the more valuable they become *provided* the company continues to adapt its product or service to meet the more and more

Box 3.1 Harley Owners Group

Harley-Davidson established the Harley Owners Group (HOG) in 1983 to build on the strong loyalty and fraternity amongst Harley enthusiasts. The term 'HOG' had in fact been associated with Harley-Davidson for decades. It was said that in the early part of the twentieth century the H-D racing team were drawn from a roughneck group of farm boys. After a win they would take the team mascot, a baby pig, on a victory circuit of the track.

From the very start the company saw HOG as a means of promoting a lifestyle rather than a product. As such, over time, Harley-Davidson reformulated its competitive strategy around its HOG brand community. HOG has also opened new merchandising opportunities for the company in the form of tie-in merchandise from biker jackets to H-D watches. Many community events are staffed by employees (not outsourced as most brand events) many of whom are themselves riders. In 1991 HOG went international with its first European Rally in Cheltenham, England. Today it has over 1400 chapters worldwide and over one million members making it the largest organisation-sponsored club in the world.

(*Sources*: Wordpress, Fournier & Lee, 2009)

specific customer needs. As customers interact more frequently with sellers they appear to gain more information which reduces uncertainty and improves trust (Palmatier *et al.*, 2006, p. 149). This learning relationship gets 'smarter and smarter' with every interaction. The relational view of developing competitive advantage identifies relationship learning as an important way to create differential advantage (Selnes and Sallis, 2003, p. 80).

Motivational investments

Dwyer *et al.* (1987, p. 14) suggest that the type of relationship that develops between a supplier and a customer is determined by the different amounts of motivational investment that buyers and sellers are prepared to commit to the relationship. They hypothesise that there are four types of active relationships in addition to 'no exchange' (see Figure 3.1):

- **bilateral relationships;**
- **seller-maintained relationships;**
- **buyer-maintained relationships;**
- **discrete exchanges.**

Figure 3.1
Hypothesised realm of buyer–seller relationships

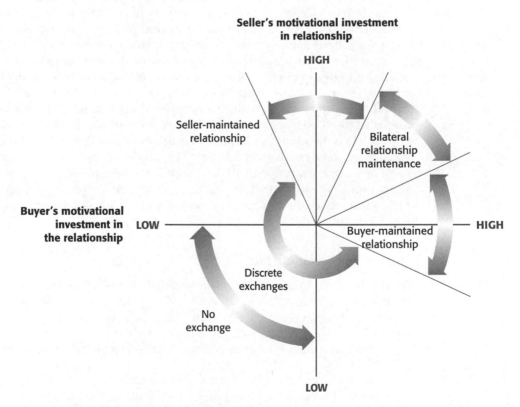

(*Source*: Adapted from Dwyer *et al.*, 1987, p. 14)

Bilateral relationships are those in which both parties are motivated highly enough to invest in a relationship. This situation reflects many of the relationship definitions and criteria discussed in Chapter 2. These bilateral relationships are particularly relevant to business-to-business markets, although some relationships of this type may be seen to exist in some consumer markets (e.g. financial services) and may relate to many brand communities. At the other end of the scale, **discrete exchanges** are low-involvement, purely transactional relationships (see Chapter 5).

That relationships might exist other than bilateral (i.e. with the active involvement of both parties) or discrete (i.e. transactional) does not, according to Dwyer *et al.* (1987, p. 15), denigrate the significance of this type of relationship, albeit that they are one-sided. In Dwyer *et al.*'s conception just because one or other party has a low motivational investment does not mean it is not a relationship – rather that it is a relationship of a different type.

Examples of **buyer-maintained relationships** may be seen in the automobile market where Toyota, Ford and other manufacturers regularly share their production information with their suppliers. Retail stores such as Tesco and Sainsbury also allow suppliers access to 'point of sale' data to facilitate distribution. It is noticeable that buyer-maintained relationships are more likely to exist when the buyer is the more dominant partner. It is, however, a significant change in attitude from past decades when such information was regarded as commercially confidential and was used to maintain an element of control over suppliers. Seller-maintained relationships are those where it is in that company's interest to foster longer-term bonds with the company. These may be worthless, however, if the customer fails to reciprocate.

In consumer markets, although it is possible that customers may actively seek a relationship (for example by joining a brand community), it is the organization that will largely manage the interaction. Exceptions do exist. Some brand communities (whether set up by the company or not) resent organizational interference. Fournier and Lee (2009) even suggest that communities generate more value when members control them. Relationships between buyers and sellers in these markets are generally considered to be much looser. In FMCG markets, many companies use tactics that have more in common with traditional marketing techniques (e.g. mass mailings, promotional websites) than RM. In these situations, according to McDonald (2000, p. 31), supplier delusions about the state of their customer relationships have reached alarming proportions.

Higher-level relationships

Although higher-level and closer relationships may be more common in business-to-business environments (see Chapters 9 and 10), it seems possible for some consumer organisations to develop relationships that appear to be higher up the 'relationship ladder' (see Figure 4.3, p. 81). The higher the level at which RM is practised, it is suggested, the greater the potential for sustained competitive advantage (Berry, 2000, p. 158).

Attachment or affinity to local football teams or voluntary organisations (e.g. a favourite charity or a political party) can result in behaviour that suggests a deep and frequently emotional relationship. When an individual joins such an organisation as a member they make a visible statement that they wish to be in a relationship with that organisation and its membership (Gruen, 2000, p. 356). This may be despite the fact that many of the activities (from the perspective of the outsider) reflect commercial considerations. Thus the blatant commercialism of the football club that changes its kit design frequently in the knowledge that its fans will buy the new version or continues to increase season ticket prices *may* have no apparent effect on that supporter's loyalty to the club (see Box 3.2). In the not-for-profit sector a high level of relationship may mean not only subscribing regularly but may also involve participating in fund-raising, volunteering or even governance of the organisation (Garbarino and Johnson, 1999, p. 9).

Some organisations with higher-level relationships may raise funds with the assistance of other, more commercial operators. Affinity partnering is a strategy in which the primary goal is to 'leverage the felt affinity, goodwill or brand name strength of a partner so as to enhance relational market behaviour' (Swaminathan

---

Box 3.2   No room for loyalty at United

For the past fortnight, my inbox has been filled with tales of long-standing Manchester United fans who cannot afford to renew their season tickets, following the 26 per cent rise in prices in the past two years.

These people have supported the club spiritually and financially for decades; now they are priced out. And what really upsets them is that the rises are to underwrite the new owners' takeover costs.

This week, those contemplating life without United learned what the club feels about them. A spokesperson observed that the defection of large numbers of committed customers wasn't a problem since there are 14,000 people on the season-ticket waiting list, happy to pick up any stack from the departures.

Perhaps we should be grateful for such honesty. Now we have it officially: for the English champions, loyalty is not a commodity of any value. All that concerns the Glazer-driven board is maximising revenues as quickly as possible.

As a model for the football business, however, the approach of the Old Trafford organisation might prove to be fundamentally wrong-headed. Logic suggests this summer is not the end of double digit ticket price rises. So what will happen next season when many of the incoming 14,000 also find they cannot afford their renewals? Will churn-over continue until we reach a point when everyone in the country has become an ex-season holder?

Perhaps only then will the administration appreciate that there is a financial value in loyalty. When that time arrives, sadly, for those who have found their long-term dedication so scandalously spurned by the administration, there will be no pleasure in saying 'I told you so'.

(*Source*: Jim White, *Daily Telegraph*, 16 June 2007)

and Reddy, 2000, p. 382). The programmes are known variously as **affinity packages, cause-related marketing, co-branding**, dual signature and other terms. Affinity packages (e.g. university credit cards, society or group insurance or assurance policies) are often arranged through companies such as MBNA, Royal Bank of Scotland and Membership Services Direct and are prompted by the consumer's close relationship with the affiliated organisation. Whether the consumer sees this as a close relationship with the actual (as opposed to the nominal) supplier is, however, doubtful. What is more realistic is that the member sees this 'relationship' as a relatively cost-efficient way of contributing to the sponsor organisation's coffers. From the actual supplier's perspective it may be a means of targeting customers with specific needs or particular profiles associated with the membership of certain organisations.

Other affinity-type relationships include those that Foxall *et al.* (1998, p. 17) call 'frequency marketing'. Frequency marketing describes those interconnected programmes designed to link customers with brands by engaging them into clubs entitling members to special discounts, newsletters, tie-in purchases, credit cards, promotions and other privileges. Examples include collectors' clubs such as those for Swatch watches and Royal Doulton bone china figurines.

Relationship loyalty

It is almost impossible to discuss relationships without discussing the concept of loyalty as customer loyalty is frequently seen as an expected outcome of RM (Palmatier *et al.*, 2006, p. 140). Indeed the phrase '**loyalty marketing**' is frequently used interchangeably with relationship marketing.

Loyalty is a state of mind (Dick and Basu, 1994, p. 99). Such is its perceived importance that it has been claimed that customer loyalty 'is emerging as the marketplace currency for the twenty-first century' (Singh and Sirdeshmukh, 2000, p. 150) and that it represents an important basis for developing sustainable competitive advantage (Dick and Basu, 1994, p. 99).

Loyalty is, however, a much used and abused term. Although it is widely utilised, most authors fail to define what they mean by the term, resulting in a lack of consistency in the marketing literature. The frequent assumption is that loyalty translates into an unspecified number of repeat purchases from the same supplier over a specified period (Kendrick, 1998). It is, however, more complex a term than this suggests. At its most profound, the term 'loyalty' suggests the highest possible level of relationship impinging upon the emotional, not to say the irrational. Its use in commercial situations has, however, debased this higher-level meaning, although some suppliers would have us believe differently. Although loyalty itself is an important concept, its nuances have been lost in the traditional brand loyalty debate (Fournier, 1998, p. 343). The idea that loyalty has some special magical powers that marketers can invoke which are 'different' or 'in addition to' their normal marketing activities has been growing (Mitchell, 1998, p. 16) despite considerable evidence to the contrary.

Defining loyalty

There appear to be two main strands of thought on the essence of commercial loyalty (Javalgi and Moberg, 1997, p. 165):

- A definition of loyalty in *behavioural* terms, usually based on the number of purchases and measured by monitoring the frequency of such purchases and any brand switching.
- A definition of loyalty in *attitudinal* terms, incorporating consumer preferences and disposition towards brands to determine levels of loyalty.

The frequent assumption is that, from whatever sources the loyalty is derived, it translates into an unspecified number of repeat purchases from the same supplier over a specified period. Neal (1999, p. 21), for example, defines customer loyalty as:

> the proportion of time a purchaser chooses the same product or service in a category compared with his or her total number of purchases in the category, assuming that acceptable competitive products or services are conveniently available.

The problem with relying on this behavioural definition is that there may be many reasons for repeat patronage other than loyalty, among them lack of other choices, habit, low income, convenience, etc. (Hart *et al.*, 1999, p. 545). Equating loyalty wholly with relationship longevity, therefore, tells us little about relationship strength (Storbacka *et al.*, 1994, p. 30).

A more comprehensive definition of loyalty[3] may be:

> The biased (i.e. non-random) behavioural response (i.e. re-visit), expressed over time, by some decision-making unit with respect to one [supplier] out of a set of [suppliers], which is a function of psychological (decision making and evaluative) processes resulting in brand commitment.
>
> (Bloemer and de Ruyter, 1998, p. 500)

Simple repatronage, therefore, is not enough. Loyalty, if it is to have any credence, must be seen as 'biased repeat purchase behaviour' or 'repeat patronage accompanied by a favourable attitude' (Dick and Basu, 1994, p. 99; O'Malley, 1998, p. 50; Hart *et al.*, 1999, p. 545). The strongest conceptualisation of customer loyalty, therefore, views it as a multi-faceted construct which takes into account both the psychological and behavioural components (Too *et al.*, 2001, p. 292). Loyalty can originate from factors extrinsic to the relationship such as the market structure in which the relationship exists (and the possible geographic limitations) but also in intrinsic factors such as relationship strength and the handling of critical episodes during the relationship (Storbacka *et al.*, 1994, p. 29).

Antecedents to loyalty

There are two distinct viewpoints as to the antecedents to loyalty. In the first, loyalty is seen as more often built on 'hard' dimensions, such as value for money, convenience, reliability, safety and functionality, and that these are the prime drivers for product or service choice (Christopher, 1996, p. 60). Fredericks and Salter's (1998, p. 64) model (Figure 3.2) shows this graphically and encompasses some of the areas that will be discussed more fully in later chapters.

This viewpoint suggests that, while a customer's positive experiences with products or services may enhance a type of temporal loyalty, it is essential to remember that 'money talks' and 'everyone has a price' (Hassan, 1996, p. 7). Such is the level and scope of price-based competition in some consumer markets (e.g. FMCG retailing) that some would even suggest that fostering 'real' loyalty in such markets is an almost impossible task (Pressey and Mathews, 1998, p. 39).

An alternative to this view is expressed by Dick and Basu (1994, p. 99). In this model, 'softer', more intangible factors such as emotion and satisfaction are seen to affect attitude in a decisive way. This viewpoint suggests that customer loyalty is viewed principally as a result of the bond between an individual's relative attitude and repeat patronage, again mediated by social norms and situational influences or experiences (Figure 3.3).

What both models implicitly suggest is that customer satisfaction sustains loyalty. The presumption is that loyalty is built upon satisfaction derived from a positive differentiation achieved by providing superior customer service (Javalgi and Moberg, 1997, p. 165). Research (Hassan, 1996, p. 9), however, suggests that loyalty should not be confused with satisfaction (though creating more satisfaction *may* reduce the likelihood of disloyalty). Satisfaction does not always result in retention (loyalty) and it is equally apparent that dissatisfaction does not necessarily result in defection (Buttle, 1997, p. 145; O'Malley, 1998, p. 48). Not only is there not a simple linear effect but there appears to be no consistency across industries (Singh and Sirdeshmukh, 2000, p. 161). Dick and Basu's (1994, p. 101) 'relative attitude/ behaviour matrix' (see Figure 6.3, p. 133) graphically shows that 'spurious loyalty' may be caused by the lack of alternatives and numerous other variables. As Storbacka *et al.* (1994, p. 28) note:

Figure 3.2
Customer loyalty: an integrated model

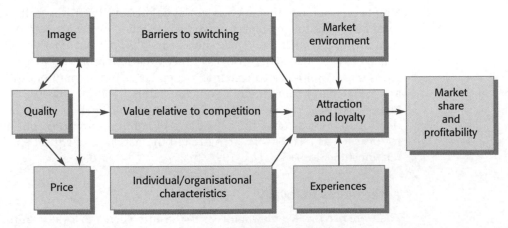

(*Source*: Adapted from Fredericks and Salter, 1998, p. 64)

Figure 3.3
Framework for
customer loyalty

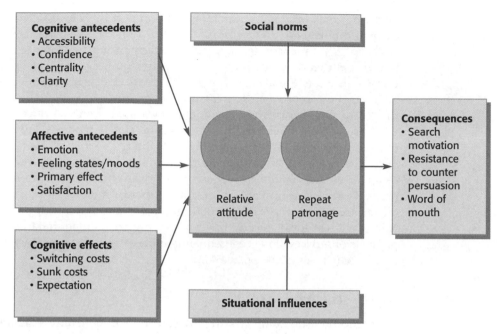

(*Source*: Adapted from Dick and Basu, 1994, p. 100)

Customer loyalty is not always based on positive attitude, and long-term relationships do not necessarily require positive commitment from customers. The distinction is important because it challenges the idea that customer satisfaction (the attitude) leads to long-lasting relationships (the behaviour).

Indeed, research suggests that neither loyalty and satisfaction (Hassan, 1996, p. 9) nor loyalty and profitability (East, 2000, p. 7) necessarily go hand in hand.

Loyalty-type behaviour

There are many ways of describing loyalty-type and non-loyal customer behaviour. For example, Uncles (1994, p. 342) proposes three ways of considering customer repatronising behaviour:

- *Switching behaviour*: where purchasing is seen as an 'either/or' decision – either the customer stays with you (loyalty) or turns against you (switching).

- *Promiscuous behaviour*: where customers are seen as making a 'stream of purchases' but still within the context of an either/or decision – either the customer is always with you (loyalty) or flits among an array of alternatives (promiscuous).

- *Polygamous behaviour*: again, the customer makes a stream of purchases but their loyalty is divided among a number of products. They may be more or less loyal to your brand than any other.

Evidence from consumer research tends to support the view that patterns of promiscuity and polygamy are the norm (Uncles, 1994, p. 344). Barnard and Ehrenberg (1997, p. 23), for example, suggest that many or most consumers are multi-brand buyers and that only one-tenth of buyers are 100 per cent loyal. In the UK and the USA for example the average number of credit cards per person continues to rise.[4] This may be because a customer's holistic requirements frequently extend beyond those capable of being effectively fulfilled by a single firm's products and services.

Consumers are, therefore, prone to 'mix and match' products and services according to their specific needs (Kandampully and Duddy, 1999, p. 316). There is also doubt over whether loyal buyers are more profitable than promiscuous or polygamous buyers. Research evidence suggests that loyalists are more often light buyers of products or services in various categories whereas multi-brand (or broad repertoire) buyers are heavier users (East, 2000, p. 7). It is not difficult to perceive a situation where the less loyal 'heavy' buyer is a more frequent purchaser of a company's products or services (and is consequently more attractive) than a buyer who is 100 per cent loyal (Uncles, 1994, pp. 346–7).

Loyalty schemes

There can be little doubt that we are surrounded by **loyalty schemes** and this has been particularly apparent with the rise of the world-wide web. Indeed, the perceived significance of such schemes seems to have reached heroic proportions. Many authors pointed to the growth of store loyalty cards in particular as evidence of the uptake of relationship marketing in the retail sector (Pressey and Mathews, 1998, p. 39) but it is developments on-line which have brought immediacy and interaction to the process. According to Uncles (1994, p. 341), the espoused view is that customers actively seek an involving relationship with 'their' brand (product manufacturer, service supplier, brand owner or retailer), which in turn offers psychological reassurances to the buyer and creates a sense of belonging. A proposed benefit for loyal and heavy or frequent customers is having this sense of belonging reinforced. According to Bolton *et al.* (2000, p. 95) the goal of such programmes is to establish a higher level of customer retention in profitable segments by providing increased satisfaction and value to certain customers.

One of the increasingly important objectives of loyalty programmes and other schemes is the collection and qualification of customer data. There is little doubt that this data has the potential to be valuable and it is frequently suggested that this offsets the costs of such schemes (see Chapter 11). Views differ on customers' motives and expectations for providing this data. According to Kelly (2000, p. 263), when you hand a customer a loyalty card you immediately create the expectation in the mind of the consumer that you are now going to study their behaviour and that, in return, they expect the supplier to do something intelligent with that information. This expectation may be equally important to consumers who volunteer information on-line. This 'cooperation' may be the basis of a future relationship. Evidence on both customer expectations and competitive advantage is, however, patchy. Khan (1998, p. 65) comments that until retailers start to make use of the information they collect there seems to be little justification for collecting it. There is at least one school of thought that suggests data collection is over-emphasised and that the costs of data collection frequently outweigh any advantages gained (O'Malley, 1998, p. 52).

Another principal reason for developing a loyalty scheme, according to Hart *et al.* (1999, pp. 541–62), is to build lasting relationships with customers. Although in some instances there may be a genuine desire on the part of the supplier to enter into a relationship with customers, most loyalty schemes seem to be tactical moves designed to defend short-term positions in highly competitive markets (Uncles, 1994, p. 337) rather than a relationship-building exercise. These schemes are little more than 'classic' sales promotions with short-term incentives to disloyal 'brand-switchers' (Palmer, 1998, p. 114; Uncles, 1994, p. 341).

Profitability is another proposed driver but here again the evidence is conflicting. While loyalty scheme pioneers (e.g. American Airlines' Frequent Flyer programme and Tesco's Clubcard) in a sector may gain additional business in the short term, these incentives rapidly become the 'sector norm' that customers come to expect (Palmer, 1996, p. 22). All too quickly, early benefits can turn into the unavoidable cost of doing business (Uncles, 1994, p. 349) as they become institutionalised and an expected part of the offering (Gruen, 2000, pp. 355/6). When loyalty rewards become the expectation in any sector it is doubtful whether anyone is ultimately any better off (Palmer, 1998, p. 117). To exacerbate the situation, once loyalty schemes become the norm and customers come to expect rewards, then there is the costly task of 'continually ratcheting up the loyalty ladder' (Uncles, 1994, p. 348). This is likely, ultimately, to affect the relationship. Over time, customers who receive, in effect, only bribes are likely to become promiscuous and seek the highest bribe available as that is the only satisfaction they receive from the exchange (Tynan, 1997, p. 992).

If there is so much doubt about the validity of these programmes, why do 'loyalty scheme saturated sectors' continue to invest so heavily? It may simply be a case of 'follow the leader'. When Tesco launched its loyalty scheme, Sainsbury were adamant that they would not follow suit, a decision reversed within 12 months.[5] Another reason may be that it is very difficult to measure the effectiveness of a loyalty programme. This stems from the difficulty of comparing the performance of companies that run them with companies that do not (Palmer, 1998, p. 114). In this situation it may be perceived as safer for the supplier to retain a scheme rather than chance losing custom.

It is perhaps ironic that attempts to apply RM in consumer markets have concentrated on 'low-involvement' categories such as **FMCG products, white and brown goods**, and services such as supermarkets and petrol retailers (O'Malley and Tynan, 1999, p. 589; see Box 3.3). Many such schemes would seem to have been introduced not for proactive but for defensive reasons (Khan, 1998, p. 65). As a result, customers, according to Mintel (quoted by Khan, 1998), are getting more out of loyalty schemes than retailers (see Box 3.2).

Loyalty in context

Features such as loyalty cards may have a part to play in relationship maintenance but they cannot realistically be taken as a proxy for the relationship marketing philosophy. Loyalty programmes are not a marketing panacea and are often not

Box 3.3   Loyalty programmes

It may appear that so-called loyalty schemes are a very recent phenomenon. The technology may be more sophisticated but the principle of 'locking-in' consumers by way of 'promotions' has changed remarkably little. The Co-operative Movement has operated a loyalty scheme since 1844, initially as the 'divi' (a dividend based on the amount of purchases made during a period), later using trading stamps and latterly using smart card technology. Pink (Sperry & Hutchinson) and green (Green Shield) stamps were an important incentive as early as the 1960s. Petrol retailers have been wedded to continuity programmes for many years, with 'low tech' collection devices (cards, stamps, etc.) being replaced later by more technologically sophisticated mediums (e.g. Esso Tiger Cards, Mobil/BP Nectar Cards). Airline frequent flyer programmes (e.g. Virgin Freeway, Air France Frequent Plus) have grown to the extent that very few non-cut-price airlines are without one. Store loyalty cards and on-line redeeming sites are but the latest ploy in marketing continuity programmes that have been around for decades.

much more than sophisticated sales promotions where costs may frequently outweigh advantages (O'Malley, 1998, p. 52). At best, loyalty schemes act as reinforcing mechanisms since it appears, on the whole, that they reward the 'already loyal' rather than anyone else (Ward *et al.*, 1998, p. 85). Participation in many of these programmes is strictly an economic decision on the part of the customer and has no influence (not even negative influence) on related behaviours (Bhattacharya and Bolton, 2000, p. 343). David Sainsbury's dismissive description of Tesco loyalty cards as 'electronic Green Shield stamps' was probably closer to the truth than many gave him credit for at the time. From a customer perspective, many loyalty schemes offer 'me too' benefits, which may be nice to have (because most people like getting something for nothing) but these are no guarantee of continued loyalty and are often marginal to their brand choice decision (Uncles, 1994, p. 341). Given the evidence, it would appear to be becoming increasingly obvious that loyalty schemes have little effect on underlying affective commitment (Palmer, 1998, p. 117) or do little to directly affect the chances of account retention (Bolton *et al.*, 2000, p. 103). As Dowling and Uncles (1997, p. 71) note 'most loyalty schemes do not fundamentally alter market structure. They might help to protect incumbents and might be regarded as a legitimate part of the marketing armoury, but at the cost of increasing market expenditure'.

Constrained relational development

In an earlier chapter it was suggested that certain industries are more or less likely to benefit from relational strategy development. On a more individualistic note, it may also be the case that, even where the general indication is that a particular business may benefit from relational strategies, there are reasons why attempting to develop such relationships may be a fruitless pursuit. These 'unrealistic' or constrained RM scenarios may be determined by either the customer or the supplier.

According to Palmer (1996, p. 20), a number of unrealistic customer scenarios exist where:

■ there is no reason why, or little likelihood that, a buyer will purchase again from a supplier;

■ buyers want to avoid a relationship as it may lead to a dependency on a seller;

■ buying processes are formalised in a way that prevents either party developing relationships based on social bonds;

■ a buyer's confidence lowers the need for risk reduction (see Chapter 6);

■ the costs associated with a relationship put the buyer at a cost disadvantage in a price-sensitive market.

Low likelihood of repurchase

With the growth of travel the percentage of purchases made at diverse, temporary locations (e.g. airports) increases. A buyer who is unlikely ever to repatronise a supplier will see no benefit from relationship formulation and may indeed be annoyed by the tactics associated with it (e.g. data capture).

Dependency avoidance

This situation may exist when any benefits associated with the relationship are outweighed by lost opportunities elsewhere. For example, some companies offer improved terms for exclusive agreements (e.g. estate agencies' commission rates). Customers may decide, however, that a sole-agent relationship would limit them (e.g. restrict the chances of a quick sale through a larger number of estate agents) and choose instead to open up the contract to other suppliers. They are forgoing any benefits of the relationship (e.g. reduced commission) in favour of the benefits of plurality (e.g. wider coverage). The implication is that, although consumers may be naturally inclined towards reducing choice, when forced to forgo all choices, or when they feel excessive pressure to conform to the beliefs of others, customers react against that pressure (Sheth and Parvatiyar, 2000, p. 185).

Formalised contracts

Formalised buying situations (such as those involving government agencies) may be compromised and jeopardised by too close an association between buyer and seller. Indeed, such relationships may be contractually or legally barred. In these situations the establishment of relationships may be neither welcomed by, nor be in the long-term interest of, either party.

Low-risk situations

In many exchange situations risk (as potentially a major driver to 'relationship seeking') is minimal (e.g. FMCG products). As a consequence consumers are unlikely to see either the need or the justification for closer relationships (see Chapter 6).

Price-sensitive markets

It may prove more profitable for buyers in certain markets to keep their eyes open for the best deal available rather than narrow the field and commit themselves to one supplier. Indeed, they may well prefer to play suppliers off against each other using an organisation's potential insecurity to gain added value.

In situations such as these, where the consumer will be unlikely to perceive any advantage from a relationship, suppliers should be looking to qualify whether costly relationship-building strategies are a viable proposition. The problem, or indeed paradox, from the perspective of the supplier, is the difficulty of knowing that some of these situations exist (e.g. where the customer is unlikely to repatronise) unless the customer volunteers this information.

Constrained supplier relationship development

This 'relationship avoidance' is not necessarily consumer-dominated and may also be sought by the supplier in certain situations. These scenarios closely mirror the previous list, and include situations where:

- there is no reason why a seller would ever see a buyer again;
- a seller seeks to avoid a relationship in which it becomes dependent on a buyer;
- buying processes become formalised in a way that prevents either party developing relationships based on social bonds;
- the seller has little opportunity to develop relationships due to the undifferentiated nature of the market;
- the ethos of the industry makes relationship-building inappropriate.

Low likelihood of repurchase

Situations where a customer is unlikely to repatronise a particular supplier (perhaps because the buyer's home base is many miles from that supplier, or where, by the nature of the product or service, a second purchase is unlikely) may suggest that investment in relationship building is unlikely to provide a profitable return.

Dependency avoidance

This may reflect the supplier's desire not to put all of their eggs in one (or a few) basket(s). This may be particularly relevant in business-to-business situations where the number of customers is, generally, lower, although it may also exist in some financial services (or other potentially high-risk associations) where the level of exposure may make the organisation vulnerable to high loss. This scenario may be very difficult to manage from the supplier's perspective if the buyer is, or has the potential of being, a substantial customer and if that customer is pushing for a closer relationship. An example of where 'dependence avoidance' may be considered is where a supplier appears overly dependent on one or a few retailers, leaving it vulnerable to changes in market circumstances (as some UK suppliers of Marks & Spencer discovered to their cost when the company changed its 'buy British' policy in 1999).

Formalised contracts

This situation mirrors the buyer's dilemma. Suppliers may be at risk (particularly in public contracts) from legal action should they even attempt to build a relationship with a public body's representative as this may be construed as bribery or corrupt practice.

Undifferentiated markets

Although RM has been presented as of potential benefit in undifferentiated markets, a different interpretation may be considered. Suppliers of largely undifferentiated products or services where customers are likely at any time to switch should consider whether 'seduction' (e.g. promotional discounts) rather than potentially costly relational strategies are more cost effective. In reality, this is what is happening in the UK supermarket industry where some of the major players (e.g. Tesco, Sainsbury's) have chosen what they would call relational strategies based upon loyalty programmes, while others (e.g. Asda, Morrisons) have opted for the promotional route.

Price-sensitive markets

This situation may exist where companies rely on market opportunism. Blois (1998, p. 258) suggests that the US company NECX Inc. is such an organisation. In a case study, Blois noted that the company exists principally to take advantage of uncertainties in both supply and demand in the computer supplies market. Blois argues that this company would feel inhibited about 'exploiting' shortage situations if it were to develop 'relationships' with its customers.

Relationships in context

Relationships are inherently dynamic and are never settled in a way that 'enables us to take a moral audit' (Smith and Higgins, 2000, p. 91). There is no doubt, however, that some companies seem to have the knack of handling relationships. Grönroos (2000, p. 4) quotes Fergal Quinn, founder and president of Superquinn stores in the Irish Republic, as saying that, if the supplier handles relationships well, the customer will come back. Quinn calls this the 'boomerang principle', the beauty of which is that 'you and the customer end up on the same side . . . so that the relationship with your customer is not an adversarial one, it's a partnership'. Tesco too is fêted as an organisation that has handled its relationships with customers well. On the other hand, companies such as British Airways and BP have been criticized for their handling of stakeholder relationships.

On the other side of the coin, the danger comes when the relationship metaphor becomes accepted as truth. Many authors treat consumer–organisational relationships as though they were literally true (O'Malley and Tynan, 1999, p. 594) when realistically they will never be more than weak associations. As Van den Bulte (1994, p. 416) notes, after long and repeated use, a metaphor may become so hackneyed that people forget that it is a metaphor and sublimate its relationship with reality. Perhaps this is happening with RM and the relationship metaphor has become a device with little meaning or relevance any more to the bulk of marketing activities (O'Malley *et al.*, 2008, p. 168).

Loyalty, as we have noted, is a very much used and abused term. Although RM and loyalty marketing (or for that matter CRM) have several common components (e.g. the use of information technology, customer knowledge and direct customer communications), it is questionable whether the association is any deeper (Hart *et al.*, 1999, p. 541). Loyalty programmes and other behaviour-based initiatives suggest that this view of relationship formation is more akin to a stimulus–response function (Barnes and Howlett, 1998, p. 15) than anything resembling a relationship. Rarely are loyalty programmes more than sophisticated sales promotions where the loyalty is to the programme and not the brand (O'Malley, 1998, p. 52). Whereas loyalty schemes may play a part in relationship maintenance, they cannot be realistically taken as proxy for the RM philosophy (Pressey and Mathews, 1998, p. 39).

Whatever the level of the relationship, it cannot be expected to last forever. Various terms exist for describing termination of relationships within marketing and these will be covered in more detail in the following chapters. Suffice to say at this stage that long-term relationships can carry with them the seeds of their own destruction (Grayson and Ambler, 1999, p. 138). It is certainly not a foregone conclusion that relationships will mature gracefully. Whether prompted by some experience within the relationship or not, many relationships will suffer and potentially disintegrate from basic boredom or fatigue. Satisfaction is certainly no defence against termination as the customer can *always* be more satisfied somewhere else. Previously loyal customers may gradually drift away and this may not be discernible until it is too late to do anything about it. Laura Ashley and Marks & Spencer may have been in the past victims of this creeping apathy.

It is important, therefore, that any reference to the term 'relationship' is made in the recognition that not all relationships are close and enduring. Relationships exist at many different levels. What might be said about all relationships, however, is that they determine the type and nature of the customer–supplier interaction. As such, and at whatever level they exist, they are of interest to the marketer.

Summary

This chapter looked at the central concepts associated with 'relationships'. It examined whether customers can have relationships with organisations and/or brands and whether relationships always have to be interpersonal. It suggested that, although personal relationships may be stronger, relationships with organisations and brands were possible and that this relationship often acted as a prelude to and/or as a mediating factor in the establishment of interpersonal and non-personal business relationships.

The chapter looked at 'learning relationships' based on 'knowing' the customer and (crucially) acting on this knowledge. It examined how 'motivational investment' affects the types of relationships that exist and how 'supplier-maintained' or 'buyer-maintained' relationships may exist in addition to bilateral and discrete exchange relationships. Higher-level relationships were discussed, including affinity, affinity packages and frequency marketing.

Loyalty as a concept close to the heart of RM was elaborated upon and the perceived antecedents to loyalty outlined. Loyalty-type behaviour was discussed and loyalty schemes put under the spotlight.

The potential for situations where relationship development is unrealistic (from either the customer or the supplier perspective) was discussed and the factors leading to such situations noted.

The chapter concluded by attempting to put relationships into perspective within the RM debate. It suggested that many levels of relationship exist, all of which are of interest to the marketer.

Discussion questions

1 In what ways are relationship metaphors used in marketing?
2 How might relationships develop between organisations and their customers?
3 What different levels of relationship can be seen to exist between buyers and suppliers?
4 What part do loyalty schemes play in relationship development?

Case study   The art of the soft sell

Walk into one of Yoforia's three frozen yogurt stores in Atlanta, and you'll get a warm hello from a server, who will encourage you to try all four of the company's frozen yogurt flavors. The server might also describe the organic milk used to make the yogurt and talk about the all-natural ingredients that go into the premium dark chocolate, mango, pomegranate, and blueberry desserts.

What you won't get is a hard sell. If you look as if you want to be left alone, you will be. Staffers are told to put themselves in customers' shoes, to interact and be pleasant, but never to nag. Although after tasting the yogurt and hearing about how healthy it is, you're certainly more likely to make a purchase. And Kim's sales are up 40% over last year.

'I take the pressure off my employees that they have to make sales,' says Jun Kim, co-founder of the 25-person, $1 million company. All of his staffers are former customers who are passionate about his yogurt. Although Kim doesn't have formal staff meetings, he works on a daily basis with his employees, instructing them to sell service as much as frozen yogurt. He awards staffers bonuses of up to $100 when he sees them going out of their way to help customers and work well with other employees. Says Kim: 'We try to focus on the customers, making sure they have a good experience when they come to the store, so they feel their money is well spent and well worth it.'

On the surface, that may not sound groundbreaking—treat your customers well, figure out what they want, give them information about your product, and sell them something you care about. But wrapping it all together and persuading your sales folks not to obsess over, well, sales, is something different: customer-centric or consultative sales. A customer-centric sales process emphasizes a low-pressure environment that lets your sales staff act as consultants, offering information and showing how your product or service can help solve a customer's problem. When it comes to yogurt, that may be as simple as helping a customer pick the best flavor. The end goal of customer-centric sales is not only to boost sales and trumpet your brand but also to make customers happy they shopped at your store, building the foundation for future sales.

(*Source*: Jeremy Quittner, *BusinessWeek*, 9 October 2009). Used with permission of Bloomberg Businessweek Copyright © 2010. All rights reserved.

Case study questions

1 What does the author mean by 'customer centric'?
2 Why does Yoforia go out of its way to reward good customer service?

References

Barnard, N. and Ehrenberg, A.S.C. (1997) 'Advertising: strongly persuasive or nudging?', *Journal of Advertising Research*, **1**, January/February, 21–31.

Barnes, J.G. and Howlett, D.M. (1998) 'Predictors of equity in relationships between service providers and retail customers', *International Journal of Bank Marketing*, **16** (1), 5–23.

Berry, L.L. (2000) 'Relationship marketing of services: growing interest, emerging perspectives', in Sheth, J.N. and Parvatiyar, A. (eds) *Handbook of Relationship Marketing*, Thousand Oaks, CA: Sage, pp. 149–70.

Bhattacharya, C.B. and Bolton, R.N. (2000) 'Relationship marketing in mass markets', in Sheth, J.N. and Parvatiyar, A. (eds) *Handbook of Relationship Marketing*, Thousand Oaks CA: Sage, pp. 327–54.

Bloemer, J. and de Ruyter, K. (1998) 'On the relationship between store image, store satisfaction and store loyalty' *European Journal of Marketing*, **32** (5/6), 499–513.

Blois, K.J. (1997) 'When is a relationship a relationship?', in Gemünden, H.G., Rittert, T. and Walter, A. (eds) *Relationships and Networks in International Markets*, Oxford: Elsevier, pp. 53–64.

Blois, K.J. (1998) 'Don't all firms have relationships?', *Journal of Business and Industrial Marketing*, **13** (3), 256–70.

Bolton, R.N., Kanna, P.K. and Bramlett, M.D. (2000) 'Implications of loyalty programme membership and service experience for customer retention and value', *Journal of Marketing Science*, **28** (1), 95–108.

Brown, S. (1998) *Postmodern Marketing II*, London: International Thomson Business Press.

Brown, S. and Patterson, A. (2000) 'Knick-knack, paddy-whack, give a pub a theme', *Journal of Marketing Management*, **16** (6), 647–62.

Bund-Jackson, B. (1985) 'Build customer relationships that last', *Harvard Business Review*, November/December, 120–8.

Buttle, F.B. (1996) *Relationship Marketing Theory and Practice*, London: Paul Chapman.

Buttle, F.B. (1997) 'Exploring relationship quality', paper presented at the Academy of Marketing Conference, Manchester, UK.

Carlell, C. (1999) 'Relationship marketing from the consumer perspective', paper presented at the European Academy of Marketing Conference (EMAC), Berlin.

Christopher, M. (1996) 'From brand values to customer values', *Journal of Marketing Practice*, **2** (1), 55–66.

Dick, A. and Basu, K. (1994) 'Customer loyalty: toward an integrated conceptual framework', *Journal of the Academy of Marketing Science*, **22** (2), 99–113.

Dowling, G.R. and Uncles, M.D. (1997) 'Do customer loyalty schemes work?', *Sloan Management Review*, Summer, 71–82.

Dwyer, F.R., Schurr, P.H. and Oh, S. (1987) 'Developing buyer–seller relationships', *Journal of Marketing*, **51**, 11–27.

East, R. (2000) 'Fact and fallacy in retention marketing', Professorial Inaugural Lecture, 1 March, Kingston University Business School, UK.

Fournier, S.B. (1998) 'Consumers and their brands: developing relationship theory in consumer behaviour', *Journal of Consumer Research*, **24**, 343–73.

Fournier, S.B. and Lee, L. (2009) 'Getting brand communities right', *Harvard Business Review*, April, 105–11.

Foxall, G.R., Goldsmith, R.E. and Brown, S. (1998) *Consumer Psychology for Marketing*, London: International Thomson Business Press.

Fredericks, J.O. and Salter, J.M. (1998) 'What does your customer really want?', *Quality Progress*, January, 63–8.

Garbarino, E. and Johnson, M.S. (1999) 'The different roles of satisfaction, trust and commitment in customer relationships', *Journal of Marketing*, **63** (2), 70.

Grayson, K. and Ambler, T. (1999) 'The dark side of long-term relationships in marketing', *Journal of Marketing Research*, **36** (1), 132–41.

Grönroos, C. (2000) 'The relationship marketing process: interaction, communication, dialogue, value', in 2nd WWW Conference on Relationship Marketing, 15 November 1999 to 15 February 2000, Paper 2, <www.mcb.co.uk/services/conferen/nov99/rm> (accessed 15 November 2000).

Gruen, T.W. (2000) 'Membership customers and relationship marketing', in Sheth, J.N. and Parvatiyar, A. (eds) *Handbook of Relationship Marketing*, Thousand Oaks, CA: Sage, pp. 355–80.

Gummesson, E. (1999) *Total Relationship Marketing: Rethinking Marketing Management from 4Ps to 30Rs*, Oxford: Butterworth Heinemann.

Gummesson, E. (2000) 'Return on relationships (ROR): building the future with intellectual capital', in 2nd WWW Conference on Relationship Marketing, 15 November 1999 to 15 February 2000, Paper 5, <www.mcb.co.uk/services/conferen/nov99/rm> (accessed 15 November 2000).

Håkansson, H. and Johanson, J. (2001) 'Business network learning: basic considerations', in Håkansson, H. and Johanson, J. (eds) *Business Network Learning*, Amsterdam: Elsevier Science.

Hart, S., Smith, A., Sparks, L. and Tzokas, N. (1999) 'Are loyalty schemes a manifestation of relationship marketing?', *Journal of Marketing Management*, **15**, 541–62.

Hassan, M. (1996) *Customer Loyalty in the Age of Convergence*, London: Deloitte & Touche Consulting Group, <www.dttus.com> (accessed 23 November 2007).

Javalgi, R. and Moberg, C. (1997) 'Service loyalty: implications for service providers', *Journal of Services Marketing*, **11** (3), 165–79.

Kandampully, J. and Duddy, R. (1999) 'Relationship marketing: a concept beyond the primary relationship', *Marketing Intelligence & Planning*, **17** (7), 315–23.

Kelly, S. (2000) 'Analytical CRM: the fusion of data and intelligence', *Interactive Marketing*, **1** (3), 262–7.

Kendrick, A. (1998) 'Promotional products vs price promotion in fostering customer loyalty: a report of two controlled field experiments', *Journal of Services Marketing*, **12** (4), 312–26.

Khan, Y. (1998) 'Winning cards', *Marketing Business*, May, 65.

Kinard, B.R. and Capella, M.L (2006) 'Relationship marketing: the influence of consumer involvement on perceived service benefits', *Journal of Service Marketing*, **21** (6), 359–68.

Levitt, T. (1983) 'After the sale is over', *Harvard Business Review*, November/December, 87–93.

McAdam, P. (2005) 'Give the customers what they want and in most cases, it's not a relationship', *Banking Strategies*, BAI Online <www.bai.org/bankstrategies/current/cover> (accessed 12 April 2007).

McDonald, M. (2000) 'On the right track', *Marketing Business*, April, 28–31.

Mitchell, A. (1998) 'Evolution', *Marketing Business*, November, 16.

Mitchell, A. (2001) 'It's a matter of trust', *Marketing Business*, April, 33.

Muñiz, A.M. and O'Guinn, T.C. (2001) 'Brand community', *Journal of Consumer Research*, March, 412–31.

Neal, W.D. (1999) 'Satisfaction is nice, but value drives loyalty', *Marketing Research*, Spring, 20–3.

O'Malley, L. (1998) 'Can loyalty schemes really build loyalty?', *Marketing Intelligence and Planning*, **16** (1), 47–55.

O'Malley, L. and Tynan, C. (1999) 'The utility of the relationship metaphor in consumer markets: a critical evaluation', *Journal of Marketing Management*, **15**, 587–602.

O'Malley, L., Patterson, M. and Kelly-Holmes, H. (2008) 'Death of a metaphor: reviewing the "marketing as relationships" frame', *Marketing Theory*, **8** (2), 167–87.

Palmatier, R.W., Dant, R.P., Grewal, D. and Evans, K.R. (2006) 'Factors influencing the effectiveness of relationship marketing: a meta-analysis', *Journal of Marketing*, **70** (October), 136–53.

Palmer, A.J. (1996) 'Relationship marketing: a universal paradigm or management fad?' *The Learning Organisation*, **3** (3), 18–25.

Palmer, A.J. (1998) *Principles of Services Marketing*, London: Kogan Page.

Palmer, A.J. (2000) 'Co-operation and competition: a Darwinian synthesis of relationship marketing', *European Journal of Marketing*, **34** (5/6), 687–704.

Peppers, D. and Rogers, M. (2000) 'Build a one-to-one learning relationship with your customers', *Interactive Marketing*, **1** (3), 243–50.

Pressey, A.D. and Mathews, B.P. (1998) 'Relationship marketing and retailing: comfortable bedfellows?', *Customer Relationship Management*, **1** (1), 39–53.

Rousseau, D.M., Sitkin, S.B., Burt, R.S. and Camerer, C. (1998) 'Not so different after all: a cross discipline view of trust', *Academy of Management Review*, **23** (3), 393–404.

Selnes, F. and Sallis, J. (2003) 'Promoting relationship learning', *Journal of Marketing*, **67** (3), 80–96.

Sheth, J.N. and Parvatiyar, A. (2000) 'Relationship marketing in consumer markets: antecedents and consequences', in Sheth, J.N. and Parvatiyar, A. (eds) *Handbook of Relationship Marketing*, Thousand Oaks, CA: Sage, pp. 171–207.

Singh, J. and Sirdeshmukh, D. (2000) 'Agency and trust mechanisms in consumer satisfaction and loyalty judgements', *Journal of Marketing Science*, **28** (1), 150–67.

Sisodia, R.S. and Wolfe, D.B. (2000) 'Information technology', in Sheth, J.N. and Parvatiyar, A. (eds) *Handbook of Relationship Marketing*, Thousand Oaks, CA: Sage, pp. 525–63.

Smith, W. and Higgins, M. (2000) 'Reconsidering the relationship analogy', *Journal of Marketing Management*, **16**, 81–94.

Storbacka, K., Strandvik, T. and Grönroos, C. (1994) 'Managing customer relations for profit: the dynamics of relationship quality', *International Journal of Service Industry Management*, **5**, 21–38.

Swaminathan, V. and Reddy, S.K. (2000) 'Affinity partnering: conceptualisation and issues', in Sheth, J.N. and Parvatiyar, A. (eds) *Handbook of Relationship Marketing*, Thousand Oaks, CA: Sage, pp. 381–405.

Too, L.H.Y., Souchon, A.L. and Thirkell, P.C. (2001) 'Relationship marketing and customer loyalty in a retail setting: a dynamic exploration', *Journal of Marketing Management*, **17** (3/4), 287–319.

Tynan, C. (1997) 'A review of the marriage analogy in relationship marketing', *Journal of Marketing Management*, **13** (7), 695–704.

Uncles, M. (1994) 'Do you or your customer need a loyalty scheme?', *Journal of Targeting, Measurement and Analysis*, **2** (4), 335–50.

Van den Bulte, C. (1994) 'Metaphor at work', in Laurent, G., Lilien, G.L. and Pras, B. (eds) *Research Traditions in Marketing*, Boston, MA: Kluwer Academic, pp. 405–25.

Ward, P., Gardner, H. and Wright, H. (1998) 'Being smart: a critique of customer loyalty schemes in UK retailing', *Customer Relationship Management*, **1** (1), 79–86.

Notes

1 As of February 2010.
2 <www.cokezone.co.uk, www.mycokerewards.com>, etc.
3 Bloemer and de Ruyter were describing 'retail store loyalty' in this definition but it is equally applicable to suppliers in general.
4 According to Data Monitor (14 February 2008) the average British adult has 2.8 credit cards and this is expected to exceed 3 by 2011. The Federal Reserve Bank of Boston reported (January 2010) that the average US adult holds 3.5 cards.
5 Sainsbury originally ran their own loyalty programme. In 2003 they joined the 'Nectar' loyalty scheme together with BP, Debenhams and others.

4 Relationship economics

Key issues

- The economic justification for relationship marketing
- Customer acquisition versus customer retention
- Stages of relationship development
- Lifetime value concepts
- Switching costs
- Relationship longevity

Introduction

It has previously been noted that there is limited agreement on a precise definition of relationship marketing, and many of the philosophical, organisational and economic concepts that surround it. There are, however, a number of key ideas or concepts that have developed through relationship marketing research which, proponents claim, underpin relational marketing theory and practice.

As was noted in Chapter 2, profitability is ultimately the driving force behind any strategy development. However, there are bad profits (usually associated with short-term exploitation) and good profits. In this chapter, therefore, we will look at the arguments for and against what are described in this context as the economics of relationship marketing or 'relationship economics'.

Relationship economics

One axiom of traditional marketing is the belief that self-interest and competition are the drivers of value creation. That axiom is challenged by relationship marketers who believe that it is mutual cooperation that delivers this value (Sheth and Parvatiyar,

1995a, p. 399). A central feature of RM is, therefore, to distinguish the concept from the microeconomic paradigm (Palmer *et al.*, 2005). However, the illusion that RM is unconcerned about profit because of its apparent philanthropic and cooperative image is false. A principal objective behind companies adopting relational strategies must, at least ultimately, be sustainable profitability. Even though in a relational exchange the focus is more concerned with the longer-term economic benefits profits remain important to all parties in the relationship (Morgan, 2000, p. 485). As Gummesson (1994, p. 17) notes, the 'language of management is money, [therefore] a good question is how the relationship portfolio pays off'.

RM is, therefore, not altruistic but based on profit-driven arguments (Buttle, 1996, p. 5) with the profitability of relationships as one of the key goals (Storbacka *et al.*, 1994, p. 22). It is, what Sheth and Parvatiyar (1995b, p. 265) call, 'enlightened self-interest'.

Leaky bucket theory

Historically, the focus of traditional marketing has been on creating new customers. This 'offensive marketing' strategy included, in addition to acquiring wholly new customers, attempting to attract dissatisfied customers away from competitors, particularly in periods of heavy competition (Storbacka *et al.*, 1994, pp. 22–3). Many authors take the view that, although the acquisition of customers is important, it is an intermediate step in the process (Berry and Gresham, 1986, p. 43). The first line of defence for any company is maintaining its existing customers (Kotler, 1992, p. 50).

RM, therefore, highlights the proposition that, in addition to 'offensive strategies', companies need 'defensive strategies' which minimise customer turnover (Storbacka *et al.*, 1994, pp. 22–3). The logic behind this double-headed approach is probably best illustrated using the metaphor of the leaky bucket (Figure 4.1). This emphasises the importance of keeping customers while recognising that acquiring customers is, of course, the basis for having any customers to keep (Grönroos, 1995, p. 253).

To succeed, a company must *both* have a flow of new customers and restrict customer exit. The aim is to keep or, where company objectives call for it, increase the number of customers available to the company. To achieve profitability the dual strategies of acquisition and retention must work in tandem.

Customer acquisition

There is a continuous need in a business for 'new blood'. Any fall in the overall number of customers has profitability implications, particularly in service industries where fixed costs (especially staffing costs) tend to be highest. *Every organisation loses customers* through relocation or other forms of termination, if not through some level of competitive switching. Any loss of customers has to be replaced merely for the company to stand still.

Companies in the past have tended to concentrate on the customer acquisition process as, in general, market growth provided a steady supply of new prospects.

Figure 4.1
Leaky bucket
theory

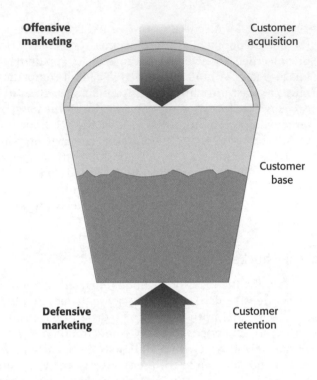

Yet, even in the halcyon days of high population growth, high sector growth and/or minimal competition the possibility always existed of substitutes or new competitors entering the market. In the third millennium, forecasters suggest low and perhaps negative population growth in many mature markets. This will particularly affect the number of potential customers at the freer spending, lower end of the adult age spectrum. Competitive pressures meanwhile are unlikely to ease and may, with the opening up of national borders, get worse. The economic downturn and credit crunch has only served to exasperate this. The likelihood is, therefore, that customer acquisition in relative terms will become more difficult.

Customer retention

Although RM has a dual focus on *both* acquisition and retention strategies, it is the latter that is often given more prominence. Indeed, it has become one of the under-pinning convictions of RM that it encourages *retention marketing* first and *acquisition marketing* second (Gummesson, 1999, p. 9). This bias exists because customer retention is perceived as offering significant advantages, particularly in saturated markets (Dawes and Swailes, 1999, p. 36). This is generally supported by academics, many of whom further promote the concept by suggesting that customer acquisition is between five and ten times more expensive than customer retention (e.g. Gummesson, 1999, p. 183). It has, therefore, become widely accepted by more and more companies that it makes a great deal of sense to try to keep existing customers happy rather than devote high levels of marketing effort to new customer acquisition (Barnes, 1994, p. 562).

To further strengthen the argument that the principal focus should be on retention, it is proposed that the longevity of relationships also provides additional profit potential. Reichheld (1996, p. 65), for example, suggests that the benefits are cumulative and that the longer the cycle continues the 'greater the company's financial strength'.

The dual benefits of customer retention can be summarised, therefore, as:

■ existing customers are less expensive to retain than to recruit;

■ securing a customer's loyalty over time produces superior profits.

These, it is proposed, are the two economic arguments that underpin RM (Buttle, 1996, p. 5). Although this is an oversimplification, there is little doubt that a major impetus for the development of RM has been a growing awareness of these *potential* long-term benefits.

Zero defections?

Despite RM's concentration on retention, no company can possibly hold on to all its customers even in monopoly situations. Although some marketing gurus call for policies leading to 'zero defections', this is neither a possible, practical nor indeed profitable objective. Total customer retention is never achievable as there is always some loss. For example, some customers will move; others will pass away. In a highly competitive market, customers may switch (temporarily or permanently) to another product or service on the basis of factors that may not necessarily be within the control of the company. It is also invariably unprofitable to attempt to achieve total (or even near total) retention as the costs (often in the form of inducements to return) involved in delivering this strategy are likely to be prohibitive. Retention strategy should not, therefore, be aimed at keeping customers at any cost (Gummesson, 1999, p. 26). The company must know when to 'cut and run'.

Retention strategies tested

As with any generalised statements, such as those made in support of RM, there is always a danger that they become accepted truths and prescriptive remedies for all varieties of assorted ills. Although the principles may hold good in many instances, there are several inconsistencies with retention economics which should be challenged before companies consider the full application of relational strategies.

Acquisition and retention costs

It is widely suggested that an important component in calculating the benefits of customer retention is that the front-end costs of customer acquisition exceed the cost

Figure 4.2
Typical profit
pattern in
financial
services and
other high
acquisition cost
industries

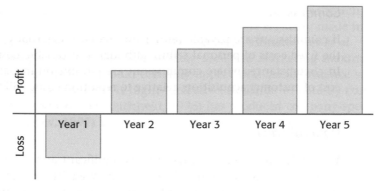

(Not to scale; for illustration only)

Low front-end-cost industries

At the other end of the acquisition costs spectrum are sectors (e.g. FMCG retailing) where the costs of customer acquisition appear marginal as intense personal selling, commissions, detailed information gathering and/or equipment supply are not always necessary to make an individual sale. The FMCG consumer would only seem to require one or more of a limited number of drivers, such as location, perceived service quality, price competitiveness, product range and quality and/or promotional offerings, to stimulate a sale. These are also the factors seen to influence the customer retention process.

Advertising and other (non-personal selling) marketing communication costs, commonly included in the customer acquisition calculations, again do not fully justify the up-front cost argument. High advertising and sales promotion costs attributed to customer acquisition fail to acknowledge the part played by those same messages in the retention process. Advertising serves to remind buyers of their purchasing preferences (East, 2000, p. 96) and may, therefore, often work defensively to protect the existing customer base rather than aggressively to bring in new buyers (Barnard and Ehrenberg, 1997, p. 38).

If drivers promoting sales to potential new customers are similar or the same as those for existing clients then the cost of acquisition must closely equal the cost of retention. Indeed, if the supplier introduces schemes that reward repeat buying over and above the single purchase (the basis of most retail and airline loyalty schemes) then the cost of retention may exceed the cost of acquisition.

Economics of retention strategies

RM appears to be an expensive alternative to mass marketing and, as such, marketers' commitment to such strategies are only valid when they are deemed to be affordable and practical (Berry, 2000, p. 154). Yet much of the current discussion about RM management ignores how the economic effects of establishing such relationships can be or are measured (Blois, 1999, p. 91). Indeed much of the RM literature depends on the mostly implicit, suggestion that a causal effect of relationships is always effective performance (Ambler and Styles, 2000, p. 499). The economics of costly relational techniques must, in circumstances where **acquisition/retention cost ratios** are small, be closely scrutinised. This is particularly evident in the case of many costly loyalty schemes which are, perhaps ironically, most prevalent in those sectors where the validity of relational strategies is most highly questionable (e.g. FMCG retailing). Incentives to retention in these schemes are costs that (if profitability is to be maintained) lead ultimately to higher prices. In such markets differentials may occur in costs between the 'loyalty incentivisors' and their lower-priced competition (Palmer and Beggs, 1997). The phenomenon is not new. The history of British supermarket retailing is peppered by swings between price wars and differential advantage strategies. The airline industry too is experiencing this anomaly in the competition between established and 'low-cost' airlines.

The evidence that exists suggests that, in industries where recognisable high front-end costs are involved, these are drivers to relational strategies that promote customer retention over customer acquisition. Where acquisition costs are low and/or where the real difference between acquisition and retention costs is marginal, the introduction of costly relational strategies may become a burden.

Claims about the effectiveness of improved retention may also frequently be overblown. According to East (2000, p. 11), authors (e.g. Doyle, 1998, p. 44; Kotler *et al.*, 1999, p. 44) who make claims of 25–85 per cent profit increases based upon increasing retention by as little as 5 per cent rarely consider how difficult (and potentially costly) this is to achieve.

Long-term benefits

Retention economics are also promoted as a time-based form of competitive advantage through the suggestion that investment in long-term relationships brings long-term advantages (Murphy, 1997, p. 1). Relationship investment refers to the time, effort and resources that the supplier invests in building stronger investments (Palmatier *et al.*, 2006, p. 140). Gummesson (1999, p. 183) has coined the phrase **'return on relationships' (ROR)** to describe the expectation that there would be a return on this investment. ROR he defines as 'the long-term net financial outcome caused by the establishment and maintenance of an organisation's network of relationships'. The long-term orientation is often emphasised because it is believed that loyalty is cumulative (Reichheld, 1993, p. 65).

Long-term benefits may be considered from two perspectives:

■ relationship stages;
■ the lifetime value of the customer.

Relationship stages

As noted in our earlier definition, relationship marketing is seen as a means of identifying, establishing, maintaining, enhancing and, where necessary, terminating relationships (Grönroos, 1996, p. 7). This definition anticipates that, once a company starts thinking about individual customers (as opposed to mass markets), it will recognise that different customers are at different stages of relational development. Importantly, it also implies that each customer type (e.g. prospect, customer, former customer) should be handled in a different way. This may include different targeted messages (rather than mass communication) and different 'value options' (e.g. rewards) from the exchange.

The recognition of different relational stages in RM also includes the implicit assumption that the higher the stage of development the greater the profitability to the organisation and consequentially the greater the benefits to the organisation. As we will discuss later, this may be an over-simplification in some industries.

Stages models

Various models exist that illustrate this concept (see Figure 4.3) and that may be seen to approximately equate to both consumer and business-to-business relationships. Dwyer *et al.* (1987, p. 15) suggest a five-stage model where each phase represents a major transition in how parties in a relationship regard each other. These are:

■ awareness;
■ exploration;
■ expansion;
■ commitment;
■ dissolution.

Awareness

Awareness is where one party recognises that the other party is a 'feasible exchange partner'. Interaction has not yet taken place although there may be 'positioning' and 'posturing' by the parties to enhance their attractiveness.

Exploration

Exploration refers to the 'research and trial stage' in the exchange. At this level potential partners consider obligations, benefits and burdens of the exchange. This may well include the psychological and actual costs involved. Dwyer *et al.* suggest that this stage includes sub-phases such as attraction, communication and bargaining, development and exercise of power (see Chapter 9), norm development (e.g. contractual arrangements) and expectation development (e.g. trust and commitment; see Chapter 6).

Figure 4.3
Relationship
ladders or
stages

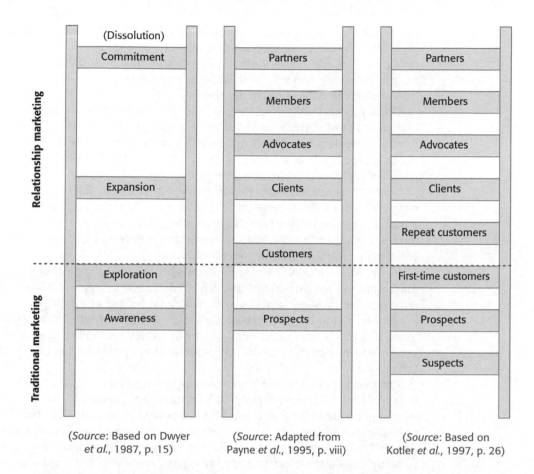

(*Source*: Based on Dwyer *et al.*, 1987, p. 15)

(*Source*: Adapted from Payne *et al.*, 1995, p. viii)

(*Source*: Based on Kotler *et al.*, 1997, p. 26)

Expansion

Expansion refers to the period where there is a continual increase in benefits obtained by exchange partners and where they become increasingly interdependent.

Commitment

Commitment relates to the implicit or explicit pledge of relational continuity between the parties.

Dissolution

The inclusion in the model of a dissolution stage reminds us that disengagement always remains a possibility in any relationship.

Dwyer *et al.* (1987, p. 25) make the important point that, although all transactions have relational properties, it makes sense to consider many exchanges as 'practically discrete' (or non-relational). In other words, relationship stages, such as those described, are not automatic and can only exist where both parties recognise the potential benefits of the relationship. Although in organisational (business-to-business) markets these types of close, bilateral relationships can be seen and are explicitly recognised (Blois, 1997, p. 53), doubt must remain whether this level of closeness could possibly exist in consumer goods or even in many consumer services markets where many of the exchange relationships are discrete.

Other models exist which suggest relational stages of customer development. The long-established concept of a 'ladder of loyalty' was adapted by Payne *et al.* (1995, p. viii) to create a 'relationship ladder'. The metaphor of the 'ladder' and 'climbing up' to higher levels of relationship is easy to visualise. Kotler (1997, p. 26) also proposes a stages model which resembles the relationship ladder.

In the three models illustrated in Figure 4.3, although each has a slightly different perspective, they all promote the idea of customers moving upward from one stage to another. They also illustrate the perception that, whereas traditional marketing's interest ends with the sale, RM's interest extends beyond this to the development and enhancement of the customer relationship.

In the Kotler model the process starts with the identification of suspects. In mass marketing terms this might be achieved through segmentation and targeting although the 'wastage' (media costs which are judged at a cost per thousand 'hits' invariably include an untargeted audience) would be high. In database marketing terms this may involve the rental of lists of names and addresses of suspected target groups. Either way, it is the identification of these potential customers which begins the process.

Prospects are at a higher level than suspects and have, most probably, given some indication that they are likely to purchase the goods or services on offer. Not all prospects are viewed as being of equal potential and, as such, there is a prospect hierarchy (see Figure 4.4). In this hierarchy former customers (known users who have already had experience of the product or service) are considered most likely to revert to being customers. Next best are those customers who have made active enquiries about a product, the assumption being that, having made the effort to contact the company, they are quite probably already motivated to purchase. Referrals are seen as next best in the knowledge that referrals carry considerable weight with most customers

Figure 4.4
Prospect
hierarchy

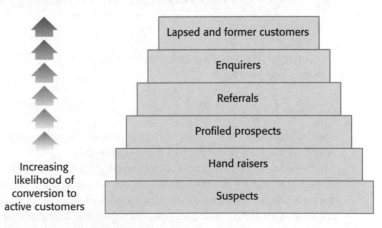

Increasing
likelihood of
conversion to
active customers

(*Source*: Adapted from Tapp, 1998, p. 150)

and again, in probability, they are likely (having sought information) to be in a frame of mind to purchase. Profiled prospects are those who, based on their profile, give a strong indication that they may purchase, while 'hand raisers' have also indicated in some other way (perhaps in a consumer survey) that they also are potential customers. Finally, suspects might be indicated by demographic or **lifestyle analysis**. This 'prospect hierarchy' is used, particularly by direct and database marketers, to prioritise customer communication and is an example of how markets may be segmentable against some sort of 'relationship proneness' variable (Buttle, 1996, p. 7).

Kotler (unlike Payne *et al.*) differentiates between first-time and repeat customers. Certainly the decision-making process will be different in each case. With repeat purchases the consumer has actual experience (as opposed to hype or hearsay) to go on. It is at this point that the relational marketer is seen to diverge from the traditional marketer, whose interest is seen to be primarily in the single transaction. The prime task of the relational marketer from this point is to become skilful at moving customers to higher stages of relationship, with each stage representing a strengthening of the company's relationship with the customer (Kotler, 1997, p. 26). This is seen to be in complete contrast with the traditional marketer, who has no ambition to encourage customers to climb the loyalty ladder (Gummesson, 1999, p. 11).

The Kotler stages model suggests that the company is looking to transform repeat customers into 'clients', which by definition implies a higher status and some (non-stated) form of psychological contract or 'bond' between the parties. The further jump to the status of 'advocate' implies that the customer moves from being responsive to the company to becoming actively involved in the marketing of the organisation, most commonly through word-of-mouth recommendation. 'Members' implies even greater affinity to the company while 'partnership' suggests a relationship on such a high level that, as predicted in some definitions (e.g. Gordon, 1998, Vargo & Lusch 2004, Ballantyne & Varey 2006, Flint 2006) of RM (see Chapter 2, page 38), the customer becomes part of the value-creating process.

Marketing reality

As with all relational concepts, it is important with 'stages' or 'ladder of loyalty' theories to separate the reality from the rhetoric. There is, for example, no research to suggest the extent to which those engaged in loyalty marketing actively pursue customers up the ladder of loyalty (Hart *et al.*, 1999, p. 545). Terms such as advocate, member or partner assume a depth of association that few consumers would recognise in relation to companies or organisations they deal with on a daily basis. It is not sufficient simply to imply an affiliation if the customer does not recognise it as such. Even if the supplier regards the process as a long-term commitment on their behalf it will be the customer who will ultimately define the relationship. The real issues are how a company identifies its best customers and how it retains them economically (Moules, 1998, p. 46). Each level also involves higher maintenance costs, so it is important for organisations to determine when (and if) it is worth going to the next level (Kotler, 1992, p. 52).

Some companies have, however, managed to introduce tactics that have successfully created membership-type relationships that assume affiliation of some sort. This does not include so-called 'consumer clubs', which do not normally fulfil the reciprocity conditions required in high-level relationships and are rarely regarded as more than registration or contractual devices by most consumers. Travel organisations are perhaps the furthest advanced and many (particularly airlines) have developed clubs where members are seen to enjoy privileges that ordinary consumers do not enjoy. Some organisations, for example British Airways, have taken this a stage further by openly differentiating between levels of membership dependent on the customer's commitment (determined by expenditure) to the airline. Executive Club members (who can be blue, silver or gold card holders) receive different levels of privileges dependent on their status.

There are also some organisations where explicit relational bonds (or higher-level relationships) are much more evident. These include those where voluntary membership of, for example, political parties or charitable organisations involves, by implication, membership commitment and, perhaps, costs or effort without monetary (but perhaps with psychological) reward (see Box 4.1). Organisations such as clubs or voluntary organisations may also make explicit that a higher level of relationship can be achieved, usually with increased status potential.[2] Membership of political parties may include the member actively involved in development of the

---

Box 4.1   Article 25

Article 25 is a UK registered charity that designs and delivers buildings and structures for those in greatest need worldwide. They are named after the 25th Article of the Universal Declaration of the United Nations Human Rights Convention which is the only article which refers to the built environment. It says that adequate shelter and housing are a fundamental human right. The charity's aim is to build bigger, better, safer, and more sustainably, in developing countries and after disasters such as the Haiti earthquake. Articles 25's vision is a world where there is never a life or a livelihood lost for the want of a built solution that can preserve or serve it.

In addition to a core team of professional staff Article 25's have a database of dedicated professionally qualified volunteers who include architects, engineers, physicists, project managers and other built environment experts. Between them they build schools, bridges, clinics and homes, and rebuild lives. They also provide free or not for profit construction services to aid agencies, charities, NGOs and communities by sharing skills, training local workers and ensuring community participation is a priority.

Amongst current projects Article 25 is working with the villagers of Lalehun, to save the 75,000 hectare Gola Rainforest and help develop sustainable livelihoods and opportunities in conservation and eco-tourism for the 100,000 people living in and around the Gola Forest. This project will help protect one of western Africa's most important natural habitats – and offer a route out of poverty for local communities.

(*Source*: Article 25 <http://www.article-25.org>)

policies of that party – the political equivalent of 'value creation'. Membership of this type can even mean the member becoming involved in the management of the organisation on a part-time or even full-time basis.

A further problem with the 'ladder' or 'stages' theories is the implicit assumption that there is a linear progression from lower to higher status. It should be recognised that a consumer may, regardless of the efforts of the company, demote themselves for a multiplicity of reasons (e.g. better source of supply) or indeed cease altogether to be a customer. Remaining at any British Airways Executive Club level, for example, is determined by the points accumulated in any one membership year. Should customers decide to utilise another (non-affiliated) airline for a number or all of their journeys they are demoted or lose altogether their Executive Club benefits. This differential status has been retained between airlines involved with British Airways in the Oneworld alliance (see Box 4.2). Change of customer status can, therefore, be in either an upward or a downward direction.

Box 4.2 Oneworld frequent flyer programmes (as at 1 September 2010)

Oneworld airline programme	Oneworld emerald status	Oneworld sapphire status	Oneworld ruby status	Entry level to programme
British Airways	Executive Club Gold	Executive Club Silver	Not applicable	Blue
American Airlines	AA Advantage Executive Platinum	AA Advantage Platinum	AA Advantage Gold	AA Advantage
Cathay Pacific	Marco Polo Club Diamond	Marco Polo Club Gold	Marco Polo Club Silver	Asia Miles
Finnair	Finnair Plus Platinum	Finnair Plus Gold	Finnair Plus Silver	Finnair Plus
Iberia	Iberia Plus Platinum	Iberia Plus Gold	Iberia Plus Silver	Blue Clasica
Japanese Airlines	JMB Diamond	JMB Sapphire	JMB Crystal	JMB Member
JAL	JGC Premier			
LanChile	LanPass Comodoro	LanPass Premium Silver	LanPass Premium	LanPass
Malév	DC Platinum	DC Gold	DC Silver	DC Blue
Mexicana	Mexicana GO Conquer	Mexicana GO Discover	Mexicana GO Explorer	Welcome
Qantas	Platinum	Gold	Silver	Frequent Flyer
Royal Jordanian	Platinum	Gold	Silver	Royal Plus

Lifetime value

Recognition of the importance of RM was driven, in part, by the realisation that people trade over lifetimes (Ambler and Styles, 2000, p. 503). The '**lifetime value**' concept suggests that a company should avoid taking a short-term view of the profit (or indeed loss) of any individual but rather should consider the income derived from that company's lifetime association with the customer. As part of a successful customer retention strategy, organisations should project the value of individual customers over time rather than focus on customer numbers (Dawes and Swailes, 1999, p. 36). The idea is not new. Banks, for example, have traditionally offered young people attractive deals to open accounts. Although this may be costly in the short term, these banks are prepared to do this in the knowledge that, traditionally in this sector, customers change infrequently to competitor organisations (although traditional allegiances may be changing, particularly with the introduction of Internet banking).

The lifetime value of a customer is an impetus to implement retention policies. Decisions concerning investment in relational strategies (to promote retention) may be made on the basis of the customer's notional lifetime value, albeit based on historical data. These investments may include those designed to enhance product or service quality in order to maintain or increase competitive advantage, or alternatively to discourage defection to the competition. In the latter case the company may effectively be building 'barriers to exit' to promote retention (see switching costs, below). An example of the average lifetime value of an organisation's customers is shown in Box 4.3.

The downside of the lifetime value concept is that there is no guarantee that the customer will continue to patronise a supplier at the same level as previously or indeed that he or she will even stay with the company. This is particularly true in businesses with low exit barriers (e.g. retailing) and in rapidly changing, competitive markets (e.g. telecommunications). It may also be the case in industries where substantial sales promotion is used. Indeed, if customers perceive that the only difference between alternative companies is the size of the 'bribe' offered them they are likely to become increasingly promiscuous, actively seeking out the highest bribe available as the only satisfaction to be derived from the exchange (Tynan, 1997, p. 992). The merit of 'lifetime value' in situations such as these must be questionable.

Switching costs

It is difficult to discuss **retention strategies** without referring to the subject of switching costs. Switching costs are effectively **barriers to exit** from the relationship from the perspective of the consumer. Perceived wisdom is that RM strategies work best not only when you have long time horizons but also high switching costs (Kinard and Capella 2006, p. 359). These are costs (monetary and non-monetary) that buyers

Box 4.3 Lifetime value calculation

For an explanation of these calculations please see the appendix to this chapter on page 101.

	Year 1	Year 2	Year 3
Referral rate	5.0%	7.0%	10.0%
Referred customers	–	2,500	2,975
Retention rate	80.0%	82.5%	85.0%
Retained customers	–	40,000	35,063
Total customers	50,000	42,500	38,037
Revenue per customer	£400	£425	£450
Total revenue	£20,000,000	£18,062,500	£17,116,650
Direct costs £225	£11,250,000	£9,562,500	£8,558,325
Acquisition cost £90	£4,500,000	0	0
Marketing costs £25	£1,250,000	£1,062,500	£950,925
Total costs	£17,000,000	£10,625,000	£9,509,250
Profit	£3,000,000	£7,437,500	£7,607,400
Discount rate	1.00	1.12	1.2544
Net present value	£3,000,000	£6,640,625	£6,064,573
Cumulative NPV	£3,000,000	£9,640,625	£15,705,198
Lifetime value	£60	£193	£314

Based on 50,000 acquired and existing customers for Year 1
The formula for the discount rate is: $D = (1 + i)^n$
i = the market rate of interest plus a factor for risk (e.g. 6 per cent and 2 = 0.12)
n = the number of years for which you have to wait (e.g. 0, 1, 2)

encounter when switching from one supplier to another. While largely self-evident in complex, **business-to-business (B2B) marketing** relationships (sunken costs, search costs, etc.), they can equally be relevant to consumers (Bhattacharya and Bolton, 2000, p. 334). It is important to recognise that the 'real' costs may be greater or less than that customer's perception of them (Stewart, 1998, p. 241).

Switching costs may be created by the supplier, by the consumer or by the relationship itself. This is a controversial area within the RM debate as some costs or barriers are seen as positive in that they are the 'natural' barriers created in any good relationship or at the behest of the consumer. Others, however, are seen as coercive and contrary to the principles (if such principles exist) associated with relational strategies. These actual or psychological 'costs' (which are not mutually exclusive), may be summarised as:

- search costs;
- learning costs;
- emotional costs;
- inertial costs;
- risk;
- social costs;
- financial costs;
- legal barriers.

Search costs

Search costs are those based on the time and energy spent searching for alternative sources of supply (e.g. searching through catalogues looking for a particular product or service). Company websites go some way to reducing these costs but can never be seen to be wholly comprehensive

Learning costs

Learning costs are based on the time and energy expended learning how to deal effectively and efficiently with a new supplier (e.g. learning the layout of a supermarket you have never used before or working with a new distribution system).

Emotional costs

Relationships over an extended period can create emotional ties with an organisation or the personnel of that organisation. Personal services (e.g. hairdressing) can engender such loyalty, as can some iconic brands (see Harley-Davidson Box 3.1, page 52). In this regard the Internet has seen the development of 'brand community' sites (e.g. Apple, General Motors and Coca-Cola) where members regularly show the depth of their devotion.

Inertial costs

The effort involved in breaking habitual behaviour is frequently underestimated. This tendency is probably best summed up by the phrase 'I can't be bothered to go elsewhere'. This is also associated with the concept of the **'zone of tolerance' (ZOT)**. The ZOT is seen as that range of service performance where small increases or decreases in performance quality do not lead to any (positive or negative) action (Yap and Sweeney, 2007, p. 137). However, poor performance, price rises or recognition of better value elsewhere can soon break through this inertia.

Risk

The move to a new supplier will always involve a degree of risk. Even where the risk is not immediately apparent there is still a general preference to stay with an existing supplier rather than risk a move to another of whom you have no experience. This is best summed up by the inclination of people to remain with the 'devil you know' rather than move to 'the devil you don't'.

Social costs

The existing supplier may, in some way, contribute to the social life of the customer. An exaggerated example might be the existence of 'singles shopping nights' in some supermarkets. A more commonplace example may be the opportunity to socialise with other customers and staff at a company organised event (e.g. preview evenings). This has become more prevalent with the development of Internet-mediated brand communities where companies such as Saab, Jeep and Harley-Davidson organise weekend events for avid fans of the product.

Financial costs

The break-up of a relationship may mean financial penalties (e.g. the costs frequently involved in switching mortgage providers) or the loss of rewards or status gained through relationship longevity (e.g. some loyalty schemes, no-claims insurance).

Legal barriers

In some situations (e.g. mobile phone contracts), the agreement ensures that the consumer stays (even against their will) for the full period of an agreement regardless of better opportunities elsewhere.

Pressey and Mathews (1998, p. 43) suggest that in developed relationships efforts are made to lock in customers using the types of barrier or cost described above. Relationship marketers, however, suggest that there is more to RM than simply 'locking them in' (Barnes, 1994, p. 556) and that companies that rely on this type of retention are on a 'hiding to nothing'. Thus, when 'enhancement and development of customers' is defined as 'more effective tethering and dissuasion from defection by threat of corrective action' (Worthington and Horne, 1998, p. 39), this is open to criticism. If marketers create excessive barriers or high switching costs, customers are likely to react negatively (Sheth and Parvatiyar, 2000, p. 185).

There does, however, appear to be a distinction between applied costs/barriers (e.g. financial penalties) and those created by the customer (e.g. emotional or social costs) or as a consequence of the relationship (e.g. search, learning or risk-associated costs). Relationships generated by companies which view RM as 'locking in' customers through penalty barriers are seen as inferior relationships to the ones where the parties engaged are willing participants. What passes for a relationship in an enforced retention situation is really a 'pseudo-relationship' in that it is one-sided with customers kept, against their will, because the cost of leaving is too high (Barnes, 1994, p. 565). According to Gummesson (1994, p. 17) this type of 'manipulative marketing' can be compared with:

the use of artificial fertilizer and pesticides which increase short-term harvests but impoverish not only the soil where the crops grow, but the whole of nature for short-term greed. Just like ecology RM sees marketing activities as part of a larger context.

Customer-created barriers, by comparison, are usually the product of mutually recognised satisfaction (or possibly absence of dissatisfaction) created by the supplier to add value to the relationship. An example may be so-called 'strategic bundling' (Payne, 2000, p. 119) where groups of associated products or services are offered with advantages of convenience and/or cost saving. Those barriers that exist as a consequence of the relationship (such as search or learning costs) may not be directly created by the supplier although it may be in that supplier's interest to illustrate the potential costs to the customer. Ultimately long service may act as a switching barrier, but not one that is insurmountable (Stewart, 1998, p. 10).

Relationship longevity

It has been suggested that, when used with skill, customer retention leads to enhanced revenue, reduced costs and improved financial performance. Reichheld (1996, p. 39) echoes this claim by proposing a list of accumulating benefits that contribute to an entire 'life cycle of profits' from the customer. The model (see Figure 4.5) presented assumes:

■ revenue growth over time;
■ cost savings over time;
■ referral income;
■ price premiums.

Figure 4.5
Profit growth
over time

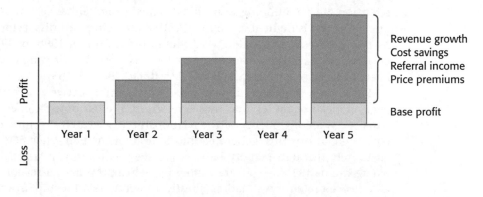

(*Source*: Reprinted by permission of Harvard Business School Press. From *The Loyalty Effect: The Hidden Force Behind Growth, Profits and Lasting Value* by F.F. Reichheld. Boston, MA 1996, p. 43. Copyright © 1996 Harvard Business School Publishing Corporation.)

relationship marketing as a 'good thing' because it leads to long-term profitability is, however, too simplistic and begs the question of how and with whom these relationships are to be established and what form they should take (Barnes, 1994, p. 562). When it is clear, from past experience, that the average customer will continue to purchase a product or service, then the benefits of relational strategies based on a lifetime value calculation may seem apparent.

The proviso must always be made that all such claims are based on historical data and cannot be guaranteed in the future. Estimates of 'lifetime value', therefore, can be valid from a strategy planning perspective but to rely over much on these forecasts may result in complacency.

Summary

This chapter looked at the economics of relationships. It investigated the arguments surrounding the costs of customer acquisition versus the costs of customer retention and concluded that whereas in many industries it can be stated with some certainty that the cost of acquisition exceeds that of retention, it is by no means a universal truth. The chapter also discussed the benefits of relationship longevity, including stages theories and the concept of lifetime value, and again suggested that although considerable benefits could be achieved under certain industry conditions, this could not be assumed in every case. The switching costs associated with relationship longevity were also discussed and a distinction made between costs positively associated with the relationship and coercive barriers to exit. The chapter concluded by suggesting that the notion that RM leads to long-term profitability is far too simplistic.

Discussion questions

1 What are the different cost drivers associated with (a) customer acquisition and (b) customer retention?
2 What are the potential advantages to be gained from long-term supplier–customer relationships?
3 How would you differentiate between the different stages models discussed in this chapter?
4 What effect do switching costs have on a relationship?

Case study   Get fat on chat

Back in 1981, Queens Park Rangers football club succumbed to madness when it dug up the perfectly adequate grass pitch at its Loftus Road ground and replaced it with astroturf. Fans watched matches aghast as the ball bounced erratically and sliding players were afflicted with 'carpet burns'. The artificial playing surface rapidly became the object of ridicule. QPR soon reverted to real grass, and the English FA eventually banned plastic pitches altogether.

▶

Fast forward more than 20 years and 'astroturfing' has been prohibited again. Only this time it's astroturfing in the fake-grass-roots sense, referring to the unethical practice of distorting word of mouth (WOM). Astroturfing means pretending to be something or somebody that you're not, in order to seek commercial gain.

Since 26 May 2008 the Consumer Protection from Unfair Trading Regulations have made astroturfing illegal in the UK and, given that the legislation is derived from the EU Unfair Commercial Practices Directive, across much of Europe too.

The nature of the Internet means that it's often difficult to tell who is behind a range of activities such as blog postings, online reviews, virals and social networking groups. In the past, some unscrupulous marketers have abused this digital smokescreen by hiding their true allegiances.

What, then, does this tightening up of regulation signify for digital WOM marketing? Will marketers be scared off?

Duncan Brown, European managing director of agency Influencer50 doesn't believe so. 'Ethical WOM has nothing to fear from tighter regulations,' he says. 'It's the paid "brand ambassadors" and stooges that give WOM a bad name. All the lessons learned so far point to transparency being the best practice. If you have a good message and target it at the right people then you'll be successful.'

Power tool
Research from Nielsen carried out in 2007 showed that WOM is the most powerful selling tool available to marketers, with 78 per cent of customers trusting consumer recommendations above all other types of marketing.

The trust consumers place in WOM means it can change the way that brands are perceived, argues Harri Owen, buzz manager at Hyperlaunch. The biggest benefits come from increasing engagement and dialogue with the target audience.

Owen cites Dell's 'Idea Storm' (www.dellideastorm.com) initiative as a great example of WOM's potential. By encouraging input from its target audience, Dell managed to shift customer perceptions of the brand away from an uncaring and remote image.

'Transparency is crucial,' says Owen. 'Connecting with communities under their terms of use and their own community tolerances is critical. Each community sets these levels differently and they should be approached with caution and respect.'

Caution and respect are indeed important watchwords, but, while they should be kept in mind, they shouldn't preclude original and engaging communication. Smart brands are stimulating WOM in clever ways.

Influential friends
Over the Christmas period, retailer Borders ran a Facebook campaign in which it challenged the wider Facebook community to create a group of friends entitled 'I want to win signed Quentin Blake artwork from www.borders.co.uk'.

The person who created the biggest group of friends won the signed prints. As a result, Borders attracted many new friends to its online community, creating a wider audience for marketing messaging.

Borders digital marketing manager Nick Atkinson describes WOM as 'a bit of a minefield'. He feels that, even with recent changes to regulations, many marketers are still not as clear and upfront about their identity and intentions online as they should be.

But putting ethics to one side, Atkinson believes this kind of deceptive marketing is lacklustre.

'You get a much higher quality and more sustainable response when you interact with people in a clear and honest way because it gives them the chance to make a considered response to your marketing,' he explains.

'There are two important aspects to a successful online campaign, and these are often the hardest things to achieve,' he says. 'One is to trigger a genuine emotional reaction in your target audience, and the second is to be the most price-competitive.'

Sometimes creativity is the way to drive that emotional reaction. American retailer JC Penney created a viral smash for itself in the festive season with its 'Doghouse' video, which benefited from high production values and a genuinely funny script (http://bewareofthedoghouse.com).

A question of taste

Burger King recently delivered a WOM campaign in the US that attracted criticism as well as plaudits. The mechanic of the 'Whopper Sacrifice' promotion, which ran on social networking site Facebook, involved consumers deleting 10 Facebook 'friends' to receive a coupon entitling them to a free Whopper. The ex-friends, meanwhile, were notified as to what had been done and why. Participants could also send each other heavily branded 'Angry-Grams'.

The Whopper Sacrifice idea took off. By the end of the promotion almost 234,000 friendships had been sacrificed. Friends joked online about sacrificing each other for the sake of a burger – and the norm was for friends to be reinstated on Facebook after free Whoppers had been claimed. Yet some observers expressed distaste, with at least one blogger going so far as to label Whopper Sacrifice as puerile and obnoxious.

Burger King's irreverent approach works well with its target audience, but may be too risky for many brands. Mobile phone brand T-Mobile is more cautious with its UK WOM activity. It has created an 'Advocate Panel' on an extranet site to create a buzz. T-Mobile market intelligence manager Gavin Sugden says that panel participants are offered rewards such as tickets to football matches to get them to participate, but that they also simply take pleasure in giving their views on products and services.

This co-creation approach is of huge benefit to the company, both in terms of new product development and seeding positive brand associations. T-Mobile is among a large number of businesses that seek to measure customer loyalty using the net promoter score as a metric, dividing consumers into those who rate products or services highly (promoters), at mid-level (passives) or poorly (detractors). Online discussion of products and services can give insight into net promoter scores.

Talk tactics

The clout behind the online words of one individual or another is not equal. Paid services such as Brandwatch, Buzzmetrics and Onalytica offer an analysis of data and claim to be able to identify conversation influencers. Services such as Radian 6 and Sysomos offer a more do-it-yourself toolkit for conversation analysis.

Influence is not something marketers can always hope to command online, but respecting certain rules will gain marketers respect in turn. Marketing guru Seth Godin stresses the importance of delivering anticipated, personal and relevant messages to people who want them. Spamming people with your message will not create a buzz.

Nor is WOM about labelling a medium with branding. Justin Kirby, chairman of online WOM opinion panel Yooster, says many marketers fail to realise that in social networks, the people themselves are the medium, not the site. He reminds marketers that a few negative consumer comments should never trigger a knee-jerk change of strategy. 'You could make some schoolboy errors by basing strategic decisions on the input of a handful of vocal disgruntled teenagers.'

It is vital, therefore, to build up a picture of who wields influence and who does not. With regard to the blogosphere, the specialist search engine Technorati produces a measure of authority for all the blogs it searches, using the inbound links to an individual blog to generate a measure of its influence.

For social networks, simple measures such as the number of 'friends' an individual has attached to their profile can help to define influence, but this can also be a measure of an individual's preoccupation with popularity, which is not the same as influence. Emerging tools such as Facebook Grader attempt to calculate an individual's influence scientifically.

Twitter offers a more immediate measure of influence in terms of number of followers of an individual profile, but the number of others they interact with and how often their messages are passed on are also worth noting. Tools such as Twinfluence aim to deliver a picture of reach and authority on Twitter, although the company may soon begin charging companies for its brand-tracking services.

'If you go to a WOM conference, 70 per cent of the presentations are about digital WOM, but 90 per cent of the conversations people have about brands happen offline,' says managing partner of agency Spring Research, Stephen Phillips.

'The difficulty you have with offline is that you can't measure it,' he says. In other words, never forget that online is only part of the picture.

Foot in mouth

■ Wal-Mart ended up with egg on its face when its PR agency Edelman was shown to be behind a fake blog, or 'flog', that followed the progress of a supposedly impartial couple driving their motorhome to Wal-Mart car parks across America. (www.guardian.co.uk/technology/blog/2006/oct/16/whatsafloga)

■ A Facebook group of Tesco employees caused embarrassment to the retailer when comments were posted labelling customers as rude, smelly and stupid. (www.guardian.co.uk/commentisfree/2009/jan/20/michele-hanson-tesco-facebook)

■ In 2006, Sony was discovered to have hired a marketing company to create a sham fan site called All I Want For Christmas is a PSP, attracting plenty of negative comment on genuine games sites and blogs once the ruse was rumbled. (http://adweek.blogs.com/adfreak/2006/12/sony_gets_rippe.html)

■ Whole Foods CEO John Mackey spent a decade praising his company on Yahoo message boards under a pseudonym before his true identity was uncovered. (www.huffingtonpost.com/2008/05/23/rahodeb-returns-whole-foo_n_103244.html)

■ Burger King fired two executives in the US last summer after anonymous comments disparaging a farm-workers' group were posted online. (www.ciw-online.org/BK_campaign_archive.html)

Deliver to people who want to hear your message – spamming will not create a buzz.

(*Source*: Robert Gray, *The Marketer*, March 2009)

Case study questions

1 Why do customers trust WOM?
2 Can WOM be managed and what are the dangers associated with this?
3 Does WOM provide proof that brand-customer relationships can exist?

References

Ambler, T. and Styles, C. (2000) 'Viewpoint: the future of relational research in international marketing: constructs and conduits', *International Marketing Review*, **17** (6), 492–508.

Ballantyne, D. and Varey, R.J. (2006) Creating value-in-use through marketing interaction: the exchangelogic of relating, communicating and knowing, *Marketing Theory*, **6** (3), 335–48.

Barnard, N. and Ehrenberg, A.S.C. (1997) 'Advertising: strongly persuasive or nudging?', *Journal of Advertising Research*, January/February, 21–31.

Barnes, J.G. (1994) 'Close to the customer: but is it really a relationship?', *Journal of Marketing Management*, **10**, 561–70.

Barnes, J.G. and Howlett, D.M. (1998) 'Predictors of equity in relationships between service providers and retail customers', *International Journal of Bank Marketing*, **16** (1), 5–23.

Berry, L.L. (2000) 'Relationship marketing of services: growing interest, emerging perspectives', in Sheth, J.N. and Parvatiyar, A. (eds) *Handbook of Relationship Marketing*, Thousand Oaks, CA: Sage, pp. 149–70.

Berry, L.L. and Gresham, L.G. (1986) 'Relationship retailing: transforming customers into clients', *Business Horizons*, November/December, 43–7.

Bhattacharya, C.B. and Bolton, R.N. (2000) 'Relationship marketing in mass markets', in Sheth, J.N. and Parvatiyar, A. (eds) *Handbook of Relationship Marketing*, Thousand Oaks, CA: Sage, pp. 327–54.

Blois, K.J. (1997) 'When is a relationship a relationship?', in Gemünden, H.G., Rittert, T. and Walter, A. (eds) *Relationships and Networks in International Markets*, Oxford: Elsevier, pp. 53–64.

Blois, K.J. (1999) 'A framework for assessing relationships', competitive paper, Proceedings of the European Academy of Marketing Conference (EMAC), Berlin, pp. 1–24.

Buttle, F.B. (1996) *Relationship Marketing Theory and Practice*, London: Paul Chapman.

Christopher, M., Payne, A. and Ballantyne, D. (1991) *Relationship Marketing*, London: Butterworth Heinemann.

Dawes, J. and Swailes, S. (1999) 'Retention sans frontières: issues for financial service retailers', *International Journal of Bank Marketing*, **17** (1), 36–43.

Doyle, P. (1998) *Marketing Management and Strategy*, London: Prentice Hall.

Dwyer, F.R., Schurr, P.H. and Oh, S. (1987) 'Developing buyer–seller relationships', *Journal of Marketing*, **51**, 11–27.

East, R. (2000) 'Fact and fallacy in retention marketing', Professorial Inaugural Lecture, 1 March, Kingston University Business School, UK.

Flint, D.J. (2006) Innovation, symbolic interaction and customer valuing: thoughts stemming from a service-dominant logic of marketing, *Marketing Theory*, **6** (3), 349–62.

Gordon, I.H. (1998) *Relationship Marketing*, Etobicoke, Ontario: John Wiley & Sons.

Grönroos, C. (1995) 'Relationship marketing: the strategy continuum', *Journal of Marketing Science*, **23** (4), 252–4.

Grönroos, C. (1996) 'Relationship marketing: strategic and tactical implications', *Management Decisions*, **34** (3), 5–14.

Grossman, R.P. (1998) 'Developing and managing effective customer relationships', *Journal of Product and Brand Management*, **7** (1), 27–40.

Gummesson, E. (1994) 'Making relationship marketing operational', *International Journal of Service Industry Management*, **5**, 5–20.

Gummesson, E. (1999) *Total Relationship Marketing: Rethinking Marketing Management from 4Ps to 30Rs*, Oxford: Butterworth Heinemann.

Harlow, E. (1997) 'Loyalty is for life – not just for Christmas', paper presented at the Advanced Relationship Marketing Conference, 23 October, Century Communications, London.

Hart, S., Smith, A., Sparks, L. and Tzokas, N. (1999) 'Are loyalty schemes a manifestation of relationship marketing?', *Journal of Marketing Management*, **15**, 541–62.

Kinard, B.R. and Capella, M.L. (2006) 'Relationship marketing: the influence of consumer involvement on perceived service benefits', *Journal of Service Marketing*, **21** (6), 359–68.

Kotler, P. (1992) 'Marketing's new paradigm: what's really happening out there?', *Planning Review*, **20** (5), 50–2.

Kotler, P. (1997) 'Method for the millennium', *Marketing Business*, February, 26–7.

Kotler, P., Armstrong, G., Saunders, J. and Wing, V. (1999) *Principles of Marketing*, 2nd European edn, New York: Prentice Hall.

Mitchell, A. (1997) 'Evolution', *Marketing Business*, June, 37.

Mohammed, R.A., Fisher, R.J., Jaworski, B.J. and Cahill, A.M. (2002), *Internet Marketing: Building Advantage in the Networked Economy*, New York: McGraw-Hill.

Morgan, R.M. (2000) 'Relationship marketing and marketing strategy', in Sheth, J.N. and Parvakiyar, A. (eds) *Handbook of Relationship Marketing*, Thousand Oaks, CA: Sage, pp. 481–504.

Moules, J. (1998) 'Stopping the exodus', *Information Strategy*, **3** (5), 46–8.

Murphy, J.A. (1997) 'Customer loyalty and the art of satisfaction', *Financial Times*, FT Mastering Series.

Palmatier, R.W., Dant, R.P., Grewal, D. and Evans, K.R. (2006) 'Factors influencing the effectiveness of relationship marketing: a meta-analysis', *Journal of Marketing*, **70** (October), 136–53.

Palmer, A. and Beggs, R. (1997) 'Loyalty programmes: congruence of market structure and success', paper presented at the Academy of Marketing Conference, Manchester, UK.

Palmer, A.J. (1998) *Principles of Services Marketing*, London: Kogan Page.

Palmer, R., Lindgreen, A. and Vanhamme, J. (2005) 'Relationship marketing: schools of thought and future research directions', *Marketing Intelligence and Planning*, **23** (3), 313–30.

Payne, A. (2000) 'Customer retention', in Cranfield School of Management *Marketing Management: A Relationship Marketing Perspective*, Basingstoke: Macmillan, pp. 110–24.

Payne, A. and Frow, P. (1997) 'Relationship marketing: key issues for the utilities sector', *Journal of Marketing Management*, **13** (5), 463–77.

Payne, A., Christopher, M. and Peck, H. (eds) (1995) *Relationship Marketing for Competitive Advantage: Winning and Keeping Customers*, Oxford: Butterworth Heinemann.

Pompa, N., Berry, J., Reid, J. and Webber, R. (2000) 'Adopting share of wallet as a basis for communications and customer relationship management', *Journal of Direct Data and Digital Marketing (Interactive Marketing)*, **2** (1), 29–40.

Pressey, A.D. and Mathews, B.P. (1998) 'Relationship marketing and retailing: comfortable bedfellows?', *Customer Relationship Management*, **1** (1), 39–53.

Reichheld, F. (1993) 'Loyalty-based management', *Harvard Business Review*, March/April, 56–69.

Reichheld, F.F. (1996) *The Loyalty Effect: The Hidden Force Behind Growth, Profits and Lasting Value*, Boston, MA: Harvard Business School Press.

Sheth, J.N. and Parvatiyar, A. (1995a) 'The evolution of relationship marketing', *International Business Review*, **4** (4), 397–418.

Sheth, J.N. and Parvatiyar, A. (1995b) 'Relationship marketing in consumer markets: antecedents and consequences', *Journal of the Academy of Marketing Science*, **23** (4), 255–71.

Sheth, J.N. and Parvatiyar, A. (2000) 'Relationship marketing in consumer markets: antecedents and consequences', in Sheth, J.N. and Parvatiyar, A. (eds) *Handbook of Relationship Marketing*, Thousand Oaks CA: Sage, pp. 171–207.

Stewart, K. (1998) 'The customer exit process: a review and research agenda', *Journal of Marketing Management*, **14**, 235–50.

Storbacka, K., Strandvik, T. and Grönroos, C. (1994) 'Managing customer relations for profit: the dynamics of relationship quality', *International Journal of Service Industry Management*, **5**, 21–38.

Strandvik, T. and Storbacka, K. (1996) 'Managing relationship quality', in Edvardsson, B., Brown, S.W., Johnston, R. and Scheuing, E.E. (eds) *Advancing Service Quality: A Global Perspective*, New York: ISQA, pp. 67–76.

Tapp, A. (1998) *Principles of Direct and Database Marketing*, London: Financial Times Management/Pitman Publishing.

Tynan, C. (1997) 'A review of the marriage analogy in relationship marketing', *Journal of Marketing Management*, **13** (7), 695–704.

Vargo, S. and Lusch, R. (2004) 'Evolving to a new dominant logic for marketing', *Journal of Marketing*, **67** (1) 1–17.

Worthington, S. and Horne, S. (1998) 'A new relationship marketing model and its application in the affinity credit card market', *International Journal of Bank Marketing*, **16** (1), 39–44.

Yap, K.B. and Sweeney, J.C. (2007) 'Zone of tolerance moderates the service quality-outcome relationship, *Journal of Service Marketing*, **21** (2), 137–48.

Appendix

The lifetime value (LV) as shown in Box 4.3 is calculated for all or a segment of customers and the supposition is that it can then be attributed back to individual customers. In the example 50,000 customers were recruited at a cost of £90 each totalling £4.5 million. There will always be customers who leave for a variety of reasons and in the example 20 per cent have been lost one year later giving a retention rate of 80 per cent. Of these customers who are carried forward 80 per cent and 82.5 per cent will be retained in Years 2 and 3 respectively. Direct and Marketing costs encourage sales and retention. There is also a healthy referral rate of 5 per cent (rising to 10 per cent in Year 3) which may be based on 'word-of-mouth' and/or as a result of a 'customer-get-customer' promotion. The profit from these customers is calculated and then discounted (to bring it back to current value) using the formula $D = (1 + i)^n$ where i is the rate of interest plus a factor for risk (6 per cent and 2 in the example). The net present value (NPV) for each year is added cumulatively and divided by the original customers (50,000) to give an individual lifetime value. From this calculation you can determine that the value of the customer in the first year is £60 rising to £314 in Year 3. To calculate the value of any individual customer you can attribute the expected behaviour of an individual to the average of the group.

NB: 3 years are shown. Year 1 is not a calendar year but the year of acquisition and may, therefore, include several years' worth of customer acquisitions. Year 2 and Year 3 are the first and second years after acquisition.

Notes

1 'Front of mind' awareness is seen as important where infrequent buying decisions are made (e.g. life insurance). The purpose is to ensure that when the consumer is ready to make a decision, the brand is 'front of mind'.

2 In the Chartered Institute of Marketing, for example, you can be a student member, associate member, member, chartered marketer or fellow. Each level of membership has different privileges and different costs.

5 Strategy continuum

Key issues

- RM's context within marketing
- The marketing continuum
- Hybrid marketing and portfolios of marketing strategies
- Continuum drivers

Introduction

The discussion concerning the economics of relationship marketing in the previous chapter suggests that, while RM may be beneficial in some instances, it is by no means certain to be beneficial in all. As time has passed and other theories and discussions have entered the marketing debate such a stark contrast between RM and traditional marketing may not be as apparent. However, contrasting these philosophically different approaches still offers insights into how we handle a diversity of strategies and how we decide when particular strategy types are relevant and appropriate.

RM in context

In the 1990s, the debate regarding RM's place within marketing theory could be summed up as a choice between four 'alternative' philosophical viewpoints (Brodie *et al.*, 1997, p. 389; Pels, 1999, p. 19):

- By adding a relationship dimension to the marketing management approach the 'anomalies' identified in traditional marketing could be incorporated into the existing marketing paradigm (see Chapter 2, page 28).

- Exchange relationships (i.e. RM) should be regarded as a new marketing paradigm, suggesting that a paradigmatic shift had taken place in marketing from traditional marketing (TM) towards relationship marketing (see Chapter 2, page 17).
- Exchange transactions (or TM) and exchange relationships (or RM) are separate paradigms and both paradigms separately coexist.[1]
- Traditional marketing (TM) and relationship marketing (RM) can coexist as part of the same marketing paradigm.

Put simply, RM may be considered as a concept, as the dominant theory, as one (of two) marketing perspectives or as an integral part of the overall marketing arsenal.

Early texts tended to view RM as a tactical influence on existing concepts, for example the marketing mix (e.g. Christopher *et al.*, 1991). This viewpoint has largely been eclipsed as the strategic value of relational strategies has increased. The argument about whether RM is a new dominant paradigm, however, still rages.

Despite RM's promotion to the highest level of marketing theory, however, there still remain doubts as to whether companies would *always* (or indeed would *ever*) find it suitable and/or profitable to develop relational strategies (e.g. Palmer, 1996, p. 18; Grönroos, 1997, p. 408). Kotler (1997, p. 26), for example, suggests that reports of the demise of traditional mass marketing are 'somewhat premature' and that companies such as Coca-Cola, Gillette and Kodak will continue primarily to practise traditional **mass-marketing** techniques (e.g. mass communication using mass media) into the foreseeable future. Mayer *et al*. (2000, p. 391) too argue that claims that mass markets and mass consumption are dead are not borne out by empirical evidence. A good example of this is the budget airline Ryanair whose strategy is blatantly transactional. In 2006 they were voted the world's most hated airline in an online poll (Ritson, 2006) yet in the same year posted record half-year profits of €329 million, a year-on-year increase of 39 per cent (*Business Weekly*, 6 November 2006). Despite years of bad press and a worldwide fall in passenger numbers they are still posting profits expected to be in the region of €275 million to March 2011.

The logical consequence of this viewpoint is that some marketing activities may remain best handled through a transaction marketing approach (Gummesson, 1994, p. 17). As Dwyer *et al*. (1987, p. 14) note, it is possible that the real or anticipated costs (to either party) of relational strategies may outweigh the benefits of relational exchange. As Grönroos (1997, p. 408) suggests, 'the main thing is . . . not whether a relational strategy is possible or not, but whether the firm finds it profitable, and in other respects suitable, to develop a relational strategy or a traditional strategy'. The implication is that, if companies cannot justify, economically, a relational approach, then they would be best advised to retain (or re-adopt) a transactional strategy.

The view that transactional marketing and relational marketing can coexist suggests that the RM should not be considered simply as a replacement for TM strategies but as another perspective in marketing. This implies that RM is not a clearly defined, delimited phenomenon but a 'helpful perspective' in approaching marketing (Gummesson, 1994, p. 8). The argument remains, however, whether RM and TM are exclusive relative to an individual company or industry or as part of the same paradigm (Brodie *et al*., 1997, p. 389; Coviello *et al*., 1997, p. 516), perhaps extremes on a 'marketing strategy continuum' (Grönroos, 1995, p. 252).

RM/TM continuum

Research conducted by Brodie *et al.* (1997, pp. 389–402) supports the marketing strategy continuum hypothesis. Their evidence suggests that, at managerial level, a combination of TM and RM approaches are used by firms and that managers maintain a 'portfolio' of strategy types. Although their case and survey results suggest that certain types of marketing (either TM or RM) are more common in some sectors than others, it did not imply exclusivity. The researchers note that firms at the transactional end of the continuum tended to be larger and longer-established businesses, but this might be an element of sluggishness in adopting new strategies. The researchers' analysis otherwise fails to identify clearly specific characteristics of firms dominated by one or the other practice. This may support the suggestion that 'drivers', other than strictly industry typology, may be involved.

Although general marketing practice did show a considerable shift towards customer orientation, Brodie *et al.*'s conclusion (p. 389) was that both transactional and relational marketing approaches can and do coexist. Möller and Halinen (2000, p. 43) too recognise that purely relational (or indeed purely transactional) types rarely exist and that it is better portrayed as a continuum of varying degrees of relational complexity. Exchanges, therefore, can be considered as falling somewhere along a spectrum ranging from the discrete to the relational (Blois, 1999, p. 4). Pressey and Mathews (1998, p. 48) also seem to suggest a multivarious approach when they note, in a retail context, that a customer's relationship cannot be classed as one that fits the characteristics of RM yet is not as 'discrete' as TM. The relationship is, therefore, between the two and, as such, has parts of both. The strategies used may, therefore, be called a 'portfolio of types'.

In this marketing continuum model RM would be placed at one end. Here the general focus would be on building relationships with customers (and other stakeholders). At the other end of this continuum is TM, where the focus is short term and based on one transaction at a time (Grönroos, 1994, p. 10). Whereas collaboration is the core property of RM, traditional marketing is prejudiced in favour of competition.

Grönroos (p. 11) suggests that industry type may influence a company's position on the continuum (see Figure 5.1). He predicts that at one extreme is the end-user, packaged consumer-goods market with a marketing mix approach based on discrete, transactional exchange and where customers are more sensitive to price than the development of any longer-term relationship. **Process services** (e.g. McDonalds, Ryanair) which are standardized, repetitive and frequently cost-based processes as opposed to personal service, also tend towards this end of the spectrum. RM, and the relationship metaphor, it is suggested, are of less value in a mass consumer and process services marketing context than in high-contact, inter-organisational and personal service marketing contexts. At this end of the continuum, traditional measures, such as the technical quality of the output and the monitoring of market share, are used. Customer opinion is determined by *ad hoc* customer surveys as face-to-face contact is limited. Internal marketing (see Chapter 8) is not seen as a priority.

Figure 5.1
The transactional/ relational continuum and drivers

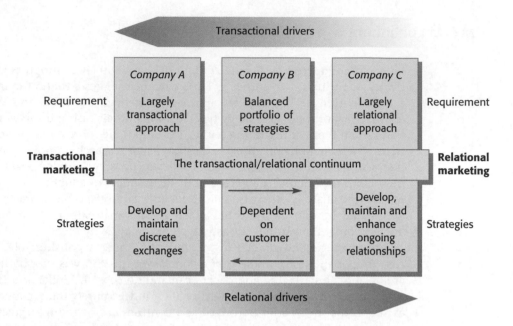

At the other end of the continuum are distribution channels, services (excluding process services) and business-to-business marketers, who, it is proposed, would benefit from the application of relationship type strategies. The concentration here is on the long term, with the use of an interactive approach based on the development, maintenance and enhancement of ongoing relationships. Sensitivity to price is much less important at this end of the continuum as customers are seeking other benefits which are delivered via the relationship with the supplier. The dominant measurement criteria here is the quality of interactions with the consumer and the successful management of the customer base. Customer feedback is in 'real time' (i.e. feedback is part of the interaction) and continuous. As the interface with the consumer is so crucial (it is often referred to as 'the moment of truth') the role of internal marketing is of strategic importance.

The strict industry division may be somewhat overstating the case by suggesting that consumer goods companies would never benefit from relational strategies and that distribution channels, services and business-to-business would always benefit from them. For example, research suggests customers perceive greater relational benefits with high contact services rather than the more standardised ones (Kinard and Capella, 2006, p. 365). Neither should there be an assumption that there is no movement over time as organisations react to the changing levels and nature of competition. What the concept of a marketing continuum suggests is that, although RM strategies may well be attractive for many products, services and markets, their application may be inappropriate for others (Palmer, 1996, p. 18). Nor does the adoption of RM strategies guarantee success. As Ambler and Styles (2000, p. 499) note, there are plenty of 'counter examples of poor but profitable relationships and those with good but unprofitable ones'.

Grönroos (1994, p. 13) notes that the more a firm moves to the right on the marketing strategy continuum and away from the transaction-type situation, the more the market expands beyond the core product (see Figure 5.2) and more has to be invested in interactive marketing (Grönroos, 1995, p. 252). Barnes (1994, pp. 566–7) hypothesises that, in moving away from TM at some point on this continuum, it may be said that a transaction approach to marketing ceases to be appropriate and the possibility for the establishment of a genuine relationship begins.

Marketing implications

Grönroos (1995, p. 253) suggests that the marketing implications across the strategy continuum (RM versus TM) are substantially different concerning:

- the dominant marketing orientation;
- the dominant quality function;
- the customer information system;
- interdependency between business functions;
- the role of internal marketing.

Dominant marketing orientation

RM suggests that marketing should not be restricted to 'marketing mix' activities nor should it be wholly the responsibility of the marketing department (see Chapter 8). In TM, the marketing role of personnel outside of the marketing department is negligible and elements such as advertising, campaigning and price promotions form the core. In RM, these elements are there but as supporting activities to interaction and internal marketing strategies.

Figure 5.2
RM/TM
continuum

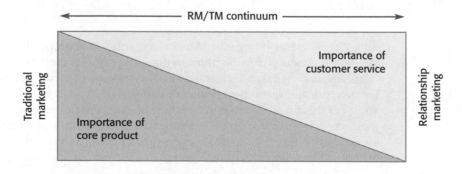

Dominant quality function

In TM it is normally enough if the output is of acceptable quality. In RM, although the technical quality has to be acceptable, it is no longer the only quality dimension. Rather, all the interactions within the firm (contact, information systems, etc.) support the quality perceptions of the customer.

Customer information system

A firm pursuing a TM strategy will normally have little, if any, direct customer contact. TM relies instead on *ad hoc* customer satisfaction surveys and market-share statistics for information about the behaviour and attitude of customers. A firm that applies RM strategies would monitor customer satisfaction by continuous contact and by directly managing its customer base (see Chapter 12).

Interdependency between business functions

The level of interdependency between functions and departments in an organisation depends on whether the firm is operating a TM- or an RM-type strategy. In traditional marketing companies the marketing department takes care of the marketing function. In companies promoting relational strategies the interaction between, in particular, marketing, operations and human resources becomes critical to success (see Chapter 8).

Role of internal marketing

Preparing the non-marketing employees – Gummesson (1999, p. 45) calls these 'part-time marketers' (see Chapter 8) – for their marketing tasks is an important element of RM strategy. Firms operating such strategies have to take a proactive approach towards getting the commitment required to develop marketing behaviour among all employees. The more people in the firm are involved in marketing, the greater the need for active internal marketing. In TM this need is limited.

Continuum drivers

A logical progression from the above arguments is the proposition that market factors determine (at any particular point in time) the value of (and thus the choice between) relational and transactional strategies. The concept of a continuum may be the basis for determining those departmental, company or industry factors, or 'drivers', that affect (or should affect) strategic decision-making in a given market situation. Drivers that may influence whether the company adopts a relational or transactional strategy are shown in Box 5.1. Some of these drivers have been discussed previously while others will be referred to in more detail in a subsequent chapter.

Box 5.1 Drivers affecting strategic decision-making

Drivers promoting relational strategies
- High acquisition costs relative to retention costs
- High exit barriers
- Competitive advantage sustainable
- Buoyant/expanding market
- High risk/high salience products or services
- High emotion involved in exchange
- Requirement for trust and commitment
- Perceived need for closeness
- Satisfaction beneficial to retention

Drivers against using relational strategies
- Acquisition/retention cost differential minimal
- Low exit barriers
- Competitive advantage unsustainable
- Saturated market
- Low risk/low salience products or services
- Low emotion involved in exchange
- Requirement for trust only
- No perceived need for closeness
- Repeat behaviour strategy beneficial

The term 'drivers' is preferred to 'antecedents' for although much RM literature describes relational factors (e.g. trust) as 'antecedents to positive relational outcomes' the empirical evidence does not always support this type of association (Grayson and Ambler, 1999, p. 132). 'Drivers', on the other hand, suggests factors that are likely to 'promote' RM rather than 'predict' it as an outcome.

The concept of the strategy continuum implies that an 'optimum position' exists (whether determinable or not) and that each company's individually tailored perspective is dependent on the balance between the various transactional or relational drivers. In business as well as in life, relationships are inherently unstable (Blois, 1997, p. 367) and this balance is constantly changing as factors ebb and flow, strengthen or weaken. Research suggests, for example, that customer relationships do not equally influence all exchange outcomes (Palmatier *et al.*, 2006, p. 147). These constantly changing circumstances suggest a permanent 'danger area' either side of the supposed optimum position owing to the difficulty (if not impossibility) of calculating the outcome of particular TM and RM strategies at any given point in time (see Figure 5.3). The two biggest dangers are:

Figure 5.3
RM/TM
continuum

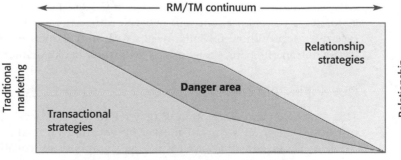

- at the transactional end of the spectrum, not recognising the desire of customer for an increased level of 'customer service';
- at the relational end of the spectrum, overestimating the level of service expected by the customer, resulting in defection to lower-cost (and lower-service) competitors.

The nearer the middle of the hypothesised continuum, the greater the danger of mis-application of strategies is likely to be. To make matters worse each situation requires individual judgement. The uniqueness of relationships makes the 'mechanical transfer of successful practices among different companies dubious at best'.

(*Source*: Håkansson and Snehota, 2000, p. 83)

Hybrid managerial approach

As rational and intuitively sensible as the introduction of relational strategies may have appeared in theory, it was only through observation of these policies, over time, that they were put to the test. Observation of real-world marketing practice indicates that a hybrid managerial approach (suggested by the continuum concept) may be the most appropriate response to prevailing market circumstances (Chaston, 1998, p. 273). An example of this is the airline industry where the advent of the budget airline has caused many international and national carriers to strip out much of the service content at the promotional end of the market while maintaining relational strategies for higher classes of travel. Möller and Halinen (2000, p. 45), for example, note that companies operating in fast-moving consumer goods industries, consumer durables, industrial goods and services often employ two modes. Grönroos (1995, p. 252) suggests that, whether a company is largely transactional or largely relational, there may be situations where both types may benefit from taking another approach. This would suggest the use of multiple marketing strategies (Voss and Voss, 1997, p. 279) that:

- develop and maintain discrete exchanges (TM);
- develop, maintain and enhance ongoing relationships (RM).

Within a single operation customers too may prefer (or demand) a differentiated approach. In a survey of US bank customers (quoted in Mohammed *et al.*, 2002, pp. 490–1) researchers noted a distinction between transactional customers, who generally tended to be relatively self-sufficient people who sought out financial information and tended to be price sensitive, and relationship-orientated customers, who wanted more face-to-face service and were less price sensitive. The survey estimated a 62 : 38 per cent split between transactional and relational types! A more recent US survey showed similar results with only 31 per cent of customers receptive to the notion of having a relationship with their bank (McAdam, 2005, p. 3).

Developing RM concepts

The continuum/drivers hypothesis may relate to other developing RM concepts. The notion of the three forces of marketing equilibrium (elaborated by Gummesson, 1996, p. 34) suggests that, even if RM puts emphasis on collaboration, it is the combination of competition, collaboration and regulatory institutions in each specific

Kinard, B.R. and Capella, M.L. (2006) 'Relationship marketing: the influence of consumer involvement on perceived service benefits', *Journal of Service Marketing*, **21** (6), 359–68.

Kotler, P. (1997) 'Method for the millennium', *Marketing Business*, February, 26–7.

Lowe, S., Carr, A.N. and Thomas, M. (2004) 'Paradigmapping marketing theory', *European Journal of Marketing*, **38** (9/10), 1057–64.

McAdam, P. (2005) 'Give the customers what they want (and in most cases, it's not a relationship)', *Banking Strategies*, BAI Online <www.bai.org/bankstrategies/current/cover> (accessed 12 April 2007).

Mayer, R., Job, K. and Ellis, N. (2000) 'Ascending separate stairways to marketing heaven (or careful with that axiom, Eugene!)', *Marketing Intelligence & Planning*, **18** (6/7), 388–99.

Mohammed, R.A., Fisher, R.J., Jaworski, B.J. and Cahill, A.M. (2002) *Internet Marketing: Building Advantage in the Networked Economy*, New York: McGraw-Hill.

Möller, K. and Halinen, A. (2000) 'Relationship marketing theory: its roots and directions', *Journal of Marketing Management*, **16**, 29–54.

Palmatier, R.W., Dant, R.P., Grewal, D. and Evans, K.R. (2006) 'Factors influencing the effectiveness of relationship marketing: a meta-analysis', *Journal of Marketing*, **70** (October), 136–53.

Palmer, A.J. (1996) 'Relationship marketing: a universal paradigm or management fad?', *The Learning Organisation*, **3** (3), 18–25.

Pels, J. (1999) 'Exchange relationships in consumer markets?', *European Journal of Marketing*, **33** (1/2), 19–37.

Pressey, A.D. and Mathews, B.P. (1998) 'Relationship marketing and retailing: comfortable bedfellows?', *Customer Relationship Management*, **1** (1), 39–53.

Ritson, M. (2006) 'Don't be scared of being despised', *Marketing*, 1, November, 23.

Voss, G.B. and Voss, Z.G. (1997) 'Implementing a relationship marketing programme: a case study and managerial implications', *Journal of Services Marketing*, **11** (4), 278–98.

Note

1 For arguments supporting 'paradigm-crossing' and the co-existence of multiple truths see Lowe *et al.*, 2004.

6 Relationship drivers

Key issues

- Risk, salience and emotion
- Trust and commitment
- Closeness
- Customer satisfaction
- Inertia

Introduction

In the previous chapter the concept of 'drivers' towards relational strategies was introduced. A number of these drivers were discussed in Chapter 4, including:

- high customer acquisition costs (see page 75);
- high exit barriers (see page 86);
- sustainable competitive advantage (see page 94);
- buoyant/expanding market (see page 91).

In this section we will look at those other drivers that appear to have an important bearing on the decision to develop a relationship marketing approach, in particular:

- risk, salience and emotion;
- trust and commitment;
- perceived need for closeness;
- customer satisfaction.

A summary of these positive drivers towards relational strategies and those that suggest an alternate strategy are shown in Box 6.1.

Box 6.1 Drivers promoting/against relational strategies

Drivers promoting relational strategies	**Drivers against using relational strategies**
■ High acquisition costs relative to retention costs*	■ Acquisition/retention cost differential minimal*
■ High exit barriers*	■ Low exit barriers*
■ Competitive advantage sustainable*	■ Competitive advantage unsustainable*
■ Buoyant/expanding market*	■ Saturated market*
■ High-risk/high-salience products or services	■ Low-risk/low-salience products or services
■ High emotion involved in exchange	■ Low emotion involved in exchange
■ Requirement for trust and commitment	■ Requirement for trust only
■ Perceived need for closeness	■ No perceived need for closeness
■ Satisfaction beneficial to retention	■ Repeat behaviour strategy beneficial

* See Chapter 4

Risk, salience and emotion

Risk, salience and emotion are all psychological aspects involved in some way in every exchange or purchase. Although they are wholly subjective, the levels of risk, degree of salience involved and the emotion generated *will* affect the choice of product or service and supplier involved, as well as the 'level' of relational involvement the customer will seek or, in some circumstances, allow.

An explanation of what is meant by risk, salience and emotion in a marketing context may be appropriate:

■ **Risk** may be defined as 'the perceived probability of loss interpreted by the decision-maker' (Rousseau *et al.*, 1998, p. 395) and presumes an element of consumer vulnerability in the exchange.

■ **Salience** may be regarded as the level of importance or prominence associated with the exchange. Intuitively one knows that some purchases have more personal relevance than others and that this has an impact on behaviour (Uncles, 1994, p. 343).

■ **Emotion** is the complex series of human responses (sometimes negatively described as 'agitation of the mind' or 'cognitive dissonance') generated as a result of the exchange.

Risk, salience and emotion are separately definable concepts, but are not mutually exclusive. There is a close association between the level of risk perceived in, the salience associated with and the emotion generated by any given exchange situation. Thus high risk is often associated with high-salience products or services and with a high-emotional outcome although any measures are *highly subjective* and may differ from individual to individual. It is quite possible to imagine, for example, that a particular exchange relationship will generate a perception of high levels of risk, salience and emotion with one customer yet, if the situation were to be replicated, only generate low levels with another.

High risk, salience and emotion

Much of the relationship marketing literature (e.g. Sheth and Parvatiyar, 1995, pp. 288–9, 2000, p. 180; Bhattacharya and Bolton, 2000, p. 334) suggests that the greater the perceived risk, the greater a customer's propensity to engage in relational-type behaviour. Consumer confidence is itself a prime relational benefit influencing relational response behaviour (Kinard and Capella, 2006, p. 365). Case studies of companies that appear to benefit from relational strategies are frequently those involving 'high-risk purchases', either with a large, single monetary outlay (e.g. vehicle purchases) or with payments over an extended period (e.g. financial services). These latter extended payments are often associated with high opportunity or actual costs as a possible consequence of incorrect decision-making at the initial sale. One reason why so-called high-risk purchases may benefit from RM strategies is that a relationship, over time, is likely (but not certain) to lower the perceived risk as the consumer 'learns' more about the terms and security of the arrangement and, more generally, gets to know the supplier. RM may also be well suited in cases where the unforeseen future is continuously defined and redefined by those involved in the relationship (Tzokas and Saren, 2000, pp. 12–3). Even in a situation where these long-term experiences create some doubt about the supplier, this learning exercise in itself may reduce risk by indicating those areas of the relationship where the supplier can and cannot be trusted. The existence of risk, therefore, creates an opportunity for trust that would not be needed if actions could be taken with certainty and no risk (Rousseau *et al.*, 1998, p. 395).

The case studies quoted in support of relational strategies are also generally highly salient to the consumer, either representing major and current status symbols or as affecting status or quality of life at some point in the future (e.g. pensions, investments). In situations characterised by high risk and high salience, the customer may enter the service encounter with certain specific expectations associated with rather intense emotions (Cumby and Barnes, 1998, p. 55) and may be seeking specific re-assurance and reduction of cognitive dissonance. These situations appear to benefit from the closer ties and more frequent communication associated with RM strategies and tactics.

There may be a built-in redundancy in risk-reducing relationships. Over time the perceived risk may reduce with increased self-confidence leading, perhaps, to consumers manifesting increased transactional marketing behaviours (Sheth and Parvatiyar, 2000, p. 180). On the contrary, leading brands are believed to offer psychological reassurances against the risk attached to purchasing and as a consequence create a sense of belonging (Wright and Sparks, 1999, p. 431). There may, therefore, be forces working both for and against the establishment of long-term relationships associated with risk.

Low risk, salience and emotion

At the other end of the spectrum are those products and services that may be defined as low (actual or opportunity) cost, decidedly low risk and low salience. As a result, suppliers at this end of the spectrum, such as FMCG retailers and process services (e.g. fast-food outlets), are rarely involved in exchange situations that generate the emotional intensity of major purchases. In these industries there is little need for the supplier to devote time and resources to anything more than basic reassurances, guarantees and warranties, and no apparent motive on the part of the customers to seek anything more than a tenuous relationship.

Personalised services

There are, however, some products and services that, seemingly, generate emotions out of proportion to their value. These tend to be highly personalised and are usually associated with self-esteem. These categories include products such as clothing and services such as hairdressing or beauty treatment. If the benefits associated with these products and services are important emotionally to a customer, then they are highly salient and the customer is likely to be risk averse. In these situations, relational strategies may help secure that customer's patronage. With most consumers these personal goods or services involve a trade-off. Thus the introduction of 'personal shoppers', personal trainers or expert stylists, at an increased cost to the consumer, may be acceptable to a percentage of the population although the core value of the service is low.

With highly personalised services there is frequently a high level of personal risk potential and salience *perceived by the customer*, and a resultant high degree of emotion generated, despite the relatively low cost in monetary terms (but perhaps a high cost in psychological terms). This situation may also promote or 'drive' RM strategies.

Trust and commitment

The requirement for trust and commitment appears to be an important indicator of when RM strategies may be potentially valuable. Equally, the existence of trust and commitment among parties is seen by some to be central to the success of relationship marketing strategies (Morgan and Hunt, 1994, p. 22; Palmatier *et al.*, 2006, p. 149) and the main means by which the affective strength of a buyer–seller relationship can be judged (Bejou and Palmer, 1998, p. 8). Trust and commitment are frequently discussed together in RM literature, with few authors mentioning one without the other (Pressey and Mathews, 1998, p. 41).

Trust

Trust is defined in various ways in the marketing literature. Both Lewicki *et al.* (1998, p. 438) and Morgan and Hunt (1994, p. 23) define **trust** as confidence in the exchange partner's reliability and integrity. This does not, however, mention the insecurity that trust is seen to overcome. In a risk-taking context partners will necessarily exhibit signs of vunerability as a precondition of trusting behaviour (Mitchell *et al.*, 1998, p. 159). A more comprehensive definition, therefore, might be 'an acceptance of vulnerability to another's possible, but not expected, ill will or lack of good will' (Blois, 1997, p. 58). Trust here is shown to be a psychological state comprising an intention to accept this vulnerability, based upon the positive expectations of the intentions or behaviour of others (Rousseau *et al.*, 1998, p. 394). Young (2006, p. 440) sees two levels of trust. The first is cognitive, calculative and rational, whereas the second is personal trust based on more emotional reasoning.

Trust is not itself a behaviour (unlike for example cooperation) nor a choice (as in taking a risk) but an underlying condition that can result from such activities (Rousseau *et al.*, 1998, p. 395). Trust evolves through reaction and assessment over time (Young 2006). Trust is seen as an important driver to both relationships and relationship enhancement in that it would appear to reduce risk perception more effectively than anything else. It is effectively a fundamental relationship model building block (Wilson, 1995, p. 337). From another perspective, trust may also be seen as a pyschological outcome of a trusting relationship (Swaminathan and Reddy, 2000, p. 400) and/or associated with outstanding performance. In this regard, trust may be a consequence rather than an antecedent or, more likely, a cumulative build-up of both (Ambler and Styles, 2000, p. 496).

Scholars have seen trust as an essential ingredient in a healthy personality, as a foundation for interpersonal relationships, as a prerequisite for cooperation and as a basis for stability in social institutions and markets (Lewicki *et al.*, 1998, p. 438). It is seen as the glue that holds relationships together across different encounters (Singh and Sirdeshmukh, 2000, p. 163). As Baier (1986, p. 234) puts it: 'we inhabit a climate of trust as we inhabit an atmosphere and notice it as we notice air, only when it becomes scarce or polluted'.

As well as generating cooperative behaviour, trust may (Rousseau *et al.*, 1998, p. 394):

■ reduce harmful conflict;

■ decrease transactional costs (e.g. negating the need for constant checks);

■ promote adaptive organisational forms (e.g. network relationships);

■ facilitate the rapid formation of *ad hoc* work groups;

■ promote effective response to a crisis.

The suggested advantages involved with organisational groups seem, however, to assume that trust negates ambition. Given human nature and the intense political manoeuvring frequently seen within organisations, this viewpoint may be questionable.

Implicit in the above definitions and descriptions of trust is the general expectation that the word of another can be relied upon. So strong is this expectancy that in certain relationships it is generally seen to supersede normal commercial decision-making. For example, customers are seen to place a high value on trust when dealing with financial services organisations (Alexander and Colgate, 1998, p. 67). Thus, when some UK financial advisers were seen to sell products designed to return their companies or principals a handsome profit (a notion encouraged in many sectors of industry) and themselves very satisfactory commissions, the British government decided it was 'mis-selling' and highly publicised action was taken to refund customers.

The importance of trust has become central to discussions concerning Internet sales. Lack of trust in (often newly created and therefore unknown) suppliers to supply to the quality expected (or indeed at all) was for many years cited as one of the major barriers to Internet sales. In response, a number of established organisations (that customers might be expected to 'trust' based on their size and/or reputation) stepped in to offer 'seals of approval' to legitimise Internet businesses. Other organisations (e.g. Amazon, ebay, W.H. Smith) offering externally sourced products and services under their own name are also acting to reduce mistrust. Guarantees from credit card providers (either voluntary or through legislation) have also helped alleviate much of the risk of trading on-line.

Trusting situations

Many different words or terms seem to be used to describe trusting situations. These, according to Mitchell *et al.* (1998, p. 160), may be summarised under the following headings:

- probity;
- equity;
- reliability;
- satisfaction.

Probity

Probity focuses on honesty and integrity that may be realised in business terms as professional understanding and reputation. Reputation matters, and in particular the historical trustworthiness of parties following previous interactions. Although trust may be managed by individuals, companies can trade on their previous trustworthiness (even if the person who was responsible for generating the trust initially has gone elsewhere) because it can be 'institutionally captured' by the organisation (Shepherd and Sherman, 1998, p. 437) (see also Chapter 3).

Equity

Factors such as fair-mindedness, benevolence, caring, values and sincerity are in evidence here. Helpful advertising and/or cause-related sponsorship or promotions may help communicate this message to the consumer. Equity may also suggest an implied contract with mutual expectations and perceived obligations (Mitchell *et al.*, 1998, p. 160). Trust is not, however, simply cooperation (which may be coercive) but is seen to have more altruistic motivations (Rousseau *et al.*, 1998, p. 394).

Reliability

Reliability relates to the firm having the required expertise to perform its business effectively and reliably. It is emphasised through dependability, quality and consistency, and may be associated with high levels of predictability on the part of consumers as to the product or service they can expect. This may be expressed through the inherent qualities associated with the corporate name or brand or through guarantees and warranties issued by the company (Mitchell *et al.*, 1998, p. 160). It may be important to note that, when customers are not able to evaluate product or service quality, it is brand reputation that often drives the exchange (Selnes, 1998, p. 318).

Satisfaction

This will be covered more fully in the following section but is included here in its capacity as a predictor of trust. There would appear to be considerable overlap between trust and satisfaction as they both represent an overall evaluation, feeling or attitude about the other party in a relationship (ibid., p. 308). Satisfaction may be developed through personal experience or, less directly, through opinion and the experience of peers. It is associated with the perceived standard of delivery and may well be dependent on the duration of the relationship. Anticipated levels of satisfaction may also have an important effect on the duration of trust (Mitchell *et al.*, 1998, p. 160). In addition to being a potential antecedent, satisfaction may also be seen as an outcome of a trusting relationship (Swaminathan and Reddy, 2000, p. 400).

Since trust is built generally through experience, the more positive experiences the consumer has with the company, the more trusting he or she is likely to become (Grossman, 1998, p. 33) Trust is, therefore, a belief in a person's (or organisation's or brand's) competence to perform a specific task under specific circumstances (Sitkin and Roth, 1993, p. 373). In other circumstances no such trust (or active distrust) may exist. This is because relationships are multifaceted. It is quite possible for parties to hold, simultaneously, different views of each other as to each party's trustfulness in particular situations. For example, a company may be trusted as regards quality but not to deliver on time. Trust (and for that matter distrust) involves movement towards certainty (Lewicki *et al.*, 1998, p. 438) although complete certainty can never be reached. Trust is almost always regarded as a beneficial force; however, excessive trust (or suppression of distrust) may be at the root of 'group-think' dynamics (ibid p. 453), where logic is suppressed in favour of group integrity, or may lead to claims of naïvety.

Commitment

Relationship commitment, it is suggested, is central to relationship marketing and, according to Wilson (1995, p. 337), is the most commonly used dependent variable used in buyer–seller relationship studies. To many it is the 'end-game state' of relationship marketing (Dann and Dann, 2001, p. 352). It is, however, frequently an ill-defined concept. In RM literature it would seem to be regarded as a situation where one or other of the party's intention is to act and their subsequent attitude towards interacting with each other (Storbacka *et al.*, 1994, p. 28). Commitment implies the importance of the relationship to the parties and their desire to continue it (Wilson, 2000, p. 250). It also suggests that both parties will be loyal, reliable and show stability in the relationship with one another (Bejou and Palmer, 1998, p. 10). It is, therefore, a desire to maintain a relationship, often indicated by an ongoing investment in activities which are expected to maintain that relationship (Blois, 1997, p. 58). As it may take time to reach a point where a commitment may be made, it may also imply a certain 'maturity' in a relationship (Bejou and Palmer, 1998, p. 10). High levels of commitment are also associated with perceptions of 'future rewards, relationship identification, limited desire to seek out alternatives, the amount of effort expended in a relationship, the investment made in the relationship and the individuals assumed responsibility' (Grossman, 1998, p. 33).

Commitment is undoubtedly connected with the notion of trust but it is less clear which, if any, assumes precedence. Whether commitment is the outcome of growing trust or whether trust develops from the decision to commit to one or a few suppliers is not immediately clear. In addition, a breakdown in commitment may be the result of a breakdown in trust or vice versa. As with trust, commitment may also be seen as a potential 'psychological outcome' of a strong relationship (Swaminathan and Reddy, 2000, p. 400). It may also be associated (negatively) with greater competition and the availability of alternative relational parties (Bejou and Palmer, 1998, p. 10). Dann and Dann (2001, pp. 352–3) distinguish between two types of commitment: affective commitment, based on a liking, emotional attachment and sense of bonding with the other party, and calculative commitment based on a balance sheet of costs and benefits. They go on to note (p. 353):

> There is an evident bias in the literature towards preferring the affective side of commitment for long-term relationships. In reality, performance of the relationship is every bit as influenced by the profit and loss calculations of calculative commitment as it is by the sensitive 'touchy-feely' approach of affective commitment.

Trust and commitment

Notionally trust and commitment appear inseparable in the RM debate. This may well indicate that, if one or other is missing, the relationship is unlikely to be more than a 'hands off' or transient arrangement. This is because trust and commitment are invariably associated with the prerequisite that the relationship is of significantly high importance to one or both parties that it warrants maximum efforts at maintaining it (Morgan and Hunt, 1994, p. 23). According to Doyle (1995, p. 38), trust and commitment often require new forms of behaviour from marketers. They may have to set aside long-held beliefs and prejudices to accommodate the relationship.

Situations which may benefit from relational strategies are, therefore, likely to be those where the consumer and/or the supplier (but not necessarily both) regard the formation of a relationship as important. Where the supplier alone recognises the importance of a relationship, relational strategies designed to 'lock-in' customers over time seem a logical development (see Chapter 4). Indeed generating relationship benefits and promoting customer dependency may be more effective strategies for increasing customer commitment than for building trust (Palmatier *et al.,* 2006, p. 149). Where the customer alone recognises the importance of a relationship (e.g. in situations of high risk) the supplier may use this desire to attract customers through the development of strategies perceived by the customer as satisfying this need.

What these descriptions of trust and commitment suggest is that, whatever the industry, it is important to build trust and commitment if the establishment of a relationship is the end goal (Pressey and Mathews, 1998). Conversely, it may be hypothesised that, if trust and commitment are generally prerequisites to a sale, then relationship building is an important step towards achieving this.

There may be a number of precursors to trust and commitment, including (Morgan and Hunt, 1994, pp. 24–5):

■ relationship termination costs;
■ relationship benefits;
■ shared values;
■ communication;
■ opportunistic behaviour.

Relationship termination costs

Relationship termination costs are *all* of the costs expected from terminating the relationship, including the lack of comparable alternative partners, relationship dissolution expenses as well as other switching costs (see Chapter 4).

Relationship benefits

Relationship benefits directly influence trust and commitment (ibid.). RM theory suggests that partner selection may be a critical element in competitive strategy as partners deliver superior 'value benefits'. Partners that receive superior benefits are likely to be more committed to a relationship.

Shared values

Shared values also directly influence both trust and commitment. The extent to which the partners have beliefs in common about behaviours, goals and policies that are important, appropriate and right for a particular situation is likely to affect commitment to the relationship.

Communication

Communication may directly influence trust and, indirectly, commitment. The sharing of meaningful and timely information is likely to build up both trust and commitment.

Opportunistic behaviour

Opportunistic behaviour (i.e. taking advantage of the relationship partner) on the part of one of the relationship participants is likely to directly influence (negatively) trust and, indirectly, commitment. When a party engages in opportunistic behaviour, such perceptions can lead to decreased trust and, as a consequence, the lessening of commitment.

It is worth noting that although trust and commitment play important roles other factors such as relationship satisfaction, efficiency, equity and reciprocity can also be important (Palmatier *et al.*, 2006, p. 152).

Transactional marketing

O'Malley and Tynan (1999, p. 593) have noted that there is empirical evidence to suggest that there is very little trust, commitment or indeed mutual respect in consumer markets. This may only be partly correct as at the more transactional end of the spectrum trust may be implicit as the consumer relies on the 'promises' of the supplier and/or the brand as regards safety, reliability and value for money for products and services. Often the customer, particularly in the case of services, must buy before 'experiencing the purchase' (Berry and Parsuraman, 1991, p. 107) basing their decision on how much they trust the supplier/brand. This implies that trust is most applicable when the outcome is unclear. The breaking of this trust may be seen to be a potential dissatisfier and a reason for defection.

A high degree of trust can, therefore, exist between parties without much feeling of commitment (Håkansson and Snehota, 2000, p. 77). In the FMCG sector consumers have no reason to commit themselves to one or a few suppliers because of the availability of supply in a largely undifferentiated market. At the other extreme, what at first might appear to be 'commitment' on the part of one party may hide the fact that they have few other exchange possibilities and are 'trapped' rather than committed to the relational exchange (Bejou and Palmer, 1998, p. 10).

The irony is that it is the FMCG sector, where commitment is low, that is the industry most heavily involved in 'loyalty schemes'. If commitment is a rarity in these businesses then loyalty is also in short supply. Indeed, most loyalty schemes, while rewarding repeat behaviour, are little more than technically advanced promotions that have little to do with retention, and may actively work against the development of long-term commitment. Exit barriers in this industry are low and the psychological costs nearly non-existent. At this end of the industry spectrum seduction is the favoured option (Tynan, 1997, p. 993). The risk is that 'promiscuous customers' will be attracted by the best deal with little regard for who supplies it. Indeed, a breakdown in commitment may well be associated with greater competition and availability of alternative relational partners (Bejou and Palmer, 1998, p. 10).

Commitment implies a state of maturity in a relationship that does not seem to exist at the transactional end of the RM–TM continuum. There is no need to commit oneself either to a brand or a supplier; rather, consumers seem content to work with a 'portfolio of brands' (including retailer brands) until such time as a better alternative is available (Barnard and Ehrenberg, 1997). If the requirement for the successful application of RM is both trust and commitment, and not just one or the other (Morgan and Hunt, 1994), then many such industries fail to fulfil this criterion.

Perceived need for closeness

Some relationships will always be closer than others. Closeness, therefore, is a construct that is integral to the notion of relationship in that very close and less close relationships exist in virtually all circumstances (Barnes, 1997, p. 229). Closeness can be physical, mental or emotional and can strengthen the feeling of security in a relationship (Gummesson, 1999, p. 17). When the 'distance' between the parties is shorter, deeper relationships are likely to develop (Pels, 1999, p. 27). Conversely, when the distance is greater the relationship (if a relationship can be said to exist) is functional and at 'arm's length'. Close relationships are acknowledged to be more solid and likely to be longer lasting – precisely the characteristics relational marketers are looking for (Barnes, 1997, p. 229).

Different groups may be more or less 'prone' to the development of close relationships (Barnes and Howlett, 1998, p. 16). Not all customers want close relationships (see Chapter 5) and some may only be interested in developing them with some parties and not with others (Pels, 1999, p. 27). A certain percentage may already have a moderately close relationship with a supplier and may wish that it were closer, while others might wish that it were less close. A continuum of closeness may, therefore, be said to exist (Barnes, 1997, p. 229) which may, to an extent, resemble the relational–transactional continuum (see Chapter 5).

According to Barnes (p. 237), degrees of closeness in a relationship may be linked, among other things, to the frequency of two-way communication with employees, and to the trust, empathy and mutuality of perceived relationship goals, and are usually associated with core products and services that involve high risk and involvement. Establishing close customer relationships in settings that are not characterised by frequent personal contact or high levels of involvement or emotion may, therefore, be a challenge. This concept seems to have bypassed some organisations. What is seen as a relationship as defined by many marketing programmes (e.g. customer contact/updates) is not likely to be a relationship in the eyes of the customer in that it is mostly one-sided and lacking in two-way communication (p. 229).

This view of the importance of 'closeness' also has implications for direct marketers whose implicit objective is to develop or otherwise exploit relationships with customers, in particular those using technology as a surrogate for 'close relationships' (see Chapter 11). Targeted mailings, in general, fail to satisfy the criteria as the 'normal' response rate is low, with many customers rejecting the 'communication'. This applies even when the 'return on investment' on the campaign is satisfactory. Companies that rely on frequent mailings to 'keep their customers informed' are merely throwing messages at consumers (in effect a refinement on mass marketing), not communicating with them.

Moves to utilise technology to save staff costs (e.g. cash machines, Internet information services) may also discourage the development of close relationships. By removing the human element in the process the company reverts to relying solely on the easily replicated 'core product and support services' (see Chapter 12) to achieve any 'differentiation' from its competitors.

Customer satisfaction

Relationship marketing theory suggests that profitability is enhanced when customer retention is high. Retention in competitive markets is generally believed to be a product of customer satisfaction (Buttle, 1997, p. 143). In addition, customer satisfaction has been shown to be positively associated with return on investment (ROI) and market value (Sheth and Sisodia, 1999, p. 80), although these are sometimes regarded as poor measures of actual company performance in the long term.

Satisfaction can be perceived from a number of different viewpoints, however, most researchers agree that satisfaction is a psychological process of evaluating perceived performance outcomes based on predetermined expectations (e.g. Sheth and Sisodia, 1999). Customers are, therefore, satisfied when their 'expectations of values' are positively disconfirmed (Buttle, 1997, p. 143). In contrast, the greater the (negative) gap between the level of expectation and the matching of such expectations, the greater the level of dissatisfaction experienced by the customer (Hutcheson and Moutinho, 1998, p. 706). Figure 6.1 illustrates these concepts.

Satisfaction drivers

What drives customer satisfaction? Fournier and Mick (1999, p. 2) note that the customer-satisfaction paradigm suggests that:

■ confirmed standards lead to moderate satisfaction;

■ positively disconfirmed (i.e. better than expected) standards lead to high satisfaction;

■ negatively disconfirmed (i.e. worse than expected) standards leads to dissatisfaction.

This may, however, be an over-simplification of a complex series of reactions. Cumby and Barnes (1998, pp. 58–60) suggest that drivers exist on five levels and that these generally involve progressively more personal contact with the service supplier:

Figure 6.1
Expectation and realisation of service

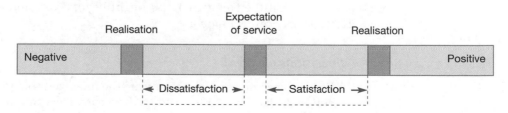

- core product or service;
- support services and systems;
- technical performance;
- elements of customer interaction;
- affective dimension of services.

Core product or service

This is the basic product or service provided by the company and, probably, provides the supplier with the least opportunity to differentiate or add value. However, in the competitive marketplace the company must get the core product or service right otherwise the whole relationship is at risk. With services in particular, the inability to patent the service and the ease of copying largely precludes the use of service features for competitive advantage (Devlin and Ennew, 1997, p. 73).

Support services and systems

These include the peripheral and support services that enhance the provision of the core product or services (e.g. staffing levels, delivery, technical support). The customer may well receive an excellent core product or service from the supplier but be dissatisfied with the supplier because of inferior support services and systems.

Technical performance

This level of the 'customer satisfaction model' deals with whether the service provider gets the core product or service *and* the support services and systems right. The emphasis is on keeping the promises made to the consumer (e.g. on-time delivery, correct billing). There may be nothing wrong with the core product or service and the supplier may have the services and systems in place but they do not (perhaps because of management failings) get them right on every occasion. Customer dissatisfaction may result from this failure to deliver to the customer's expectations.

Elements of customer interaction

This level relates to the way the service provider interacts with the customer either face-to-face or through technology-based contact (e.g. telephone, etc.). How do we treat customers? Are they treated with courtesy? Do we make it easy for them to do business with us? Understanding of the importance of applying this level of consideration implies that the company has thought beyond the simple provision of core products and services and support.

Affective dimensions of service

Beyond the basic interactions of the company are the messages, sometimes subtle and often unintentional, that companies send to their customers that leave them with either positive or negative feelings towards them. Cumby and Barnes (1998, p. 58) note that research evidence exists showing that a considerable amount of customer dissatisfaction has nothing to do with core products and services or with how that 'core' is delivered or provided to the customer. Indeed, the customer may be satisfied with most aspects of the interaction. The problem is with the 'little things' that may not even be noticed by staff (see Box 6.2).

Box 6.2   Frustrations

- I used to be able to telephone my bank if I had a problem and my problem would normally be sorted out then and there. Now my bank uses a 'customer care centre'. I now have to call this centre (which is frequently engaged), try to remember the first, third and fourth letter of my password (which I frequently forget) and explain (usually from the very beginning as the call centre operator does not know me) my problem. They cannot usually answer my question because they need first to speak to my bank, which they promise to contact. I may then receive a telephone call at home during office hours (usually taken by my answerphone so I have no opportunity to question what I am told) a few days later either part-answering or not answering my query. I then have to call the customer care centre back and the cycle begins again. Not only was my query not answered immediately but it would seem to me that the duplication of effort on the part of the bank hardly suggests efficiency.
- A large cable telephone operator has written to me on two separate occasions urging me to join them. As I am less than happy with my current telephone provider I called the company on both occasions to find out more. Both times the company told me that cables have yet to be laid in my street. Discussing this with some students, I find that the same thing has happened to many of them. I am beginning to think that it is not a mistake, as I had been told, but that the company is 'mass mailing' to judge whether it would be worth laying cables in the first place. Is this ethical or sharp practice?
- A well-known insurance company wrote to me a while ago suggesting that they could 'almost certainly' cut the cost of my home insurance. I called them only to be quoted a premium almost £200 more than my current insurer. The operator said it was because of the area in which I lived. As these rates are based almost always on post codes why did this company bother writing to me in the first place?
- I was involved for many years with a UK ceramics company for which I was (on behalf of a large North American department store) that company's largest customer. Towards the end of each year I would contact the company to check on the January/February shipments. Each time, without fail, I would be told there was a delay. When I asked why, I would be told (each and every time) that the problem was that the factory was closing for Christmas. The fact that Christmas happened every year did not seem to influence the company's planning programmes in any way.
- How annoying is it when you want to talk to a real live person rather than a machine. You have been to the website and gone through the FAQs with no success. You search for a phone number which is rarely given and sometimes you don't even get an e-mail address. The Internet should be about improving communication not frustrating it.

Cumby and Barnes (ibid.) make the point that it is quite possible for the supplier to get things right on the first four levels and to dissatisfy the customer because of something that happens on the fifth level. This emphasises the importance of 'critical episodes' in the exchange process, as discussed in the following section.

Episode value

Service researchers have long argued that the consumer's experience and subsequent satisfaction are primarily an outcome of the interaction between personnel and the consumer (Möller and Halinen, 2000, p. 33; Palmatier *et al.*, 2006, p. 141; Kinard and Capella, 2006, p. 365) and that these may be described in the form of 'episodes'. Indeed, one definition of relationships in RM is as 'the sum of meaning-filled episodes which relational partners co-produce' (Buttle, 1997, p. 148). Bitner *et al.* (1990, p. 73) define them as 'specific interactions between customers and . . . employees that are especially satisfying or unsatisfying' [*sic*]. Not all of these episodes have the same importance or carry the same weight (Storbacka *et al.*, 1994, p. 30). Some are routine and others critical. Customer satisfaction can be increased, it is suggested, if episode value is improved by increasing the benefit and/or reducing the sacrifice for the buyer (Selnes, 1998, p. 305).

According to Storbacka *et al.* (1994, p. 30), the definition of a '**critical episode**' is an episode that is of 'great importance to a relationship and upon which the continuation of a relationship is dependent'. Not keeping up the standard expected by the customer in an exchange may be seen to have a negative effect that may trigger a critical episode. Critical episodes are customer specific, and even a 'routine episode' can become critical if the *perceived* level of service is not met. Thus episodes indicative of high quality in one relationship may be deemed indicative of poor quality in another (Buttle, 1997, p. 153). These 'critical episodes' within the relationship are seen to have a considerable effect on customer satisfaction. The importance of episode value will be returned to in Chapter 7.

The customer satisfaction process

While the literature differs on the definition of satisfaction most descriptions share common elements, including (Giese and Cote, 2000, p. 1):

■ customer satisfaction is a response (emotional or cognitive);
■ the response relates to a specific focus (e.g. expectation, experience);
■ response occurs at a particular time (before, during or after consumption).

Although this may be the case in certain instances, this does not take account of satisfaction (or dissatisfaction) that develops over time and is based upon episodes in the relationship (see Chapter 7).

Jones and Sasser (1995, p. 93) suggest that the ability to 'listen to the customer' is at the heart of any successful strategy to 'manage' customer satisfaction. They suggest five categories of approach to this process:

- customer satisfaction indices;
- feedback;
- market research;
- front-line personnel;
- strategic activities.

Customer satisfaction indices

Customer satisfaction indices are among the most popular methods of tracking or measuring customer satisfaction. Indeed, businesses of all sorts now divert considerable energies into tracking customer satisfaction in this way (Mittal and Lassar, 1998, p. 178). These studies are, however, 'static and cognitively orientated' (Strandvik and Storbacka, 1996, p. 73) and are frequently criticised for reporting overly positive results (Nowak and Washburn, 1998, p. 443). There is also a problem with how questions are asked. Different results can be achieved with the same satisfaction survey dependent on how it was operationalised (Giese and Cote, 2000, p. 1). There is an added difficulty of equivalence across countries and/or cultures where knowledge and meaning may make comparisons difficult (see Reynolds and Simintiras 2000). Jones and Sasser (1995, p. 91) point out that, as important as they believe 'satisfaction surveys' to be, it would be fatal for a business to rely solely on them.

Mittal and Lassar (1998, p. 178) note that many companies measure satisfaction in the hope that, if the scores are high, the customer will stay with them. They warn, however, that even a satisfied customer will leave for the lure of a competitor's offer. Their research (p. 183) suggests that, even at a satisfaction rating of five (on a five-point scale) nearly 20 per cent of healthcare customers and over 30 per cent of car repair customers were 'willing to switch' to another supplier. At a score of four (a level most companies would be quite happy with) the potential desertion figures reached 32.4 per cent and 78.6 per cent respectively. Reichheld (1993, p. 71) also recognises that customer satisfaction is not a surrogate for retention. According to his research, between 65 per cent and 85 per cent of customers who defected claimed they were satisfied or very satisfied before leaving. Whatever else satisfaction indices tell us, they do not predict loyalty.

Feedback

Feedback in this context includes comments, complaints and questions. It may be among the most effective means of establishing what the customer regards as a satisfactory level of performance and what 'dissatisfiers' exist within the operation as it is based on actual performance rather than contrived situations (e.g. market research).

Market research

In addition to research among customers and non-customers into potential 'satisfiers', 'dissatisfiers' and 'customer expectations', market research can be used (once they have become customers) to establish those drivers that brought them there and

The view that customer satisfaction is the key to securing customer loyalty is, therefore, far from a fully robust concept. It is not sufficient to have customers who are merely satisfied. In addition, satisfying customers that have the freedom to make choices is not enough to keep them loyal (Jones and Sasser, 1995, p. 91; Stewart, 1997, p. 112). Satisfaction does not always result in retention and it is equally apparent that dissatisfaction does not necessarily result in defection (Buttle, 1997, p. 145; O'Malley, 1998, p. 48). Indeed, the gap that appears to exist between satisfaction and loyalty calls into question the assertions managers often make about the direct association between them (Mittal and Lassar, 1998, p. 178) (see Chapter 3).

Traditional customer satisfaction theory assumes that the customer has expectations and comparison standards (Strandvik and Storbacka, 1996, p. 73) to compare with product or service performance in deriving satisfaction judgements (Fournier and Mick, 1999, p. 11). It also presumes objectivity. This assumption of rationality is perceived to be a problem, not just in this particular scenario but generally in marketing theory, which emphasises positive decision-making as being at the centre of consumer behaviour (East, 1997a, p. 41) when real-life observation suggests customers can be fickle. Research calls into question the continued dominance of the customer-satisfaction paradigm (Fournier and Mick, 1999, p. 18) and suggests 'value-expectation' is a flawed measure because of its multifacetedness, complexity (Ravald and Grönroos, 1996, p. 19) and subjectivity.

Inherent satisfaction may be the basis of one form of loyalty, particularly where the customer has exerted some effort in establishing the 'best deal' available in the marketplace. Other situational drivers (such as time and opportunity costs) may, however, result in 'default loyalty' where satisfaction plays little or no part. Research by East (1997b, p. 7), for example, notes that convenience of location may be a stronger motivator in FMCG retailing than supermarket loyalty schemes.

In FMCG retailing in particular, strategies designed to encourage simple repeat behaviour or to minimise disruption of consumer inertia (see the following section) may be considerably more beneficial than costly, interactive, relational strategies. In industries with lower or more complex comparability a different need exists. Continual reassurance and frequent comparison may be required to ensure that customers remain relatively satisfied.

Inertia

One further element in the 'customer satisfaction' debate that is frequently underrated is the part played by **'inertia'**. Customer satisfaction is regarded, generally, as a positive, proactive force that drives behaviour patterns. Satisfaction is not, however, always the result of positive input but may be simply the result of things not going wrong (Johnson and Mathews, 1997, p. 536). In other situations the level of 'satisfaction' may be due to a lack of motivation and/or the ability of a customer to evaluate the level of service (Bloemer and de Ruyter, 1998, p. 501).[1] In the former case this may be described not as satisfaction but as inertia. Rather than 'driving' a customer to repatronise a supplier, this non-response to other external attractions suggests habitual behaviour. This may be similar to what Fournier and Mick (1999, p. 10) refer to as 'satisfaction-as-resignation', which involves 'passive submission and unresisting acceptance of that which is imposed'.

Inertia-type behaviour might be defined as behaviour that would occur anyway, assuming no external stimuli. This variety of satisfaction is passive and simply reflects the willingness of customers to stay with a supplier until they perceive (if ever) that something better is available in the market or other factors (e.g. customer moves away) cause a change. Stability in markets occurs because habits may rarely change (East, 1997a, p. 40). It may be hypothesised, therefore, that in many situations it is not positive 'customer satisfaction' driving consumers to act but lack of stimulation to act otherwise. The distinction between positive and neutral satisfaction (or inertia) is important as, in certain industries, it again challenges the idea that customer satisfaction leads to long-lasting relationships (Storbacka *et al.*, 1994, p. 28). Marketers should not equate inertia with loyalty (Cumby and Barnes, 1998, p. 56).

It is quite probable (although not a universal truth) that consumer inertia or unwillingness to change from the present behaviour may be the norm in many industries. The 'comfort zone'[2] described is the difference between an adequate and a desired level of service (Storbacka *et al.*, 1994, p. 26), which becomes a 'zone of inertia' where customers do not act or react to increased levels of service quality. Effectively customers are indifferent to small increases or decreases within the zone (Yap and Sweeney, 2007, p. 137). In this situation, any small increase in service level or quality (all other things being equal) merely helps maintain inertia or habitual behaviour rather than actually driving the competitive process (see Figure 6.4). This inertial form of routine human behaviour may help explain why aggregate responses to surveys are very weak measures (East, 1997a, p. 41). In relationship terms, an analogy to marriage suggests that, whatever bond holds couples together, it is largely responsive rather than proactive, particularly after time has elapsed. The natural tendency of relationships is towards erosion of sensitivity and attentiveness over time. Familiarity may not always breed contempt but it may well create inertia! In commercial situations, it has been observed that individuals who remain 'loyal' in the long term indeed show signs of this inertia (Bejou and Palmer, 1998, p. 16).

The concept of inertia in many ways runs counter to one of the main planks of the customer satisfaction paradigm, that excellent services necessarily improve profitability (e.g. Buttle, 1996, p. 9). Rather it suggests that, in certain industries, no benefit is achieved from the extra effort expended. Once resources have been allocated to the

Figure 6.4 The inertia effect on expectation and realisation of service

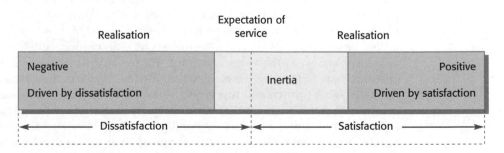

achievement of latent customer satisfaction (or, more descriptively, customer inertia), up to a threshold level (and not beyond) any additional investment will not yield any return in the form of increased customer retention (Hassan, 1996, p. 9) or, ultimately, increased profitability. Indeed, if keeping up with customers' needs in a highly competitive market involves ever greater investment, the potential is forever falling, not rising, profits as expectations on quality is believed to have diminishing returns (Strandvik and Storbacka, 1996, p. 74). An increased level of satisfaction *may*, in itself, be counter-productive as it may well increase expectations and, therefore, increase dissatisfaction rates (Hutcheson and Moutinho, 1998, p. 718). This is directly contrary to another fundamental principle of RM in that its concern is to meet, or preferably exceed, customers' expectations (Buttle, 1996, p. 8).

By direct contrast, any decrease from whatever level of service the customer now expects, possibly regardless of what the market generally has to offer, may ferment switching behaviour. The marketing emphasis here, far from being upon increasing satisfaction, may be directed at retaining the *status quo*. This may be achieved not by increasing customer satisfaction but by minimising dissatisfaction as the switching costs of dissatisfaction may well outweigh the benefits of satisfaction (Hutcheson and Moutinho, 1998, p. 706). The danger is that the competition may move the goalposts and what was previously acceptable is no longer the standard to be achieved.

The reason that 'inertial behaviour' seems to contradict some widely held concepts of RM may be because its application appears to coincide with more repetitive transactional exchanges at the TM end of the transactional–relational continuum (see Chapter 5). In situations where RM is seen to be beneficial the development of customer satisfaction through differential, relational strategies may be advantageous. In repetitive, more transactional relationships, strategies that promote repetitive behaviour may be more profitable.

Satisfaction – the reality

The simple model (customer satisfaction→customer retention→profitability) is too simplistic and possibly misleading for many businesses. While intuitively a useful goal, an increased level of satisfaction could prove counterproductive in certain industries as it may well increase expectation and, ultimately, lead to increased dissatisfaction rates (Hutcheson and Moutinho, 1998, p. 718). This may simply reflect the obverse of the Buddhist principle that when you decrease your desire you increase your chances of happiness. Evidence from the US market suggests that, despite the increased focus on satisfaction and service quality among many American companies, customer satisfaction rates in that market are at an all-time low and other expressions of dissatisfaction at an all-time high (Fournier *et al*., 1998, p. 42). Jan Lapidoth Sr, in an interview about his time at SAS (quoted by Gummesson, 1999, p. 185), describes a concept known as the 'service paradox' (Box 6.3). This suggests that less profitable customers are frequently the most satisfied while the more profitable are frequently less satisfied. A further, and supporting, paradox has emerged in research by Gwynne *et al*. (2000, p. 559). This is that customers who are generally happy about what they have received thus far and are generally positively disposed towards the supplier are likely to be more demanding in terms of their future expectations. Conversely customers who are disgruntled appear to temper their expectations.

Box 6.3 The service paradox

Gummesson (1999, p. 185) introduces the notion of a 'service paradox', which suggests that the most loyal customers do not always mean the most satisfied or the most profitable. Gummesson quotes a definition of the service paradox as described to him by Jan Lapidoth Sr on his experiences at SAS. He states that 'the less profitable customers are, the more satisfied they are, while the more profitable customers are less satisfied'. Lapidoth illustrates this with the example of flights between New York and Europe. The prices of fares on this route differ dramatically. Full Business Class is $3,000.00. The business traveller is highly profitable but highly demanding. Value for the business traveller is high quality, punctuality, comfort, etc. The Economy Class customer contributes marginally to profits but is grateful for the low price and not so demanding. Value for the economy traveller is in low prices. The likelihood is that the business traveller is less satisfied than the economy traveller despite the business traveller getting better service.

(*Source*: Based on Gummesson, 1999, p. 185)

Summary

A model was introduced at the end of Chapter 5 that suggested that there were a number of perceived 'drivers' to relational and transactional strategies. In this chapter additional drivers were introduced and discussed.

The existence of high risk, high salience and, consequently, high emotion in an exchange transaction appears to suggest that RM strategies would be beneficial as the customer may perceive that a close relationship is necessary in such situations. At the other end of the spectrum, low risk, low salience and low emotion suggest that the customer does not perceive the benefits of staying with one or a few suppliers and is, consequently, more opportunistic.

The perceived need for trust and commitment in deep relationships provided another indicator of those situations where relational strategies may be seen as beneficial. At the transactional end of the continuum, although there are indications that a certain level of trust is a necessary ingredient, the existence of commitment is not usually observed.

The concept of closeness was also discussed. When the 'distance' between the parties is shorter, deeper relationships are likely to develop. Conversely, when the distance is greater, the relationship is functional and at arm's length. Again, observation of these characteristics in a relationship may be an indicator of whether RM strategies are likely to be beneficial.

The complexities surrounding the concept of customer satisfaction were examined and it was concluded that the widely accepted model (customer satisfaction *leads to* customer retention which *leads to* profitability) is too simplistic and may cause difficulties in certain industries. The perceived need for positive customer satisfaction in a relationship may, however, prove a reasonable indicator (or driver) of the benefits of relational strategies. At the other end of the continuum, strategies which promote habitual behaviour may be more indicative of transactional marketing.

The importance of these themes is such that they will be referred to again in later chapters.

Discussion questions

1 Explain the association between risk, salience and emotion.
2 Explain the association between trust and commitment.
3 Why will close relationships be stronger than arm's length relationships?
4 Describe a situation where inertia may determine the duration of a relationship.

Case study   Find a way into the hearts of customers

By Philip Delves Broughton
Published: November 8 2010 22:26   Last updated

Imagine a couple goes in to see a doctor who tells them their child will be born with a genetic disorder. It is mid-morning and when they emerge from their consultation, they see a row of parents bouncing their healthy children on their laps. The emotional shock they have just experienced with the doctor will now be compounded by feelings of appalling unfairness. Why us?

While the genetic test results cannot be changed, the process by which prospective parents are informed could be. The couple could be asked in to the clinic in the early morning or evening, when there are no other patients around. They could be shown out through a side door, so they don't have to see babies right after they receive their bad news.

It is not just doctors' offices that could find ways to improve the process by which they handle emotions. Airlines dealing with delayed passengers, insurance companies dealing with traumatised claimants, management consultants explaining their bill could all benefit from a better understanding of the emotional peaks and troughs experienced by their customers.

In Designing the Soft Side of Customer Service, a paper recently published in the MIT Sloan Management Review, Sriram Dasu and Richard Chase of the Marshall School of Business at the University of Southern California argue that emotions are too rarely included in operations design.

Operations managers, Prof Dasu told me, regard emotions as too soft an issue to be integrated into the blinking lights and spinning discs of their world. 'They don't realise that emotions are very process driven.'

Let's say you have bought a laptop and within the first month of owning it, it fails three times. Your third call will be a more emotionally intense call than your first. But will the laptop manufacturer assign a more seasoned service agent to deal with you? Or will you simply be led through the same complaint process you experienced with your first call? In the paper, the profs say that companies should design 'emotion prints' of the customer experience and tailor their processes accordingly. Emotions are far more predictable and manageable than many operations managers believe. You do not need heroic individuals with extraordinary levels of emotional intelligence to make dramatic interventions. Rather, the process can be designed more like a factory line, with variables that can be managed and measured.

One advantage of this approach is that it takes broad intentions such as improving customer service and makes the process detailed and actionable. You do not need to train

Part II

The core firm and its relationships

As has been previously noted, a feature of 'older' definitions of relationship marketing was a concentration on the 'traditional' supplier–customer relationship. Later contributions to the RM debate were seen to widen the scope to incorporate other relationships. The rationale behind this was that in order to serve your customer properly you had to attend to all the firm's core relationships. As Grönroos (2004, p. 101) noted:

> if marketing is to be successful, other suppliers, partners, distributors, financial institutions, the customer's customer and sometimes even political decision-makers may have to be included in the management of the relationship in the network of relationships.

Although there are numerous models, and no single definition, there was a growing consensus that, in addition to a customer focus, a company should be considering a range of partnerships with suppliers, internal customers, institutions and intermediaries (Clarkson *et al.*, 1997, p. 173). In this respect RM is similar to the much older 'stakeholder theory' (Tzokas and Saren, 2000, p. 6). These 'network' or extended relationship theories, ideas and concepts have been advanced by a number of eminent marketing writers, including Christopher *et al.* (1991, 1994), Kotler (1992), Millman (1993), Hunt and Morgan (1994), Doyle (1995), Peck (1996), Buttle (1996) and Gummesson (1996). These writers adopted a view of marketing that continued to acknowledge the importance of managing customer relationships, but recognised that this is only one part of the relationship marketing equation. Although this view has, more recently, been challenged (see Chapter 13) it still best represents what distinguishes RM from other relational concepts and strategies. The common theme is that firms should compete through the development of relatively long-term relationships with all their stakeholders (Hunt, 1997, p. 431; Reichheld, 1996, p. 3). Whether the relational model is represented as 'six markets' (Christopher *et al.*, 1991, p. 13; 1994, p. 21), 'ten players' (Kotler, 1992), 'four partnerships' (Buttle, 1996, p. 3), 'four partnerships and ten relationships' (Hunt and Morgan, 1994, p. 21), or '30Rs' (Gummesson, 1996; 1999, pp. 20–2), the common ground between these theories appears to be the concept of 'the core firm and its partnerships' (Doyle, 1995, p. 34).

The move to RM is seen, therefore, as a move from a dyadic relationship to a multifaceted series of interrelationships not necessarily dominated exclusively by the supplier–customer interaction. This view of marketing represents a change of emphasis over and above traditional marketing. No longer is marketing simply about exchange (i.e. the transfer of goods and money in the marketplace). It also entails the creation and maintenance of dialogue between suppliers, sellers, customers, clients and others such that all parties are satisfied with the purchasing process (Uncles, 1994, p. 335). Different authors give varying prominence to each stakeholder group, and Gummesson (1999, pp. 20–2) in particular goes into considerable detail regarding the possible relationships a company and its stakeholders can be involved within. For relative simplicity, however, these various relationships may be broken down into four principal groupings. These are customer partnerships, internal partnerships, supplier partnerships and external partnerships. In Part II we will look at each of the four principal groupings in turn. Box II.1 and Figure II.1 show how the relationships types suggested by the different authors are related to each other.

Box II.1 Core relationships

	Customer partnerships	Supplier partnerships	Internal partnerships	External partnerships
Doyle (1995) The core firm and its **partnerships**	**Customer partnerships**	**Supplier partnerships**	**Internal partnerships** Employees Functional departments Other SBUs	**External partnerships** Competitors Governments External partners
Hunt and Morgan (1994) Four partnerships and ten relationships	**Buyer partnerships** Intermediate Final consumer	**Supplier partnerships** Goods suppliers Service suppliers	**Internal partnerships** Business units Employees Functional department	**Lateral partnerships** Competitors Non-profit organisations Government
Christopher et al. (1991; 1994) Six markets	**Customer markets**	**Supplier markets**	**Internal market** **Employee market**	**Referral market** **Influence market**
Gummesson (1996, 1999) 30Rs	**Classic market relationships** Classic dyad (customer/supplier) Classic triad (above+competitor) Classic network (distribution channels) **Special market relationships** Full-time/part-time marketers The service encounter Many-headed customer/supplier Customer's customer relationship Close versus distant relationship The monopoly relationship The customer as a member The electronic relationship Parasocial relationship (symbol etc.) The non-commercial relationship The green relationship The law-based relationship The criminal network		**Meta relationships** Profit centres Internal customer Quality (e.g. design manufacturing) Employee Matrix relationships Marketing services Owner/financiers	**Mega relationships** Personal/social Mega (e.g. government) Alliances Knowledge relationship Mega alliances (e.g. EU, NAFTA) Mass media

Figure II.1
The core
firm and its
relationships

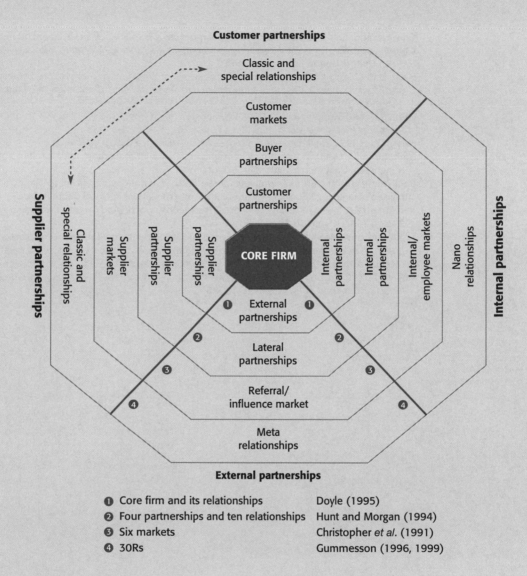

① Core firm and its relationships   Doyle (1995)
② Four partnerships and ten relationships   Hunt and Morgan (1994)
③ Six markets   Christopher *et al.* (1991)
④ 30Rs   Gummesson (1996, 1999)

References
Buttle, F.B. (1996) *Relationship Marketing Theory and Practice*, London: Paul Chapman.
Christopher, M., Payne, A. and Ballantyne, D. (1991) *Relationship Marketing*, London: Butterworth Heinemann.
Christopher, M., Payne, A. and Ballantyne, D. (1994) *Relationship Marketing*, Oxford: Butterworth Heinemann.
Clarkson, R.M., Clarke-Hill, C. and Robinson, T. (1997) 'Towards a general framework for relationship marketing: a literature review', paper presented at the Academy of Marketing Conference, Manchester, UK.
Doyle, P. (1995) 'Marketing in the new millennium', *European Journal of Marketing*, **29** (12), 23–41.
Grönroos, C. (2004) 'The relationship marketing process: communication, interaction, dialogue, value', *Journal of Business & Industrial Marketing*, **19** (2), 99–113.

Gummesson, E. (1996) *Relationship Marketing: From 4Ps to 30Rs*, Malmö: Liber-Hermods.

Gummesson, E. (1999) *Total Relationship Marketing: Rethinking Marketing Management from 4Ps to 30Rs,* Oxford: Butterworth Heinemann.

Hunt, H.K. (1997) 'CS/D: overview and future research direction', in Hunt, H.K. (ed.) *Conceptualisation and Measurement of Customer Satisfaction and Dissatisfaction*, Cambridge, MA: Marketing Science Institute.

Hunt, S.D. and Morgan, R.M. (1994) 'Relationship marketing in the era of network competition', *Journal of Marketing Management*, **5** (5), 18–28.

Kotler, P. (1992) 'Total marketing', *Business Week*, Advance Executive Brief No. 2.

Millman, A.F. (1993) 'The emerging concept of relationship marketing', in Proceedings of the 9th Annual IMP Conference, Bath, 23–25 September.

Peck, H. (1996) 'Towards a framework for relationship marketing: the six markets model revisited and revised', Marketing Education Group (MEG) Conference, University of Strathclyde, UK.

Reichheld, F.F. (1996) *The Loyalty Effect: The Hidden Force behind Growth, Profits and Lasting Value*, Boston, MA: Harvard Business School Press.

Tzokas, N. and Saren, M. (2000) 'Knowledge and relationship marketing: where, what and how?', *2nd WWW Conference on Relationship Marketing* <www.mcb.co.uk/services/conferen/nov99/rm> (accessed 15 November 1996 to February 2000, Paper 4).

Uncles, M. (1994) 'Do you or your customer need a loyalty scheme?', *Journal of Targeting, Measurement and Analysis*, **2** (4), 335–50.

7 Customer partnerships

Introduction

As was discussed in the opening chapter, one of the most significant perceived differences between relationship marketing and traditional marketing is that RM is seen to extend marketing's focus beyond the single dyadic relationship of buyer and seller (Gummesson, 1999, p. 1) and to embrace other organisational relationships. Despite this overall change in emphasis, the customer–supplier relationship is still a core issue in RM and indeed across the whole marketing discipline (Möller and Halinen, 2000, p. 31). Relationship marketing is first and foremost directed towards the management of this relationship Grönroos (2004, p. 101).

Customer focus

Another supposed difference between traditional marketing and RM is in the way customers are perceived and valued. Traditional marketing stands accused of treating customers as pawns in a competitive game. By its very nature, this 'market focused' approach is seen to concentrate on increasing market share and emphasising short-term profitability. The priorities of traditional marketers are seen as the 'capture' of anonymous customers, either before competitors or away from them, and manipulating these captives for short-term gain. Target segments were as personal as it got in this marketplace battlefield.

RM, in contrast, focuses not on what you can do *to* your customer but on what you can do *for* your customer (Worthington and Horne, 1998, p. 39) and what you can do *with* your customer, to ensure customer satisfaction. The aim is to treat your customers as valued partners, to establish their needs and develop their loyalty through quality service. As the company statement quoted in Box 7.1 elegantly puts it, 'obsession with the customer should be the most vital factor in business success'.

Customer focus motivation

This change of emphasis is not, as has been discussed, wholly altruistic. Company prosperity is still the long-term aim. What is different is that this is perceived, in particular circumstances, to be better achieved by focusing on the individual needs of the customer rather than the agglomerated marketplace. Neither is this change in attitude wholly associated with better and/or more advanced strategy development *per se*. The development of relational strategies may be seen, in part, as a recognition that the balance of power has shifted from producer to consumer and that many of the strategies of the past are no longer appropriate. Buyers of today are more knowledgeable, less naïve than in the past. In such a marketplace the supplier can no longer count on unquestioning brand loyalty and must offer something more in return for patronage than promotional bribery if sustainable advantage is to be achieved and maintained.

In today's competitive markets there are more and more undifferentiated or little differentiated products and services. Storbacka *et al.* (1994, p. 29) conclude that the degree of differentiation in provider strategies seems to be inversely dependent on the degree of market concentration. In oligopolistic markets there are seldom major differences between the providers. If the core product or service offering leaves little scope for competitive advantage then competitive advantage must be found elsewhere. To this end the development of a 'relationship' with your customer *may* be the most effective way of building something unique and sustainable that your competitor will find difficult to replicate (Buttle, 1996, p. 1).

Box 7.1   Customer focus

The following is a statement from the Burnley Building Society:

> Obsession with the customer should be the most vital factor in business success. The main priority of any business must be to win and keep customers, as failure to do so results in no profits, no growth, no jobs, therefore, no business.

This very 'modern' statement of the importance of the customer was issued by the Burnley Building Society in 1850 yet it appears as relevant today as it did over a century and a half ago.

The realisation that marketing's focus on traditional models was insufficient in the modern marketplace was highlighted (if not driven) by the dramatic changes in western economies. The marketing priority was shifting away from products to services with the growing domination of service economies in major western markets, what Vargo and Lusch (2004, p. 2) call 'service-dominant logic' (see Chapter 13). The realisation of the importance of the customer-focused approach in service marketing, over and above the market focus, was a major factor in further promoting the relationship marketing concept.

The importance of the reconceptualisation of both products and services in the development of RM cannot be overstated. For this reason a discussion of the nature of services and the importance of customer interaction may, at this stage, be appropriate.

Services

The word 'service'[1] is a frequent feature in the modern marketing vocabulary and never more so than when discussing relationship marketing in general and the supplier–customer partnership in particular. The extensive use of the word and its rapid evolution and development demonstrate the importance of this sometimes elusive concept. Service, in a marketing context, is regarded principally in two ways. The term is used firstly to describe those businesses where the greater part of the company's central offering is intangible. These '**service industries**' are generally seen to have a number of characteristics that appear to differentiate them from physical goods industries. In addition to **intangibility**, these are **inseparability**, **variability**, **perishability** and non-ownership. These characteristics are outlined in Box 7.2.

Box 7.2   Special characteristics of services

Intangibility: A 'pure' service cannot be assessed in the physical sense. It is an abstraction that cannot be directly examined before purchase. The intangible process characteristics that define services include such factors as reliability, personal care, attentiveness, friendliness and these can only be verified once a service has been purchased and 'consumed'. Few services are wholly intangible, however, and many include a tangible element (e.g. a concert programme). Intangibility has a number of implications for the consumer, including increased uncertainty and potential risk.

Inseparability: Products may be produced in one location and sold in another. The production and consumption are, therefore, said to be separable. This is not the case for services, which are produced and consumed at one time and place. This inseparability occurs whether the producer is human (e.g. a doctor) or machine (e.g. an ATM machine). With services, marketing becomes a means of facilitating complex producer–consumer interactions, rather than being merely an exchange medium.

Variability: There are two dimensions to variability. These are the amount the production varies from the norm and the extent it needs to be varied to suit the individual customer. As the customer is usually involved in the production process of a service at the same time as they consume it, it can be difficult to carry out monitoring and control of the production to ensure consistent standards. This is exaggerated in situations where personnel are providing services on a one-to-one basis (e.g. hairdressers) where they must adapt the 'service production' to fulfil an individual customer's needs.

Perishability: Services cannot be stored. For example, if a hotel fails to fill all of its rooms on a particular night, these cannot be 'carried over' to subsequent nights.

Non-ownership: The inability to 'own' a service relates to the characteristics of intangibility and perishability. Where a service is performed no ownership is transferred from the buyer to the seller. The buyer is merely buying the right to a service process (e.g. a solicitor's time).

(*Source*: Adapted from *Principles of Services Marketing*, 2nd revised ed., London: McGraw-Hill (Palmer, A.J. 1998) p. 11, reproduced with the kind permission of The McGraw-Hill Companies, all rights reserved)

There is a danger in too rigidly defining services as distinct from products (see goods *v.* services) because there is little if anything that could be called a pure service or pure good. Service characteristics can, therefore, help identify particular marketing situations but they do not wholly separate goods from services (Gummesson 2007, p. 137).

The second most frequent use of the word 'service' is in connection with the phrase 'customer service'. The definition of customer service is difficult to qualify accurately but the term is generally used to describe those features of the offering or exchange that extend beyond the 'core' product or service. The phrase is further seen to imply added value (or, over time, relational benefits) derived as a result of contact between buyers and sellers. Although the two concepts of 'service industries' and 'customer service' are related they are best approached, from an analytical perspective, separately.

Service industries

As noted above there is a lack of precision when it comes to the term 'service industries'. It can only, therefore, be a generalized term for a value-laden offering which has a number of characteristics that seemingly differentiates it from a product.

The intangible nature of service industries has always posed a problem for traditional marketers. Marketing research and teaching has for decades been dominated (and to an extent still is) by 'corporate product marketing'. The realisation that traditional marketing models were proving imprecise when applied to services drove some marketers to consider new approaches and concepts. Indeed, service marketers (together with their industrial marketing colleagues) can be said to have driven marketing research into new areas and been largely responsible for the development of the 'modern' RM approach. As Grönroos (1995, p. 252) notes:

It is quite natural that the seeds of modern relationship marketing first started to grow in service marketing research. In fact, service marketing started to develop as a discipline because the marketing mix management paradigm and some of its key models fitted service firms' customer relations badly.

Service firms have in theory always been 'relationship orientated' as the very nature of service businesses is relationship based (Grönroos, ibid.). The reasons behind this are manifold. In service industries a process or performance takes place where the customer is seen to be heavily involved in the creation and delivery (see Box 7.2, inseparability). Service delivery is, therefore, simultaneous with consumption (Johns, 1999, p. 963) and indeed may be said to be both defined and co-created with the consumer (Vargo and Lusch, 2004, p. 4). This recognition of a customer's active involvement in the value-creation process is one which is driving current debate and a reassessment of supplier and customer roles (Gummesson, 2007, p. 137).

As most service providers compete with companies very similar to themselves (resulting in so-called 'parity offerings') they frequently counter the effect of direct competition by building relationships with their customers. The services literature is clear on the difficulty that consumers have about judging the quality of the service as the 'intangibility' aspect makes it difficult to examine or sample the service (Czepiel, 1990, pp. 315–16). The difficulty in evaluating services may suggest it is less likely that consumers will switch after they have developed a relationship with a service supplier (Javalgi and Moberg, 1997, p. 166). In services marketing there is always some form of direct contact (although not necessarily physical) between the customer and the service firm. The repeated encounters provide the occasions where the parties are able to develop a more complex relationship (Czepiel, 1990, p. 316). This '**service encounter**' is such an important part of service delivery that it is frequently called the 'moment of truth'[2] (Johns, 1999, p. 965). This phrase underlines the crucial role each service encounter plays in customer evaluation of a service (Odekerken-Schröder *et al.*, 2000, p. 107).

This customer involvement in service industries can vary considerably. It may sometimes be for a long time, sometimes for a short time, sometimes on a regular basis and sometimes as a one-off encounter (Grönroos, 1995, p. 252). Services can also be defined on the basis of the closeness of the contact. Relationships play an important part in high-contact services (e.g. hairdressers, financial advisers). In low-contact or 'process' services (e.g. fast food, FMCG retailing), however, suppliers provide a more standardised service and the best investment here will be in hiring and training staff rather than developing relational programmes (Kinard and Capella, 2006, p. 365).

There is also a significant social aspect to any service relationship. Czepiel (1990, p. 13) sums up the importance of the social nature of services when he comments:

Service encounters are interesting phenomena with short-run and long-run effects. In the short-run they are the social occasion of economic exchange in which society allows strangers to interact . . . In the long-run encounters provide the social occasions in which buyer and seller can negotiate and nurture the transformation of their accumulated encounters into an exchange relationship. The concept of a marketplace-relationship, the mutual recognition of some special status between the exchange partners, is especially interesting in services marketing.

Contemporary service marketers, therefore, view marketing as an interactive process within a social context where relationship building and management are the vital cornerstones (Grönroos, 1994, p. 5). Indeed, service encounters can be regarded, first and foremost, as social encounters (McCallum and Harrison, 1985, p. 35), the variety of which goes a long way to explaining the problem of variability (see Box 7.2). It is this social contact that makes it feasible to envisage creating a relationship with the customer, if both parties (or perhaps either; see Chapter 3) are interested in such an association (Grönroos, 1995, p. 252).

Goods versus services

Although RM was (and is) principally seen as a development of, and of particular benefit to, services marketing, its application in the field of consumer goods appears to be growing (see Chapter 13). Although criticism of this broad application exists it reflects a recognition that the boundaries between goods and services (i.e. the distinctions between the tangible and the intangible dimensions of the offer) are becoming blurred (Pels, 1999, p. 2). Although services are frequently described as 'intangible' and their central offering as an 'activity' rather than a tangible object, much 'service output' has a tangible component (Johns, 1999, p. 959). Examples of the importance of this tangible component in service industries can be seen when it is recognised that a restaurant's reputation is, in part, built on the provision of food and drink and a retailer's classification based on the type of physical goods supplied. As Gummesson (2007, p.117) notes a pleasant waiter may or may not compensate for bad food or an unpleasant waiter may or may not destroy the pleasure of good food. There is, therefore, a context-driven trade-off between the goods and service element.

Products, meanwhile, are more than ever recognised as having intangible attributes. Indeed, many manufactured products are marketed on the basis of these attributes rather than the hard components or features of the offering (e.g. an automobile's prestige status or a beer's macho image). It is indeed a paradox of marketing that these product manufacturers look to promote the intangible element of their offering while service providers frequently look to create tangible features such as physical evidence (e.g. a bank's impressive façade) to establish their credibility (see Shostack, 1977).

The traditional view of marketing saw services as the occasion where the producer's production process and the consumer's consuming process intersected (Strandvik and Storbacka, 1996, p. 68). In other words, services augmented the product but the product remained the core of the exchange. The RM perspective goes beyond product specifications. Goods and services become part of a holistic, continuously developing service offering (Grönroos, 1999). It implies that the goal of marketing is to customise offerings, to recognise the consumer is always the co-producer and that the more that the customer can be involved in the process the better the fit with their needs (Vargo and Lusch, 2004, p. 11).

Thus the line between products and services and the dominance of the core product appears to be fast fading. Firms are having to alter their structures to accommodate this sea-change. Some are even reinventing their businesses. Supermarkets are becoming financiers and major manufacturers are finding ways to operate other than remaining dependent on sales (e.g. leasing, financing). Movement away from core product towards a total service offering is apparent.

Such is the overlap that Strandvik and Storbacka (1996, p. 68) suggest that the goods/services distinction should be removed altogether and that all companies should regard themselves as service companies. In their 'service management' conception, physical products (goods) are seen as 'frozen services' where the real quality or benefit of the purchase is not revealed until it is actually used (consumed) by the buyer. Grönroos (1996, p. 11) too notes that successfully executed RM demands that the firm defines its business as a service business and understands how to create and manage a total service offering. Vargo and Lusch (2004, p. 9) propose a wholly service-centred view where goods are the distribution mechanism for service provision (Vargo, 2008, p. 213). This idea of service being the fundamental concept in an exchange has important implications for marketing theory and practice (Lusch and Vargo, 2006, p. 283). This 'service-dominant logic,'[3] implies that the marketing role is less about supplying goods/services and more about helping customers to create experiences at all stages in the consumption process (Flint, 2006, p. 350).

Customer service

Customer service is regarded, in the RM literature, as a separate though related concept to service marketing. Whereas service marketing is seen as embracing all aspects relating to services industries, customer service is seen as wider in application (in that it relates to both product and service suppliers) but narrower in focus, being directly and intimately connected to the customer satisfaction process.

Although definitions of customer service vary, what they all have in common is that they are concerned with relationships at the buyer–seller interface (Clark, 2000, p. 213). Customer service is associated with the building of bonds to ensure long-term relationships of mutual advantage to both parties (Christopher et al., 1991, p. 5). The provision of high levels of customer service involves understanding what (and how) a customer buys and determining how additional value can be added to differentiate it from competing offers (Clark, 2000, p. 212). According to Buttle (1996, p. 9), relationship marketers must believe that excellent customer service produces improved profitability. The quality of this service leads (it is suggested) to customer satisfaction that leads in turn to relationship strength and longevity and (ultimately) results in relationship profitability (Storbacka et al., 1994, p. 23). As we have previously discussed (see Chapter 6), this is rather a simplistic model that is unlikely to stand up to close scrutiny across a wide range of industries. It may, however, be used as a starting point in establishing why customer service is regarded, by relationship marketers, as a crucial element in the marketing process and why so much time and money is being spent by practitioners on measuring customer service levels (see Chapter 6).

Customer service and RM

From the earliest days of relationship marketing research, customer service (created at the supplier–customer interface) has been regarded as a core component in the RM process. Christopher *et al.* (1991, p. 4) saw relationship marketing as the unifying concept that brought the individual concepts of customer service, quality and marketing together. It was their judgement that one of the biggest challenges to an organisation was to bring these three critical areas into closer alignment (see Figure 7.1).

Christopher *et al.* (1991, p. 4) suggest that customer service, quality and marketing work in harmony with:

■ customer service levels being determined by research-based measurement of customer needs and competitor performance, and in recognition of the needs of different market segments;

■ quality being determined from the perspective of the customer based on regular research and monitoring;

■ the total quality concept influencing the *process* elements (e.g. managing the 'moments of truth' in the customer encounter) associated with the marketing (or more strictly the relationship marketing) concept.

Traditional marketing, they suggest (p. vii), conceived these three elements as independent 'rather like spotlights shining on a stage and beaming light, often of different intensity at different points on a stage'. The task facing the organisation,

Figure 7.1
Relationship
marketing
orientation

Customer service levels should be determined by research-based measurement of customers' needs and competitors' performance and must recognise the needs of different market segments

Quality must be determined from the perspective of the customer based on regular research and monitoring

The total quality concept should influence the *process* elements (e.g. managing the 'moments of truth' in the customer encounter)

(*Source*: Adapted from Christopher *et al.*, 1991, p. 4)

they suggest, is to bring about an alignment of the three 'beams' so that the impact upon the customer is more effective. Their conviction was that the point of overlap best describes what RM is all about.

Customer service, therefore, can be seen as playing an important role in the realisation of RM strategies. Its influence at the macro level is complemented by its importance at the micro level of individual relationships and interactions. At this end of the scale customer service may be seen as being concerned with the building of relationships (Clark, 2000, p. 213) through the management of an ongoing sequence of episodes. These episodes, it is suggested, require analysis on an episode by episode basis as well as at the long-term relationship level (Storbacka *et al.*, 1994, p. 22) to establish the success or otherwise of customer service strategies. The influence of customer service at the macro and micro levels emphasises that, although RM takes a holistic view of relationships, it should not ignore the importance of the constituent parts.

Episodes

The concept of a relationship made up of a series of episodes (some of which are 'critical episodes') was introduced briefly in Chapter 6. In terms of customer service it is perhaps the transition from a routine episode to a critical episode that may be seen as determining the adequacy (or otherwise) of customer service performance. As Storbacka *et al.* (1994, p. 30) note:

> Every episode does not carry the same importance or weight in the customer's evaluation of the relationship. Some [are] routine ... others [are] 'critical episodes'. A 'critical episode' can be defined as an episode that is of great importance for the relationship. The continuation of the relationship is dependent (both in a negative and positive way) on 'critical episodes' ... The definition of 'critical episode' is customer specific ... A routine episode can become critical if, according to the customer, the adequate level of performance is not met.

Critical episodes[4] are, therefore, those specific interactions between customers and the firm's employees that are especially satisfying or especially dissatisfying (Bitner *et al.*, 1990, p. 73). According to Strandvik and Storbacka (1996, p. 73), long-term relationships can be defined as being made up of a 'string of episodes'. They emphasise that when analysing relationship benefits and when attempting to calculate relationship costs the configuration of these episodes has to be understood.

Configuration of episodes

Every relationship will have a number of different types of episodes that differ in content, frequency, duration, etc. and so will be configured differently. During an episode, the customer experiences one or several 'interactions' during which the actual service is produced. As former SAS president Jan Carlzon points out, 'SAS is created 50 million times a year, fifteen seconds at a time' (quoted in Grossman, 1998, p. 32). These interactions may be said to constitute a 'service chain' that can be analysed from both the customer's and the provider's perspective. The customer's perspective of the service chain may be called the 'customer's service path'. Problems frequently come about because managers rarely have responsibility for, or focus upon, the whole service episode. The customer, meanwhile, sees no such distinction, viewing it all as part of the complete service (Strandvik and Storbacka, 1996, p. 72). It may also be problematical when part of an offering is outsourced as the customer believes (rightly) that the company they have dealt with should maintain full responsibility. The association between interactions, episodes and the service chain/customer service path are illustrated in Figure 7.2.

A company that is service orientated has learnt the importance of service elements of the overall transaction and customer service in the development of added value. A service orientation carries with it the need for a shift in managerial thinking from emphasising the value of transactions to developing the value in relationships (Ballantyne, 2000, pp. 3–6).

Building customer relationships

Relationships rarely develop overnight. Relationships evolve, sometimes over a great amount of time. During this period customers may be seen to move through stages of development. Dwyer *et al.* (1987, p. 15) identified five general phases through which relationships evolve with each phase representing a major transition in how parties regard one another (see Figure 7.3). This model may apply to both business-to-consumer and business-to-business relationships and there is likely to be considerable variation in the length of each stage dependent on the type and purpose of the relationship. The phases are:

- awareness;
- exploration;
- expansion;
- commitment;
- dissolution.

Figure 7.2
Interactions
and episodes

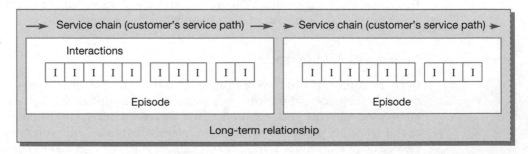

(*Source*: Based on Strandvik and Storbacka, 1996, pp. 71–4)

Figure 7.3
Evolution of
relationships

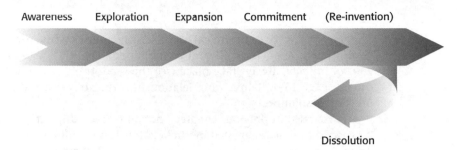

Awareness   Exploration   Expansion   Commitment   (Re-invention)

Dissolution

(*Source*: Based on Dwyer *et al.*, 1987, pp. 15–20)

Awareness

Awareness refers to one party's recognition that the other party is 'a feasible exchange party'. Interaction has yet to take place but there may be considerable 'positioning' and 'posturing' to enhance each other's attractiveness.

Exploration

This refers to the 'search and trial period' in the relational exchange. It is in this phase that potential relational partners consider the 'obligations, benefits and burdens' of the relationship. Trial purchases may be made but 'the exploratory relationship is very fragile in the sense that minimal investment and interdependence make for simple termination' (Dwyer *et al.*, 1987, p. 16). The exploration phase is conceptualised in five self-explanatory subprocesses:

- attraction (i.e. why is this likely to be a worthwhile relationship?);
- communication and bargaining;
- development and exercise of power;
- norm development (i.e. normalisation of the relationship);
- expectation development (i.e. what do we want from the relationship?).

Expansion

Expansion refers to the continual increase in benefits obtained by the exchange partners and their increasing interdependence. The critical distinction between this and the previous phase is that 'the rudiments of trust and joint satisfaction established in the exploration stage now lead to increased risk-taking' (ibid., p. 18).

Commitment

Commitment refers to the implicit or explicit pledge, made by the partners, to continue the relationship. At this stage the benefits include the 'certainty' developed from mutually anticipated roles and goals, the 'efficiency' established as a result of bargaining and the 'effectiveness' that comes from trust.

Dissolution

The possibility of withdrawal or disengagement, while not being relationship development as such, is integral to the model. Dissolution is always an option and will, ultimately, always take place (see the section on customer/supplier dissolution or exit, page 159). Reinventing relationships that have passed their sell-by date may prevent dissolution.

As discussed in previous chapters, not all relationships are as complex or as highly motivated as those suggested by the relationship formulation process outlined above. All relationships, however, have some elements that are recognisable in this model.

Customer service failure

Customer service failures test the commitment of an organisation's customers (Bejou and Palmer, 1998, p. 11). When such a situation exists, however, it may not be the problem *per se* that causes a critical episode to develop but the company's response to that problem (Stewart, 1998a, p. 9). Every customer will react differently. Each has a propensity to 'stick to' or 'switch' from the *status quo* and the magnitude of this propensity will depend on the profile of that individual (Hassan, 1996, p. 4) at any point in time. It is also likely that amounts of tolerance will vary from industry to industry or situation to situation. Tolerating a problem does not mean that a 'negative critical incident' is forgotten. Incidents within a relationship are not wholly discrete and further negative incidents may trigger 'memories' of past incidents (Stewart, 1998a, p. 11). Customers are, therefore, seen to engage in a historical evaluation process over time. This evaluation process includes not only the problem itself but also a review of previous problems and how these were handled (p. 10).

Problems may not necessarily lead to long-term dissatisfaction or desertion. Satisfactory response by the supplier *may* lead to renewed levels of satisfaction or, as is sometimes claimed (e.g. Bejou and Palmer, 1998, p. 11), greater satisfaction than existed prior to the incident. Described as the 'recovery paradox' it suggests that if the recovery is highly effective this offers the possibility of achieving higher satisfaction levels than if the failure never happened (Magnini *et al.*, 2007, p. 213). Research by Andreassen (2000, p. 160) suggests that the complainer is usually focused on restoring justice or equity and that a customer's judgement is driven by perceived fairness of the outcome. As Andreassen (p. 167) points out, fairness does not imply that the customer is right. Even when the customer has received an unsatisfactory response from the supplier this may not immediately lead to 'exit' from, or dissolution of, the relationship (for a definition of 'exit', see page 160). The negative impact may be compensated by the fact that the overall service quality is perceived to be high enough to sustain the relationship (Odekerken-Schröder *et al.*, 2000, p. 110). There may also be substantial switching costs that are powerful barriers to relationship discontinuation with a particular supplier (Stewart, 1998a, p. 10).

Relationship duration

Relationship duration, as one would intuitively suppose, is a mediating influence on the dissolution and a barrier to 'exit'. The effect of relationship duration may, however, not be as straightforward as it would seem. There would appear to be evidence (Bejou and Palmer, 1998, pp. 15–16) that in the early stages of a relationship there is a 'honeymoon period' when some teething problems or even critical episodes may be tolerated. There is no clear evidence why this aberration should exist. Perhaps it is as simple as a reluctance to admit the failings of a new supplier in whom research resources (time and effort) have been expended. Bejou and Palmer's research suggests that this level of 'toleration' drops to a low point after a short period before building up slowly again over time (see Figure 7.4).

Relationship duration may have other effects. Exiting the relationship may be seen as less complicated at an earlier stage than later when heavy investment in the relationship may result in high switching costs (Boote and Pressey, 1999, p. 8). Alternatively, it has been claimed that an individual with a history of positive experiences may be more forgiving of a failure than a first-time customer (Magnini *et al.*, 2007, p. 215).

Customer/supplier dissolution or exit

Although many RM models imply continual customer development (e.g. 'the ladder of loyalty', Chapter 4) these fail to acknowledge that some relationships (ultimately *all* relationships) will be terminated.[5] In the real world there is *always* the possibility of dissolution of, or 'exit' from, a relationship.

If the concept of relationship breakdown is examined more closely it may be seen to include three distinct types:

- **dissolution;**
- **customer exit;**
- **supplier withdrawal.**

Dissolution

Dissolution suggests some form of agreed separation. This can be either where both parties agree that it would be in their best interests to go their separate ways

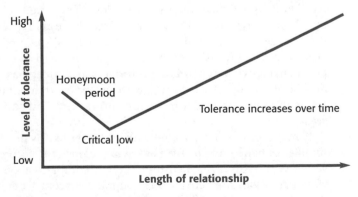

Figure 7.4
Tolerance of critical negative incidents

(*Source*: Based on Bejou and Palmer, 1998, pp. 15–16)

or where one party (usually the more powerful of the two) forms this view and the other acquiesces. This form of agreed separation is most likely, but not exclusively, to manifest itself in business-to-business markets, where higher levels of relationship are observed to develop, rather than in consumer markets, where relationships are less likely to be formally acknowledged or contractually arranged. An example of an exception to this generalisation is, for example, a solicitor–client relationship. In the case of most day-to-day commercial relationships there would appear to be little driving or compelling either party to formally acknowledge dissolution.

Customer exit

Customer 'exit' has been defined as a 'term used to denote the economic phenomenon of a customer ceasing patronage of a particular supplier' (Stewart, 1998b, p. 235). In more everyday language, it is where the customer decides to end the relationship. Unlike dissolution, the supplier has little input into the final decision although they may use argument or incentives in an attempt to prevent it. Exit may be most prevalent where competition is high and many alternative sources of supply exist. What is most important, however, is that the customer is aware of these alternatives. Customers who do not have (or know about) alternatives, even when generally dissatisfied, are likely to remain 'spuriously loyal' (Dick and Basu, 1994, p. 101; see Figure 6.3, page 133). In these situations customers may use their 'voice' (i.e. complain) but effectively stay 'loyal'.

Exit is normally seen to be considered when the customer recognises a (relative or actual) decline in performance although, as we have argued previously, customer dissatisfaction does not necessarily result in exit. This perceived decline does not necessarily mean that quality standards have fallen but may mean that better quality is seen or perceived to be available elsewhere. Stewart (1998b, p. 235) summarises those situations when exit can be expected as:

> where competition prevails and alternatives are available to the customer, who is aware of them and alert to any absolute or relative deterioration in performance.

'Exit' and 'voice' have their positive sides. They are traditionally seen as the means by which 'wayward businesses and organisations respectively, are made aware of their lapses and can begin to right their affairs' (p. 236). Customer 'voice' has long been seen as a means of recovering a critical situation (so-called '**problem recovery**'). Problem recovery remains a controversial concept as any satisfaction exhibited may be as a result of satisfaction with the 'bribe' (if a bribe such as a refund, discount, etc. is used as settlement to a problem) rather than satisfaction with the company *per se*.

A major problem associated with customer exit is how it can be recognised by the supplier as happening or even as having happened. According to Clark (2000, p. 212), 98 per cent of dissatisfied customers never complain about poor service but as a result 90 per cent will not return to the supplier. Except where customers choose to voice their decision to leave or where the relationship is particularly close and of high

Box 7.3   Complaining on the Internet

Over the past decade the Internet has become a popular medium for individuals or groups who wish to complain about public and private organisations. There are even websites such as www.howtocomplain.com and www.thecomplaintstation.com that advise newcomers on the best way to go about it. Some websites, known as 'gripe sites', are specifically aimed at particular companies such as United Airways (www.untied.com), Ryanair (www.ihateryanair.co.uk), Starbucks (www.starbucked.com) and McDonald's (www.mcspotlight.org). Some organisations pay considerable attention to the views of its customers while others do their best to shut the sites down (see Case study).

enough volume that desertion is quickly noticed, exit may go unrecognised. Customers may also choose to use negative 'word-of-mouth' as part of that complaining behaviour (Boote and Pressey, 1999, p. 3). This may cause significant, yet largely unseen, damage to the supplier. Since the advent of the Internet this behaviour has been taken to a new level (see Box 7.3). To complicate matters further exit may only be temporary, particularly in areas such as FMCG. Customers may choose, in the short term, to sample from another supplier or they may be temporarily attracted away by the incentives of competitors only to return at a later date.

Supplier withdrawal

As the phrase implies, supplier withdrawal is where the separation is at the instigation of the supplier. In our earlier definition of relationship marketing it was suggested that terminating relationships was part of the RM marketing process (see Chapter 2). Without doubt, some (many, perhaps, in certain industries or companies) customers are definite loss-makers. It is indeed quite possible that a small number of highly profitable customers may subsidise a larger number of customers on which the company actually loses money (Sheth and Sisodia, 1999, p. 83). It may even be the case that increasing customer retention in some firms may actually *decrease* profitability and *destroy* value (Reichheld, 1996, p. 34). For these reasons supplier withdrawal must always remain an option.

Supplier withdrawal or termination, as we noted previously, may be managed in two ways. The first is 'customer de-selection' or 'adverse selection' (Smith, 1998, p. 4), effectively 'dumping' the customer. This may be easier said than done (particularly if the customer believes they are on to a good thing). Withdrawal of certain services and/or discriminatory pricing may be ways that this could be achieved, but the danger is that dissatisfaction may spread from the immediate customer to a wider audience. The general outcry in the UK over the closure of Post Office branches in 2007 was an example of this. The second option is by managing the database (see Chapter 12) in such a way as to reduce the cost base of unprofitable customers. Neither is an easy option but may be necessary to protect future prosperity.

Profit chains

Many RM authors have visualised the benefits of RM customer–supplier partnerships through the medium of 'customer relationship life cycles' or 'profit chains' (Gummesson, 1999, p. 184). Probably the simplest model was discussed in Chapter 6 and is shown again in Figure 7.5.

As has been noted, this model may be inherently flawed as it is based on an oversimplification that, in many industries, creates problems (Storbacka *et al.*, 1994, p. 23). Customer satisfaction does not always lead to retention, nor does retention always lead to profitability (see relationship economics, Chapter 4).

Gummesson (1999, p. 184) describes a broader model (Figure 7.6) which suggests that building good internal quality operations leads to happy and contented employees producing quality products, which in turn results in customer satisfaction, retention and profitability (see Chapter 8). This model stems from what Gummesson calls the 'indisputable logic' that when everybody is happy the company will do well. Simple logic should, however, always be treated with a degree of scepticism. As Gummesson himself admits, the general validity of such an argument can be questioned as 'market logic' sometimes follows other patterns.

Storbacka *et al.* (1994, p. 23) also challenge the basic assumption that improving quality leads directly to customer satisfaction and that this necessarily drives profitability. Instead they put forward their own model (Figure 7.7) that reflects some of the many complexities associated with relational strategy development. This model implies that, although a linkage of sorts can be made between the basic components (highlighted in the model), there are so many intermediary stages that any direct association is tenuous. As the old saying goes, 'there's many a slip 'twixt cup and lip'.

Figure 7.5
Simple 'return on relationship' model

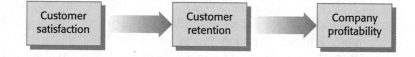

Figure 7.6
'Return on relationship' model

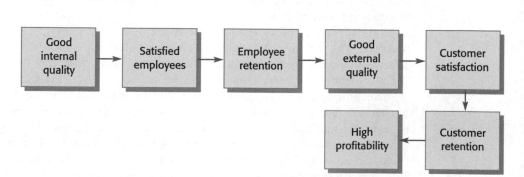

(*Source*: Gummesson, 1999, p. 184)

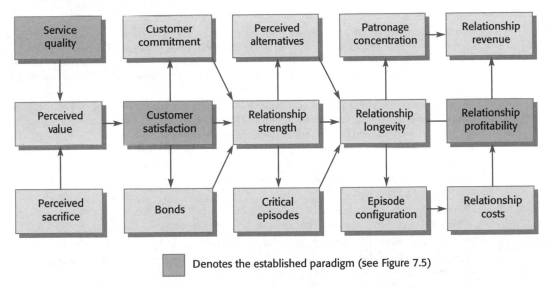

Denotes the established paradigm (see Figure 7.5)

Figure 7.7 Complex 'return on relationship' model   (*Source*: Adapted from Storbacka *et al.*, 1994, p. 23)

The Storbacka *et al.* model shows a much more complex route to profitability fraught with dangers for the relationship marketer. More in-depth descriptions of the arguments associated with these concepts are shown in Box 7.4.

The lesson that appears to be emerging is that paths to sustained profitability through customer–supplier partnerships are fraught with complexity beyond the scope or control of most companies. This is one reason why the argument for greater accountability in marketing (often called 'marketing metrics') is so fraught with danger. Many things that matter most in marketing are immeasurable! On the other hand, while firms continue to strive to outperform their competitors, offering 'legendary service' can be risky (Kotler, 1992, p. 51) as again there is no guarantee that this will translate into retention.

Box 7.4   Description of factors in complex return on relationship model (Figure 7.7)

Perceived service quality: Customer's cognitive evaluation of the service across episodes compared with some explicit or implicit comparison standard.

Perceived sacrifice: Perceived sacrifices (e.g. price, physical effort) across all service episodes in the relationship compared with some explicit or implicit comparison standard.

Perceived value: Service quality compared with perceived sacrifice.

Customer satisfaction: Customer's cognitive and affective evaluation based on the personal experiences across all service episodes within the relationship.

Customer commitment: The parties' intentions to act and their attitude towards interacting with each other; high relationship value will affect commitment positively (see Chapter 6).

Relationship strength: Measured both as purchase behaviour and as communication behaviour (word of mouth, complaints). Loyalty (repetitive purchase behaviour), which is based also on positive commitment by the customer, indicates a stronger relationship (see Chapter 3). The bonds between the customer and the service supplier also affect the behaviour.

Bonds: Exit barriers that tie the customer to the service provider and maintain the relationship. These are legal, economic, technological, geographical, time, knowledge, social, cultural, ideological and psychological bonds (see Chapter 4).

Critical episodes: Episodes that are of critical importance for the continuation of the relationship. Episodes can be critical based on the size of the values exchanged during the episode compared with the parties' resources and based on the experiences during the episode (see Chapter 6).

Patronage concentration: The share of a customer's cash-flow in a certain industry in which the customer chooses to concentrate on one provider.

Relationship longevity: The length of the relationship.

Episode configuration: The episode types and number of each type that occur over time in the relationship between a provider and a customer.

Relationship revenue: The total revenue generated from a customer relationship during a fiscal year.

Relationship costs: The total cost incurred from serving a customer relationship – including direct and indirect costs – during a fiscal year.

Relationship profitability: Relationship revenue minus relationship costs.

(*Source*: Based on Storbacka *et al.*, 1994, p. 25)

Summary

This chapter looked at the central relationship between a customer and supplier. It discussed the focus of RM as being what you can do *for* or *with* as opposed to what you do *to* your customer. Service industries were reviewed initially from the perspective of their influence on RM and what effect this has on the customer–supplier strategy. Customer service was discussed extensively, both as a component central to RM and from the perspective of breaking down customer service into episodes and interactions. Relationship formulation was analysed, as was the nature of relationship dissolution and customer satisfaction. Customer service failures and the concepts surrounding dissolution and exit were examined. Finally the ideas surrounding profit chains and the 'return on relationships' were analysed and debated.

Discussion questions
1 How might organisations operationalise their 'obsession with the customer'?
2 Why are the boundaries between products and services becoming blurred?
3 Imagine a frequent flyer's relationship with an airline. What situations have the potential to become critical episodes if service failure occurs?
4 What, according to your judgement, are the most important factors in the 'profit chain' illustrated in Figure 7.7?

Case study   Where customers go to praise (or bash) you

If you run a consumer business, chances are pretty good a few of your customers are posting their opinions about it on the dozen or so Web sites that review local businesses across the country. These sites attract tens of thousands of daily posts and position themselves as online destinations for consumers to offer or get an unvarnished take on a business – to be both the critics and lobbyists. The largest of these sites, in terms of July monthly unique visitors, include YellowPages.com (roughly 18 million uniques), YELP (roughly 17.8 million), Yahoo! Local (YHOO) (roughly 13.2 million), and City search (roughly 10 million), according to Web analytics firm Compete.com. 'These sites are going to become more important,' says Matt Booth of Kelsey Group, a research firm that specializes in local search. 'And there are going to be an increasing number of them.'

In a 2007 study of over 2,000 Internet users by online analytical firm comScore (SCOR), 24% of respondents said they looked at an online review before making an offline service purchase in the three months prior to being surveyed. The study showed that local review sites are attracting new visitors at a rate four times as high as the rate at which overall Internet use is growing. It also found that more than three-quarters of respondents call online reviews 'influential' in their purchase decision process.

Replying to gripes

Most of these sites let businesses monitor their company profiles and respond directly to reviewers. Usually for a fee, businesses can 'claim' their listing on a site and then post photos or special promotions. On City Wahoo, for example, businesses can reach out to frequent customers to offer them a coupon or discount. On Merchant Circle, businesses in towns with less than 1,000 people can set up company profiles, and customers can review the businesses – some of which don't have Web sites. On Yelp, company owners can set up alerts so that every time someone reviews their business, they receive a message and can respond directly to the customer – without either party having to give away an e-mail address.

The best way for small companies to track how this world of online critics is driving business is to do it the old-fashioned way: by asking customers how they found the business when they walk in the door. 'That continues to be the most prevalent way [businesses] can track what's working for them and what isn't,' says Yelp co-founder Jeremy Stoppelman.

Sites edit reviews differently. Some take a relatively hands-off approach, leaving comments alone unless they are indecent or defamatory. Citysearch doesn't alter the placement or wording in its reviews as a general rule, says Chief Executive Jay Herratti, and this can sometimes frustrate business owners. 'Some owners are traumatized when they get negative reviews that they feel are unjust,' he says, 'but we try to give them a voice so they can reply to reviews and tell their story.' On Angie's List, members pay a monthly fee to read and write reports on home service companies like plumbers or carpenters. As such, no reviewers can post anonymously, and the company's data department reviews all reports before posting them to ensure that they are accurate and valid. 'The key is providing a trustworthy venue,' says founder Angie Hicks.

Pay to play

Businesses that want to take advantage of these sites have to pay for it. Almost all sites offer businesses 'premium' or 'enhanced' features that give them ad placement priority (Yelp), the ability to join an ad network (Citysearch), or the power to track loyal customers. For instance, BooRah.com, a site that aggregates online restaurant reviews, recently launched a loyalty program that helps restaurants track repeat customers with a discount card. Advertising packages at Citysearch can range from $199 to $5,000 per month, say Herratti. City Waboo's premium features cost about $40 monthly. Before signing up for the various programs, businesses should know how much traffic a site attracts.

Considering that dealing with online critiques is becoming the new norm for local businesses, it behooves owners to know the sites, read the reviews and complaints, and, as Hicks of Angie's List advises: 'Take them with a grain of salt.'

(*Source*: Ricky McRoskey, *Sales & Marketing*, 15 August 2008)

Case study questions

1 Why do customers use these review sites?
2 How should companies react to complaining behaviour?

References

Andreassen, T.W. (2000) 'Antecedents to satisfaction with service recovery', *European Journal of Marketing*, **34** (1/2), 156–75.

Ballantyne, D. (2000) 'Interaction, dialogue and knowledge generation: three key concepts in relationship marketing', in 2nd WWW Conference on Relationship Marketing, 15 November 1999 to 15 February 2000, Paper 7. <www.mcb.co.uk/services/conferen/nov99/rm> (accessed 15 November 2007).

Bejou, D. and Palmer, A. (1998) 'Service failure and loyalty: an exploratory empirical study of airline customers', *Journal of Services Marketing*, **12** (1), 7–22.

Bitner, M.J., Booms, B.H. and Tetreault, M.S. (1990) 'The service encounter: diagnosing favorable and unfavorable incidents', *Journal of Marketing*, **54**, 71–84.

Boote, J.D. and Pressey, A.D. (1999) 'Integrating relationship marketing and complaining behaviour: a model of conflict and complaining behaviour within buyer–seller relationships', European Academy of Marketing Conference (EMAC), competitive paper, Berlin.

Buttle, F.B. (1996) *Relationship Marketing Theory and Practice*, London: Paul Chapman.

Christopher, M., Payne, A. and Ballantyne, D. (1991) *Relationship Marketing*, London: Butterworth Heinemann.

Clark, M. (2000) 'Customer service, people and processes', in Cranfield School of Management, *Marketing Management: A Relationship Marketing Perspective*, Basingstoke: Macmillan, pp. 110–24.

Czepiel, J. (1990) 'Managing relationships with customers: a differentiating philosophy of marketing', in Bowen, D., Chase, R. and Cummings, T. (eds) *Service Management Effectiveness: Balancing Strategy, Organisation and Human Resources*, San Francisco, CA: Jossey-Bass, pp. 299–323.

Dick, A. and Basu, K. (1994) 'Customer loyalty: toward an integrated conceptual framework', *Journal of the Academy of Marketing Science*, **22** (2), 99–113.

Dwyer, F.R., Schurr, P.H. and Oh, S. (1987) 'Developing buyer–seller relationships', *Journal of Marketing*, **51**, 11–27.

Flint, D.J. (2006) Innovation, symbolic iInteraction and customer valuing: thoughts stemming from a service-dominant logic of marketing, *Marketing Theory*, **6** (3) 349–62.

Grönroos, C. (1994) 'From marketing mix to relationship marketing: towards a paradigm shift in marketing', *Management Decisions*, **32** (2), 4–20.

Grönroos, C. (1995) 'Relationship marketing: the strategy continuum', *Journal of Marketing Science*, **23** (4), 252–4.

Grönroos, C. (1996) 'Relationship marketing: strategic and tactical implications', *Management Decisions*, **34** (3), 5–14.

Grönroos, C. (1999) 'The relationship marketing process: interaction, communication, dialogue, value', in 2nd WWW Conference on Relationship Marketing, 15 November 1999 to 15 February 2000, Paper 2 <www.mcb.co.uk/services/conferen/nov99/rm> (accessed 15 November 2000).

Grönroos, C. (2004) The relationship marketing process: communication, interaction, dialogue, value, *Journal of Business & Industrial Marketing*, **19** (2), 99–113.

Grossman, R.P. (1998) 'Developing and managing effective customer relationships', *Journal of Product and Brand Management*, **7** (1), 27–40.

Gummesson, E. (1999) *Total Relationship Marketing: Rethinking Marketing Management from 4Ps to 30Rs*, Oxford: Butterworth Heinemann.

Gummesson, E. (2007) 'Exit services marketing – enter service marketing', *Journal of Consumer Behaviour*, **6** (2), 113–41.

Hassan, M. (1996) *Customer Loyalty in the Age of Convergence*, London: Deloitte & Touche Consulting Group <www.dttus.com> (accessed 23 November 2007).

Javalgi, R. and Moberg, C. (1997) 'Service loyalty: implications for service providers', *Journal of Services Marketing*, **11** (3), 165–79.

Johns, N. (1999) 'What is this thing called service?', *European Journal of Marketing*, **33** (9/10), 958–73.

Kinard, B.R. and Capella, M.L. (2006) 'Relationship marketing: the influence of consumer involvement on perceived service benefits', *Journal of Service Marketing*, **21** (6), 359–68.

Kotler, P. (1992) 'Marketing's new paradigm: what's really happening out there?', *Planning Review*, **20** (5), 50–2.

Lusch, R.F. and Vargo, S.L. (2006) 'Services-dominant logic: reactions, reflections and refinements', *Marketing* Theory, **6** (3), 281–8.

McCallum, J. and Harrison, W. (1985) 'Interdependence in the service encounter', in Czepiel, J.A., Solomon, M.R. and Surprenant, C.F. (eds) *The Service Encounter: Managing Employee/Customer Interaction in Service Businesses*, Lexington, MA: Lexington Books, pp. 25–48.

Magnini, V.P., Ford, J.B., Markowski, E.P. and Honeycutt, E.D. (2007) 'The service recovery paradox: justifiable theory or smoldering myth?', *Journal of Service Marketing*, **21** (3), 213–25.

Möller, K. and Halinen, A. (2000) 'Relationship marketing theory: its roots and direction', *Journal of Marketing Management*, **16**, 29–54.

Odekerken-Schröder, G., Van Birgelen, M., Lemmink, J., De Ruyter, K. and Wetzels, M. (2000) 'Moments of sorrow and joy', *European Journal of Marketing*, **34** (1/2), 107–25.

Palmer, A.J. (1998) *Principles of Services Marketing*, London: McGraw-Hill.

Palmer, A.J. (2005) *Principles of Services Marketing*, 4th edn, London: McGraw-Hill.

Pels, J. (1999) 'Exchange relationships in consumer markets?', *European Journal of Marketing*, **33** (1/2), 19–37.

Reichheld, F.F. (1996) *The Loyalty Effect: The Hidden Force behind Growth, Profits and Lasting Value*, Boston, MA: Harvard Business School Press.

Sheth, J.N. and Sisodia, R.S. (1999) 'Revisiting marketing's lawlike generalizations', *Journal of the Academy of Marketing Sciences*, **17** (1), 71–87.

Shostack, G.L. (1977) 'Breaking free from product marketing', *Journal of Marketing*, **41**, April, 73–80.

Smith, P.R. (1998) *Marketing Communications: An Integrated Approach*, 2nd edn, London: Kogan Page.

Stewart, K. (1998a) 'An exploration of customer exit in retail banking', *International Journal of Bank Marketing*, **16** (1), 6–14.

Stewart, K. (1998b) 'The customer exit process: a review and research agenda', *Journal of Marketing Management*, **14**, 235–50.

Storbacka, K., Strandvik, T. and Grönroos, C. (1994) 'Managing customer relations for profit: the dynamics of relationship quality', *International Journal of Service Industry Management*, **5**, 21–38.

Strandvik, T. and Storbacka, K. (1996) 'Managing relationship quality,' in Edvardsson, B., Brown, S.W., Johnston, R. and Scheuing, E.E. (eds) *Advancing Service Quality: A Global Perspective*, New York: ISQA, pp. 67–76.

Vargo, S.L. (2008) 'Customer integration and value creation: paradigmatic traps and perspectives', *Journal of Service Research*, **11** (2), 211–15.

Vargo, S. and Lusch, R. (2004) 'Evolving to a new dominant logic for marketing', *Journal of Marketing*, **67** (1), 1–17.

Worthington, S. and Horne, S. (1998) 'A new relationship marketing model and its application in the affinity credit card market', *International Journal of Bank Marketing*, **16** (1), 39–44.

Notes

1 The distinction between service and services is also a discussion point in the service-dominant logic debate discussed in Chapter 13.
2 The phrase 'moment of truth' is often ascribed to Jan Carlzon of SAS.
3 The ideas and concepts associated with service-dominant logic will be discussed in Chapter 13.
4 Bitner *et al.* (1990) call these 'critical incidents'.
5 Dwyer *et al.*'s (1987, p. 15) five-stage model discussed previously (see Chapter 4) is an example of one that includes the possibility of separation although most models appear (sometimes conveniently) to ignore it.

8 Internal partnerships

Key issues

- The internal market
- Functional interfaces
- Organisational climate and culture
- Empowerment
- Implementing internal marketing

Introduction

Relationship marketing has, as the concept developed, wholeheartedly embraced the idea of a 'broadened view of marketing' (Christopher *et al.*, 1991, p. 21). To this end, aspects of RM theory development have mirrored, and to a certain extent borrowed from, events taking place in other areas of business research, including trends in organisational structure (Gummesson, 1999, p. 7). Whereas traditional marketing focused wholly on the external customer, RM stresses the additional significance of the internal customer (Gummesson, 1991, p. 69). The RM concept calls, therefore, not only for an external marketing orientation but also for an '**internal marketing**' **(IM)** focus on employees (Javalgi and Moberg, 1997, p. 173). A variety of terms, including **internal partnerships, internal relationships** and internal marketing, have been used to describe the concepts discussed in this chapter. Although authors in some cases imply certain nuances and priorities, the terms are used here interchangeably to avoid confusion. If a distinction is required *internal marketing* can be seen as the process towards the development of *internal partnerships*.

Customer–employee interface

Recognition of the importance of the employee–customer interface has, in large part, promoted interest in internal marketing. Research suggests that the quality of relationships a company has with its customers is largely determined by how employees at the front line make customers feel (Barnes and Howlett, 1998, p. 21). It is also suggested that where the customer–supplier interface is more immediate, the internal climate has a strong impact upon employee satisfaction and customer retention (Payne, 2000, p. 118). Indeed, contact employees are one of the means of communication with customers through which it expresses its business orientation (Macintosh 2007, p. 155). As service offerings are largely through human interaction of some kind, the suggestion is that in service organisations a 'relationship' between employees and customers is almost inevitable (Kandampully and Duddy, 1999, p. 320). Furthermore, relational strategies are more effective when they are built with individual front line staff rather than the firm itself (Palmatier *et al.*, 2006, p. 136).

Internal marketing strategies in service companies in particular are recognised as being of the utmost importance. Whereas a service firm's contact with its customers is normally through its own employees, manufacturing firms (and process services) in contrast rely on intermediaries or (increasingly) technology (e.g. call centres) to develop some type of relationship. Another factor particularly promoting IM in service companies is that these organisations are invariably labour intensive. As such, internal marketing can help these organisations attract, keep and motivate quality personnel, which in turn helps them improve their capacity to offer quality services.

The stimulus for this internal marketing concern was, therefore, the growth in the importance of services marketing. Despite this, there is no insurmountable reason why internal marketing strategies should be limited to this area (Gummesson, 1991, p. 69). Although the importance of the internal dimension is seen to be particularly relevant to service industries, any organisation's final output, be it a good or service, is almost always the product of a series of operations and processes performed by employees (Buttle, 1996, p. 3). If we accept Vargo and Lusch's (2004, p. 9) hypothesis that value is defined and co-created with the consumer rather than being imbedded in outputs the distinction may actually be superfluous.

Theory development

The ideas associated with internal marketing and internal partnerships have had a chequered career. The early views of internal marketing were more akin to the 'persuasion of staff to a management-determined situation' (Varey and Lewis, 1999, p. 929), whereas the concept of the internal customer evolved originally through the idea of 'selling jobs' and making them more attractive for employees (Reynoso, 1996, p. 77). In more recent times internal marketing and internal partnerships have become associated with a wide number of (sometimes overlapping) concepts, among them:

- The concept of employees as (internal) suppliers and customers (Gummesson, 1991, p. 69; Christopher *et al.*, 1991, p. 79). This assumes chains of internal customers (administrative and manufacturing/processing) within an organisation. An employee who, in the normal course of a job, would not deal directly with an external customer would be expected to treat internal customers as if they were external to the organisation.

- The breaking down of functional barriers within the organisation (Doyle, 1995, p. 29).

- Efforts to 'sell' the message of an organisation to its internal audience, using similar techniques to those used in the organisation's relationship with its external audiences (Palmer, 1998, p. 201).

- Marketing that takes place between profit centres inside a decentralised company (Gummesson, 1991, p. 69).

- The orchestration of staff working together and attuned to the company's mission, strategy, goals (Christopher *et al.*, 1991, p. 29) and the wider operations of the company with its environment (Hogg *et al.*, 1998, p. 893).

- Any activity within an organisation that focuses staff attention on the internal activities that need to be changed in order to enhance the external marketplace performance (Ballantyne, 1997, p. 346).

- Activities that improve internal communication and customer consciousness among employees (Hogg *et al.*, 1998, p. 880).

- Meeting the needs of employees so that they can meet the needs of their customers (Shershic, 1990, p. 45).

- The development of a company marketing orientation (Gummesson, 1991, p. 69; Varey and Lewis, 1999, p. 926; Hogg *et al.*, 1998, p. 879).

- How to get and retain customer-conscious employees (Grönroos, 1990, p. 88).

Varey and Lewis (1999, p. 931) while acknowledging the diversity of meanings and usage for the internal marketing concept, see it from a different viewpoint. They conceive that internal marketing can be seen as:

- a metaphor;
- a philosophy;
- a set of techniques;
- an approach.

Internal marketing as a metaphor suggests that organisational jobs and employment conditions are 'products' to be marketed with the employee as both buyer and consumer. As a philosophy, internal marketing suggests that human resource management (HRM) requires 'marketing-like' activities to 'sell' the requirement of management. The concept also implies that HRM should adopt marketing techniques such as research, segmentation, promotional communications and advertising internally to inform *and* persuade. Finally, internal marketing may be regarded as a style of management with key (and perhaps contradictory) objectives of flexibility and commitment.

These ideas, together with contributions from the corporate communications and branding[1] literature, converged to suggest the prime constituents of IM. It was this broader concept that Christopher *et al.* (1991, p. 30) were describing when they noted that internal marketing was:

> recognised as an important activity in developing a customer-focused organisation. In practice, internal marketing is concerned with communications, with developing responsiveness, responsibility and unity of purpose. Fundamental aims of internal marketing are to develop internal and external customer awareness and remove functional barriers to organisational effectiveness.

Internal marketing is perceived as a holistic approach to the business in general but to HRM and marketing in particular (Hogg *et al.*, 1998, p. 880). As internal interactions inevitably occur between departments in organisations, organisational dynamics are of particular relevance to both the service products and service delivery (Reynoso, 1996, p. 77; Reynoso and Moores, 1996, p. 55). Indeed, it is perceived as so important to the success of an operation that Gummesson (1991, p. 74) proposes that marketing in the future should be presented and taught from this holistic perspective and be truly integrated with other functions of the firm. In practical terms this would encompass HRM policies designed to attract, select, train, motivate, direct, evaluate and reward personnel (Palmer, 1998, p. 201) and indeed extend this influence to other parts of the organisation by breaking down the traditional functional barriers that exist in many companies. Gummesson (1991, p. 72) sees this as a change from 'marketing management' to 'marketing-orientated company management'.

The internal market[2]

Internal marketing, in the general sense, is seen to describe 'any form of marketing within the organisation which focuses attention on the internal activities that need to be changed in order that marketing plans can be implemented' (Christopher *et al.*, 1991, p. 26) and that enhances external marketplace performance (Ballantyne, 1997, p. 346). Internal marketing is essentially a way of enabling an organisation to recruit, motivate and retain customer-conscious employees in order to boost employee retention and customer satisfaction levels (Clark, 2000, p. 217). It can be broadly interpreted as those activities that improve internal communications and customer consciousness among employees, and the link between those activities and external marketplace performance (Hogg *et al.*, 1998, p. 880). In addition to this general meaning, the term can be applied to the concept that every person in an organisation is both a customer and a supplier (Buttle, 1996, pp. 3–4). The essence of internal marketing is not, according to Varey and Lewis (1999, p. 926), a phenomenon of the post-industrial era since there is some evidence of associated attitudes and methods in literature produced early in the twentieth century. What is new is the active market-orientated approach.

Internal marketing benefits

Internal marketing focuses on the three core value-adding activities, innovation, effective processes and customer support, and builds networks which design in quality (Doyle, 1995, pp. 26–7). It involves retaining customer-conscious employees and the development of employee empowerment to better satisfy the needs of the customer. Internal partnerships reflect the belief that if management wants its employees to deliver an outstanding level of service to customers, then it must be prepared to do a great deal for its employees (Reynoso, 1996, p. 77).

Internal marketing, therefore, is seen as a requirement for the successful implementation of the internal partnership concept and, ultimately, of RM. According to Buttle (1996, p. 12) the goal is to promote the development of the new culture, to persuade employees that it is sensible to buy into the new vision and to motivate them to develop and implement RM strategies. In this way internal marketing partnerships become a core business philosophy (Palmer, 1998, p. 201) rather than solely the preserve of the marketing department.

The functional interface

The CIM definition of marketing as 'management process' implies a functional marketing department responsible for a fixed number of responsibilities, aimed at the customer and closely associated with the traditional marketing mix. RM strategies imply breaking down functional barriers in an organisation. The oft-repeated maxim (at least in marketing circles) that 'whereas not everything is marketing, marketing is everything' (see McKenna, 1991, p. 18 and Ballantyne, 1997, p. 345 for variations on this theme) suggests that a **marketing orientation** means more than can possibly be handled by the marketing department alone. Rather, marketing orientation means 'the organisation-wide generation of market intelligence, dissemination of that intelligence across departments and organisation-wide responsiveness to it' (Kohli and Jaworski, 1990, p. 4). This organisational-wide stance is supported by evidence from experienced marketers who see little distinction between a business plan and a marketing plan. Marketing in this context should be leading the effort of designing and building cross-functional business processes and should, therefore, be at the heart of the organisation's strategic planning. Regretably, according to Doyle (1995, p. 23):

> Marketers have generally made the mistake of seeing the subject [Marketing] as a fundamental discipline rather than an integrated business process. Marketing Directors have sought to make Marketing decisions rather than share responsibility for satisfying customers with cross-functional teams. Unfortunately the only decisions where Marketing has sole responsibility tended to be tactical; promotions, line extension and superficial positioning policies.

Human resources

Over the past few decades, firms have begun to recognise that, more often than not, the limiting factor to their success is far more predicated on the availability of satisfactory skilled people than the availability of other resources such as capital or raw materials (Christopher *et al.*, 1991, p. 26). Studies on the major concerns of managers back up the importance of internal resources. They show employee communication and involvement, the redesign of business processes and the importance of the perceived relationship between employees and customer satisfaction as being top of managers' hit-lists (Varey and Lewis, 1999, p. 926).

Nowhere is the importance of human assets more evident than in service operations, many of which can no longer be valued on the basis of their physical assets but on the basis of 'intellectual capital'. This intellectual capital, according to Gummesson (1999, p. 190) comes in two types:

- individual capital;
- structural capital.

Individual capital

Individual capital covers the employees and their qualities, including knowledge, skills and motivation, plus the individual's network of relationships inside and outside the company.

Structural capital

Structural capital, as we have noted previously (see Chapter 3), is the embedded knowledge inseparable from its environment and which does not evaporate when an employee leaves. This includes established relationships, the climate and culture, systems, contracts, image and branding. Core competencies, based on specific knowledge, reside in the organisation's staff and the systems that it has developed (Doyle, 1995, p. 28). As the success of 'individual capital' development has the potential to enhance 'structural capital', maintaining the former is crucial. The firm has a responsibility, therefore, to develop company-specific skills and to motivate its staff to harness these skills energetically to deliver superior value to the customer (p. 28).[3]

Teamwork

Research by Reynoso and Moores (1996, p. 58) suggests that one of the key factors contributing to any discrepancy between service quality specifications and the actual service delivered is poor teamwork. It is the existence of **'functional silos'** that are seen to act independently and with little coordination that is frequently the major cause both of disagreement and 'non-goal congruence' (a frequent criticism coincidentally of CRM). For a firm pursuing RM strategies, the internal interface between marketing, operations, personnel and other functions is of strategic importance (Grönroos, 1994, p. 12). This viewpoint acknowledges that all activities in a company are interrelated – what Gummesson (1991, p. 65) calls 'inter-functional dependency'. The interesting issue is whether a holistic marketing orientation calls for more marketing department direct authority over the operating activities of the firm (Ballantyne, 1997, p. 345) or whether the marketing function *per se* has reached its sell-by date and that cross-functional teams are the answer to the functionality problem. In many ways this conundrum is at the heart of the current RM/CRM debate (see Chapter 13). It is unlikely that any solution is right in every case. Each company will need to find an organisational form that is both effective and complements its climate and culture.

Part-time marketers

Many companies have centralised marketing and sales staff, who might be called 'full-time marketers'. These employees do not, however, represent all the marketers and salespeople the firm has at its disposal (Grönroos, 1996, p. 8). Gummesson (1990) has coined the phrase '**part-time marketers**' **(PTM)**, in his book of the same name, to describe these non-marketing specialists who, regardless of their position in the company, are crucial to the company's marketing effort. These PTMs include all of those employees who, in any way, influence customer relations, customer satisfaction and the customer's perceived quality (Gummesson, 1991, p. 60). As Grönroos (1996, p. 8) notes, in many situations their impact on customer satisfaction and quality perception is more important to long-term success in the marketplace than that of the full-time marketer.

Christopher *et al.* (1991, p. 17) too recognises the part that both marketers and part-time marketers play in the marketing process. They further subdivide these categories based on the frequency of contact with the company to produce four types, as shown in Figure 8.1:

Figure 8.1
Employee influence on customers

	Involvement with marketing	Not directly involved with marketing
Frequent or periodic customer contact	**Contractors**	**Modifiers**
Infrequent or no customer contact	**Influencers**	**Isolateds**

(*Source*: Adapted from Christopher *et al.*, 1991, p. 17)

■ *Contractors*: Contractors have frequent or periodic customer contact and are heavily involved with 'conventional' marketing activities, including sales and customer service roles. They should be well versed in the company's marketing strategy, well trained and motivated to serve the customer on a day-to-day basis. They should be recruited based on their potential to respond to customer needs and evaluated and rewarded on this basis.

■ *Modifiers*: Modifiers, while not directly involved with conventional marketing activities, have frequent customer contact. This group includes receptionists, accounting staff, delivery personnel, etc. Modifiers should have a clear view of the organisation's marketing strategy and the part they play in it. They should be trained in the development of customer relationship skills and monitored and evaluated on this basis.

■ *Influencers*: Influencers are involved with elements of conventional marketing, but they have infrequent personal contact. They are, however, very much part of the implementation of the organisation's marketing strategy. Roles include research and development, market research, etc. A major skill to be nurtured here is 'customer responsiveness'. Influencers should be evaluated and rewarded according to customer-orientated performance standards. Opportunities to meet customers in a programmed way may be also be valuable.

■ *Isolateds*: Although these employees have neither regular contact with customers nor regular input into conventional marketing activities, their performance could affect successful fulfilment of the company's marketing strategy. Included in this category, for example, are staff members from personnel and data processing departments. The appropriate attention should be given to maximising the impact of their activities on marketing strategy and they should be rewarded accordingly.

Climate and culture

The management of individual encounters is, according to Bitner (1990, p. 69):

> nested within broader management issues of organisational structure, philosophy and culture that also can influence the service delivery and, ultimately, customer perception of service quality.

Organisations are not, after all, tangible objects but rather social constructs made up of people, activities, thoughts, emotions and other intangibles (Gummesson, 1994, p. 10). As Payne *et al.* (1995, p. 95) note, **organisational climate** and **organisational culture** have become recognised as the foundation of long-term marketing effectiveness. They define these linked concepts as:

■ *climate*: the policies and practices that characterise the organisation (and, in turn, reflect its cultural beliefs).

■ *culture*: the deep-seated, unwritten system of shared values and norms within the organisation (which in turn dictates its climate).

The climate and culture of an organisation are dependent on how the employees view that organisation and its goals (Hogg *et al.*, 1998, p. 881). In particular, they affect both how the individual perceives his or her role within the organisation and how those roles relate to the wider operation of the organisation with its environment (p. 893). Internal marketing and the development of internal partnerships suggest the creation of an organisational climate where cross-functional quality improvements can be sponsored and worked upon by the people whose job processes are involved (Christopher *et al.*, 1991, p. 79).

Change within organisations frequently causes concern among employees even if that change will ultimately benefit them in some way. With the dramatic change inherent in today's strategy development, a supportive organisational culture is required to successfully implement changes. Dangers are also inherent in change. Climatic problems can quickly develop if issues are not dealt with before extensive change takes place.

Employee retention and loyalty

It is unarguable that the longer an employee stays with a company, the more familiar he or she will become with the business. It may also be generally true that longevity of employment increases learning. According to Reichheld (1993, p. 68) this learning increases the value of the employee to the company based upon how long the worker is expected to stay and grow with the business. This may be somewhat overstating the point in that 'longevity' in itself cannot guarantee 'value', and 'long service' can sometimes be associated with fixed ideas and inflexibility. The general point being made, however, is that experience is frequently sacrificed in favour of expediency, particularly in cost-cutting exercises, a situation highlighted (April 2000) in a British government report. Although the expression 'our employees are our greatest assets' is often heard, it is frequently no more than a platitude (Christopher *et al.*, 1991, p. 16).

Empowerment

Empowerment lies at the heart of the relationship-based company. An important driver towards empowerment strategies came from the difficulty of non-homogeneity of delivery in service markets and the need for speedy decision-making at the customer interface. According to Bowen and Lawler (1992, p. 37) the more enduring the relationship, and the more important it is in the service package, the stronger the case for empowerment. The firm must be able to create an intra-organisational environment in which employees are flexible and prepared to take decisions without referring back to management (Chaston *et al.*, 2000, p. 637). Empowerment, however, appears to have been the second-choice solution. In the 1970s, in a bid to overcome the non-homogeneity difficulty, companies (e.g., McDonald's) took a 'production-line' approach to services (Bowen and Lawler, 1992, p. 31). Through duplication of activities, simplification of tasks and clear divisions of labour, companies were able to keep organisational control and produce efficient, low-cost, high-volume service operations with satisfied customers. This system would appear to work well in highly repetitive and relatively simple operations (e.g. fast food outlets or FMCG retailers).

It is, however, one of the oft-repeated social criticisms of the move from manu-facturing economies to service-led economies that skilled jobs are being replaced by low-paid and little-skilled service operations. To an extent (and particularly where there is a production-line or process service approach) this is true. In general, how-ever, it is the rules and lines of authority which most restrict the innate personal skills of employees being fully (and satisfactorily) realised. Empowerment, therefore, according to Tom Peters, is necessary to 'dehumiliate' work by eliminating those policies and procedures of the organisation that demean and belittle human dignity (quoted in Zemke and Schaaf, 1989, p. 68).

In other areas of service (and indeed some product) provision there is a need for more complex interactions than suggested by the production-line approach. In some cases these interactions may involve instant decision-making on the part of the employee (e.g. information desk, complaints office). In these cases, organisational control cannot be maintained at the point of interaction (although guidance may be involved beforehand and, potentially, censure afterwards). Effectively, the manager must trust the employee to make a decision that will be best from the company's perspective. It is this trust that underlies empowerment.

Empowerment looks to the performer of the tasks for solutions to problems, and to these employees to suggest new services and products and to solve problems creatively and effectively. Jan Carlzon, former CEO of SAS (quoted in Bowen and Lawler, 1992, p. 32), sees it as freeing employees from 'rigorous control by instructors, policies and orders, and to give freedom to take responsibility for ideas, decisions and actions'. This, he predicts, will 'release hidden values that would otherwise remain inaccessible to both the individual and the organisation'.

Operationalising empowerment

Bowen and Lawler (ibid.) define 'empowerment' as the sharing, with front-line employees, of four organisational ingredients that in process services and many product industries would be in the hands of senior managers. These are:

■ information about organisational performance;

■ rewards based on organisational performance;

■ knowledge that enables employees to understand and contribute to organisational performance;

■ power to make decisions that influence organisational direction and performance.

Research by Lindgreen and Crawford (1999, p. 235) suggests that, for employee empowerment to work, there has to be investment in proper customer-focused staff training to enhance such different skills as industry knowledge, customer service, communications, presentation and teamwork. When managers in organisations establish policies, procedures and behaviour that show concern for the organisation's customers they are, according to Schneider (1980, p. 53) 'service enthusiasts'. This contrasts strongly with managers interested simply in systems maintenance and routine adherence to uniform operating guidelines and procedures ('**service bureaucrats**').

As well as recognising the value of interpersonal relationships and the importance of showing concern for the customer, the difference between the 'service enthusiast' and the 'service bureaucrat' is the former's emphasis on the flexible application of rules, procedures and systems maintenance. This assumes that all employees' workplace objectives are congruent with those of the organisation and that some form of consent must exist between employers and employees (Palmer, 1998, p. 200).

Empowerment benefits and cautions

Empowerment has a number of perceived benefits. According to Bowen and Lawler (1992, pp. 32–3), it results in:

- quicker online response to customers' needs during service delivery;
- quicker online response to dissatisfied customers during service recovery;
- employees feeling better about their jobs and themselves;
- employees interacting with customers with more warmth and enthusiasm;
- empowered employees being a great source of service ideas;
- great 'word of mouth' advertising and customer retention.

As with most management concepts, empowerment benefits should be considered against the potential downside. To begin with, although the benefits are clear, the implementation is fraught with difficulty. Most commonly, problems involve managers who wish to retain authority or employees who have no wish to have such a responsibility. It is also clear that some customers may prefer to be served by non-empowered employees, for example in self-service situations. Empowerment may not, therefore, always be the preferred option. Despite Peter's warnings about the belittling nature of some service jobs, Bowen and Lawler (1992, p. 37) note that the production-line approach makes sense if a company's core mission is to offer high-volume service at the lowest cost because 'industrialising' services can take advantage of economies of scale by leveraging volume throughput. The added value of this may be seen to be cheap, quick and reliable service versus high-level customer interaction or alternatively performing a straightforward 'transaction' versus 'managing a relationship'.

There are also (and inevitably) costs associated with empowerment. These are summarised by Bowen and Lawler (pp. 33–4) as:

- higher investment in selection and training;
- higher labour costs;

- slower/inconsistent service delivery as individual treatment slows down the operation;
- poor reaction of customers who see employees negotiating 'special deals' or terms with other customers;
- too many 'give-aways' and bad and costly decisions.

Empowerment, therefore, may produce benefits, particularly, but not exclusively, in service industry settings. It must be recognised, however, that it is not a panacea for every internal management problem.

Internal marketing implementation

Obtaining and understanding the employee perspective is a critical tool in managing customer satisfaction as it enables managers to exercise internal marketing – in effect meeting the needs of employees so that they can meet the needs of customers (Shershic, 1990, p. 45). Internal marketing, it is claimed, is a relationship development process in which staff autonomy and know-how combine to create and circulate new organisational knowledge. This process will highlight those existing internal activities that require change to enable enhanced quality in marketplace relationships (Ballantyne, 1997, p. 354). It is built on the premise that employees want to give good service just as customers want to receive it, and managers who make it easier to achieve this will find that both customers and employees are likely to respond positively (Schneider, 1980, p. 54).

At a tactical level internal marketing may include ongoing training and encouragement of formal and informal communications (such as newsletters), whereas at a strategic level internal marketing extends to the adoption of supportive management styles and personnel policies, customer service training and planning procedures (Hogg *et al.*, 1998, p. 880). Doyle (1995, p. 29) suggests that the development of internal strategies requires a three-stage approach:

- The organisation has to demonstrate a commitment to the security and development of its employees that ranks at least equal to that of its shareholders.
- The organisation has to create a structure where functional barriers are torn down. It will have 'flatter' organisational levels, empowerment for front-line staff and will focus efforts on the three core value-adding processes of operations, customer support and innovation.
- Top management must then provide leadership by reinforcing these values and offering a vision of what the organisation will become.

Reynoso and Moores (1996, p. 57) suggest that implementing an internal customer approach involves a number of processes. These include the creation of internal awareness, the identification of internal customers and suppliers, the identification of the expectations of the former, the communication of those expectations to internal suppliers and the development of a measure of internal customer satisfaction and feedback mechanisms. The danger inherent in all of these proposals is that internal marketing may be limited in what it contributes to the wider issues of organisational culture as it all too often defaults to an internal communications exercise (Meldrum, 2000, p. 13).

Staff development

It appears that the satisfaction of staff with their work is positively related to customer satisfaction only when that work is customer orientated. In a detailed analysis of over 16,000 bank staff, over 25 per cent of employees revealed that they were dissatisfied, in particular, with the key support mechanisms provided by management intended to facilitate deeper relationships with customers (McAdam, 2005, p. 5). There is no evidence, however, that a broader causality between staff satisfaction and customer satisfaction exists (Ballantyne, 1997, p. 356). Grönroos (1996, p. 10) advocates what he terms a **'process management perspective' (PMP)**. PMP, he suggests, is very different from the traditional functionalistic management approach based on 'scientific management' principles. A PMP approach would see department boundaries broken down and the work-flow (including sales and marketing activities, productive, administrative and distributive activities and a host of 'part-time' marketing activities) organised and managed as a value-creating process.

Knowledge may be the key driver to staff effectiveness (and indeed satisfaction). As Gummesson (1987, p. 23) notes, all 'contact personnel' must be well attuned to the mission, goals, strategies and systems of the company otherwise they would be unable to handle those crucial 'moments of truth' that occur during the interaction with customers. This is particularly evident in service firms where the interface with the customer is broad and intense, but may also be generally true of all companies.

Reward systems too may play a crucial role in internal partnership development. At present, sales and marketing management are widely rewarded with a mix of basic salary and performance-related bonus or commission. As Buttle (1996, p. 13) notes, the common performance criteria include sales volume and customer acquisition data that only reflect the short term. Under an RM strategy employees are more likely to be rewarded by customer profitability, account penetration and customer retention (see Box 8.1).

According to Kandampully and Duddy (1999, pp. 321–2) an RM programme should:

> be considered the firm's life-blood – percolating through all ranks, departments, functions and assets of the firm – with the ultimate aim of simultaneously offering and gaining value at all levels. The firm's marketing, management, operations, finance and human resources should constitute nurturing organs assisting the firm to develop, create and nurture the continuous flow of value between the respective stakeholders inside and/or outside the organisation.

Box 8.1 Partnership in action

John Lewis Partnership (JLP) is a retail organisation that has always treated its staff as integral to the business. Staff members, from Waitrose, John Lewis and Greenbee, are called 'partners' because all 70,000 of them share in all 'partnership benefits', including dividends, and have a say in the strategic and tactical development of the store group. Each year the organisation surveys its partners on subjects including job satisfaction, pay and career development. According to the JLP Strategy Statement 'partners should gain personal satisfaction by being a member of a co-owned enterprise in which they have worthwhile, secure and fulfilling employment and confidence in the way the Partnership conducts its business. In an age of intense retail competition, will John Lewis be forced to restructure more in line with other UK retailers? It would seem not if communiqués from head office are to be believed.

Conclusion

RM's environment is not only the market and society in general but also includes the organisation and it is, therefore, dependent on changes in organisational design (Gummesson, 1994, p. 10). Internal marketing is widely seen as a prerequisite for the successful implementation of RM, although responsibility for its implementation may not be solely the domain of marketers (Clark, 2000, p. 220). According to Grönroos (1994, p. 13), if internal marketing is neglected then external marketing suffers or fails. Research by Barnes and Howlett (1998, p. 21) suggests that the quality of relationships a company has with its customers is very much determined by how employees make customers feel. Schneider (1980, p. 63) reports research which concludes that if employees perceive a strong service orientation customers declare they receive superior service. It works both ways. The success of RM is itself dependent, to a large extent, on the attitudes, commitment and performance of employees. If they are not all committed to their role as marketers (full-time and part-time) and are not motivated to perform in a customer-orientated fashion, RM strategy will fail (Grönroos, 1996, p. 12).

The adoption of RM concepts internally suggest a recognition of the need for a new type of organisation with a new type of management (Gummesson, 1994, p. 10). There is a broad recognition of the failure of conventional 'chimney stack' management with its functional bunkers (including marketing) 'embodying an abstract notion of marketing orientation . . . but a practical unwillingness to get out in the field and deliver on customer service and satisfaction' (O'Driscoll and Murray, 1998, p. 395). Doyle (1995, p. 35), predicted that:

> Marketing Managers will have to work more effectively as team players; proactively putting teams together and co-operating with other functions to enhance the core processes of innovation, order fulfillment and customer service. Functional boundaries in the 'professional core' will be seen as irrelevant and general management skills will be much more prized.

Marketing researchers in general strongly endorse these sentiments. Chaston (1998, p. 280) sees internal marketing as requiring priority over any other organisational process when seeking to achieve the goal of customer satisfaction. Grönroos (1996, p. 12) sees RM success as highly dependent on a well-organised and continuous internal marketing process. Buttle (1996, p. 193) cites evidence from the service sector (including the Post Office, banking, hospitality and not-for-profit organisations) that also suggests that organisations are 'likely to be less effective externally if the expectations of internal relational partners are not met'.

Increasing numbers of companies have recognised the need for internal marketing programmes, and the implementation of such programmes has gained momentum in recent years (Clark, 2000, p. 220). On a cautionary note, Varey and Lewis (1999, p. 927), while acknowledging that internal marketing is an evolving subject, report that there is not yet any firm theory or a strong base of empirical evidence to show how and why it is of value to managers. Adoption of internal marketing strategies is, therefore, no guarantee of success. In 1995, Doyle (1995, p. 26) cited Marks & Spencer as an example of a company which had eliminated functional boundaries and which had no marketing directors or conventional marketing departments. Despite this it went on to face considerable operational problems over the next few years. British Airways, cited as the 'most famous' of internal marketing advocates (Clark, 2000, p. 220), has also had continuing difficulties despite the introduction of its 'hearts and minds' employee programme. The argument for internal marketing is strong in theory although, perhaps, more difficult to implement and sustain.

Summary

This chapter looked at internal partnerships (also referred to as internal marketing). It highlighted the importance of the employee–customer interface and the development of an internal marketing approach to the overall success of relational strategies. It reviewed the significance of human resource management in the development of internal marketing and the broader need to remove all functional barriers from the organisational environment. The importance of full-time and part-time marketers was acknowledged and the advantages of teamwork considered. The benefits of employee retention and loyalty were noted and the effect of climate and culture on that employee loyalty discussed. Empowerment was seen as a recognisable feature of internal marketing, but it was noted that costs as well as benefits accompany such a policy. Finally, the means of implementing internal marketing was discussed.

Discussion questions
1 What are the basic concepts that underlie internal marketing strategies?
2 Suggest ways in which functional barriers (e.g. between marketing and human resource management) could be broken down.
3 What are the principal advantages and disadvantages of empowerment?
4 What type of organisational climate and culture might best suit the implementation of relationship marketing?

Case study   Resetting the sun

The brief

Providing insurance services in over 130 countries and operating in more than 28, Royal and Sun Alliance's brand portfolio was somewhat schizophrenic. 'The business had 48 active brands across the world,' says marketing and customer director Claire Salmon. 'There were 300 different brands in total, including the inactive ones for trademarks that we owned.'

Salmon wasn't only worried about the brand identity, she also had a bone to pick with the company's convoluted name. 'It was a sort of accident of destiny left over from when Royal and Sun Alliance merged in the mid-nineties,' she admits. 'The management team simply joined together the two merging names and created something that was pretty unpronounceable in most of the territories where we operate, and too long to put on the average business card – much less an advert.'

With this blurry identity, the insurance company's brand meant little to its customers and, perhaps more importantly, to its employees. 'Insurance is an incredibly intangible business, you're basically selling a promise to people to pay if things go wrong,' explains Salmon. 'So the most important asset you've got is your staff, because that's who the customer talks to on the phone, and that's who is making those promises.'

The strategy

The rebranding process started from the inside. 'We ran events that we called World Cafes, which united groups of employees from every functional area in a structured discussion about what they liked and didn't like about Royal and Sun Alliance and its competitors.'

'Keeping you moving' was the brand proposition generated by feedback from 1,000 employees worldwide. 'While most insurance companies use either fear or greed as their customer motivator, we are the Ronseal of the insurance industry – what you see is what you get,' says Salmon. 'We don't promise to make your life glamorous and wonderful, nor do we scaremonger. We just want to put our customers back in the position they were in before any kind of catastrophe happened.'

Brand consultancy Interbrand was commissioned to assess the relative value of each brand in Royal and Sun Alliance's sprawling portfolio. 'We wanted to know whether we should opt for a masterbrand approach in the vein of companies such as General Electric, for example,' says Salmon. 'Or a "house of brands" such as Royal Bank of Scotland, which incorporates everything from Churchill to Directline.'

With strong brands including Trygg-Hansa, the third biggest brand in the Danish insurance market, and More Than in the UK, Interbrand had plenty of RSA brand equity to analyse. 'We arrived at an endorsement group strategy,' says Salmon. 'In the same way that Santander has been gradually introducing its livery and logo to the recently acquired Abbey, we decided that we'd build equity in the core Royal and Sun Alliance brand and use that to support the powerful brands in the portfolio.'

Shortening its chewy title to RSA and transforming the logo livery from blue and yellow to a more modern magenta and purple, the business was ready for its makeover.

The execution

Communication of the new brand identity began with internal talks between the top 100 leaders in the business. 'We are a self-effacing organisation,' says Salmon. 'So we felt it was important that we launch in a way that would keep our employees involved and that wouldn't make it look to customers as though the company had suddenly lost the plot.'

On the day that the new brand name and identity was launched, 256 presentations in 21 different languages were made to business employees across the organisation, during which a film demonstrating the meaning of the 'Keeping you moving' proposition was shown.

'We explained what we wanted the business to stand for, and how we therefore wanted our workers to behave. We were concerned to illustrate that the rebrand was about the beliefs at the heart of the brand rather than just saying, "look, we've invented a new logo",' says Salmon.

All websites and marketing material were rebranded with the new name and livery, and workshops across all of the company's 130 countries were run to instruct employees on the brand beliefs and how to deliver them.

The PR campaign sent press releases to multiple business and consumer publications and the brand was formally presented to the shareholders at the company's annual general meeting.

Every employee was given a guide to the RSA brand and the values of responsiveness, straightforwardness, planning ahead and being focused on delivery are now intrinsically tied to the company's performance targets. 'An employee's performance appraisal is linked specifically to how well their work delivers the ideals of the brand,' says Salmon. 'We mark them for brilliant service, getting the job done, doing the right thing, having bright ideas and being positive people – those are the underlying values that help support us in delivering the brand proposition and they are all words that I think our employees would now recognise.'

The outcome

Salmon claims that anecdotal evidence proves that the rebrand has been well received by both employees and customers, but she confesses that there are not yet any solid statistics to illustrate the new brand identity's success. 'We will be sending out a tracking survey and an employee opinion survey in order to get a quantitative sense of how well the rebrand has done,' she says. 'But it's obvious that it's gone down very well across the group. We've had lots of letters from customers telling us how much they like what we've done, and our employees are very excited about it – sometimes it's difficult to slow them down in terms of what they want to do.'

RSA's rebrand has certainly impressed its peers – it won an award for best stand with its presentation of the new brand at the British Insurance Brokers Association conference in April.

A brand survey was sent out to employees in spring 2008 asking them to mark out of 10 how well they understand the brand and the benefits of changing it. Hoping for at least an average rating of seven out of 10, RSA was delighted with an 8.5 average score. Employees in countries such as Chile and Norway averaged nearly 9.5 for enthusiasm and understanding of the new brand.

Salmon points out that it will take time for the effects of the rebrand to filter through such a large organisation. 'With any brand migration, you're talking about years rather than months. I would expect us to spend a three-year period looking at the migration path and building equity in the RSA brand before we can really judge whether it has delivered against our original directives,' she explains.

Analysis

After the excitement of the first push, Salmon says the next challenge will be sustaining the rebrand's momentum. 'We have been surprised by how rapidly the brand has developed and we are doing a number of things next year to improve effectiveness, including workshops with our employees on what the brand values mean for the different segments of our customer base across the group.'

RSA has invested in Interbrand's digital management system, Brand Wizard, which stores all the brand's imagery and advert templates in one place so that advertising can be created quickly and simply.

Salmon remains true to her quest of paring down: 'We'll be working to reduce the number of agencies we use across the group. We've had too many in the past and need a smaller group of real partners in the process.'

With a customer base of 30 million already, retention is the most important aim for RSA. 'In the insurance business it is actually very easy to increase your customer base simply by reducing your rates. But we want to be a premium brand in the insurance marketplace. If people understand and respect our brand, that will lead to profitable growth and customer retention.'

(*Source*: Tabitha Barda *The Marketer*, December/January 2009)

Case study questions

1 Why was this rebranding necessary?
2 What were the positive aspects for employees?

References

Ballantyne, D. (1997) 'Internal networks for internal marketing', *Journal of Marketing Management*, **13** (5), 343–66.

Barnes, J.G. and Howlett, D.M. (1998) 'Predictors of equity in relationships between service providers and retail customers', *International Journal of Bank Marketing*, **16** (1), 5–23.

Bitner, M.J. (1990) 'Evaluating service encounters: the effects of physical surroundings and employee responses', *Journal of Marketing*, **54**, 69–82.

Bowen, D.E. and Lawler, E.E. (1992) 'The empowerment of service workers: what, why, how and when', *Sloan Management Review*, **33** (Spring), 31–9.

Buttle, F.B. (1996) *Relationship Marketing: Theory and Practice*, London: Paul Chapman.

Chaston, I. (1998) 'Evolving "new marketing" philosophies by merging existing concepts: application of process within small high-technology firms', *Journal of Marketing Management*, **14**, 273–91.

Chaston, I., Badger, B. and Sadler-Smith, E. (2000) 'Organisational learning style and competencies', *European Journal of Marketing*, **34** (5/6), 625–46.

Christopher, M., Payne, A. and Ballantyne, D. (1991) *Relationship Marketing*, London: Butterworth Heinemann.

Clark, M. (2000) 'Customer service, people and processes', in Cranfield School of Management, *Marketing Management: A Relationship Marketing Perspective*, Basingstoke: Macmillan, pp. 110–24.

Doyle, P. (1995) 'Marketing in the new millennium', *European Journal of Marketing*, **29** (12), 23–41.

Grönroos, C. (1990) 'Relationship approach to the marketing function in service contexts: the marketing and organization behaviour interface', *Journal of Business Research*, **20**, 3–11.

Grönroos, C. (1994) 'From marketing mix to relationship marketing: towards a paradigm shift in marketing', *Management Decisions*, **32** (2), 4–20.

Grönroos, C. (1996) 'Relationship marketing: strategic and tactical implications', *Management Decisions*, **34** (3), 5–14.

Gummesson, E. (1987) 'Using internal marketing to develop a new culture: the case of Ericsson quality', *Journal of Business and Industrial Marketing*, **2** (3), 23–8.

Gummesson, E. (1990) *The Part-time Marketer*, Karlstad: Centre for Service Research.

Gummesson, E. (1991) 'Marketing orientation revisited: the crucial role of the part-time marketers', *European Journal of Marketing*, **25** (2), 60–7.

Gummesson, E. (1994) 'Making relationship marketing operational', *International Journal of Service Industry Management*, **5**, 5–20.

Gummesson, E. (1999) *Total Relationship Marketing: Rethinking Marketing Management from 4Ps to 30Rs*, Oxford: Butterworth Heinemann.

Hogg, G., Carter, S. and Dunne, A. (1998) 'Investing in people: internal marketing and corporate culture', *Journal of Marketing Management*, **14**, 879–95.

Javalgi, R. and Moberg, C. (1997) 'Service loyalty: implications for service providers', *Journal of Services Marketing*, **11** (3), 165–79.

Kandampully, J. and Duddy, R. (1999) 'Relationship marketing: a concept beyond the primary relationship', *Marketing Intelligence and Planning*, **17** (7), 315–23.

Kohli, A.K. and Jaworski, B.J. (1990) 'Market orientation: the construct, research propositions and managerial implications', *Journal of Marketing*, **54**, 1–18.

Lindgreen, A. and Crawford, I. (1999) 'Implementing, monitoring and measuring a programme of relationship marketing', *Marketing Intelligence and Planning*, **17** (5), 231–9.

Macintosh, G. (2007) 'Customer orientation, relationship quality, and relational benefits to the firm', *Journal of Service Marketing*, **21** (3), 150–9.

McAdam, P. (2005) 'Give the customers what they want (and in most cases, it's not a relationship)', *Banking Strategies*, BAI Online <www.bai.org/bankstrategies/current/cover> (accessed 12 April 2007).

McKenna, R. (1991) *Relationship Marketing*, London: Addison-Wesley.

Meldrum, M. (2000) 'A market orientation', in Cranfield School of Management, *Marketing Management: A Relationship Marketing Perspective*, Basingstoke: Macmillan, pp. 3–15.

O'Driscoll, A. and Murray, J.A. (1998) 'The changing nature of theory and practice in marketing: on the value of synchrony', *Journal of Marketing Management*, **14** (5), 391–416.

Palmatier, R.W., Dant, R.P., Grewal, D. and Evans, K.R. (2006) 'Factors influencing the effectiveness of relationship marketing: a meta-analysis', *Journal of Marketing*, **70** (October), 136–53.

Palmer, A.J. (1998) *Principles of Services Marketing*, London: Kogan Page.

Payne, A. (2000) 'Customer retention', in Cranfield School of Management, *Marketing Management: A Relationship Marketing Perspective*, Basingstoke: Macmillan, pp. 110–24.

Payne, A., Christopher, M. and Peck, H. (eds) (1995) *Relationship Marketing for Competitive Advantage: Winning and Keeping Customers*, Oxford: Butterworth Heinemann.

Punjaisri, K. and Wilson, A. (2007) 'The role of internal branding in the delivery of employee brand promise', *Brand Management*, **15** (1), 57–70.

Reichheld, F.F. (1993) 'Loyalty based management', *Harvard Business Review*, March/April, 1993, 64–73.

Reynoso, J. (1996) 'Internal service operations: how well are they serving each other?', in Edvardsson, B., Brown, S.W., Johnston, R. and Scheuing, E.E. (eds) *Advancing Service Quality: A Global Perspective*, New York: ISQA, pp. 77–86.

Reynoso, J.F. and Moores, B. (1996) 'Internal relationships', in Buttle, F.B. (ed.) *Relationship Marketing: Theory and Practice*, London: Paul Chapman, pp. 55–73.

Schneider, B. (1980) 'The service organization: climate is crucial', *Organizational Dynamics*, Autumn, 52–65.

Shershic, S.F. (1990) 'The flip side of customer satisfaction research', *Marketing Research*, December, 45–50.

Varey, R.J. and Lewis, B.R. (1999) 'A broadened conception of internal marketing', *European Journal of Marketing*, **33** (9/10), 926–44.

Vargo, S. and Lusch, R. (2004) 'Evolving to a new dominant logic for marketing', *Journal of Marketing*, **67** (1), 1–17.

Zemke, R. and Schaaf, D. (1989) *The Service Edge: 101 Companies that Profit from Company Care*, New York: New American Library.

Notes

1 Including the concept of 'internal branding' described as a means of facilitating the integration of individual behaviours with desired brand promises (see Punjaisri and Wilson 2007).

2 This should not be confused with the term 'internal market', associated with systems used in some public service and other organisations.

3 This view is consistent with resource advantage theory, core competence theory and service-dominant logic (Vargo and Lusch, 2004).

9 Supplier partnerships

Key issues

- Vertical versus horizontal relationships
- Partnering
- Partnership costs
- Partnership benefits

Introduction

As the boundaries between organisations have become less clear and organisations have started to recognise the benefits of collaboration, researchers have become interested in understanding the dynamics of these relationships (Shaw, 2003, p. 147). Relationship marketing theory suggests that interdependence reduces transaction costs and generates better quality while keeping management costs lower (Sheth and Parvatiyar, 2000, p. 123). Relationships of this kind have value beyond the immediate transactions that take place between the participants (Håkansson and Ford 2006). Reciprocity is important to RM because without any reciprocal basis there would be no relationship (Tadajewski 2009). Relationships become resources because they contribute to the organisation's ability to efficiently and effectively produce market offerings that have value (Hunt *et al.*, 2006, p. 77).

An organisation's external relationships can be seen to have a vertical and horizontal dimension (Palmer, 2000, p. 689). These can be described as:

- vertical relationships representing those that integrate all or part of the supply chain through component suppliers, manufacturers and intermediaries;
- horizontal relationships represented by organisations that are at the same point in the channel of distribution (including competitors) who seek to cooperate and collaborate for mutual benefit.

These horizontal and vertical relationships are not mutually exclusive (see Figure 9.1) and it is quite possible for an organisation to have a number of bilateral and multi-lateral relationships of both sorts. When it comes to relationships of this type, not only is polygamy allowed – it is highly recommended (Gummesson, 1999, p. 129)! Whereas joint ventures have clear legal boundaries, other forms of relationships and channel partnerships seldom have legal structures that define them (Wilson, 2000, p. 260). They may instead involve an understanding between the parties to cooperate in the expectation that both parties will benefit.

Although many aspects of these relationship types have similar features, it may be valuable to investigate them separately. This chapter will, therefore, concentrate on **vertical relationships** (described as supplier partnerships or partnering), whereas Chapter 10 will look more closely at **horizontal relationships**. To differentiate the latter, horizontal relationships are termed 'collaborations'.

Supplier partnerships

Partnerships between customers and suppliers come in many forms and under many different guises: for example, Christopher *et al.* (1991, p. 24) note that electrical and healthcare company Phillips called them in the past 'vendor partnerships' and AT&T labelled them 'co-makerships'. Although 'supplier partnerships' is the term used here for these vertical relationships, it refers, more broadly, to any two-way relationship within the vertical chain and is sometimes more simply known as 'partnering'.

Figure 9.1
Horizontal and vertical relationships

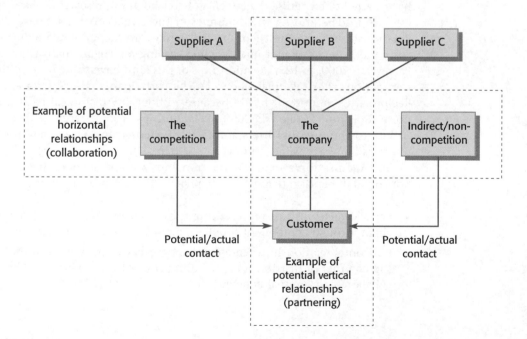

Supplier partnerships are, evidently, the other side of the 'customer partnerships' coin, so aspects relating to general relationships between 'partners' discussed previously apply. There is, therefore, no need to repeat again those aspects of the supplier–customer relationship outlined in Chapter 7. However, whereas the earlier chapter largely (but not exclusively) looked at the relationships from the consumer goods and services perspective (popularly referred to as **business-to-consumer**, or **B2C**) this chapter will concentrate on relationships further back in the supply chain. The most common way of describing this is as '**business-to-business' (B2B)** relationships, this term having largely replaced the term 'industrial goods and services marketing'.

We referred earlier to the concepts of organisational as well as personal relationships. As Håkansson and Snehota (1989, p. 187) note, when it comes to B2B, 'no business is an island', thus, by the very nature of the interdependency of most B2B markets, business relationships of one sort or another are inevitable. Whereas infinite supply would mean there would be little need for organisational interaction, under conditions of scarcity inter-organisational exchanges are essential (Levine and White, 1961, p. 587). Interdependence might be defined as where the interests of one party cannot be achieved without reference upon another (Rousseau et al., 1998, p. 395). Because each partner's individual success is linked to the success of the other, the organisations may actively pursue common goals (Hunt et al., 2006, p. 72).

The problem with discussing B2B relationships is that such is the wide variety of relationship types that the all-encompassing term 'relationship' may be too general to provide wholly constructive insight (Blois, 1999, p. 1). This chapter will attempt as far as possible to overcome this difficulty.

Business-to-business relationship research

It was the pioneering research work of the Industrial Marketing and Purchasing Group (IMP) into the complexities of the B2B markets and the relationships within them (Naudé and Holland, 1996, p. 40) that, in part, led to the development and application of relationship theory in this sector. Indeed, even the earliest development of theory by the group implicitly assumed that relationships enhanced performance (O'Toole and Donaldson, 2000, p. 328) and provided a grounding for what has developed since in relational marketing research. The recognition of the importance of 'relationships' came from real-life evidence that was slowly building up of a movement away from the traditional adversarial relationships between suppliers and their customers towards a new form of relationship based on cooperation (Christopher et al., 1991, p. 24). As Brennan (1997, pp. 759–60) notes:

> In the field of business-to-business marketing researchers associated with the International Marketing and Purchasing (IMP) Group ... published evidence to support the assertions that inter-firm buying and selling must be seen as related activities, and that the marketing function must be at least as concerned with inter-firm relationship development and management as with conventional marketing mix management.

IMP researchers also suggested that a two-level approach was evident, the first 'including short-term episodes . . . exchange of goods and services, information, financial and social aspects' and the second, and longer-term, 'processes leading to adaptation and institutionalisation of roles and responsibilities' (Grönroos, 2000, p. 7). These latter relationships require action and investment today whilst offering the prospect of reward in the future (Håkansson and Ford 2006, p. 250). Webster (1992, p. 10) also saw a 'clear evolution away from arm's length transactions and traditional hierarchical, bureaucratic forms of organisation towards more flexible types of partnerships, alliances and networks' within the B2B sector. Håkansson and Snehota (2000, p. 75), meanwhile, saw the four cornerstones of the IMP research into B2B markets as:

- relationships that exist between buyers and sellers;
- business relationships that are connected (by networks);
- a relationship being a combination that includes elements of both market and hierarchy;
- relationships that are confrontational (and therefore innovative).

Business relationships

Although the importance of IMP industrial research cannot be over-emphasised, the existence of 'trading partnerships' is not new. In the B2B field marketing concepts associated with long-term relationships have a long history of acceptance and effective practice (Barnes, 1994, p. 562). For example, personal relationships between the employees and owners/directors of companies have for some time been explicitly recognised by both buyer and seller organisations and individuals within those organisations (Blois, 1997, p. 53). Relational 'bonding' between B2B traders is not even a twentieth-century phenomenon. In the pre-Industrial Revolution world such associations were quite prevalent between traders, partly because of the need, in turbulent, minimally legislated and sometimes dangerous markets, to do business with others you could trust (Sheth and Parvatiyar, 1995, p. 403). As early as 1915 A.J. Eddy, in his book *The New Competition* noted 'the history of every industry has been a story of the rise and fall of cooperation' (quoted in Tadajewski 2009). Indeed, it was only with the growth and formalisation of mass-market distribution that traditional relationships between traders in the distribution chain became so strained and only with the advent of mass production and mass consumption that marketers began to accept a more transactional approach (Sheth and Parvatiyar, 2000, p. 130).

This observable tension in the distribution chain was most evident in relationships between brand suppliers and their retail intermediaries. Both parties had their minds focused on the final consumer but, while their individual objectives overlapped, they frequently differed considerably in strategy implementation. During the so-called 'golden age of marketing' from the mid-1950s to the mid-1970s, it was the brand owner who financed the development of individual brands and dominated and manipulated the means of distribution. Only rarely did brand owners and retailers work together to achieve a result that would satisfy both parties. Most often suppliers used 'pull strategies' with the objective of attracting customers 'over the heads' of the retailer. When 'push strategies' (effectively using trade incentives and promotions to 'push' product through the distribution chain) were used they tended to be one-off tactics rather than strategic cooperative activity. The retailers, on their part, felt no responsibility to any one supplier, being concerned more with overall profit margins than with specific brands.

The third quarter of the twentieth-century saw a change in the balance of power between suppliers and retailers, particularly in the FMCG sector, although initially little movement towards cooperation. As the power of larger supermarket retailers grew, suppliers were often played off against each other. Information regarding production capacity on one side and sales on the other was regarded as commercially sensitive and distrust of one's supplier or customer was the norm.

Only when vertical integration took place through 'acquisition' (forward or backward in the supply chain) was information seen to flow up and down the chain and, even then, somewhat hesitantly. The commonest justification for acquisition of this sort was protection of either the sources of supply (backward integration), or product markets (forward integration) with the improvement of information flow as a secondary benefit. The problems with these forms of integration were often that capital requirements and lack of flexibility typically led to inter-business subsidisation and transfer pricing as a way of shielding the internal business units from market forces (Sheth and Sisodia, 1999, p. 82). Despite these weaknesses, the acquisition route to effective and efficient distribution synergy dominated corporate strategy in the 1970s and 1980s. As the twentieth century came to a close, however, there was a growing recognition that the theoretical benefits sought through coordinating elements of the distribution chain might be better achieved in other ways. Rather than attempting to encompass all or a significant part of the distribution chain, companies were encouraged to concentrate their organisational efforts on their 'core competencies'. This thinking led to consideration of alternative strategies such as outsourcing and partnering.

Outsourcing was another approach that was not new. As Gummesson (1999, p. 128) notes, the 'make or buy' choice has always been an issue in manufacturing although the outsourcing of services is a more recent (but rapidly growing) phenomenon. Nor was partnering without precedent. Despite the general distrust in the typical distribution chain, there were partnerships which proved to be the exceptions to the rule. Partnering-type relationships existed between companies such as Whirlpool and Sears, and McDonald's and Coca-Cola, the latter of which has lasted for over 50 years (Sheth and Parvatiyar, 1995, p. 408). Similarly, Mitsubishi Electric and Westinghouse Electric have been engaged in an alliance for more than 60 years, as have Phillips and Matsushita (Sheth and Parvatiyar, 2000, p. 132). What had before been limited to a few companies was now, however, developing as mainstream strategy.

Partnering

Partnering can take many forms, so a rather generalised definition must suffice:

> Partnering is a relationship between customer and supplier organisations, recognised as such by the parties involved, whose principal objective is a shared increase in the effectiveness and efficiency of joint responsibilities within the remit of their relationship.

The *raison d'être* of a partnership approach is, therefore, to improve the efficiency and effectiveness with which a value-adding system functions (Brennan, 1997, p. 770; Hunt *et al.*, 2006, p. 77). Sheth and Sisodia (1999, p. 82) suggest that, through partnering, buyers and sellers can gain many of the advantages of vertical integration without the drawbacks associated with acquisition. These advantages include:

■ lower transaction costs;
■ assurance of supply;
■ improved coordination;
■ higher entry barriers.

This type of cooperation between buyers and sellers may manifest itself in a number of ways. They may engage in cooperative behaviour and coordinated activities in areas such as marketing, production, finance, purchasing or research and development (Hunt *et al.*, 2006, p. 72). They may include the establishment of long-term contractual commitments, the divulging of personal information and the adaptation of the production, delivery and buying processes to meet the requirements and needs of both the buyer and the seller (Palmer, 2000, p. 693). This adaptation of processes has become particularly prevalent in the motor vehicle manufacturing and FMCG distribution sectors where strategies for fast-flow replenishment are seen as necessary for competitive advantage. In the retail field, such replenishment strategies are often referred to as supplier/retailer collaboration (SRC). The GEA Consulting Group (1994), in a study for Coca-Cola, defined SRC as where:

> both retailers and suppliers share proprietary internal and external data and/or share policies and processes used in decision-making with the clear objective of sharing the benefits.

Technology has driven this information exchange even further than was envisaged in the past and systems have been developed that allow selected suppliers to monitor sales in real time. The development of customer–supplier partnering agreements has grown considerably in the past decade. Margins in the B2B sector are continually tightening, further promoting the requirement for greater efficiency and effectiveness. Rapid technological development has increased the cost of research and development (R&D) and the 'window of opportunity' for getting products and services to market has shortened, forcing companies to work together in joint research projects and joint product development programmes (Sheth and Parvatiyar, 1995, p. 410). Ideas associated with (but not dominated by) total quality management and efficient and effective management of the channels of distribution have also created a need for the flow of information between customers and suppliers.

As a result of changing markets and available technology, suppliers and retailers appear to be changing the habits of a lifetime. Whereas before they regarded each other with suspicion many now see each other as allies in the distributive chain.

Culture gap

Critical to partnering is a good understanding between partner firms. In particular, a knowledge and acceptance of each other's organisational cultures would appear crucial to successful business relationships (Phan *et al.*, 1999, p. 8; Arnett *et al.*, 2002, p. 87). Kanter (1994, pp. 99–100) talks about the need for 'chemistry' and 'compatibility' when selecting partners and that success will have more to do with people-centred factors than financial or strategic ones. Not only should there be an acceptance of cultures between organisations but also the adaptation of cultural styles and organisational mind-sets to allow partnerships to flourish. Brennan (1997, p. 766) notes the scale of the cultural divide to be bridged when he compares the 'old' with the 'desired' inter-organisational cultures that promote relationship development (see Box 9.1).

Box 9.1   Company organisational cultures

Old inter-organisational culture
We are involved in a zero sum game; if we gain then they must lose.

Desired organisational culture
We are involved in a positive sum game; together we must aim to increase our business success.

Old inter-organisational culture
Information is power; the more we know about them the better. The less they know about us the better.

Desired organisational culture
Information sharing is the key; unless we share information on a large scale, we will be unable to maximise our joint efficiency and effectiveness.

Old inter-organisational culture
Trust is for mugs; I respect my counterpart as a tough negotiator; I trust him as far as I could throw him.

Desired organisational culture
Trust will emerge naturally; gradually we will learn that each other is trustworthy, and this will improve relationship-effectiveness since we will no longer have to keep checking up.

Old inter-organisational culture
They are out to screw us and we're out to screw them.

Desired organisational culture
This is a valuable relationship; it is very unlikely that my counterpart will risk damaging it to obtain short-term advantage.

Old inter-organisational culture
Personal success is about winning; if I can consistently negotiate concessions from my counterpart then my career will go from strength to strength.

Desired organisational culture
Personal success is about mutual success; if I can demonstrate that the strength of this relationship has contributed to my company's success my career will go from strength to strength.

(*Source*: Brennan, 1997, p. 767)

Customer and supplier organisations are represented in these partnering arrangements by their employees leading to relationship development on a personal as well as organisational level. These personal bonds can be powerful and enduring although empirical evidence would suggest that they can lessen or break down once one of the participants leaves their respective organisation. Social bonds have been observed to reduce a buyer's perceived levels of risk and simplify the reordering process (Palmer, 1996, p. 22). They help build up trust between parties in the relationship by creating other situations, outside of formal meetings, by which to observe a partner. As partners interact more frequently, they tend to gain more information about their partner which reduces uncertainty (Palmatier *et al.*, 2006, p. 149).

Partnership costs and benefits

According to Brennan (1997, p. 770), the purpose of a partnership approach must be to improve the efficiency with which a value-adding system functions. He candidly notes:

> If there is no improvement in overall systematic efficiency, then the only way one party can gain is at the expense of another, in which case the firms are playing a 'zero-sum game' and are back to old-style adversarial relations. Partnering can only flourish in a 'positive-sum game' where there are real economic advantages associated with this approach to doing business.

From his research in the automobile industry, Brennan notes that the primary benefits for the supplier and the customer of the partnership approach are that:

- The supplier gains an in-depth understanding of the customer's requirements and can be proactive in suggesting product improvements.
- The supplier's personnel become familiar with the customer's 'way of doing things', potentially reducing misunderstandings and improving the speed of response.
- Greater supplier involvement (as a 'member of the team') at an early stage in new projects and new product development can increase the 'speed to market'.
- There is a reduction or elimination of the 'cost of sales' (or marketing costs) for the customer.
- The supplier is not exposed to the hazards of the marketplace, implying greater certainty about future revenues.
- The 'partner–supplier' usually gains privileged access to information about long-term customer plans, enabling a proactive stance to be taken and subsequent reinforcement of its 'preferred supplier' position.
- There is an increased information flow and greater information trustworthiness.
- The ability of both partners to focus on those aspects of the value-added chain that are their 'core competencies' is increased, enabling them to leave other aspects to their trusted partner.

Although these advantages are substantial, there is always a downside to any strategy. Partnership costs are, therefore, inevitable. Brennan (1997, p. 771) describes the potential costs to the customer and/or supplier of the partnership approach as:

■ The reduction (or dulling) of 'market incentivisation' normally created by vigorous competition (i.e. the risk that the supplier or customer becomes complacent).

■ The likelihood that external suppliers will be unwilling to bid against favoured suppliers.

■ The risk of becoming heavily committed to the wrong partners (effectively 'backing the wrong horse').

■ The sunken (i.e. committed) costs (related to customer-specific or supplier-specific investment in physical or human assets) that are more or less worthless outside of the partnership.

As with any strategy development, the costs and benefits need to be carefully considered before progressing to any partnership agreement.

Power

Power imbalance is directly related to the degree of one partner's dependence on another and this has been a focal issue in traditional and relational research (Wilson, 2000, p. 253). In organisational relationships, the 'balance of power' is rarely symmetrical (Gummesson, 1999, p. 16) with one party usually the stronger of the two. As Gummesson (1994, p. 9) notes, this is acceptable to a degree in an imperfect market but from a welfare perspective it may prove unacceptable over the long term. The balance of power will often affect how partners behave. If, for example, during a dispute the aggrieved party has the upper hand, they may adopt a more aggressive complaint resolution strategy than the aggrieved party with less authority over the situation (Boote and Pressey, 1999, p. 9).

Power and dependency in a relationship are very much a function of the relative importance of the relationship to both parties (Storbacka et al., 1994, p. 29). Imbalance of power, where one partner is seen as dominant and the other dependent,[1] creates opportunities for individual parties to pursue short-term advantage, whereas 'balanced or symmetrical dependence represents a mutual safeguard and a collective incentive to maintain a relationship' (Palmer, 1996, pp. 20–1). According to Weitz and Jap (2000, p. 235), partners in a relationship are more likely to engage in constructive conflict resolution when they are power-equals. If the power is imbalanced, then the more powerful party has little incentive to engage in joint problem-solving. It will come as no surprise to many small and medium-sized enterprises (SMEs), therefore, that relationship power imbalances are most evident when larger companies are involved. As a consequence there is a strong suggestion that the quality of buyer–seller relationships is higher among small-scale businesses operating in 'closed communities', as typified by many less developed economies (Palmer, 2000, p. 700).

An imbalance of power is potentially disruptive to any relationship. Successful partnerships appear to design agreements so that, as far as possible, power/dependence issues are avoided. However, at any particular time one partner may be a net-gainer in the partnership. The disincentive to 'cut and run' is based on the view that future gains can only be made through continuance of the relationship (Dodgson, 1993, p. 92).

The downside of B2B partnerships

As may be expected, other pitfalls (in addition to those related to costs or imbalances of power) exist for potential partners. In all relationships disagreements are probable, indeed inevitable. Complaining behaviour within a buyer–seller context can be seen as different from complaining within a consumer behaviour setting as organisational buying may involve more complexity (Boote and Pressey, 1999, p. 3). In one respect a positive 'spin' can be put on this if parties perceive these disagreements as an effective way of bringing problems out into the open, as opposed to bristling with anger and looking for new partners (Hunt and Morgan, 1994, p. 25). Even in the most serious of disagreement situations, the opportunity to threaten the ultimate sanction of leaving the relationship may be heavily restricted by barriers to exit, in particular those sunken costs of relationship development. Structural bonds develop over time as the level of investment, adaptation and shared technology grows until a point is reached when it may be difficult to terminate a relationship (Wilson, 1995, p. 339). The limited room to manoeuvre within a relationship may be a major negative. Partners trapped in such a situation are reminiscent of the 'spurious loyalists' discussed in Chapter 6.

Another potential downside relates to the length of the relationship. Despite the generally held view that the longer the association the more profitable it can be, there is also a darker side to relationships in the longer term. Inherent drawbacks exist in relationships that last any duration (Grayson and Ambler, 1999, p. 132). There is, for example, an intellectually coherent point of view that suggests that there are considerable disadvantages associated with getting 'too cosy' over time with your supplier (or customer) and that in practice these disadvantages outweigh the advantages of partnering (Brennan, 1997, p. 766). Moorman *et al.* (1992, p. 323) observe that long relationships between service providers show evidence of becoming stale or that the partners become too similar in thinking and, therefore, have less value to add. Palmer (2000, p. 696) suggests that a 'dynamic tension' in the buyer–seller relationship may be essential to achieve continuous improvements in value delivery. Long-term relationships settle into predictable patterns and lack the tension of newly formed associations. A lack of such tension, Palmer suggests, is characterised by 'gullible buyers with a low propensity to complain' and 'results in less collective benefit available to the partners'.

There appears, therefore, to be an in-built redundancy factor in relationships that do not reinvent themselves from time to time. Indeed, research suggests (Grayson and Ambler, 1999, p. 132) that many partners reach a stage where they begin to believe it is time for a change. It is interesting to note that it is in those industries where creative, fresh ideas are an important currency (e.g. advertising) that the turnover of relationships (e.g. client and agency) is perceived as greatest.

One complaint made against B2B partnering relationships is that, rather than representing a new style of business development, they are often 'old style' transaction marketing under a new guise. It may be perceived in certain industries, for example, that, whereas individual companies no longer compete against each other, 'supply chain' now competes against 'supply chain' (Christopher, 1996, p. 62) and 'network' competes against 'network' (Doyle, 1995, p. 24). There is a further serious charge that partnering relationships can have anti-competitive implications where partnering is used as a process by which a seller seeks to restrict the choice set of buyers (Palmer, 1996, p. 22). An additional danger exists when social bonds associated with close inter-organisational relationships become so pervasive that they lead to economic inefficiencies and, at the extreme, corrupt networks of buyers and sellers (p. 21).

Finally, although academics as well as the popular and business press highlight the trends towards increased buyer–seller cooperation, the trend is not universal and there is some evidence of the benefit of a spectrum of strategies. Cannon and Perreault Jr (1999, p. 6) note, for example, that while GM (General Motors) uses adversarial tactics to drive down costs, Chrysler actively cooperates with suppliers to achieve similar goals! Whether or not to partner is another example of selecting the most appropriate strategy.

Summary

This chapter has distinguished between vertical supplier–customer relationships (partnerships) and horizontal (collaborative) relationships within the business-to-business (B2B) sector. It has looked at the types of vertical relationship associated with supplier–customer partnerships (or partnering) and established that the generic objectives of these relationships is to improve the efficiency and effectiveness within the value-adding system. The importance of understanding organisational cultures was noted and the likelihood that failure is possible without changes to these cultures proposed. The reasons for the development of partnering were discussed as well as the perceived benefits and costs. The 'darker side' of longer-term relationships was also debated.

Discussion questions
1 Distinguish between vertical and horizontal relationships.
2 What part does the balance of power between the parties play in a relationship?
3 Why are closer ties likely to develop in business-to-business rather than business-to-consumer relationships?
4 Why might partnering relationships lead to 'the reduction (or dulling) of market incentivisation'?

Case study   How to . . . choose the perfect partner

The continued turbulence in the economy will result in a multitude of changes to the way the business world operates over the next few years. But it looks set to accelerate one trend – partnerships between companies and charities or non-government organisations (NGOs).

With consumer trust in the commercial world at a new low, borrowing credibility from organisations with 'social justice' and environmental change built into their mission statement could be a wise move.

Those involved in these partnerships (on both sides) agree that creating something that operates long term is the most effective route, rather than the one-off, cause-related marketing hits that were popular a few years ago.

Working wonders

Impressive results can be gained even in the short term. Procter & Gamble (P&G) is just moving into the third year of its relationship with Unicef, a deal under which P&G donates one child's vaccine for every pack of Pampers nappies sold.

In the first year, Unilever pushed its already market-leading 58 per cent of overall market spend on disposable nappies through the 60 per cent barrier, which the brand team had been aiming at for some time. By the end of the second year another percentage point had been added to market share – without any other significant marketing activity taking place over that period.

Consumer research has also shown that the partnership is bringing a long-term brand advantage to Pampers. Focus groups of consumers are regularly asked whether the brand is 'in touch with the things that are important to me'. The percentage of those who responded positively to this question increased by 13 percentage points after the first year of the Unicef tie-up – a spectacular rise in a category as stable as nappies.

Unicef has also benefitted, having received enough money from P&G to buy 23m vaccines over the two years. The duo are now globalising their activity, taking their joint-branded packs to more than 40 countries.

Jon Plant, brand manager of Pampers UK & Ireland, believes that the partnership struck such a chord with consumers 'because it's a very simple mechanic and allows a mum to instantly feel that she's made a difference to other mothers less fortunate than her'.

The authority of a non-commercial partner is valuable. Pampers buyers trust Unicef's expertise on child immunisation and P&G receives some of the halo effect of association, adding to its long-term brand strength.

Fringe benefits

Beyond sales and brand, the value of a partnership can also extend to engaging staff. Spirits firm Maxxium, owner of Famous Grouse whisky, has partnered with the Royal Society for the Protection of Birds (RSPB) for the launch of its Black Grouse brand; each bottle sold will result in a 50p donation to the charity. The money will be spent improving the habitat of the endangered Black Grouse – and Maxxium staff will be taking part in the necessary tree-planting.

'This is truly a joint partnership,' says Alison Connelly, head of marketing development at RSPB Scotland. 'We've both taken part in the Islay Whisky Festival, we've run tastings of the new whisky for our members and we feed into each other's PR plans.'

Indeed, integrating the partnership across as many of the company's activities as possible is seen as key to success. P&G has brought its major retail partners in on the Unicef tie-up for the second year of its operation, with Tesco and Asda agreeing to match P&G's donations for each pack of Pampers sold. Parenting title Prima Baby also joined in, donating a vaccine for every sale of a magazine.

The current scale and complexity of the partnership, says Plant, vindicates P&G's initial effort in finding a partner with a good fit: 'Unicef was always our first choice – its mission of securing health and equality for all the world's children fits well with our brand objective of caring for babies' development. It was also important to find a partner with the same kind of global scale as Procter & Gamble.'

Family values
A good cultural match is also important. Aunt Bessie's is a family-owned firm that has just begun a partnership with charity Age Concern. Marketing director Clare Field says that the relationship fits nicely with the company's 'family values'.

In the same way, the RSPB found the Maxxium marketing team to be 'our sort of people', according to Connelly, a belief underscored by the fact that both organisations are Scottish. Market research showed that the two organisations' customers were similarly well matched – 33 per cent of RSPB members have drunk whisky in the past year, compared with 25 per cent of the general population.

Much work was put in at the outset of the deal to ensure that the most senior people on both sides were brought into the partnership. RSPB directors were invited to a Maxxium board meeting where a toast was drunk to the deal.

This reflects a concern common among charities: 'It's really important for us to feel that the majority of senior management is behind the partnership or there's a danger that you're dropped as soon as the next big idea comes along,' says Connelly.

Everyone involved in these partnerships emphasises the importance of getting together in person, as early and as often as possible, to discuss plans. This can be challenging, especially if the activity is being extended right across the marketing mix, involving PR, media and creative agencies.

'It's essential to have an open and honest relationship,' says Aunt Bessie's Field. 'Both sides need to be very clear from the start about what they want to get out of the deal and understand that the process will involve a substantial amount of consultation before any decisions are agreed upon. We all understand that there are both commercial and social objectives to this project.'

Success for Aunt Bessie's Big Sunday Lunch, says Field, lies in three criteria: raising a significant amount of money for Age Concern; consumers feeling that the partnership is a relevant one; and, ultimately, the selling of more Aunt Bessie's products. The link will be promoted on three product lines felt to be most appropriate to the event – through Yorkshire puddings, apple pies and custard.

Raising money for a charity as a by-product of a marketing partnership might seem like a fairly straightforward element to build in. But some NGOs are realising the value of their own brand and are becoming more demanding about the terms of their associations with the commercial world.

Good business
The World Wildlife Fund (WWF) is known to be one of the environmental pressure groups most amenable to partnering with the corporate world in order to realise its

objectives of encouraging consumers and businesses to live and operate in a more sustainable way.

But, says Dax Lovegrove, head of business and industry at WWF, the organisation is now keen to move away from project-based, cause-related marketing schemes and instead to strike more lasting relationships with companies, 'to drive transformational change'.

WWF is now targeting six business sectors – food and drink, transport, finance, utilities, marine and the media – hoping to establish links that will bring in funds and raise brand awareness, as well as playing a part in establishing 'greener' business models in the corporate world.

Lovegrove argues that the latter objective doesn't necessarily work against a company's basic objective of making money. 'With all the environmental legislation about to be brought into UK law, companies will be on the back foot unless they become more carbon efficient. Both consumers and investors are more aware of these issues than ever before, and will avoid companies not seen to be embracing the new thinking.'

Partnering with an environmental group can also immediately benefit the bottom line by securing scarce resources. WWF's Forest and Trade Network consists of more than 40 companies, including B&Q and Sainsbury's, that buy timber. By partnering with WWF and agreeing to source from sustainably managed forests alone, members can all protect their future business.

One of WWF's most high-profile partnerships is with high-street bank HSBC. The HSBC Climate Partnership also involves The Climate Group, the Earthwatch Institute and the Smithsonian Tropical Research Institute, and will spend $100m (£57.5m) over five years on researching the effects of climate change on the Amazon, Ganges, Thames and Yangtze rivers.

But WWF's relationship with the bank runs even deeper than this – it claims it has helped to develop responsible lending guidelines and contributed to decisions over ethical investments.

As public-private partnerships go, this is one of the most substantial, requiring a complex set of agreements between partners. But even at a lesser level it's essential to respect the right of everyone involved to contribute to decisions, according to those with experience in the area. In practical terms, this means building in plenty of time for signing off materials at every stage of any project.

'I've had to be ruthless by insisting we build time into the approvals schedule for our Unicef contacts to sign off,' says P&G's Plant. 'The nature of Unicef means it's not unusual to find that someone has gone for a 45-day field trip – so we either need to manage that or arrange for someone else to approve the material.'

They might be more complex and time-consuming to plan than other marketing activity, but charity partnerships can offer significant benefits to the brand as well as to the bottom line. Who, in the current climate, can afford to ignore that?

(Claire Murphy, *The Marketer*, November 2008 (modified 11 May 2010))

Case study questions

1 What are the benefits to commercial organisations of the partnering described in this article?

2 What are the potential dangers for both the commercial and charitable organisation?

References

Arnett, D.B., Laverie, D.A. and McLane, C. (2002) 'Using job satisfaction and pride as internal marketing tools', *Hotel and Restaurant Administration Quarterly*, **43** (2), 87–96.

Barnes, J.G. (1994) 'Close to the customer: but is it really a relationship?', *Journal of Marketing Management*, **10**, 561–70.

Blois, K.J. (1997) 'When is a relationship a relationship?', in Gemünden, H.G., Rittert, T. and Walter, A. (eds) *Relationships and Networks in International Markets*, Oxford: Elsevier, pp. 53–64.

Blois, K.J. (1999) 'A framework for assessing relationships', competitive paper, European Academy of Marketing Conference (EMAC), Berlin, pp. 1–24.

Boote, J.D. and Pressey, A.D. (1999) 'Integrating relationship marketing and complaining behaviour: a model of conflict and complaining behaviour within buyer–seller relationships', competitive paper, European Academy of Marketing Conference (EMAC), Berlin.

Brennan, R. (1997) 'Buyer/supplier partnering in British industry: the automotive and telecommunications sectors', *Journal of Marketing Management*, **13** (8), 758–76.

Cannon, J.P. and Perreault Jr, W.D. (1999) 'Buyer–seller relationships in business markets', *Journal of Marketing Research*, **36** (4), 439.

Christopher, M. (1996) 'From brand values to customer values', *Journal of Marketing Practice*, **2** (1), 55–66.

Christopher, M., Payne, A. and Ballantyne, D. (1991) *Relationship Marketing*, London: Butterworth Heinemann.

Dodgson, M. (1993) 'Learning trust and technological collaboration', *Human Relations*, **46** (1), 77–95.

Doyle, P. (1995) 'Marketing in the new millennium', *European Journal of Marketing*, **29** (12), 23–41.

GEA Consulting Group (1994) 'Grocery distribution in the 90s: strategies for the fast flow replenishment', GEA/Coca-Cola consultancy report.

Grayson, K. and Ambler, T. (1999) 'The dark side of long-term relationships in marketing', *Journal of Marketing Research*, **36** (1), 132–41.

Grönroos, C. (2000) 'The relationship marketing process: interaction, communication, dialogue, value', in 2nd WWW Conference on Relationship Marketing, 15 November 1999 to 15 February 2000, Paper 2 <www.mcb.co.uk/services/conferen/nov99/rm> (accessed 15 November 2000).

Gummesson, E. (1994) 'Making relationship marketing operational', *International Journal of Service Industry Management*, **5**, 5–20.

Gummesson, E. (1999) *Total Relationship Marketing: Rethinking Marketing Management from 4Ps to 30Rs*, Oxford: Butterworth Heinemann.

Håkansson, H. and Ford, D. (2006) 'IMP – some things achieved, much more to do', *European Journal of Marketing*, **40** (3/4), 248–58.

Håkansson, H. and Snehota, I. (1989) 'No business is an island: the network concept of business strategy', *Scandinavian Journal of Management*, **4** (3), 187–200.

Håkansson, H. and Snehota, I.J. (2000) 'The IMP perspective, assets and liabilities of business relationships', in Sheth, J.N. and Parvatiyar, A. (eds) *Handbook of Relationship Marketing*, Thousand Oaks, CA: Sage, pp. 69–93.

Hunt, S.D. and Morgan, R.M. (1994) 'Relationship marketing in the era of network competition', *Journal of Marketing Management*, **5** (5), 18–28.

Hunt, S.D., Arnett, D.B. and Madhavaram, S. (2006) 'For dynamic relationship marketing theory: a reply to Rese', *Journal of Business and Industrial Marketing*, **21** (2), 92–3.

Kanter, R.M. (1994) 'Collaborative advantage', *Harvard Business Review*, July/August, 96–108.

Levine, S. and White, P.E. (1961) 'Exchange as a conceptual framework for the study of inter-organisational relationships', *Administrative Science Quarterly*, **5**, 583–601.

Moorman, C., Zaltman, G. and Deshpande, R. (1992) 'Relations between providers and users of market research: the dynamics of trust within and between organisations', *Journal of Marketing Research*, **29**, 314–28.

Naudé, P. and Holland, C. (1996) 'Business-to-business marketing', in Buttle, F. (ed.) *Relationship Marketing Theory and Practice*, London: Paul Chapman.

O'Toole, T. and Donaldson, W. (2000) 'Relationship governance structures and performance', *Journal of Marketing Management*, **16**, 327–41.

Palmatier, R.W., Dant, R.P., Grewal, D. and Evans, K.R. (2006) 'Factors influencing the effectiveness of relationship marketing: a meta-analysis', *Journal of Marketing*, **70** (October), 136–53.

Palmer, A.J. (1996) 'Relationship marketing: a universal paradigm or management fad?', *The Learning Organisation*, **3** (3), 18–25.

Palmer, A.J. (2000) 'Co-operation and competition: a Darwinian synthesis of relationship marketing', *European Journal of Marketing*, **34** (5/6), 687–704.

Phan, M.C.T., Styles, C.W. and Patterson, P.G. (1999) 'An empirical examination of the trust development process linking firm and personal characteristics in an international setting', European Academy of Marketing Conference (EMAC), Berlin.

Rousseau, D.M., Sitkin, S.B., Burt, R.S. and Camerer, C. (1998) 'Not so different after all: a cross discipline view of trust', *Academy of Management Review*, **23** (3), 393–404.

Shaw, E. (2003) 'Marketing through alliances and networks', in Hart, S. (ed.) *Marketing Changes*, London: Thomson, pp. 147–70.

Sheth, J.N. and Parvatiyar, A. (1995) 'The evolution of relationship marketing', *International Business Review*, **4** (4), 397–418.

Sheth, J.N. and Parvatiyar, A. (2000) 'The evolution of relationship marketing', in Sheth, J.N. and Parvatiyar, A. (eds) *Handbook of Relationship Marketing*, Thousand Oaks, CA: Sage, pp. 119–45.

Sheth, J.N. and Sisodia, R.S. (1999) 'Revisiting marketing's lawlike generalizations', *Journal of the Academy of Marketing Sciences*, **17** (1), 71–87.

Storbacka, K., Strandvik, T. and Grönroos, C. (1994) 'Managing customer relations for profit: the dynamics of relationship quality', *International Journal of Service Industry Management*, **5**, 21–38.

Tadajewski, M. (2009) 'The foundations of relationship marketing: reciprocity and trade relations', *Marketing Theory*, **9** (1), 9–38.

Webster Jr, F.E. (1992) 'The changing role of marketing in the corporation', *Journal of Marketing*, **56** (October), 1–17.

Weitz, B.A. and Jap, S.D. (2000) 'Relationship marketing and distribution channels', in Seth, J.N. and Parvatiyar, A. (eds) *Handbook of Relationship Marketing*, Thousand Oaks, CA: Sage, pp. 209–44.

Wilson, D.T. (1995) 'An integrated model of buyer–seller relationships', *Journal of the Academy of Marketing Science*, **23** (4), 335–45.

Wilson, D.T. (2000) 'An integrated model of buyer–seller relationships', in Sheth, J.N. and Parvatiyar, A. (eds) *Handbook of Relationship Marketing*, Thousand Oaks, CA: Sage, pp. 245–70.

Note

1 Palmer (1996, p. 20) alternatively calls this 'absence of symmetrical dependence'.

10 External partnerships

Key issues

- Horizontal partnerships
- Networks
- Industry collaboration
- External collaboration
- Relationship life cycles
- Legislative, agency and pressure group relationships

Introduction

In the previous chapter, a distinction was made between vertical relationships (partnering) and horizontal relationships (collaboration). This chapter will concentrate on those horizontal relationships that were earlier described as being represented by organisations at the same point in the channel of distribution[1] (including competitors) who seek to cooperate and collaborate for mutual benefit. In addition, this chapter will look at other relationships (e.g. with governments) that are, strictly speaking, non-commercial, but which have the potential to affect the commercial viability of an organisation.

Horizontal partnerships

Over the past two decades there has been considerable growth in the number of horizontal partnerships between competitors or other complementary players. These types of collaboration have significantly changed the competitive landscape as well as greatly extending the complexity of inter-firm relationships. The rise of strategic network competition, where firms compete within networks with other networks (Hunt *et al.*, 2006, p. 72), has further changed the competitive nature of whole industries including aviation and automobile manufacturing. **Resource dependence theory** (Varadarajan and Cunningham, 2000, p. 282) suggests that few organisations are self-sufficient in critical resources, but this is more than casual relationships. Internationalisation, rapid advances in technology, a changing industrial base and increasingly active customers are among the reasons why organisations are entering these alliances, partnerships, joint ventures, licensing agreements and networks (Shaw, 2003, p. 149).

As with the previous chapter, the concentration here is almost wholly on the business-to-business (B2B) sector. The growth in consumer networks (particularly via the Internet; see Box 10.1) is apparent, and may prove to be very significant in the future (see Chapter 12). It is in the B2B sector, however, that collaborations and networks of associations and relationships are currently more obviously developing. It is also more evident that many of the 'higher forms' of relationship discussed in previous chapters are more likely to develop in the B2B sector than in most consumer markets.

Box 10.1   Consumer network developments

Although consumer networks (effectively consumers collaborating to achieve a particular objective) are rare in today's economy, they do exist and there is some evidence to suggest that they are likely to increase in the future. In the past families and friends have got together to buy in bulk (e.g. a whole carcass from the butcher) at a much reduced price. Indeed the origins of the Co-operative Movement had the collective spending power of the consumer as its driving force. In more recent years 'share portfolio' clubs have developed where pooled resources cut costs and shared decision-making potentially increases efficiency and effectiveness.

The limitation with these types of collaboration is usually geographical as extended distribution arrangements add to costs. It is also generally true that the more widespread the membership, the less collaborators have an opportunity to meet. The Internet has the potential to remove this geographical dependence. Already there is the example of the American consumer who, unhappy about the price quoted for her new car, used the Internet to trawl for other potential buyers. As a result she was able to return to the dealership with multiple orders for which she was now quoted a significantly lower price.

That consumer networks have potential is evident. To succeed they invariably rely on a 'leading partner' who effectively fulfils the function of an intermediary, or 'middleman'. The distinction between the leading partner as the customer or the supplier becomes, therefore, very blurred. Chaffey *et al.* (2000, p. 196) see an alternative in the form of market intermediaries working on behalf of clients. They suggest that 'as customers become aware of the value of information and as technology on the Internet enables them to protect private information relating to site visits and transactions so the opportunity for intermediaries to act as customer agents grows'. The sole source of revenue for these new 'infomediaries' will derive from the value they generate for their clients.

Relationship research

According to Blois (1998, p. 256), an observer watching two organisations' behaviour is able to make an assessment of the current state of the relationship between them when:

■ the observer has knowledge of the contractual terms under which the exchange is being conducted;

■ the observer can observe the exchange process over an extended period of time;

■ the participants give explanations of the reasons why the observed actions were undertaken.

Subject to some measure of access, research of this type may be seen as relatively straightforward in the B2B sector. Indeed, many researchers (especially from the IMP Group) have taken advantage of the relative visibility in the sector to examine, sometimes in great detail, the interactions between partner companies and their employees. This contrasts with the consumer goods sector (B2C), where most relationships are non-contractual and where consumers' motivations (despite the valiant attempt of researchers) are largely hidden, making assessment of relationships considerably more difficult. Add to this the probability that many consumers have little motivation to explain their actions (if indeed they actually know why these actions took place) and the difficulties of RM researchers in the B2C area are evident.

As a result of the greater openness in B2B marketing a considerable volume of research literature has been produced. While not always consistent (particularly in the language used to describe these relationships), this has provided a wealth of evidence about why networking and collaboration are becoming so widespread.

Networks and collaborations

There is considerable confusion in the usage and meaning of terms such as **networks**, **collaborations** and other associations (e.g. **alliances**). These terms change meaning with different authorship and are frequently used interchangeably depending on the circumstances described. In respect to this chapter the following descriptions are offered:

■ *Networks*: Networks are seen as relationships between individuals (as opposed to organisations). 'Networkers' utilise their 'contacts' in a sometimes systematic, but more often *ad hoc*, way. These 'personal contact networks', according to Chaston (1998, p. 276), are 'constituted of formal and informal co-operative relationships whereby individual owners/managers seek to build links with each other in their market with the aim of obtaining the necessary information and knowledge to optimise organisational performance'.

■ *Collaborations*: Collaborative relationships are perceived as more formal relation-ships between organisations in the sense that they are recognised on a company-wide basis. These may be contractual, but as Gummesson (1999, p. 130) notes, 'trust cannot be assured through contracts and those that believe that lawyers can prevent the risks and hurdles of collaboration are bound to be disillusioned'. By the very nature of business, however, they are likely to include more formal meetings and involve the establishment of agreements and procedures on the form and nature of the collaboration.

Networks

Networking is a managerial buzzword which continues to have resonance in the new millennium. As networking is more individual than organisational it may be valid to suggest that 'networking' is more effective on a smaller rather than a larger scale. It has been suggested, for example, that personal networks offer opportunities for small firms, in particular, to compete more effectively with larger companies (Chaston, 1998, pp. 275–6).

A network consists of a collection of individuals (see Figure 10.1), albeit individuals who are likely to have organisational affiliations and can use the benefits derived from networking for the good of their individual companies. According to Keegan (1999, p. 175), executives from global organisations obtain as much as two-thirds of the information they receive through personal sources. Certain businesses thrive on networking while others actually depend on the network of contacts developed by their employees (e.g. financial services). In general most companies recognise

Figure 10.1
Business-to-business networks

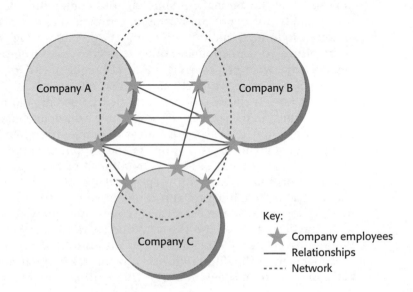

Key:
★ Company employees
—— Relationships
- - - - Network

the value in knowledge terms of their staff developing a network of contacts with associate and competitive companies, other industries and other influential players (e.g. government) and explicitly encourage it.

Informal and *ad hoc* contact is of considerable importance. Formal relationships between these network players are unlikely and may even be barred by government legislation (e.g. if there is any attempt by networkers to manipulate a market). Despite this informality, such networks can be both strong and enduring. Social relationships are not discouraged and can indeed be the 'glue' that holds these networks together.

Networks are not a new phenomenon nor is the blur between acceptable and unacceptable behaviour in commercial relationships a new debate. Where, for example, should the line be drawn on corporate entertainment? Is it an unfair advantage that a decision-maker and potential supplier see each other socially? Is the membership of organisations that promote kinship ethical? Social membership of organisations such as the Freemasons, Rotary Clubs and even working men's clubs has always had a self-help element to it that is clear to members, if sometimes less acceptable to those outside. What is evident is that the growing complexity of network organisations and the interdependency of members renders much subsequent analysis simplistic (Palmer, 2000, p. 690).

Collaboration

To many the future of business is collaboration. Firms are engaging in cooperative behaviour and the coordination of activities in all areas of business including marketing, manufacturing, finance, purchasing and research and development (Hunt *et al.*, 2006, p. 72). Over the past decade authors have battled to describe systematically the types of cooperation that were apparent in the marketplace. The number and range of such relationships typically defy neat pigeonholing. Brandenburger and Nalebuff (1996), for example, coined the phrase '**cooptition**' to describe what at first sight appears to be the anomaly of simultaneous competition and collaboration. Even before the term 'cooptition' was used, terms such as alliances, partnerships, joint ventures, joint R&D, minority investments, cross-licensing, sourcing relationships, co-branding, co-marketing and other cooperative descriptions were being used to describe what was being recognised as a 'key requirement' for successfully competing in the global marketplace (Sheth and Sisodia, 1999, p. 81).

So pervasive is collaboration seen to be that decades-old marketing concepts are being rewritten in the language of cooperative behaviour. Gummesson (1999, p. 127), for example, updates the 1980s 'forces of competition' model (involving present and potential competitors, customers and suppliers; Porter, 1985, p. 5) which he interprets, 'in the spirit of RM', as 'relationships forces giving birth to alliances'. Governments too have noted the spectacular increase in 'collaborative agreements' and are having to reinterpret anti-competitive legislation to take this into account. In 2010, for example, the European Commission approved British Airway's alliance with American Airlines and Iberia. While US regulators gave these and their 'One World Alliance' partners immunity from anti-trust legislation.

Collaboration should not, however, be mistaken for altruism or an end to competition. Indeed, in some industries competition is more intense than ever as one 'alliance' battles with another in a bid for greater market share (e.g. the airline industry – see Box 10.2). It is also widely recognised that collaborative relationships can, if restrictions are not observed, have anti-competitive implications (Palmer, 1996, p. 22). They can give birth to 'power networks' which create partly locked markets (Gummesson, 1999, p. 131). So potentially powerful are these collaborations that legislators around the world keep a very close eye on such agreements and have developed powers, where necessary, to prohibit them.

Collaboration types

Collaboration can be crudely divided into two types:

- *Industry collaboration*: with competitors in the same market sector and where objectives may include effectiveness and efficiency of distribution channels, servicing or other support facilities and market sector growth or market sector dominance. Distinguishing features of intra-industry strategic collaborations are that the partners tend to be rivals competing for market share in the same product/service market, in the same market segments, in different segments or in different geographic markets (Varadarajan and Cunningham, 2000, p. 216).

- *External collaboration*: where collaborators (usually from different industries) bring different skills, competencies and assets to the relationship. The objective of external collaboration is often to take advantage of a new sector or to promote existing sector differentiation (e.g. Mercedes and Swatch – see Box 10.5).

Industry collaboration

Industry collaboration is becoming a key marketing strategy as firms recognise the possibilities of a 'positive-sum game' where a degree of cooperation results in greater value creation and enlargement of the market for all participants (Sheth and Sisodia, 1999, p. 81). Industry collaboration is not new. Trade associations have existed for centuries and were set up with the aim of setting of agreed standards. They often used generic advertising to encourage market growth (e.g. Meat Marketing Board, International Wool Secretariat).

According to Sheth and Sisodia (p. 82), market share will continue to be an important concept but it is fundamentally a 'zero-sum' or 'win–lose' proposition compared with industry collaboration. Most authors agree that collaboration (like partnering) should aim to be a 'win–win' relationship if it is to succeed. Equity is also seen as vital. In this type of relationship, parties must treat each other as equals and partners, otherwise there is the likelihood that one party will act covertly to out-manoeuvre the other (Gummesson, 1999, p. 130).

Market-share thinking, therefore, has to be counterbalanced with a 'market-growth orientation' as an industry growing the total market collaboratively is often less costly to its individual firms (Sheth and Sisodia, 1999, p. 82). There is also what

Gummesson calls 'tacit alliances', which emerge through such industry consensus and which result in all members acting in the same way. The plus side of these 'tacit alliances' is that they can instil ethical behaviour into an industry. On the negative side they may uphold past bad practices at the expense of the future of the industry.

The current growth area in industry collaboration is in so-called alliances. This is where a group or groups of competitors (as opposed to the whole industry) collaborate to achieve cost and efficiency objectives. At one extreme a strategic alliance can encompass all the functional areas; at the other extreme it may be limited in scope to a single functional area (e.g. marketing) or value activity (Varadarajan and Cunningham, 2000, p. 274). It is in the airline industry that the development of alliances is most prevalent (see Box 10.2 and 10.3). An airline may, for example, belong to one group for sales purposes but to another for engine maintenance – even if that

Box 10.2 Airline Alliances

One World Alliance	Star Alliance	Sky Team
American Airlines	Adria	Aeroflot
British Airways	Aegean	Aeromexico
Cathay Pacific	Air Canada	Air Europe
Finair	Air China	Air France/KLM
Iberia	Air New Zealand	Alitalia
Japan Airlines (JAL)	ANA	China Southern
LAN	Asiana Airlines	Czech Airlines
Malév	Austrian	Delta
Mexicana	Blue	Kenyan Airways
Quantas	BMI	Korean Air
Royal Jordanian	Brussels Airline	Tarom
	Continental Airline	Vietnam Airlines
	Croatia Airline	
	Eygptair	
	LOT Polish Airlines	
	Lufthansa	
	SAS Scandinavian Airline	
	Shanghai Airline	
	Singapore Airline	
	South African Airways	
	Spanair	
	Swiss Airlines	
	TAM	
	TAP	
	Thai	
	Turkish Ailines	
	United	
	US Airways	

means servicing its sales competitor's aircraft (Palmer, 2000, p. 689). For the airlines involved the objectives of such alliances are improved competitiveness, increased sales, increased revenue and lower cost through coordination of destinations, time-tables, reservation systems, ticketing and staffing (Gummesson, 1999, p. 129).

Industry-driven alliances have a history that stretches back across the twentieth century. A good example is the Associated Merchandising Corporation (AMC). AMC was formed at the beginning of the twentieth century to source merchandise for a number of North American department stores, including Bloomingdales of New York, Filenes of Boston, Bullocks of Los Angeles and other, originally independent, stores, each of which held a 'share' of AMC's equity. Although the ownership of these stores is now concentrated in fewer hands, it still operates on the basis of delivering collaborative gains in merchandise cost and distribution efficiency and effectiveness to its 'member' stores. In Japan conglomerate-type industrial groups, known as *Keiretsus*, have existed since after the Second World War (and their precursors, *Zaibatus,* since the nineteenth century). These *Keiretsus* are made up of a complex web of interacting independent companies, often with interlinked ownership, which cooperate with each other as 'systems' through which to share skills and resources to achieve competitive advantage (Chaston, 1998, p. 275; Varadarajan and Cunningham, 2000, p. 289).

Alliances come in all shapes and sizes. They can vary considerably in intensity and duration, may be 'one-shot projects', continuous cooperation or take parties so close that the next step is to consider merger (Gummesson, 1999, p. 127). The recent mergers between Air France and KLM, and British Airways and Iberia[2] are notable examples of this.

External collaboration

Collaboration frequently (and with growing regularity) means arrangements between organisations from different market sectors, each of which bring different skills, competencies and assets to a relationship. Inter-industry collaborations[3] are often propelled by 'the convergence of industries and the complexity and muliplicity of

---

Box 10.3   Aer Lingus: changing face

Aer Lingus is a former member of One World Alliance which, because of the airline's decision to drop certain services, it had to leave on 31 March 2007. Whilst it is not officially connected any more to one of the airline alliances (see Box 10.2) it code-shares with One World, Star Alliance and Sky Team members as well as other independent carriers. It also has a shared frequent flyer programme with British Airways, Cathay Pacific, United Airlines and Quantas. The airline is currently operating a strategy to compete with the European 'no-frills' airlines such as Ryanair, Easy Jet and German Wings and plan their own 'no-frills' intercontinental flights in the future. Business Class travel and cargo provision for short-haul flights (a requirement for One World Alliance members) have been phased out.

technologies underlying the product [or service] of these emergent industries' (Varadarajan and Cunningham, 2000, p. 288). These relationships may be for the purposes of improving the total package offering (e.g. the collaboration between British Airways and Hertz) or to create a distinctive advantage in an existing market sector (e.g. Sky Television and Granada Television with a variety of Premier League football teams). Alternatively, they may be developed to take advantage of a new market sector (see Boxes 10.4 and 10.5). It is in the area of 'new sector development', particularly those associated with recent technological advances, that collaborations are expected to have the greatest growth potential.

Box 10.4   Handbag.com

Handbag.com is, in Internet parlance, a 'vertical portal' (or 'vortal') aimed at women. Vertical portals are Internet sites which include links to other (often retail) sites and where revenue is largely derived from advertising and sponsorship. Handbag.com was launched in October 1999 as a 50/50 joint venture between the pharmaceutical and beauty product retailer Boots and Hollinger Telegraph New Media. Boots brought to the venture extensive experience of retailing to the site's target female market. Hollinger Telegraph New Media (the media management and investment division of Hollinger International) brought extensive experience of Internet publishing, including the *Electric Telegraph*, one of the UK's best online news websites. The typical Handbag.com user (or handbagger) is said by the company to be between 25 and 45, likely to be in the higher earning ABC_1 demographic and either married or living with a partner in the house she owns. Having established itself as a highly successful portal Handbag.com became part of the Hearst Digital Network, the digital division of the National Magazine Company Limited in October 2006.

Box 10.5   The Smart Car

The concept of the Smart Car was initially championed by Swiss Watch manufacturer Swatch. As Swatch had no experience of automobiles they sought to collaborate with established car manufacturers. Initially they approached Volkswagen before teaming up with the Mercedes division of Daimler-Benz. Designed as a fun, sporty vehicle for young people it was originally nicknamed the Swatchmobile. The eventual name, 'Smart', was nothing to do with its perceived advantages of an electronic car designed for the city but an anagram for Swatch Mercedes Art. In 1994, a joint venture was established. The first concept car was premiered at the Atlanta and Paris Car Shows in 1996 and the first production line model, the Smart Fortwo, came out in 1998. Although Swatch were to pull out of the venture because of initial heavy losses, the project would probably never have got off the ground without them and the vision of the Swatch CEO Nicholas Hayek.

Developing collaborative relationships

Successful collaborations of any sort are not created overnight but develop over time, dependent upon the desired level of closeness and/or the complexity of the relationship. Collaborative relationships mature with interaction, frequency, duration and the diversity of challenge that relationship partners encounter and face together (Lewicki *et al.*, 1998, p. 443), ultimately becoming part of the structural capital of the organisation (Gummesson, 1999, p. 5). Tzokas and Saren (2000, p. 8) suggest that this development can be represented by a 'relationship life cycle' that develops through different stages. Each of these stages, they suggest, presents unique requirements and opportunities for those involved. These life cycle stages are shown in Figure 10.2.

Tzokas and Saren suggest that specific knowledge requirements are a necessity at each stage of the cycle. At the introduction stage partners seek a mutual understanding of each other's capabilities and concerns and their potential for strategic, behavioural, cultural and purpose 'fit'. Trust at this stage is based on rational evaluation. At the experimental stage the first joint tasks are undertaken, testing the effectiveness and efficiency of the relationship and helping develop appreciation by the collaborators of each other's capabilities. Trust is, at this stage, seen to be based on a working knowledge of the partnership. At the identification stage closer and more ambitious collaboration may be undertaken and the boundaries between the organisations may begin to dissolve. Organisational and relational skills are required at this point to maintain the strategic purpose and direction of the collaboration.

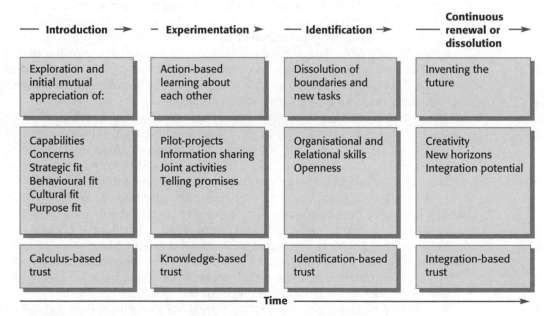

Figure 10.2 Relationship stages   (*Source*: Adapted from Tzokas and Saren, 2000, p. 8)

Identification-based trust, characterised by a mutual sharing of values, becomes more evident. In the final (continuous renewal or dissolution) stage two options are put forward. If the relationship has run its course (e.g. if it has become stale or less productive), then dissolution may be the end result. Alternatively, renewal may take place if partners identify new tasks to be performed and have the ability to reinvent the relationship. Trust at this stage is integral to the operation.

Tzokas and Saren's model illustrates the potential for collaborative relationships. The existence of such relationships implies a degree of mutual dependency that blunts the ability of either partner to part from the other without some degree of inconvenience (Brennan, 1997, p. 770). The 'usual warnings' must, however, be made concerning models of this type. The movement is not necessarily unidirectional as relationships can be scaled down as well as up, depending on perceived needs at a particular point in time. In addition, many relationships will never reach the stage where organisational boundaries are seen to dissolve if partners are content to operate at a lower relationship intensity.

Downsides

A variety of environmental factors influence the stability (and indeed the acceptability) of cooperative relationships, including the general values of the society in which the exchanges occur and the specific history of actions and reactions by individuals within that society (Palmer, 2000, p. 690). There is a very fine line between cooperation and collusion (Sheth and Sisodia, 1999, p. 81) and different societies are prone to draw the line according to established national practice. Thus, what is acceptable cooperation in Japan may be regarded as anti-competitive in the USA and the European Union. Even within national boundaries regulators are prone to 'move the goalposts' in support of their own companies' self-interest. For example, whereas in the UK it is acceptable for former public utilities to come under foreign ownership, UK companies cannot do the same in some European countries.

Operational defects may also prove damaging. According to Palmer (2000, p. 687), cooperation that is too pervasive may have the effect of reducing efficiency and effectiveness in a market. For example, the extensive networks of cooperative relationships among Japanese distributors can add three levels to the distributive system with a consequent increase in costs. A further common occurrence in systems where social relationships become intermingled with business relationships is that 'altruism' may be extended by one partner (e.g. accepting goods which fail to meet their expectations of value) to preserve the standing of the other partner (Palmer, 2000, p. 700). Another problem associated with making relationships work is 'culture clash' (see Chapter 9). The potential battle between two corporate cultures can be hazardous. Confrontation between value systems and cultural shock are, according to Gummesson (1999, p. 130), the rule rather than the exception.

The value of replacing one competitive system with another (albeit collaborative) system must also be questioned. As Palmer (2000, p. 700) notes:

The development of co-operative marketing alliances, which result in competition between networks of organisations, rather than between individual organisations may transfer this selfish instinct to the network rather than the individual firm.

The danger also exists that marketers are misreading the partnership and collaboration runes and that relationships of this type are a phase rather than a wholly new direction. Certainly, while the number of collaborative agreements continues to rise, there are still examples of mega-mergers continuing apace. There is also evidence of a growing number of equity investments between collaborators that may drive further mergers in the future. Alternatively, this may simply reflect the diversity of the marketplace and the need for a spectrum of strategies.

Collaborations need to be constantly worked upon if they are to succeed. Gummesson (1999, p. 131) recognises the problems associated with maintaining relationships when he proposes:

The advice provided by a marriage councillor is surprisingly well suited for the advice needed for a company entering an alliance – choose your partner carefully, invest in a win–win relationship, stay attractive to your partner, develop a sound economy, and search for a division of labour that works for all parties. Good vibrations are needed, even if it is not passionate love. Still we know that decisions on cohabitation are taken under uncertainty with no guarantee whatsoever of the outcome.

Other relationships

Other important external liaisons exist in addition to those so far discussed in this and the previous chapter. These include relationships with:

- local, national and supranational legislators;
- national and international agencies;
- pressure groups.

Legislators

Companies have long recognised the importance of maintaining good relationships with legislators. After all, legislators have it within their power to considerably benefit or jeopardise the health of commercial organisations. There is, however, a significant difference between the types of relationship permitted with legislators and those between commercial firms. Whereas commercial companies (within the scope of anti-competitive legislation) are free to establish whatever depth of relationship the parties see fit, relationships with legislators at anything less than arm's length are perceived as potentially corrupt practice in most developed economies. To suggest it never happens would be naïve. Both parties are, however, aware that there are boundaries (albeit unclear) that they should avoid crossing.

'Lobbying'[4] is the all-embracing term most often used to describe the methodologies applied to influence government. Although the term implies influence through argument, the general meaning is 'to influence or solicit' (politicians) and a wider range of techniques are used in addition to straightforward argument. Thus, lobbying may take the form of information transmission (ensuring legislators have the information to make a decision), influence (ensuring that the company's or industry's position is clear), general 'public relations' activities (e.g. social events, trips) or political party funding.

Having the ear of government (or the potential future government) is seen as so important that substantial sums are spent (and sometimes mis-spent) on funding such activities. It is often said that only companies with monetary resources can indulge themselves in political lobbying. On the other hand democracy works best when governments can discuss proposals with appropriate interest groups (Baines *et al.*, 2004, p. 372). Companies also see it as useful to bring political appointees into their businesses for advice and lobbying purposes. In the UK, for example, the most common type of interest declared in the House of Common's Register of Members' Interests is payment from organisations that employ them although a number of recent scandals have led to some curbing of this. The line between acceptable and unacceptable influence is, however, still very blurred.

In addition, it should not be forgotten that governments (local, national and supranational) are large existing and potential customers and that, from the supplier perspective, relationship maintenance will be directed to this end (Zineldin, 2000, p. 20). Given the level of public accountability for this expenditure, however, the development of personal relationships is (technically) severely restricted.

Agencies

As with legislators, local, national and international agencies (or quangos) can be influential in many industries (e.g. road building and construction) in that they often have the ear of governments and, in many cases, have substantial buying power. There has been a considerable growth in 'agencies' in many countries (e.g. UK, New Zealand), with a growing number of previously directly controlled departmental operations being privatised. As with legislators, the level of relationship will be determined by acceptable practice. The greater freedom of previously government-run businesses (e.g. the UK Post Office) has meant some easing of the 'rules' (written and unwritten) covering formal and informal relationships between these organisations and those in the private sector. The high public profile of such organisations, however, normally ensures that such relationships rarely reach the levels established between other commercial companies.

Pressure groups

There are a growing number of pressure groups whose actions can influence and affect the commercial viability and long-term success of a business. Direct conflict with such pressure groups can appear inequitable at times with apparently small, ill-financed groups taking on large, multinational corporations. The Internet has only served to heighten such groups influence (see Box 7.3). Such groups' can have an influence with consumers and legislators sometimes considerably out of proportion to their size, as companies such as Shell and McDonald's can testify. Frequently (but by no means always) commercial organisations find themselves in opposition to such groups. Whereas complete agreement may not always be possible, maintaining a dialogue with such groups may be in an organisation's best interest.

Conclusion

There is little doubt that horizontal relationships are of current and growing importance in many industries. Gummesson (1999, p. 127) suggests that, for companies such as Corning, collaboration is so central to their business strategy that the corporation calls itself a 'network of organisations'. He goes on to note (p. 129) that five US corporations were represented in 400 formal alliances and countless informal ones. These include IBM (136), AT&T (77), Hewlett-Packard (65), Digital Equipment (63) and Sun Microsystems (45). In those industries driven by new technologies, the value of such strategies is particularly apparent with partners and collaborators bringing diverse skills and knowledge to the relationship.

There is, however, no guarantee that such collaborations will always produce results. In a study by McKinsey (quoted in Gummesson, 1999, p. 130), of 49 collaborations studied, one-third failed. Whereas collaboration in general is seen as beneficial and can contribute to the effectiveness and efficiency of an operation, such outcomes are far from a foregone conclusion. Important decisions need to be made concerning the validity of all such collaborations, the level of closeness and the probable duration. In addition, companies should not just have 'collaboration'-forming strategies but plans in place to be implemented when such relationships have run their course.

Summary

This chapter looked at horizontal partnerships and other potential partnerships external to the organisation. It noted the considerable increase of such arrangements between competitors and other complementary players, which may or may not come from a single industry. The chapter differentiated between 'networking' and 'collaborations', subdividing the latter into 'industry collaboration', usually with competitors, and 'external collaboration' with other companies that could offer different skills, competencies and assets to a partnership. The chapter noted that successful collaborations are not created overnight and presented a 'relationship life cycle', describing the factors observed at each stage in the relationship. The importance of other relationships with, for example, governments, agencies and pressure groups was also highlighted.

Discussion questions
1 Distinguish between network and collaborative strategies.
2 Where would you draw the line between collaboration and collusion?
3 Suggest examples of (a) industry collaboration and (b) external collaboration.
4 Why might organisations wish to maintain relationships with consumer or other pressure groups?

Case study   Mumsnet's the word

When the 2010 general election is scrutinised by academics a few decades from now, one phrase is sure to bob to the surface. 'The Mumsnet election' will either be seen as an important early milestone in the evolution of the great national – and maybe global – institution that Mumsnet has become. Or it could prove to be no more than a footnote relating to an enterprise that flourished briefly at the dawn of the 21st century before it was overtaken by a more cutting-edge social networking phenomenon and drifted to the fringes of cyberspace, only to disappear for ever.

Which of these scenarios will come to pass is hard to call right now. But the fact that an enterprise set up by two mothers at the height of the dot.com boom on little more than a wing and a prayer has survived at all, let alone managed to persuade leading politicians of all hues that it is indispensable, ranks as quite an achievement.

Gordon Brown was the first of the leaders to visit Mumsnet's offices for a webchat last October; he was followed a month later by David Cameron and, in January, by Nick Clegg. Other politicians who have been falling over themselves to hitch their keyboard to the Mumsnet server include Ed Miliband, Harriet Harman, Ed Balls and David 'two brains' Willetts.

For the uninitiated – which means you're probably male, childless or both – Mumsnet is a kind of web portal that describes itself as 'by parents for parents', albeit, in practice, just 1% of users have a Y chromosome. Its main business is talk, with the conversation embracing conception tips, pregnancy, childbirth, breastfeeding, baby foods, nursery and schooling, plus a raft of topics that have less to do with children, including relationships, sex, books, travel and, of course, politics. A particularly popular strand is dubbed 'Am I being unreasonable?' and allows users to rant about just about anything.

The 'Mumsnet election' tag was dreamed up by Rachel Sylvester of *The Times*, who noted that 'all the parties have decided that women are the key to electoral success, that the family will be a critical issue when the country goes to the polls and that the Internet is a vital campaign tool'.

And it's a label that Mumsnet co-founder Justine Roberts is in no hurry to disown. 'We are totemic of something, even if that doesn't mean we hold the key to the election,' she reflects. 'Women are important in this election because they are less tribal and more floating, more swingable than men. And all three leaders have young children, so family issues are naturally at the forefront.'

The question is, can the remarkable degree of influence and the impressive user base of Mumsnet be converted into something that is financially sustainable and even commercially successful? Will it make the leap from community to become a gold-plated brand and money-making machine such as Saga is for the over-fifties? Or would success be seen by its loyal followers as treachery, a betrayal of the community values that attracted them in the first place?

These are just some of the questions I'd been mulling over before meeting Roberts at the cringingly named 'Mumsnet Towers', which turned out to be a floor in an anonymous office building in Kentish Town, north London. Considering the volume of chatter on the site, the place is eerily quiet, with only half a dozen of the 25-odd staff there, thanks to flexible working.

Back in 2000, Roberts had the idea that became Mumsnet during her first holiday with her twins at a resort in Florida. 'All the parents were moaning how un-child friendly it was, and how they wished they'd known,' she says. 'So the idea I had was for parents to provide each other with peer-to-peer information and advice.'

Roberts was not entirely lacking in business acumen: she'd worked as an economist and strategist at Warburg, quitting the City when she concluded it was incompatible with children, to become a sports journalist. Even that didn't work, as it was male-dominated and meant working mainly evenings and weekends, so she was looking for an occupation that would fit in with family life. She roped in TV producer Carrie Longton from her ante-natal class, on the promise that they could work when it suited and hold meetings in the Jacuzzi at the gym.

With the dot.com boom raging, they set out to grab a slice of the riches on offer. 'We were close to raising €4.5m, but it fell through when boo.com went bust. It's probably a good thing, because we would have been saddled with huge overheads.'

Instead, they set up with a €25,000 loan from a friend, and adopted a less pressured organic route to growth. Mumsnet quickly evolved in a way that hadn't been entirely predicted: a piece of forum software purchased for €25 became the Talk section, which now accounts for 85% of traffic; and it was soon clear that mums were the main audience. ('Men don't chat in the same way – we do have a section for them, but they tend to use the site mainly searching for information.')

For five years, neither founder even took a salary, as Mumsnet slowly built up its numbers and developed a modest income stream from advertising. What first put Mumsnet on the map was a row with parenting guru Gina Ford in 2007; she sued when parents posted comments that she considered defamatory, and although the company ended up making an apology and paying undisclosed damages, the publicity sent the number of users soaring.

Now Mumsnet receives 20 million hits a month and 20,000 posts a day, with 200,000 signed-up members and an estimated one million users. (The only incentive to sign-up is that you can post, but Roberts says: 'Our survey indicates we have 20 lurkers to every poster.') These are numbers that should make it of serious interest to advertisers, as they have to politicians. Roberts is quick to point out that Mumsnetters are a highly educated group with 75% having a degree.

Indeed, advertising is the mainstay of Mumsnet's business, accounting for about three-quarters of last year's revenues of approximately €1.7m. Banner advertisers range from the predictable parent categories of pushchairs, washing detergents and educational publishers to those with more of a lifestyle angle: Boden and Mark Warner are two prominent supporters.

The challenge has been to broaden the advertiser base. 'Advertisers do tend to look at us as mums with babies,' says Jules Kendrick, Mumsnet's commercial manager. 'But our users buy clothes, perfumes, property, everything.'

Surveys and consumer testing of products have provided a more subtle form of advertiser revenue and have landed Mumsnet's biggest fish to date, carmaker Ford. Mumsnet may have put off some advertisers by taking an ethical stance: it declared itself a 'Nestle-free zone' and turned away McDonald's after consulting users. 'We won't do cosmetic surgery advertising and we're very sceptical about slimming,' says Roberts. 'We also won't take formats like expandables and pop-ups. Our policy is not to take any advertising that contradicts our aim to make parents' lives easier.'

Other income comes from click-through to the stores in Mumsnet Mall and from a fledgling move into offline content, most notably a range of Mumsnet guidebooks.

But although the potential for commercial exploitation may look huge, it's an idea that Roberts baulks at. 'It's not that we don't want to make money, but it hasn't been our priority,' she says. 'I'd like to create a different model, where we can ethically make money, with the consent of our community.'

This ambivalence towards raw commerce is reiterated when she describes Mumsnet as 'something that is not quite a business'. The community, as she sees it, is Mumsnet's stakeholders, and there's no room for investors or moneymaking activities that would alienate them.

Plans are, nevertheless, afoot for new moneymaking ventures and Roberts does not rule out introducing pay-walls for some of Mumsnet's content in the manner of Rupert Murdoch's newspaper empire, but is determined not to exclude people who can't pay.

And further evidence that Mumsnet is not a conventional business comes from its campaigning activities. So far, it has taken up the cudgels on a range of issues, from opposing formula milk to helping families in the developing world. An advertising campaign that declared 'Career women make bad mothers' was pulled after a mass letter-writing campaign on Mumsnet; while an 11-point code of practice to get better care for women suffering miscarriage is set to be adopted in large part by the Department of Health.

The picture, then, is of an enterprise that is more than just a business, bringing together a community of parents, wielding significant influence, campaigning on ethical issues and providing fulfilling employment to its people. So far, so good. Yet Mumsnet also has its critics – quite a few of them – and their viewpoint is damning. Libby Purves recently wrote: 'The Mumsnet obsession is a patronising sideshow.' Many women complain that while Mumsnet garners all the attention, it doesn't represent them, while more specific is the complaint that its Talk forum is full of bullying and abuse rather than the sisterly love it is meant to enshrine. As one reader puts it: 'Foul-mouthed and vicious I found it, in my one brief venture. Hunting in packs. Nasty.'

And there's another, potentially more serious charge; that Mumsnet is not in control of its message. Newspapers and other traditional media decide on their own editorial stance, which enables them to set the tone of their conversation and pitch it to their audience. In this way, they can effectively manage and strategically guide their own brand. But it is Mumsnet's users who decide what they want to post about, and nothing is censored before it appears on the site. The Gina Ford case highlighted the ease with which a forum such as Mumsnet can be hijacked by one vociferous group, resulting in potentially costly litigation.

Roberts' response is to argue that Mumsnet is not a publisher but a platform on which it is the community members who provide the content, and which Mumsnet facilitates. Users are all encouraged to be moderators; by reporting unacceptable comments, they can draw attention to them and get them removed – which provides a handy defence mechanism, if nothing else.

And she's unapologetic about the robust nature of argument and debate on the site. 'People say Mumsnet is more aggressive than other parenting sites, and it's true that we don't delete people for being unsupportive to the original poster.' There are, she concedes, those who complain that Mumsnet is no longer what it was and preferred it when it was smaller, but her response is blunt. 'Mumsnet is there to make lives easier and the moment it's not doing that for you, perhaps you should log off.'

It's inevitable, she feels, that as their children grow older, many women will no longer find Mumsnet so relevant, while the pipeline of 'newbies' – usually new mothers – are what provides the community with its lifeblood.

In any case, she proudly defends the real support and connectedness that Mumsnet provides to a group that has too often suffered from feelings of isolation. 'Our busiest time is during the evening, when many women log on and settle down with a glass of wine just to have a good chat,' she says. 'I get 10 e-mails a week saying: "This has saved my life." It has become a labour of love.'

Election aside, Mumsnet is a social phenomenon of our time – one that you can love or hate – and whether or not it finds a way to convert into a truly profitable and sustainable business, it has certainly trodden a path that demonstrates the power of communities in the digital age.

Roberts says her greatest sense of achievement comes not from having tea with Gordon Brown in Downing Street but from 'the overwhelmingly supportive nature of most users and the small acts of kindness that take place between them every day'. It is, she adds, 'replacing a wider community that we've lost.'

(*Source*: Alexander Garrett Saturday, *Management Today*, 1 May 2010)

Case study questions

1 What external relationships have Mumsnet developed?
2 Why is the portal so successful and what might it need to do to maintain this success in the future?

References

Baines, P., Egan, J. and Jefkins, F. (2004) *Public Relations: Contemporary Issues and Techniques*, Oxford: Elsevier.

Blois, K.J. (1998) 'Don't all firms have relationships?', *Journal of Business and Industrial Marketing*, **13** (3), 256–70.

Brandenburger, A.M. and Nalebuff, B.J. (1996) *Cooptition*, New York: Doubleday.

Brennan, R. (1997) 'Buyer/supplier partnering in British industry: the automotive and telecommunications sectors', *Journal of Marketing Management*, **13** (8), 758–76.

Chaffey, D., Mayer, R., Johnston, K. and Ellis-Chadwick, F. (2000) *Internet Marketing*, Harlow: Pearson Education.

Chaston, I. (1998) 'Evolving "new marketing" philosophies by merging existing concepts: application of process within small high-technology firms', *Journal of Marketing Management*, **14**, 273–91.

Gummesson, E. (1999) *Total Relationship Marketing: Rethinking Marketing Management from 4Ps to 30Rs*, Oxford: Butterworth Heinemann.

Hunt, S.D., Arnett, D.B. and Madhavaram, S. (2006) 'For dynamic relationship marketing theory: a reply to Rese', *Journal of Business and Industrial Marketing*, **21** (2), 92–3.

Keegan, W. (1999) *Global Marketing Management*, 6th edn. Englewood Cliffs, NJ: Prentice Hall.

Lewicki, R.J., McAllister, D.J. and Bies, R.J. (1998) 'Trust and distrust: new relationships and realities', *Academy of Management Review*, **23** (3), 438–58.

Palmer, A.J. (1996) 'Relationship marketing: a universal paradigm or management fad?', *The Learning Organisation*, **3** (3), 18–25.

Palmer, A.J. (2000) 'Co-operation and competition: a Darwinian synthesis of relationship marketing', *European Journal of Marketing*, **34** (5/6), 687–704.

Porter, M.E. (1985) *Competitive Advantage*, New York: Free Press.

Shaw, E. (2003) 'Marketing through alliances and networks', in Hart, S. (ed.) *Marketing Changes*, London: International Thomson Business Press, pp. 147–70.

Sheth, J.N. and Sisodia, R.S. (1999) 'Revisiting marketing's lawlike generalizations', *Journal of the Academy of Marketing Sciences*, **17** (1), 71–87.

Tzokas, N. and Saren, M. (2000) 'Knowledge and relationship marketing: where, what and how?', in 2nd WWW Conference on Relationship Marketing, 15 November 1999 to 15 February 2000, Paper 4 <www.mcb.co.uk/services/conferen/nov99/rm>.

Varadarajan, P.R. and Cunningham, M.H. (2000) 'Strategic alliances: a synthesis of conceptual foundations', in Sheth, J.N. and Parvatiyar, A. (eds) *Handbook of Relationship Marketing*, Thousand Oaks, CA: Sage, pp. 271–302.

Zineldin, M. (2000) 'Beyond relationship marketing: technologicalship marketing', *Marketing Intelligence and Planning*, **18** (1), 9–23.

Notes

1 Strictly speaking, organisations that collaborate *at* the same point in the distribution but not necessarily *from* the same point in the chain. This is particularly relevant when 'complementary relationships' are discussed.
2 At the time of writing the BA/Iberia merger has been announced but not yet finalised.
3 Varadarajan and Cunningham use the word 'alliances' but the meaning in the context of this chapter does not change.
4 There is some doubt about the derivation of the word 'lobbying'. Depending which side of the Atlantic you are on it derives either from the practice of UK Members of Parliament meeting visitors in the lobby of the House of Commons or from the habit of US politicians meeting their petitioners in the lobby of the Willard Hotel in Washington, DC.

Part III

Managing and controlling the relationship

In this third and final part, important aspects of the management and control of relationships are discussed. It should be noted, however, that this is not a prescriptive approach; rather, an attempt to illustrate the various routes taken and the opportunities available dependent on a company's individual requirements.

Chapter 11 discusses the concepts surrounding the planning and control of RM and the potential management of relationships. The text deliberately avoids the promotion of a prescriptive 'checklist' of solutions, although some models are generally accepted as valuable from a planning perspective. Instead, it recommends the need to 'design in' relational strategies, initially within the current planning process. The chapter also confronts head on the criticisms of RM, in part as a warning against 'prescriptive complacency' and in part to rebalance (if this is needed) any over-enthusiastic claims made on its behalf.

Chapter 12 looks at the enormous impact that new technologies are having on marketing and the management of relationships. As Brad DeLong, an economist at the University of California at Berkeley, has stated: "IT and the Internet amplify brain power in the same way that the technologies of the industrial revolution amplified muscle power" (quoted in Woodall, 2000). Even he would be surprised by the developments in the last 10 years and their affect on commercial life.

Chapter 13 looks at the direction in which RM research is heading and what forms and influences it is taking. It discusses customer relationship management (CRM) and perceived associations and conflicts with RM. In this edition two other developments, social marketing and service-dominant logic, are discussed as they are both seen as having RM at their core.

Reference
Woodall, P. (2000) 'Untangling e-conomics: a survey of the new economy (Part 1)', e-business forum.com, *The Economist Intelligence Unit*, 27 September.

11 Relationship management

Key issues

- The management of relationships
- The marketing plan
- High/low involvement management
- Managing personal information
- Criticism of RM

Introduction

How do you manage relationships of the type discussed in previous chapters? Perhaps the idea of managing relationships is itself illusory as it implies controlling, or attempting to control, a notoriously fickle and increasingly independent customer base. Evans (2003, p. 263) has described the phrase 'relationship management' as an oxymoron in that it represents two reactionary and opposing elements. According to O'Toole and Donaldson (2003, p. 208), the application of a planning framework to relationship marketing is 'taking a managerial perspective to something that cannot be managed'. This should not mean the equivalent of commercial anarchy. Management planning and decision-making are necessary to coordinate the direction and resource allocation of any organisation and important factors in creating the organisational climate in which relationships can flourish. Simply overlaying RM onto an existing organisational structure and systems, however, without any consideration of how relationships are pursued and developed, will undoubtedly cause problems (O'Malley, 2003, p. 142). So how can this be orchestrated? It probably starts with the realization that RM does not imply is a formulaic or prescriptive solution that guarantees success. Both the decision to apply relational strategies and the ways in which these are designed and implemented are, if they are to be successful, situation specific.

The suggestion has been made that little has been provided by way of practical recommendation as to how to implement RM or what that implementation entails

(Too *et al.*, 2001, p. 290). Predictably this lack of specific guidelines has led to criticism that it is not systematic and that relationship marketers are 'happy-clappy, touchy-feely, weepy-creepy, born-again zealots without any underpinning process' (McDonald, 2000, p. 8). This criticism is perhaps partly dependent upon whether you view marketing as an art or a science. A scientific view of marketing demands systematic solutions and has little room for the subjective. Viewing marketing as an art, however, suggests creating the 'best-fit' and perhaps unique solution to an individual situation that may not be replicated elsewhere. There is little point, therefore, duplicating a strategy simply because it worked elsewhere. The science versus art debate has continued for decades with little hope of resolution. However, many marketing researchers agree with Tapp (2004, p. 582) when he suggests that 'marketing as a science is now so seriously in doubt that even the most die-hard positivist would struggle to dismiss the need for mixed philosophies'. Perhaps the worst outcome is when polarisation of opinion takes place and marketers reject alternative perspectives and (at the extreme) claim that success is only achievable by adopting their particular prescriptive solution. There is room for alternate opinions and approaches of both a scientific and artistic nature. To paraphrase Voltaire, those who are certain they are right should be certified!

Advocates of direct marketing, database marketing and customer relationship management, in particular, are prone to advance generalised solutions, often with too little consideration as to appropriateness to individual situations. Not that all RM advocates are innocent of such overstatement. Relationship marketing, whatever its faults, is conceptually distinct from direct marketing, database marketing, customer relationship management, loyalty marketing, etc., in so much as these are tactical methodologies, by definition short term, although they might contribute in various ways to longer-term relational development.

There is no claim (at least in this text) that RM is right for every, or even the majority of, situations (see Chapter 13); further, that one particular standpoint has no credible right to be dominant or superior over any other (Littler, 1998, p. 1). As Micklethwait and Wooldridge (1996, p. 22) somewhat sarcastically note:

> Dig into virtually any area of management theory and you will find, eventually, a coherent position of sorts. The problem is that in order to extract that nugget you have to dig through an enormous amount of waffle.

The application of relational strategies should be a response to a need and implies an element of flexibility and cunning. Neither are relational strategies mutually exclusive. Rather than single, narrow, one-concept strategies, companies need a 'portfolio of strategy types' (see Chapter 5) of which relational strategies can play an important part. Ideas ebb and flow, concepts come and go. Industrial priorities change, which calls for adaptable strategies. What is right for one generation may have no place in the next. Indeed, the uniqueness of relationships makes the mechanical transfer of successful practices among different companies dubious at best (Håkansson and Snehota, 2000, p. 83). After all, isn't differentiation at the heart of marketing? If so, why are marketers peddling generalisable solutions?

An organisation needs to examine the ideas generated and adopt or reject them as appropriate. After all, observation of 'real world' marketing practice suggests that a hybrid managerial approach is the most appropriate response to prevailing marketing circumstances (Chaston, 1998, p. 273). It is even possible to envisage a company using a relational approach for some customers who need or require this, or in situations where it is profitable for the company. Other customers may not seek such services, or may contribute nothing to profit. There are dangers in such tactics. In 2007 HSBC attracted negative comment for its decision to use UK call centres for top clients whilst diverting less valuable ones to its call centres overseas. The skill (or art) of the marketer is not in the application of RM or TM strategies *per se* but in applying the strategies most appropriate to its customers in any given situation.

Relationship management

None of the foregoing should suggest that management has no role. Neither is there any pretence that managing relational strategies is easy. Indeed, making RM work in practice, by means of a system within the company, is one of the most difficult of marketing tasks (Ryals, 2000, p. 231). What should be avoided is 'throwing the baby out with the bath water'. In our headlong rush for instant results (prompted by prophets of doom) there is the danger of applying inappropriate relational strategies to a given situation. The biggest risk of all is creating relationships without considering how value will be created (Ballantyne, 2000, p. 4). Ballantyne calls this the 'lobsterpot approach' to RM, characterised by an over-enthusiastic rush into the unknown. If we accept (as it is suggested) that every customer is uniquely individual, we must accept that every company is unique too. So beware of following the herd too far and too fast. As Damarest (1997, p. 375) notes, it is not 'what is right' but 'what works' or even 'what works better'.

Marketing, perhaps more than any other discipline, is prone to the 'new broom' syndrome (Mazur, 2000, p. 33). Attempting to restructure everything overnight is more than chancing fate. Flexible adaptation over time is the key. Using a scalpel, not a hatchet (Micklethwait and Wooldridge, 1996, p. 21), is the appropriate metaphor; reviewing and adapting current strategies, the most appropriate solution. According to Grönroos (2000, p. 11):

> We know too little about how relationship marketing should be best integrated into the planning of a company. The only way to find out is through trial and error in our companies and through research. Under these circumstances it seems reasonable to start by adding RM dimensions to the marketing plan in use, retaining its basic format.

The advantage of using the 'current format' and 'adding RM dimensions' is direct comparability: the ability to establish what works and why. Although most marketing plans tend towards being overly systematic and to be applied prescriptively, it is better to adapt than replace one system for another, as yet untried. There is, however, a downside. The language of strategy, tactics, power and intelligence gathering coexists rather uncomfortably with that of trust, harmony and commitment (O'Malley and Tynan, 1999, p. 595). Where practical, 'new' language might be adopted that recognises the value of cooperation over confrontation and competition.

The marketing plan

The traditional marketing plan usually follows the pattern of analysis, design, implementation and control. Various formats exist so no generic form is proposed as necessarily better than any other. The plan presented in Figure 11.1, for example, is represented by the acronym SOSTAC (Situation, Objectives, Strategies, Tactics, Action, Control) and follows, approximately, the 'standard' format. One difference from most is that, rather than a linear approach, the model recognises that marketing plans are not 'one-off' but need to be continually revisited. Rather than a list, the model is seen as a continuous circle of activities.

Alternatively, other, perhaps more traditional, marketing plan formats exist. In Figure 11.2, for example, Brassington and Pettitt's (2006) 'stages in the planning process' and McDonald's (2007) '10-step strategic marketing planning' model are shown for comparison. The similarities may be noted although different authors give different prominence to different parts of the plan. In any marketing plan, although they appear sequential, several stages may happen simultaneously and information is being constantly updated. As systematic as they appear, flexibility is again the key. Decisions are rarely made in neat stages and planning happens in 'an evolutionary, organic way emerging from organisations and their interaction over time' (O'Toole and Donaldson, 2003, p. 199).

Developing a marketing plan

It is not the purpose of this book to go into the minutiae of a marketing plan. Other authors (including those represented in Figure 11.2) have covered this extensively. What follows is a series of observations concerning the development of a marketing plan particularly as it relates to the incorporation of relational strategy development. The structure is based on the SOSTAC model in Figure 11.1 but might well apply to any chosen plan.

Figure 11.1
Basic SOSTAC
planning model

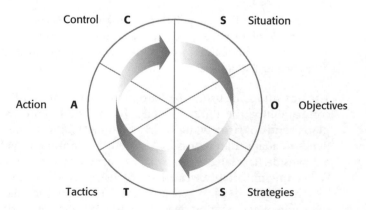

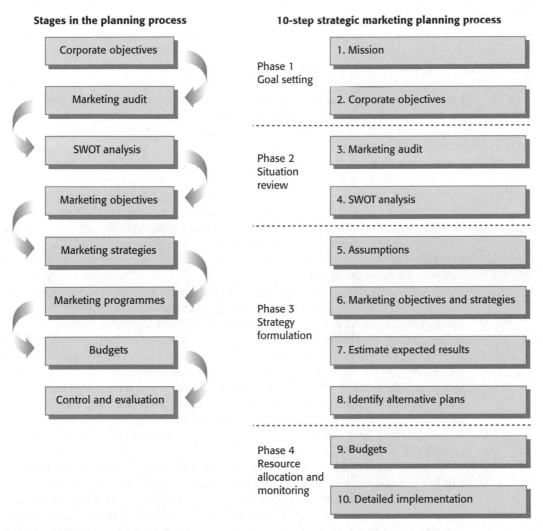

Stages in the planning process

- Corporate objectives
- Marketing audit
- SWOT analysis
- Marketing objectives
- Marketing strategies
- Marketing programmes
- Budgets
- Control and evaluation

10-step strategic marketing planning process

Phase 1
Goal setting
- 1. Mission
- 2. Corporate objectives

Phase 2
Situation
review
- 3. Marketing audit
- 4. SWOT analysis

Phase 3
Strategy
formulation
- 5. Assumptions
- 6. Marketing objectives and strategies
- 7. Estimate expected results
- 8. Identify alternative plans

Phase 4
Resource
allocation and
monitoring
- 9. Budgets
- 10. Detailed implementation

Figure 11.2 Alternative marketing plans
(*Source*: '10-step strategic marketing planning process', McDonald, 2007)

(*Source*: 'Stages in the planning process', based on Brassington and Pettitt, 2006, p. 1000)

Situation (situational analysis)

The old adage rings true: how do you know which direction to go when you don't know where you're coming from? Most companies begin (or resume) the planning process by establishing (or reiterating or adapting) their mission and scope. The mission and scope relate to the 'attitudes and expectations within the organisation with regard to the business that the organisation is in, how the organisation rates against competition and how it fits into its environment' (O'Malley *et al.*, 1999,

p. 37). Corporate and/or business objectives need to be known so that the priorities (often financial) of the organisation can be attended to and incorporated into the plan.

The situational analysis, upon which decisions will be based, is a comprehensive assessment of the organisation and its competitive and macroenvironment. Analysts have commonly used versions (both simple and complex) of **PEST(L)**, **SWOT** and competitive market models to develop such analyses.[1] As RM emphasises the importance of customer retention and the existing customer base, a 'customer analysis' is considered vital. Buyer–seller relationships rarely exist in pure types. Conceptualising where the company and the individual customer types are on the strategy continuum could provide useful insight. Review of the drivers towards relational and/or traditional marketing could help in this process. Understanding when to utilise RM strategies requires distinguishing between the discrete transaction, which has a distinct beginning, short duration and sharp ending, and relational exchange, which traces back to previous agreements and is longer in duration. In addition, the consequences of other relationships require consideration as to how they affect the strategic direction of the company.

Although much has been said about the advantages of the 'segment-of-one', current capabilities are such that aggregation of customer types is likely to still be the most practical in all but a very few industries. The identification and profiling of target markets is, therefore, important. For 'customer acquisition' purposes this may still require the use of sociodemographic, geodemographic and/or life style (including propensity to buy) data, whether exercised through rented 'lists' or communications media audience classifications. The Internet enables the tracking of actual behaviour (see Chapter 11) that has revolutionised customer profiling. Not all customers are equal and part of the 'skill' of the relational marketer is targeting the 'right' customer, not necessarily the easiest to attract or the most profitable in the short term (Reichheld, 1993, p. 65).

From the customer retention and development perspective the company database will be of considerable importance as it should indicate customer preferences and profitability. Direct marketers, for example, use recency, frequency and monetary value (RFV) models that incorporate data on a customer's most recent purchases and the frequency and value of previous purchases to target offerings (including 'cross-selling' and 'up-selling'). In addition to establishing customer traits, an RM perspective implies segmentation by type of relationship that can profitably be engaged (Smith and Higgins, 2000, p. 87).

Objectives

Objectives are what drive an organisation. They are the 'where we want to be' of any business. They should be **SMART** (strategic, measurable, actionable, realistic and timely), communicable and aspirational. Traditionally, marketing objectives are derived (or cascade down from) business objectives. The development of technologies that can interrogate databases and establish objectives from this information has led to the incorporation of this 'bottom-up' approach to objective setting into the existing model.

To ensure that everyone in the company is working to the same agenda, there is a need for all employees to be aware of top-level and marketing objectives. The RM approach further suggests that this information should be available to all other core relationship partners. This is seen as a particular failing with many CRM implementations.

Strategies

If the objectives are 'where we want to be', then the strategies are 'how we are going to get there'. Marketing strategies may include sub-strategies (e.g. media strategy, creative strategy). Box 11.1 indicates a number of different strategic options that may prove useful in strategy development, dependent on whether the aim is transactional or relational. They should, however, be recognised as a range of indicators rather than as a prescription for either TM or RM. Keep the customer at the core of the planning and avoid strategies that promote behaviours positive for the bottom line but destructive to customer relationships (Young, 2006, p. 116), or what Reichheld has called 'bad profits' (Schulz and Levy, 2006, p. 1).

Tactics

Tactics are the operational element and, by necessity, short term. The choice may be between different media (including the Internet) or techniques (e.g. direct marketing).

Box 11.1   Transactional versus relationship marketing

Transactional marketing	Relationship marketing
■ Do the deal and disappear	■ Negotiate a 'win–win' sale situation and stay around being a resource for better results
■ Push price	■ Promote value
■ Short-term thinking and acting	■ Long-term thinking and acting
■ Build the business on deals	■ Build the business on relationships
■ Getting new customers	■ Keeping customers
■ No structure for ongoing business	■ Structure created to support relationships
■ Selling focused	■ Relationship focused
■ Short-term empathy	■ Long-term empathy and rapport
■ Incentive for 'doing the deal'	■ Incentive for long-term relationship and revenue
■ Foundation of sale telling and selling	■ Foundation of revenue trust
■ After-sales service at additional cost	■ After-sales service as investment in relationship
■ Product service focused	■ People expectations and perception focused
■ Rewards incentives for 'doing deals'	■ Rewards incentives for maintaining and growing relationships and revenue
■ The deal is the end	■ The sale is the beginning

(*Source*: Adapted from Thomas, 2000, p. 531)

The danger here is confusing the tactical with the strategic. For all its influence on business habits in general, the Internet is a tactical tool. It is part (certainly not all) of a company's armoury. It may promote different approaches but it is, in strict terms, another media channel. In the same way, database marketing, direct marketing and CRM are, within a RM strategy, tactical responses rather than strategic approaches to company development.

Action

Action plans provide the means by which the organisation's ideas are turned into reality by being given a structure and format through which they can be implemented (O'Malley *et al.*, 1999, p. 59). The action plan is the blueprint through which the objectives are realised. As with the objectives, there is a need to disseminate information to employees and, increasingly, to suppliers, customers and strategic partners.

Control

The control element involves setting clear evaluation criteria (e.g. target response levels). It may also involve testing prior to full execution. Testing differs from research in that it is actual response (albeit on a smaller scale) as opposed to forecast response. In this regard technology has a considerable part to play in the control element of any marketing plan.

Managing relationships

When an RM dimension is incorporated into a company's marketing plan this should be done in the knowledge that certain additional factors will need to be incorporated and subsequently managed.

Handling relationships

While there is nothing new in the desire of businesses to develop ongoing relationships with their customers, developments in information technology offer new opportunities (see Chapter 12). Ultimately it may lead to a greater ability to attend to individual customer's concerns (or one-to-one marketing). If, as many authors suggest, organisations should be treating each customer as an individual then 'one-to-one marketing' is the ultimate aim. It emphasises that every customer requires a different form of communication and (in an ideal world) individual attention. The danger of replacing personal contact with technology is a real one. Such a decision must be taken in the knowledge that depersonalisation may do harm.

The management of customer relationships will differ from industry to industry. In 'low involvement' consumer markets the relationship with the customer is likely to be managed through technologies such as a database and/or the World Wide Web

(O'Malley and Tynan, 1999, p. 589). Databases can be used to target customers with customers having little or no knowledge of the company in question or the existence of the database (Barnes and Howlett, 1998, p. 15). This database view of RM, according to Copulsky and Wolf (1990, pp. 16–17), incorporates three key elements:

■ identifying and building a database of current and potential customers;

■ delivering differentiated messages;

■ tracking each relationship.

The 'low involvement' customer may be quite happy with technology-based relationships where technology substitutes for physical proximity (Zineldin, 2000, p. 16). This may contrast with the 'high involvement' consumer who may need a more personal, less mechanised and individually tailored approach that technology (currently) finds difficult to duplicate.

The management of relationships is prone to pitfalls. The problem is that many marketers take their eye off the ball. Rather than viewing a database as simply an 'enabling technology' too many firms have focused their energies on 'database building' rather than 'relationship building' (O'Malley et al., 1997, p. 553). In addition, now that it is possible to manipulate a database in such a way that relationship development is feasible does not mean that all customers want or need such a relationship. Contacting customers on too regular a basis can be worse than not contacting them at all. As Pels (1999, p. 33) points out, this 'technology-allows-me-to-do' approach has more in common with a production type orientation than a marketing orientation.

Managing personal information

The management of customer information through advanced technology can create problems regarding privacy, and privacy concerns tend to erode buyer–seller relationships (Prabhaker, 2000, p. 160). Although these concerns are not peculiar to marketing – medical records being an example – what is different is the quantity and depth of data collected (see Box 11.2). The three major concerns would appear to be that:

■ the handing over or collection of personal information is an infringement of personal liberty.

■ the handing over of information will result in unwanted attention being paid to that customer.

■ if companies are permitted to hold such information then they should utilise the information wisely.

Infringement of personal liberty

The commercial incentive to collect, merge, warehouse and sell customer information is enormous while the safeguards tend to be weak and easily ignored (ibid., p. 158). In

Box 11.2   MPs quiz Tesco and Nectar card executives on data privacy: Commons committee continues investigation of 'surveillance society'

MPs are set to grill executives from supermarket giant Tesco and Nectar loyalty card firm LMG on how they use customer data – and how privacy is protected. The retail executives will give evidence to the Commons home affairs committee's inquiry into the 'surveillance society'.

The investigation has already heard the [UK] information commissioner, Richard Thomas, call for his office to be given new powers allowing uninvited investigations to examine data protection measures. Today's hearing will examine commercial companies' use of monitoring information, such as the data collected for marketing purposes or the financial information gathered by credit checking agencies. The MPs will examine how the information is collected, how it is used and how it is protected from abuse. Witnesses include Nick Eland, legal services manager of Tesco, which gathers information on consumers' spending habits through its Clubcard loyalty scheme and tailors special offers accordingly. Martin Briggs, corporate affairs director of LMG, the firm behind the Nectar loyalty cards, will also give evidence to the MPs. Earlier this year, LMG renewed its contract with Sainsbury's, beefing up the level of analytics on customer spend provided to the supermarket firm. Under the new contract Sainsbury's will receive analysis based on data from its checkout tills as well as Nectar information.

Also appearing at the evidence session are officials from the International Association of Privacy Professionals, credit reference firm Experian and the Finance & Leasing Association trade body.

(*Source*: Tash Shifrin, published 11:37, 7 June 2007, Computerworld <http://www.computerworlduk.com> (accessed 1 September 2010))

the UK, which has data protection legislation, there is continued pressure from the regulator for tighter control. There is little doubt that legislation will only get tougher and already many markets have introduced rules that require customers to opt in (rather than opt out) if they wish to use their customer's data. Practitioners have, however, developed techniques for encouraging customers to 'opt in' or 'join' them. This may include the provision of information or services (e.g. online news) in exchange for data. This range of customer-authorised data collection strategies has been called '**permission marketing**'.

There is also some suggestion that customers react badly when they believe their personal details are being indiscriminately passed on. The covert acquisition of information, rather than representing a phase in relationship building, may actually undermine the relationship building process (O'Malley *et al.*, 1997, p. 552). On the other side of the coin, there is the irony that strictly regulating the collection of personal information could ultimately limit the quality and level of service that a business can deliver (Prabhaker, 2000, p. 160).

Nowhere is this privacy debate more pertinent than with the Internet.[2] As Prabhaker (ibid., p. 159) notes:

Every time an individual interacts with the web she leaves behind a trail of extraordinary detailed information about who she is, her buying habits, financial status, maybe her medical records and other intimate personal details. She has very little control over who can have access to this information and what they will do with it. It is unrealistic to expect profit driven businesses not to infringe on consumer privacy in an environment that makes it increasingly profitable and a technology that makes it easier than ever to collect and share personal information.

Another technology with ethical implications is mobile telephony. The ability to pinpoint the location of individual users, using satellite navigation, offers considerable marketing opportunities (including text offers and directions to local purchase points) but raises issues regarding personal privacy.

Undoubtedly what some marketers imagine as a means of developing the relationship through information exchange some customers will see as intrusion into their private lives. Finding an acceptable balance may become marketing's greatest challenge.

Unwanted attention

O'Malley et al. (1997, p. 553) quote one respondent in their research into consumer's views on data management as commenting that 'handing over personal details just means more rubbish coming through the letterbox'. Fournier et al. (1998, p. 43) report that a woman interviewed concerning the number of approaches made to her every day stated 'it's overkill . . . one is more meaningless than the next'. These are not isolated perceptions and it is easy to see why. Direct mail, for example, while being described as a more targeted and flexible medium, may have a response rate of 4 per cent, a return generally seen as satisfactory in some industries. This means that for every one customer evidently interested enough in the offer to respond 24 are not. The cost of sending e-mails is so low[3] that unrestricted and unwanted e-mails (or spam) has quickly become a source of pollution. According to Techcrunchies,[4] an Internet statistics website, 90 trillion e-mails were sent in 2009 of which 200 billion were classed as spam. Although many consumers will, as a consequence of modern life, take this in their stride, a percentage will be annoyed about what they regard as untargeted junk mail. Whether the direct marketing industry likes it or not, the ever-growing number of postal and especially electronic mailshots will ensure that this will become an even greater cause for concern in the future.

Utilising information

The poor utilisation of information is surprisingly commonplace. Another customer in the O'Malley et al. (1997, p. 551) study showed her frustration with companies that have the information (they suppose) but do not use it (see also Box 6.3). She explains:

I go overdrawn at the end of every month and have trouble making the repayments but my bank are (sic) constantly making me loan offers. They should know that I can't afford to take out another loan. They, of all people, should know because they have all my details and I often deal with them person-to-person.

This type of irresponsible behaviour was clearly brought to a head following the exposure of valueless 'toxic loans' largely blamed for the all too recent financial difficulties.

Fournier *et al.* (1998, p. 47) note what they call 'the forgotten rule': that intimacy and vulnerability are intertwined. If a company routinely asks its customers for sensitive information, but does not put that information to good use, it should stop asking those questions. Marketers must use the information they already have more effectively and develop appropriate processes to initiate and maintain meaningful dialogue with customers (O'Malley *et al.*, 1997, p. 553). Today's 'interactive age customers' are accustomed to having their needs met immediately, conveniently and inexpensively (Peppers and Rogers, 2000, p. 243) by companies utilising the information they already have at their disposal. Nothing can be more frustrating than having to repeat the details of problems over and over again to assorted customer service personnel. Studies support this. Participants in the O'Malley *et al.* (1997, p. 551) research believed that, if companies used the data they already had more effectively, it would reduce the quantity of irrelevant communications they received.

Appropriateness

Used appropriately, technology can help the company learn from every customer interaction and deepen the relationship by advancing ideas and solutions likely to suit the customer (Gordon, 1998, p. 168). Used inappropriately, the backlash is likely to ensure restrictive controls. Ultimately the evolution of any technical advances in information gathering is dependent on its acceptance by the public (Prabhaker, 2000, p. 161). The compromise is likely to settle around what is becoming known as 'permission marketing' (Chaffey *et al.*, 2000, p. 233) where consumers actively cooperate in the supply of data. The potential downside is if, having received permission from the customer, the organization abuses it.

Criticisms of RM

An important aspect of management is knowledge of the (actual or perceived) weaknesses of any strategy. Although this book chronicles and generally supports the development of relational strategies in marketing, it would be inappropriate to ignore any perceived weaknesses or criticism of the RM concept or indeed the dangers inherent in the introduction of any new management ideas. Although some of these criticisms have emerged earlier in the text it may be valuable, at this stage, to consolidate them. It is only by acknowledging the weaknesses that the strengths of relational strategies can be fully appreciated.

Management fads

Is RM a fad? It is now over 15 years since it hit the marketing headlines. Will companies 15 years from now regret adopting RM strategies, as has happened with other fads in the past? In their introduction to a collection of writings on RM, Payne *et al.* (1995, p. vii) include this warning:

> There is a tendency when new ideas in management emerge to embrace them keenly for a while and to see them as the ultimate solution to whatever problems we currently perceive to exist. Equally there is a tendency to put them aside after the initial novelty has worn off, and they are found to be not quite the panacea that we once thought. Marketing particularly has been prone to this 'flavour of the month' syndrome ... Already there are some who would claim that 'relationship marketing' is another of these short-lifecycle management phenomena.

Dholakia (2001, p. 1), talking about CRM in financial services, might as well have been talking about RM or indeed any of the managerial developments of the last 100 years when noting:

> Ideas that become buzzwords typically begin as clever, useful concepts of great practical value. Then others add bells and whistles to make them more marketable and profitable. As more and more people get acquainted with the concept and become convinced of its value, the 'bandwagon' effect results in certain aspects of the concept getting emphasised, while others remain overlooked.

Already some writers see RM as already having moved on to embrace newer schools of thought (e.g. service-dominant logic – see Chapter 13). However, RM, like all successful ideas, has initial intuitive appeal (Blois, 1997, p. 53) and there have been a number of successful interpretations that have helped to promote the concept. It would, however, also be true to suggest that, with the rapid development of RM, the boundaries have often been stretched and claims made which could never be universally justified. As East (2000, p. 1) notes, some of these propositions have little evidence to support them and/or rest on invalid or over-simplified reasoning. As is often the case with radical change, there is a tendency to over-correct (Baker, 1999, p. 212) and consequently over-hype a concept. Care should be taken, therefore, when implementing relational strategies, to clarify that the concept is right for particular industries or individual situations. This involves seeing through the rhetoric to the core of what RM purports to be all about.

RM as a new marketing concept

Is RM really a new phenomenon? Haven't RM objectives always been important to marketing? If the answer is yes to either or both of these questions, then how is it different? It is frequently debated whether RM is a 'new' concept or simply an old concept given a new lease of life by marketing's spin doctors: a new paradigm or an old idea in a revised format. Brown (1998, p. 173) is particularly scathing when he suggests it is not new and was already anticipated as part of the original marketing concept. His view is that to regard RM as something novel is 'arrant nonsense'. There is certainly a justifiable criticism regarding RM's novelty. The emergence of RM in the 1980s was not so much a discovery as a rediscovery of long-held and successful strategies (Payne, 2000, p. 41), a return to practices of a pre-industrial era when producers and consumers dealt directly with each other and 'a potential for emotional bonding that transcends economic exchange' (Sheth and Parvatiyar, 2000, p. 123). The concept of 'relationships in marketing' is, indeed, not new as traders have been practising it for centuries. Cynics might suggest, therefore, that RM is nothing but a marketing makeover, the latter-day version of changing the sign on the departmental door from 'sales' to 'marketing' (Brown, 1998, p. 173).

In RM's favour, it is frequently suggested that its biggest achievement is that it has brought back 'relationships' into the mainstream of marketing. That it is really a rebirth of marketing practices of the pre-industrial age. This may be largely true; however, while relationships may have been 'rediscovered in western corporate markets' they have remained a fundamental part of exchange in many eastern cultures (Palmer, 1996, p. 19). Perhaps, even in our own culture, the concept may have also been kept alive in 'less sophisticated' village and suburban communities or small companies previously largely ignored by marketing academics. According to Gummesson (1999, p. 6):

> The renewed interest in RM may imply that marketing theorists are getting closer to reality; that we are beginning to discern the marketing content of Japanese *Keiretsus*, Chinese *Quanxies*, global ethnic networks, the British school tie, trade between friends, loyalty to the local pub and so on. Marketing has not invented these phenomena, practice has!

In these terms RM is merely re-emphasising certain neglected areas of marketing (Brown, 1998, pp. 173–4) rather than creating something wholly new – the equivalent of 'going back (or is it forward?) to basics' (Gummesson, 1999, p. 13). RM's biggest benefit is that it has caused marketers to question the process-led 4Ps (or 7Ps) approach of the traditional marketing paradigm and to consider the importance of the core firm and its relationships.

Selective research

Another valid criticism of RM is that the universal success implied in case studies is frequently based on selective organisations in a limited number of industries. These claims are usually implied rather than directly stated when, in promoting RM (or indeed direct marketing (DM), database marketing (DbM) or customer relationship management (CRM)) strategies, writers frequently omit industries where relational strategies may be of marginal, if any, importance. A potential hazard is where this selective research leads to a polarisation of opinions. This in turn causes some marketers to reject alternative perspectives and, at the extreme, begin to claim that firms can only succeed by adapting their particular prescriptive solutions (Chaston, 1998, p. 277).

These prescriptive solutions are of particular concern when it comes to dealing with consultant agencies that promote the RM (or any other) concept. Any search of the Internet using the phrase 'relationship marketing' (or 'customer relationship management') will produce a host of these consultants each extolling the virtues of their vision. Marketers should, therefore, take care, when examining the evidence supporting RM, that the factors which led to its successful implementation in one industry or in other contexts are comparable to their own.

O'Malley and Tynan (2000, p. 12) also point out that, although marketers have appropriated the technology, it remains unclear whether they have internalised the philosophy, particularly in consumer markets. They note that, in many markets, all that is apparent is a resource shift from above (i.e. advertising) to below the line (other marketing communications tools; e.g. sales promotion), indicating that RM may, on occasion, be more rhetoric than reality.

One-sided communication

It is suggested that, despite claims to co-produce value, the voice of the customer is often missing especially in consumer goods marketing. Caught up in the enthusiasm for the rapid increase in information gathering techniques and for the benefits that long-term engagement with customers may hold, many companies that claim to have adopted RM techniques and concepts have forgotten that relationships take two (Fournier et al., 1998, p. 42). The term 'relationship' has often been used by practitioners to underpin a supplier's marketing activities without the customer necessarily being conscious that they are even participating in an RM campaign (Blois, 1997, p. 53).

This viewpoint raises the question (discussed in Chapter 3) of whether it is legitimate to use the term 'relationship' for the interaction between the consumer and a company. Perhaps predictably, much RM research is designed not for the benefit of the consumer but in the interest of the selling firm (Mattsson, 1997, pp. 43–4). This has meant a focus on suppliers' needs regardless of whether or not the buyer wants to develop an ongoing relationship (Palmer, 1998, p. 118). There is also concern over pseudo-relationships (Barnes, 1994, p. 565), where what passes for a relationship is one-sided, with customers locked in, effectively kept in the relationship against their will, because the costs of leaving the relationship are seen to be too high.

Corruption

Social bonds (particularly in business-to-business situations) can, without doubt, become pervasive to the point where they allow economic inefficiencies to develop. In extreme cases networks of corrupt buyers and sellers may acquire sufficient market power to result in an overall loss of economic welfare (Palmer, 1998, p. 118). In addition many of the basic tenets of cooperative marketing would appear to be contrary to competitive philosophy (Palmer, 2001, p. 762). Indeed, anti-competitive legislation has been introduced in most developed markets of which some cooperating companies have, or may in the future, fall foul. Gummesson's (1999, p. 6) reference to the

'British school tie' and 'trade between friends' also raises possible moral issues into cooperative trade. There is indeed a fine line between cooperative behaviour and collusion (Sheth and Sisodia, 1999, p. 84).

Outmoded marketing

It has been said that marketing in general is going through a 'mid-life crisis'. Perhaps it is just that it has not yet matured. Certainly the heat generated by the RM debate suggests less rationality than juvenile pride. Micklethwait and Wooldridge (1996, pp. 15–17) in their critique of management theory list four grounds which link to a description of a management discipline as adolescent:

- it is constitutionally incapable of self-criticism;
- its terminology usually confuses rather than educates;
- it hardly rises above basic common sense;
- it is faddish and bedevilled by contradiction that would not be allowed in more rigorous disciplines.

RM could be accused of all four – but again so could many of the alternative theories, many of which are put forward as solutions. It is hoped that this text has avoided the trap!

Summary

This chapter looked at the management of RM. It noted the criticism that RM was not systematic enough for some although this may be more to do with whether marketing is viewed as an art or a science. The chapter suggested 'using a scalpel not a hatchet' by introducing RM strategies into an existing marketing plan. This allows for comparability with existing strategies. A number of aspects, specific to RM, were discussed within the context of the marketing plan.

The chapter looked specifically at how relationships might be managed, particularly in relation to available technology. It reviewed the concerns relating to information handling, notably the infringement of personal liberty, unwanted attention and poor utilisation of information.

The chapter concluded with a review of some of the criticisms of RM as it was proposed that knowledge of RM's actual or perceived failings may contribute to the development of successful relational strategies. Specifically, it challenged and clarified claims that RM is a 'management fad', a reworked (and therefore not new) concept, based on selective research and one-sided communication, and prone to corruption.

Discussion questions
1 What factors distinguish a marketing plan that incorporates relational strategies from a more traditional plan?
2 Why might the management of customer information become even more important in the future?
3 What, in your judgement, are the most sustainable and least sustainable criticisms of RM?

Case study   A decisive edge

Your company is in a crisis. Its pole position as the producer of a best-selling consumer brand is under attack from a long-term rival. The competitor's new marketing campaign has focused consumer attention on a particular characteristic of its otherwise identical brand – an aspect you had considered unassailable. Your company is desperate to win this highly public battle. In a tense board meeting, it's suddenly your turn to speak. The company's future rests on the board's decision. What do you suggest?

Coca-Cola found itself in this predicament in the 1980s, when its arch-rival launched the Pepsi Challenge taste tests. Faced with a fight on the one area they'd never worried about before – taste – Coca-Cola ran focus groups that seemed to confirm it as the issue. Yet the company made a primary error – it failed to look for contradictory evidence before settling on a solution. It did everything else by the book – including reformulating the Coca-Cola recipe (at great expense). But the result, New Coke, was an embarrassing flop. Changing the flavour was the wrong decision.

Coke's case illustrates the truism that a great team, a fast brain and a lot of data don't guarantee a good decision. For a manager, decision-making skills are essential to continued success. Get a decision like this right and you're likely to be congratulated. Get it wrong and you'll be sidelined by your boss and lose the confidence of your team. A bad decision can stall a promising career.

The quest is on, then, for smarter decision-making. Academic research divides this subject roughly into three areas: structures, styles and thinking errors. Knowing how to use the structure is of course helpful, but it's an awareness of decision-making styles and avoidance of common errors in thinking that can turn a bright individual into a reliable decision-maker. 'Structures allow a perspective on the problem and on the risks,' says Derek Bunn, professor of decision sciences at the London Business School. 'They also enable you to make decisions that are defensible, credible and that you can easily communicate.'

But structures are only as good as the person using them. 'There's no panacea,' explains Bunn. 'You can't automate decision-making. All that structures can do is provide an extra level of analytic capability. No one believes that you can delegate an intuitive decision to a quantitative model anymore.'

What Bunn is driving at is that a bad decision is less likely to be a result of the decision-making process than of the mindset of the decision-maker. Different decision styles include those of the snap decision-maker, who boasts of 'gut instinct'; the fence-sitter, who keeps the options open; the democratic decider, who canvasses colleagues' opinions; and the uncertain manager, who's easily led.

Says Professor Nigel Nicholson of the London Business School, author *of Managing the Human Animal* (Texere): 'Styles vary across cultures, over time, with maturity and experience, and with background. There is a bias towards one of two models. Model 1 is the collegial first-among-equals style: high in involvement and low in power. Model 2 is the lead-from-a-distance style: top-down, goal-setting, sometimes visionary, often empowering (by leaving people to their own devices), yet driving for action and results.'

Both styles can work, and it's possible for one person to switch between them. 'Model 1 suits situations where you have to constantly adjust to change and work together,' explains Nicholson. 'And you can be very successful in model 2 if you have highly skilled, self-managing professionals reporting to you.'

High-flyers know that once you've found your style, you don't stop there. Talented managers adapt their decision-making as their career progresses. Kenneth Brousseau, CEO of US software house Decision Dynamics, and Gary Hourihan at Korn/Ferry International have identified the decision-making patterns that permeate an individual's career (*Harvard Businesss Review*, February 2006). Junior managers favour a 'decisive' style that focuses on choosing and implementing one option, with an emphasis on speed and simplicity. But as managers progress, the most successful adopt a flexible and integrative style, which enables them to solicit, choose from and adapt solutions as the situation changes.

This more participative and responsive style is clearly evident across the highest-performing 20 per cent of managers studied by Brousseau and Hourihan. Failure to evolve, they say, 'can be fatal to your career'. As evidence, they point to the lowest-performing managers, whose styles do not develop over time.

What about those who find it hard to make decisions? According to LBS's Nicholson, it's rare for hopeless prevaricators to get into positions of leadership – one good reason to brush up on your decision-making skills. Yet some leaders are accused of inconsistency because they can see everyone's point of view. Says Nicholson: 'If you're lost in a forest, you need a compass. The compass for decision-making is an overarching concept of the company's vision and purpose, and of your own identity. If you don't have this, you need to spend time digging down into yourself and thinking about what sort of leader you want to be.' In other words, to become better at decisions, look at the bigger picture – the company's aims and your own career objectives – and use that as your decision frame.

Of course, not all decisions are entirely your own. Some you inherit, others are partially or wholly dictated by a boss, the context, a competitor's actions or your predecessor's choices. Says Ralph Keeney, a research professor at the Fuqua School of Business at Duke University, North Carolina: 'There are three things that unambiguously frame your decisions: what is the problem, what are the objectives, and what are the alternatives? It's after this that the decision-making takes off. Too often, that initial framing is left to someone else. The fundamental thing is to recognise that this occurs and try to put it right. You need to ask the right questions. Don't just decide what your objectives are by reacting to the moves of others – whether competitors, colleagues or bosses.'

But your mind can trip you up even when you've developed your decision-making style, such is the faulty psychology underpinning many of our decisions. Social scientists recognise the tricks our minds play on us, such as discounting important information, misremembering facts and acting on our biases – all while we think we're doing no such thing.

According to Max Bazerman, professor of business administration at Harvard Business School, such flaws are rife, even among seasoned decision-makers. 'While there is plenty of good advice available, most people do not follow it. Why not? Because we fall victim to a variety of predictable errors that not only destroy our intuition but also hinder our tendency to implement good advice.'

Imagine you're choosing a new software package to process sales data and bring you up to the speed of your competitors. A consumer report lists a particular package as the best, but a friend who has just installed the system says it's nothing but trouble. The friend represents one isolated, unrepresentative incident, whereas the consumer report has tested thousands of software packages and is far more accurate. Yet you're now very unlikely to buy that particular software.

Bazerman calls this the 'availability trap'. The more salient, memorable or recent information is, the more we rely on it to make our decision. An anecdote is far more available, and therefore persuasive, than dry data – but that doesn't make it the right information on which to base a decision. Instead, examine data, information and statistics carefully and don't let colourful information or anecdotes influence you. The availability trap is one of several decision-making errors we're prone to, particularly under pressure. Faced with cognitive overload, our minds use shortcuts – known as heuristics – to see us through. These rely on a combination of received wisdom, previous experience, habit and emotion – all of which can go against rational calculation.

For some theorists, heuristics is enjoying a resurgence over old-fashioned deliberative decision-making. Author and New Yorker journalist Malcolm Gladwell recently devoted a whole book, *Blink* (Allen Lane), to instinct, or 'thinking without thinking'. Research from decision-making experts in the Netherlands suggests that 'unconscious thought' (akin to 'sleeping on it') leads to better decisions than the slow, analytical approach. And business leaders like Jack Welch have popularised the 'from the gut' leadership style so that many now see instinctive decisions as the hallmark of a great leader. As *Harvard Business Review* suggested in January 2006: 'Pragmatists act on evidence. Heroes act on guts.'

And, indeed, most of the time heuristics works. Imagine if, when you got up in the morning, you stopped to consider which side of the bed to get out of or whether to put on your right or left sock first. If you deliberated over each decision, colleagues might soon call, wondering why you weren't at work. Heuristics avoids this problem as it enables you to make decisions fast, but largely unconsciously.

Think back to this morning. Why did you put your socks on in that particular order? It's unlikely you'll have a reasoned answer. This highlights two main problems with heuristics: we use it all the time, but we're not always aware that we're doing so; and it may conceal basic flaws in our thinking and judgment.

Keeney has compiled common pitfalls in his book, *Smart Choices: A Practical Guide to Making Better Decisions* (HBS Press), co-written by John Hammond and Howard Raiffa. A common error he picks out is our tendency to seek confirming evidence. We often sub-consciously decide we do or don't like a particular solution or decision and then look for evidence to confirm our hunch. This might explain the New Coke débâcle. Coca-Cola went about its decision-making the right way – carefully analysing and weighing evidence. But Pepsi's campaign lured it into chasing the wrong information and falsely confirming taste as an issue.

To avoid this, Keeney recommends being honest about your motives in making a decision. Are you really scrutinising data with a view to making a smart choice, or looking for evidence that supports your favourite option? If you are decision-making with your team, don't ask leading questions – encourage team members to play devil's advocate rather than yes-men.

Another common pitfall is anchoring. As an example, ask yourself the following: Are there more than 150 nations in the UN? Got an answer? Now try this: What's your best guess of how many nations belong to the UN? For most of us, the number 150 influences our answer to the second question. If the first had said 'are there more than 50 nations in the UN?', our answer to the second would have been much lower. Our minds seize on initial impressions, data or estimates and use them to anchor subsequent thoughts and judgments.

Even the way a problem is presented can serve as an anchor. If your manager highlights an issue – say, poor sales – and suggests spending more on advertising, you and your team are more likely to focus on this solution than to explore new, unrelated avenues. Your boss's comments, however throwaway, have become your anchor. To get round the problem, Keeney suggests approaching decisions from different angles, deliberately abandoning your first line of thought, and not taking the first thing you hear as gospel. Push yourself to seek fresh perspectives.

We're also biased in favour of the *status quo*. Maintaining it means we avoid sticking our necks out. Faced with a plethora of options, choosing the *status quo* is easier – which is why so many of us fail to switch mortgage lenders when the honeymoon period of low rates expires; we just can't face the choice and look for reasons to stick with what we know.

Keeney suggests asking yourself: 'Would I consider the *status quo* as a good option if it wasn't already the *status quo*?' Don't dramatise the difficulty of changing the old order. And if there are many possible options, force yourself to choose rather than default to what you know.

Even once we're aware of these pitfalls, we will inevitably still make poor decisions at times. What then? First, admit your mistake – to yourself if no one else. It's tempting to keep metaphorically throwing good money after bad – persisting with that dying project, hanging on to the underperforming member of staff you hired. To do otherwise would be to admit your mistake – particularly hard if your company doesn't tolerate errors of judgment. But it's imperative to cut your losses and start afresh. Imagine you are approaching the situation as an outsider – what would you change? Don't waste time on recriminations, instead, start the search for new solutions.

We can be our own worst enemy. Even if we know which decision-making strategy to use, we can trip ourselves up with our unconscious biases, lazy thinking and failure to seek out as many options as possible. Because taking mental shortcuts is pretty much bar-coded into our brains, it requires constant attention to adjust our decision-making. As Keeney points out: 'The best defence is always awareness.'

Be prepared to evolve your style, to spot the tricks your mind plays on you, and to guard against them, and you're well on the way to being an excellent decision-maker.

(*Source*: Rebecca Alexander, *Management Today*, May 2007)

Case study questions

1 What makes a good decision-maker?
2 What part does intuition play in decision-making?
3 Explain the 'availability trap' and 'anchoring'.

References

Baker, M.J. (1999) 'Editorial', *Journal of Marketing Management*, **15**, 211–14.

Ballantyne, D. (2000) 'Interaction, dialogue and knowledge generation: three key concepts in relationship marketing', in 2nd WWW Conference on Relationship Marketing, 15 November 1999 to 15 February 2000, Paper 7, <www.mcb.co.uk/services/conferen/nov99/rm>.

Barnes, J.G. (1994) 'Close to the customer: but is it really a relationship?', *Journal of Marketing Management*, **10**, 561–70.

Barnes, J.G. and Howlett, D.M. (1998) 'Predictors of equity in relationships between service providers and retail customers', *International Journal of Bank Marketing*, **16** (1), 5–23.

Blois, K.J. (1997) 'When is a relationship a relationship?', in Gemünden, H.G., Rittert, T. and Walter, A. (eds) *Relationships and Networks in International Markets*, Oxford: Elsevier, pp. 53–64.

Brassington, F. and Pettitt, S. (2006) *The Principles of Marketing*, 4th edn. London: Pitman.

Brown, S. (1998) *Postmodern Marketing II*. London: International Thomson Business Press.

Chaffey, D. (2006) *Internet Marketing: Strategy, Implementation and Practice*, 3rd edn, Harlow: Pearson Education.

Chaffey, D., Mayer, R., Johnston, K. and Ellis-Chadwick, F. (2000) *Internet Marketing*, Harlow: Pearson Education.

Chaston, I. (1998) 'Evolving "new marketing" philosophies by merging existing concepts: application of process within small high-technology firms', *Journal of Marketing Management*, 14, 273–91.

Copulsky, J.R. and Wolf, M.J. (1990) 'Relationship marketing: positioning for the future', *Journal of Business Strategy*, 11 (4), 16–20.

Damerest, M. (1997) 'Understanding knowledge management', *Long Range Planning*, 30 (3), 374–84.

Dholakia, P. (2001) 'Customer relationship management: the three myths of financial services CRM', *Financial Services Marketing*, 3 (2), 40–1.

East, R. (2000) 'Fact and fallacy in retention marketing', *Professorial Inaugural Lecture*, 1 March, Kingston University Business School, UK.

Evans, M. (2003) 'Marketing communications changes', in Hart, S. (ed.) *Marketing Changes*, London: International Thomson Business Press, pp. 257–72.

Fournier, S., Dobscha, S. and Mick, D.G. (1998) 'Preventing the premature death of relationship marketing', *Harvard Business Review*, January/February, 42–9.

Gordon, I.H. (1998) *Relationship Marketing*, Etobicoke, Ontario: John Wiley & Sons.

Grönroos, C. (2000) 'The relationship marketing process: interaction, communication, dialogue, value', in 2nd WWW Conference on Relationship Marketing, 15 November 1999 to 15 February 2000, Paper 2, <www.mcb.co.uk/services/conferen/nov99/rm>.

Gummesson, E. (1999) *Total Relationship Marketing: Rethinking Marketing Management from 4Ps to 30Rs*, Oxford: Butterworth Heinemann.

Håkansson, H. and Snehota, I.J. (2000) 'The IMP perspective: assets and liabilities of business relationships', in Sheth, J.N. and Paryatiyar, A. (eds) *Handbook of Relationship Marketing*, Thousand Oaks, CA: Sage, pp. 69–93.

Littler, D. (1998) 'Editorial: perspective on consumer behaviour', *Journal of Marketing Management*, 14, 1–2.

McDonald, M. (2000) 'On the right track', *Marketing Business*, April, 28–31, 28.

McDonald, M. (2007) *Marketing Plans: How to Prepare Them, How to Use Them*, Oxford: Elsevier.

Mattsson, L.G. (1997) 'Relationships in a network perspective', in Gemünden, H.G., Rittert, T. and Walter, A. (eds) *Relationships and Networks in International Markets*, Oxford: Elsevier, pp. 37–47.

Mazur, L. (2000) 'A difficult age', *Marketing Business*, December 1999/January 2000, 33.

Micklethwait, J. and Wooldridge, A. (1996) *The Witch Doctors: What the Management Gurus are Saying*, London: Heinemann.

O'Malley, L. (2003) 'Relationship marketing', in Hart, S. (ed.) *Marketing Changes*, London: International Thomson Business Press, pp. 125–45.

O'Malley, L. and Tynan, C. (1999) 'The utility of the relationship metaphor in consumer markets: a critical evaluation', *Journal of Marketing Management*, 15, 587–602.

O'Malley, L. and Tynan, C. (2000) 'Relationship marketing in consumer markets: rhetoric or reality?', *European Journal of Marketing*, 34 (7).

O'Malley, L., Patterson, M. and Evans, M. (1997) 'Intimacy or intrusion? The privacy dilemma for relationship marketing in consumer markets', *Journal of Marketing Management*, **13** (6), 541–59.

O'Malley, L., Patterson, M. and Evans, M. (1999) *Exploring Direct Marketing*, London: International Thomson Business Press.

O'Toole, T. and Donaldson, W. (2003) 'The strategy to implementation cycle of relationship marketing planning', *Marketing Theory*, **3** (2), 195–209.

Palmer, A.J. (1996) 'Relationship marketing: a universal paradigm or management fad?', *The Learning Organisation*, **3** (3), 18–25.

Palmer, A.J. (1998) *Principles of Services Marketing*, London: Kogan Page.

Palmer, A.J. (2001) 'Co-operation and collusion: making the distinction in marketing relationships', *Journal of Marketing Management*, **17** (7/8), 761–84.

Payne, A. (2000) 'Relationship marketing: the UK perspective', in Sheth, J.N. and Parvatiyar, A. (eds) *Handbook of Relationship Marketing*, Thousand Oaks, CA: Sage, pp. 39–67.

Payne, A., Christopher, M. and Peck, H. (eds) (1995) *Relationship Marketing for Competitive Advantage: Winning and Keeping Customers*, Oxford: Butterworth Heinemann.

Pels, J. (1999) 'Exchange relationships in consumer markets?', *European Journal of Marketing*, **33** (1/2), 19–37.

Peppers, D. and Rogers, M. (2000) 'Build a one-to-one learning relationship with your customers', *Interactive Marketing*, **1** (3), 243–50.

Prabhaker, P.R. (2000) 'Who owns the on-line consumer?', *Journal of Consumer Marketing*, **17** (2), 158–71.

Reichheld, F.F. (1993) 'Loyalty based management', *Harvard Business Review*, March/April, 64–73.

Ryals, L. (2000) 'Planning for relationship marketing', in Cranfield School of Management, *Marketing Management: A Relationship Marketing Perspective*, Basingstoke: Macmillan, pp. 231–48.

Schulz, R. and Levy, R.H. (2006) 'Reichheld's new metric: the net promoter score', *Chief Marketer*, 22 February, <http://chiefmarketer.com/crm_loop/roi/new-metric/022206/index.html>.

Sheth, J.N. and Parvatiyar, A. (2000) 'The evolution of relationship marketing', in Sheth, J.N. and Parvatiyar, A. (eds) *Handbook of Relationship Marketing*, Thousand Oaks, CA: Sage, pp. 119–45.

Sheth, J.N. and Sisodia, R.S. (1999) 'Revisiting marketing's lawlike generalizations', *Journal of the Academy of Marketing Sciences*, **17** (1), 71–87.

Smith, W. and Higgins, M. (2000) 'Reconsidering the relationship analogy', *Journal of Marketing Management*, **16**, 81–94.

Tapp, A. (2004) 'A call to arms for applied marketing academics', *Marketing Intelligence and Planning*, **22** (5), 579–90.

Thomas, M.J. (2000) 'Commentary: princely thoughts on Machiavelli, marketing and management', *European Journal of Marketing*, **34** (5/6), 524–37.

Too, L.H.Y., Souchon, A.L. and Thirkell, P.C. (2001) 'Relationship marketing and customer loyalty in a retail setting: a dynamic exploration', *Journal of Marketing Management*, **17** (3–4), 287–319.

Young, L. (2006) 'Trust: looking forward and back', *Journal of Business and Industrial Marketing*, **21** (7), 92–3.

Zineldin, M. (2000) 'Beyond relationship marketing: technologicalship marketing', *Marketing Intelligence and Planning*, **18** (1), 9–23.

Notes

1 PEST (or STEP) macro-environmentental issues: political, economic, sociological and technological, to which is frequently added legal (L); SWOT: strengths, weaknesses, opportunities and threats.
2 It is not within the scope of this chapter to distinguish between terms such as World Wide Web, Internet, intranet, etc. For a full explanation, see Chaffey, 2006.
3 E-consultancy.com estimate that the cost of sending 1.8 million e-mails is about £6,000/€7200.
4 <http://gorumors.com/crunchies>.

12 Relationship technology

Key issues

- The language of e-commerce
- Mass customisation
- Loyalty schemes and data gathering
- One-to-one marketing
- Database, direct and digital marketing
- Internet marketing and the changing marketplace

Introduction

Developments in information technology (IT) and manufacturing technology have had an enormous impact on the theory and practice of marketing in general and relationship marketing in particular. Recent developments (e.g. social media) have provided exciting new opportunities for developing communications between companies and their customers. Such is the influence of this new technology that it has been claimed that without these advances RM could never hope to be an effective strategy (Zineldin, 2000, p. 9; Sheth and Parvatiyar, 2000, p. 196). Certainly, without these developments few companies would be able to handle the growing complexity of their customer and other core relationships. O'Malley and Tynan (2000, p. 799) suggest that having been initially ignored by strategists, who considered it more appropriate in services and business-to-business (B2B) industries, RM was apparently not 'discovered' by consumer goods marketers until the advent of the technology that made effective data storage and communications processes possible.

The pace of technological change is frantic. Developments are unfolding 'so fast, in so unsettling and complex a manner, that it is very easy to see only thousands of different trees and get thoroughly lost in the wood' (Mitchell, 2000, p. 355). It is easy to get carried away by the prospects of IT and it can be very difficult to tell the genuine from the hype (Gummesson, 1999, p. 89), which may account for the oft-quoted 70–80 per cent failure rate on CRM projects. The speed of this change makes discussion of new technology difficult as even new technology can become outdated quickly. The Internet is also fast evolving. For example three of the biggest social media sites, MySpace (2003), Facebook (2006) and Twitter (2006) were launched after the publication of the first edition of this book. Therefore, to avoid potential embarrassment, this chapter, whilst noting important trends, will concentrate on the actual or potential strategic effects of current technology and its likely successors rather than on the specific technology developments.

Buzzwords

A growing problem when discussing the effects of new technology on marketing theory and practice is the myriad of ways these developments are described by different authors. Buzzwords and phrases are created (and subsequently dumped) at a rate that reflects the technocrat's needs to move on to the next best thing. The evident danger is that this form of technological development will lead rather than facilitate the marketing imperative.

The language of electronic commerce is used to convey the strategic priorities of many companies. At the simplest level the prefix 'e-' is seen to imply updated techniques utilising the tools of the technological age (e.g. e-business, e-commerce, e-tail). The ubiquitous suffix '.com' (or 'dot com'), over and above other suffixes (e.g. co.uk), is seen to convey (despite the bubble bursting) the message that this businesses wishes it to be known that they are competing in this technologically developed marketplace. On an educational level the number of different concepts with the suffix '-marketing' directly associated with IT and technological developments in manufacturing are growing fast (e.g. one-to-one, permission, virtual). To add to the chaos, it is frequently the case that:

■ many conceptual terms have definitions that appear to overlap;
■ different authors use the same terms to describe different concepts or different terms to describe the same concept;
■ some terms 'evolve' into differently named yet apparently similar concepts;
■ terms are denigrated and ditched as the next 'new' idea (if indeed it is new) comes along.

Ground rules

The 'rule' followed in this chapter has been to describe the impact of IT developments on marketing relationships using those terms that appear to offer maximum clarity and/or best represent the industry consensus. It is also seen fit to discuss IT developments in both manufacturing and service delivery as they are both driving and being driven by such developments.

Manufacturing/Service delivery technology

Mass manufacturing and mass marketing may have dominated commercial activity in much of the nineteenth century and nearly all of the twentieth, but this has not always been the case. In earlier times most people traded for basic needs within a confined geographical area. Suppliers knew their customers well and frequently made or supplied to order. It was only with the coming of the Industrial Revolution that the cost advantages of mass production were fully recognised and the consequent need to market on a mass scale developed. Mass production and mass marketing together drove the enormous increase in consumer spending during the twentieth century and were arguably both responsible for the growing wealth (and so-called consumerism) of developed economies.

Mass customisation

The final decade of the twentieth century saw the beginnings of a reaction against 'mass production' and 'mass marketing' both prompted by and promoting technological developments of every sort. The term '**mass customisation**' has come to refer to 'the notion that, by leveraging certain technologies, companies can provide customised products while retaining the economic advantages of mass production' (Sheth and Sisodia, 1999, p. 80). In many ways, the mass-customisation concept can be seen to have developed from service markets where customisation is necessary because of the simultaneity (see Chapter 7) of delivery and consumption (Bhattacharya and Bolton, 2000, p. 327). In manufacturing industries, mass customisation 'entails the use of flexible processes, structures and management to produce varied and even individualised products' at the same low cost of standardised products (Bhattacharya and Bolton, 2000, p. 327). Mass customisation differs from individually crafted products or services (for which there also appears to be a growing trend) in that it maintains the economies of scale advantages of mass production. In many industrial sectors, the capability is becoming available to produce more and more varieties and choices for the customer although, as Box 12.1 points out, there is still a gap between the vision and the reality.

The individual tailoring of products suggested by 'mass customisation' has been described by Ira Matahia (quoted by Chaffey *et al.*, 2000, p. 292), CEO of Brand Futures Group, as 'complicated simplicity'. Matahia goes on to suggest that as consumers crave individually tailored products there will be a strong demand for unique items. For businesses, this will mean the end of a mass audience orientated approach and the beginning of an 'audience-of-one' (or 'segment-of-one') approach to marketing.

Although these developments should not be over-emphasised (most consumers are still happy to benefit from the cost savings of mass-manufactured products or mass-supplied services), the growing wealth of consumers (relative to the cost of living) has meant more and more are looking for more individual, personally tailored offerings (see Box 12.1). While mass marketing is not yet dead (companies such as Coca-Cola or Nestlé certainly have some life left in them) there is evidence that 'mass customisation' is a recognisable, although occasionally faltering, trend.

Box 12.1   Unto This Last – 'local craftsmanship at mass production prices'

Unto This Last is a furniture studio and workshop, based on two sites in London. Its name comes from the title of a book by John Ruskin, published in 1862, in which he advocated a return to localised, craftsman/artisan workshops as an antidote to the conditions which industrialisation had imposed on much of Britain's working class. As a fore-runner of William Morris and the Arts and Crafts Movement, Ruskin's thoughts were influential, but the rising standard of living which mass manufacturing brought to the West meant that his pleas were ultimately seen as anachronistic. But according to Olivier Geoffrey, founder of Unto This Last, CNC machining* and on-demand manufacturing open up possibilities for the craftsman in the community which may yet see Ruskin's vision realised.

Unto This Last's designs are . . . a reflection and a result of distribution systems and logistics. A customer who visits the store can see some examples of the products on sale, but with the exception of a few small gift items, no products are held in stock, instead they are manufactured to order. This reduces the costs of storage and inventory, whilst also allowing the company to carry more than 2000 items in its catalogue. Orders are made in-store and delivered pre-assembled, and because the furniture is shipped direct from the store it means packaging is also greatly reduced. In this way, by using digital manufacturing processes and some of the techniques recognisable from other mass customisation initiatives, Unto This Last can offer custom-made furniture at close to mass-production prices.

*CNC is a machine tool that uses programs to automatically execute a series of machining operations.

(*Source*: Matt Sinclair, 26 February 2010, <http://no-retro.com/home/category/mass-customisation> (accessed 26 August 2010))

Process services

Technology has also changed the way many services are delivered often replacing costly face-to-face interaction. This has happened in many industries including travel, digital retailing and banking. For example, in the past banking was considered a high contact service with customers regularly visiting the bank premises, many of whom knew their bank manager and staff on some personal level. One of the side-effects of the introduction of technology is that customers are no longer required to ever again visit bank premises and interact with staff. This, coupled with depersonalised call centres, often based overseas, has demoted banking from a personalised service to an anonymised, technology-driven process. There is an evident benefit for the customer in that Internet banking has made the costs and rewards of banking more transparent and encouraged customers to shop around. For the banks, however, there is a potential downside. In the USA a survey of senior banking executives revealed that 90 per cent of US banking institutions emphasised relationship banking or service quality as their primary value proposition (McAdam 2005). Yet technology is causing theses relationships to break down (if they ever formed in the first place). Research has shown that when people evaluate another individual they make stronger, quicker, more confident judgements than when they evaluate organisations (Palmatier *et al.*, 2006). It also suggests consumers see greater relational benefits when they are in a relationship with high contact, customised services versus the more standardized, moderate contact service (Kinard and Capella 2006). This issue, therefore, has significant managerial implications for firms who try to increase their service efficiencies through the intercession of technology (Palmatier *et al.*, 2006).

Time to market

In technological industries (i.e. those companies producing, as opposed to simply using, this new technology) time to market is a key factor. Windows of opportunity for any new technically innovative product are smaller than before and product life cycles (PLCs) appear to be getting shorter. The pressure to get a new product to market means that, in general, there is less time than before to spend on research. As Gordon (1998, p. 6) notes, 'marketers used to use market research to help identify issues and assess customer response' but under the more pressurised conditions that now exist this research can 'take more time than the marketer has got'. This can lead to problems (see Box 12.2). Market conditions are, Gordon notes, changing so fast that a company addressing current research may quickly find itself dealing with yesterday's issues. In many instances, instead of pre-launch research, companies are using the marketplace as their testing ground. The 'beta testing of prototypes' is a common technique employed online by software development companies and is becoming common in technology-orientated firms (Dann and Dann, 2001, p. 211). These firms are using the flexibility of technologically advanced development methods to 'roll out' (and at the same time adapt) early versions of products while simultaneously testing their response. This testing (as opposed to research) has the advantage of producing results based on actual as opposed to forecast sales while at the same time generating revenue.

Box 12.2   Apple iphone

Even the biggest and best technology companies are prone to criticism when things don't go quite right. When Apple launched its iphone in 2007 it was seen as the latest in the line of technologically superior products from the company. However, ever since the launch there have been a variety of problems ranging from connectivity, missing functions and one that led to the issue of 100+ pages of phone bills. In 2010 the launch of the iphone 4 led to complaints relating to the phone's antenna. Specifically customers were complaining that signal strength dropped and calls terminated when the phones were held in a certain way. According to BBC News there have been requests to recall the phones. It seems unlikely, however, that Apple will do this as it would affect its bottom line (a recall might cost $1.5 billion) and its reputation.

Source: BBC News, 15 July 2010

Information technology

It is generally acknowledged that IT has potential for relationship building, if used effectively. Developments in IT allow a relationship-orientated management to store and manipulate information about their customers and, ultimately, to provide those customers with a better service. Unfortunately it frequently falls short. According to Peppers and Rogers (2000, p. 243) in today's 'interactive age' customers:

> are accustomed to having their needs met immediately, conveniently and inexpensively. That's why, for many people, contacting customer service representatives can be an excruciating experience. Between navigating lengthy menus of push-button options, waiting on hold for what seems an eternity, never getting a reply to an e-mail, and not having you or your problems remembered the next time you call back, it's no wonder many customers think customer 'service' is a cruel joke.

Loyalty programmes

One of the most prominent uses of IT has been in the management of loyalty (or more strictly usage) programmes, although some would suggest that this has more to do with sales promotion than relationship development. According to Bejou and Palmer (1998, p. 7), for example, many such loyalty programmes are nothing more than crude attempts to increase short-term sales without adding to the long-term relationship with the customer. Others would argue that 'loyalty technology' has augmented the traditional usage programme (based on 'low-tech' stamps or tokens) and can be very successful in driving up turnover.[1] Uncles (1994, p. 339) suggests three reasons why they might be successful:

■ The range of organisations involved in promotions and programmes is much wider, extending beyond high street retailers and petrol stations to encompass international travel, financial services and all levels in the distribution chain.

■ National borders are no longer a constraint (e.g. Dunnes Stores' loyalty scheme operates in Northern Ireland and the Republic of Ireland).

■ Recognition of some usage schemes is widespread, leading to fairly complex offers to retain customers (e.g. British Airways and Air Miles, Nectar and Sainsbury, BP, Expedia and others).

Customer 'data', captured as part of the loyalty scheme process, is considered to have value and the potential to augment a relationship. (Storing data for later retrieval is known as 'data warehousing'; manipulation of 'warehoused' data is known as 'data mining'.) Much of the captured and stored data, however, would appear to be surplus to current requirements, although it holds out the possibility of being utilised at a later date.

One-to-one marketing

One-to-one marketing has become, according to Mitchell (2000, p. 354), 'an almost ubiquitous buzz phrase, almost a cliché, used to cover everything from good old-fashioned junk-mail to the most sophisticated forms of mass customised communications and products'. Data collection does offer potential for one-to-one communication where it improves the information flow and the systems are in place such that knowledge will be derived from it. Linking suppliers, distributors and customers through electronic data interchange (EDI) in a network of closer relationships potentially provides enormous cost advantages (Zineldin, 2000, p. 20). Used appropriately, technology can help a company learn from every customer interaction and deepen a relationship by advancing ideas and solutions likely to appeal to that customer (Gordon, 1998, p. 168). As Marty Abrams (2000, p. 7) vice-president of Experian notes:

> manufacturing expertise is a given. If you do not make a great product that you deliver at a great price, you do not have a ticket to play. What will differentiate the winners [from] the losers is their ability to reap the efficiencies that come from understanding the nature of individual demands. Not only will the market make goods better, cheaper and quicker, but it will produce the right goods based on an information driven understanding of individual consumer demand applied at an aggregate level.

However utopian this vision may appear, technology can theoretically make this possible. The Internet already enables users to customise what consumers see and hear, how they choose to buy and what specification the product or service should be. This attention to individual customer needs is already close to the dream of 'one-to-one marketing'. Here the implication is the development of long-term relationships with each customer in order to better understand that customer's needs and better deliver the 'service' that meets the individual's requirements (Chaffey *et al.*, 2000, p. 290). RM theory provides the conceptual underpinning to one-to-one marketing as it emphasises customer service through knowledge of the customer and deals with the markets segmented at the level of the individual.

Database, direct and digital marketing

The 'database' has been described as the engine that enables RM (ibid., p. 194) and as being at the heart of direct marketing. More recently the term 'digital marketing' has become vogue for many of the same ideas albeit extended from databases to platforms on-line. By way of definition:

- **database marketing (DbM)** is using a database to hold and analyse customer data and helping create strategies for marketing;
- **direct marketing (DM)** focuses on using the database to communicate (and sometimes distribute) directly to customers so as to attract a direct response;
- **digital marketing (DgM)** the promotion of products and services using the Internet, mobile telephony and other interactive channels.

Möller and Halinen (2000, p. 33) suggest that rapidly developing information technology has created a 'primarily practice based and consultant-driven literature on managing customer relationships through databases'. These programmes (under the auspices of RM) are often criticised for not being 'customer-focused'. Rather, it is suggested, they are designed more to raise switching costs and/or rely on database-driven information to 'market at' customers who may or may not want a relationship (Barnes and Howlett, 1998, p. 15).

Caught up, as we are, in the enthusiasm for technology's information-gathering capabilities, it is possible that companies are forgetting that relationships take (at least) two (Fournier *et al.*, 1998, p. 42). Often DbM is little more than enhanced manipulation of customer data to create an illusion of a customised response. Despite this some authors suggest that RM, DM and DbM are converging to create a powerful new marketing paradigm (Chaffey *et al.*, 2000, p. 290) where RM provides the conceptual underpinning, direct and digital marketing provides the tactics and DbM is the technical enabler. The paradox is that as technology develops and more information becomes available through different media, the importance of human contact may actually be increasing.

The turn of the century saw the rise of **customer relationship management** (CRM) as the new strategy for the digital age. This is covered in more detail in Chapter 13.

Internet marketing[2]

Although database technology is important, perhaps the greatest change now and in the future will be in the market itself. Nowhere is this change more evident than the medium of the Internet. The Internet is affecting every facet of business life. In 2010 there are an estimated[3] 1,966,514,816 users, up over 445 per cent since 2000 with the biggest increases in Asia (621 per cent) and Europe (352 per cent). This means 28 per cent of the world's population are capable of going online.

Although the Internet has become indispensable in many people's lives, the argument rages as to the effect of online marketing on the customer retention and/or relationship building process. To some the Internet is the very encapsulation of 'one-to-one marketing' and, as such, gives companies the ability to establish enduring relationships with individual customers. On the other hand, encouraging customers to go online could lead to desertion in the long term.

In many, if not most, organizations today the Internet has become the shop window to the world and principal means of communication. Internet data capture (particularly 'cookies' and related technology) gives the marketer the opportunity to establish actual as opposed to predicted behaviour as the customer moves from site to site (this has data protection implications as noted in Chapter 11). Woodall (2000, p. 5) suggests:

> The Internet (in theory) allows customers to seek the lowest price, and firms to get quotes from more suppliers; it reduces transaction costs and barriers to entry. In other words it moves the economy closer to the textbook model of perfect competition, which assumes abundant information, many buyers and sellers, zero transaction costs and no barriers to entry. It makes these assumptions a bit less far-fetched.

The Internet is, however, a passive medium and the means by which one attracts customers to commercial and other organisational websites has become an art. Advertising, stationery, vehicles invariably promote website addresses. E-mails direct potential visitors to specific sites and **search engine optimization (SEO)** has become a subject of intense interest.

Another area of potential for organisations has been the growth in popularity[4] of **social media** (or **social networking**) sites. Boyd and Ellison (2007) define social media websites as web-based services that allow individuals to:

- construct a public or semi-public profile within a bounded system;
- articulate a list of other users with whom they share a connection;
- view and traverse their list of connections and those made by others within the system.

In 2010 it has been estimated[5] that 940 million people will use social media networks. Although principally designed to stimulate personal relationships their commercial importance has gradually been recognized. Many organizations and brands have their own pages on Facebook, Twitter and other such sites and aim to build communities around them.

Other communities exist that have been formed specifically around brands or organizations rather than social networks. According to Baron *et al.* (2010, p. 154) there are three (not mutually exclusive) communities. They are:

- **communities of practice:** networks linked by their behaviour e.g. Buzznet (music and culture);
- **values-based communities:** neo-tribes where members share values, lifestyles or self images rather than demographic traits e.g. Harley-Davidson (see Case Study);
- **issue-based communities:** specific issues that band people together in a community even if only temporarily (e.g. Save our South London Line[6]).

Technology and marketplace relationships

With the growth of commercial and social media sites marketing relationships are changing. Adaptations of established associations (e.g. customer/supplier/internal/external) are appearing as Internet technology holds out the potential of new types of relationships (see Figure 12.1). (Mitchell 2000, pp. 356–9) suggests these include:

- marketer–customer;
- agent–customer;
- marketer–marketer;
- customer–customer.

Figure 12.1
Virtual
exchange:
potential new
types of
relationships

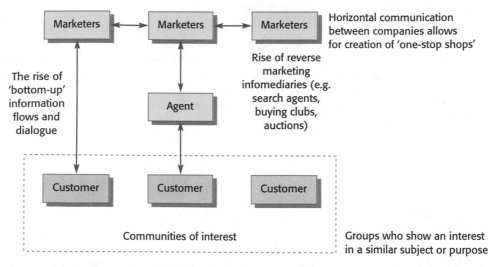

(*Source*: Adapted from Mitchell, 2000, pp. 356–9)

Marketer–customer

The traditional market relationship has seen changes with the rise of 'bottom-up' information flows' and 'dialogues' between the marketer and their customers. These flows are frequently initiated by the customer.

Agent–customer

The 'death of the intermediary' predicted by many in the early days of the Internet has proved incorrect. Indeed, the rise in the number of 'cybermediaries', such as Amazon and Lastminute.com, continue apace. Traditional retailers, albeit after a slow start, have begun to master the Internet and in some cases make it their own. The success of price comparison sites such as Moneysupermarket.com and LastMinute.com is also an indication that consumers welcome mediation (if the mediator is trusted). One area that may develop further is that of 'reverse marketing'. This includes 'infomediaries' such as search agents, buying clubs and 'reverse auctions'. The principal difference will be that 'infomediaries' will (theoretically) be working on behalf of the consumer rather than as an agent for the supplier.

Marketer–marketer

The growth of 'alliances' was discussed in Chapter 10 and the Internet has, and will in the future, promoted this trend. The Internet relies heavily on customers actively approaching the company. The importance of 'visibility' is, therefore, of considerable importance. Collaboration between companies, whether through links, vertical portals (e.g. handbag.com) or online communities (e.g. HSBC Business Network), will undoubtedly increase.

Customer–customer

The rise of consumer groups (or communities of interest) has become a feature of the new marketplace. These will comprise groups of individuals who share an interest in a similar subject or purpose (see **Box** 3.1). It stands to reason that marketers will find these communities very valuable for targeting purposes and it may be in the interest of marketers to sponsor or otherwise support such ventures.

Summary

This chapter discussed the effects of developments in manufacturing and information technologies. It noted the confusion of terms, particularly when describing relational strategies and tactics. It suggested that there is evidence to suggest that consumers are reacting against mass production and mass marketing, both promoted by and promoting technological development. As a result of this trend and the creation of technologies to support it, 'mass customisation' (the customisation of products while retaining economies of scale) may be of growing importance in the future. In technology-driven industries, time to market is now a major priority. This is affecting companies' ability to undertake market research as it can take more time than marketers have available.

Information technology development has enormous potential for building one-to-one relationships although developments in this area may not always meet with customers' wholehearted approval. Loyalty programmes were highlighted as a prominent utilisation of technology, although, in general, they are perceived to be more akin to short-term promotions than longer-term relationship building.

The concepts of direct marketing, database marketing, digital marketing, customer relationship management and Internet marketing were discussed and the danger of substituting technology for 'relationship proximity' highlighted. Although RM has been accused of being too much 'theory based' and not concerned enough with practical and measurable relationship management, it serves to underpin the principles associated with these tactics albeit the reality may be different.

The changing marketplace, particularly as a result of developments in Internet technology, was highlighted. The requirement for the customer to be proactive and the 'democratising' of information processing are adapting current, and developing new, relationships.

Discussion questions
1 Why is marketing research expenditure perceived to be difficult to justify?
2 What do you understand by the term 'one-to-one marketing'?
3 Distinguish between the terms 'relationship marketing', 'direct marketing', 'database marketing' and 'digital marketing'.
4 How is the Internet changing the marketplace?

Case study   Social networks; cash cow or corporate headache?

Social networks and social media generally are a great opportunity for marketers. We can gain feedback and insight into our customers. The problem is that we might not like what we hear, and this is the double-edged sword facing the marketing world.

The general approach has been one of non-engagement. Social networks are fast moving, mostly unregulated places that tend to give a platform to the most vocal. This has led many companies, especially those with compliance departments, to bury their heads in the sand with a policy of not getting involved – nothing can go wrong if you're not doing it in the first place. Unfortunately, this completely misses the point.

Whether your company is big or small it's likely somebody is saying something about you somewhere online. That may be on a blog, through Twitter or via another social network. If you aren't aware of what is being said and where it is being said, you are missing a trick.

First, you're losing out on the chance to understand what people think. You're also missing an opportunity to engage, react and try to improve people's perception of your brand. As many of us already know, quite often the vocal minority can cause us the most problems, and engagement, when done badly, can often make things worse. But this is no excuse for shying away. Customer service doesn't improve by ignoring people.

Most customer services activity does not occur in an arena as public as an online social network so we need to tread carefully. Often the best approach to take with those being unreasonable online is to drive the conversation offline. This has two positive effects – the conversation will not remain in Google for ever and people are often more reasonable when speaking to a 'real' person.

In contrast, those who are vocal about our businesses in a positive way offer one of the best opportunities we have as marketers. By nurturing advocates we can improve brand image and drive more traffic and conversions to our websites. This comes down to peer-to-peer recommendation.

The amount of searches done online with the words 'online review' appended has more than quadrupled in the past four years, according to Google Insights. We only have to look at the influence that TripAdvisor.com now has in the travel sector to see what the effects of this have been.

Social networks can and do drive the bottom line – we just don't always see the connection because we don't see what has motivated our customers' purchases. Very often the motivator is what a customer's peers think, what they have said, or what they have reviewed online.

The first practical step to engaging with social networks and social media more widely is to be aware of what is being said. Happily there are now many cost-effective digital brand-monitoring tools available. The next, and more difficult step, is to engage with these audiences, build advocacy and manage negative feedback. The bottom line is that ignoring things doesn't make them go away.

(*Source*: Daniel Rowles, *The Marketer*, April 2010)

Case study questions

1 What are the pitfalls associated with non-engagement?
2 What is the best response to those who are 'vocal about our business' in positive and in negative ways?

References

Abrams, M. (2000) 'Contribution to debate paper', *Interactive Marketing*, **2** (1), 6–11.

Barnes, J.G. (1994) 'Close to the customer: but is it really a relationship?', *Journal of Marketing Management*, **10**, 561–70.

Barnes, J.G. and Howlett, D.M. (1998) 'Predictors of equity in relationships between service providers and retail customers', *International Journal of Bank Marketing*, **16** (1), 5–23.

Baron, S., Conway, T. and Warnaby, G. (2010) *Relationship Marketing: A Customer Experience Approach*, London, Sage.

Bejou, D. and Palmer, A. (1998) 'Service failure and loyalty: an exploratory empirical study of airline customers', *Journal of Services Marketing*, **12** (1), 7–22.

Bhattacharya, C.B. and Bolton, R.N. (2000) 'Relationship marketing in mass markets', in Sheth, J.N. and Parvatiyar, A. (eds) *Handbook of Relationship Marketing*, Thousand Oaks, CA: Sage, pp. 327–54.

Boyd, D.M. and Ellison, W.B. (2007) 'Social network sites: definition, history and scholarship', *Journal of Computer-mediated Communication*, **13** (1), 210–30.

Chaffey, D., Mayer, R., Johnston, K. and Ellis-Chadwick, F. (2000) *Internet Marketing*, Harlow: Pearson Education.

Dann, S.J. and Dann, S.M. (2001) *Strategic Internet Marketing*, Milton, Qld: John Wiley & Sons.

Fournier, S., Dobscha, S. and Mick, D.G. (1998) 'Preventing the premature death of relationship marketing', *Harvard Business Review*, January/February.

Gordon, I.H. (1998) *Relationship Marketing*, Etobicoke, Ontario: John Wiley & Sons.

Gummesson, E. (1999) *Total Relationship Marketing: Rethinking Marketing Management from 4Ps to 30Rs*, Oxford: Butterworth Heinemann.

Kinard, B.R. and Capella, M.L. (2006) 'Relationship marketing: the influence of consumer involvement on perceived service benefits', *Journal of Service Marketing*, **21** (6), 359–68.

McAdam, P. (2005) 'Give the customers what they want (and in most cases, it's not a relationship)', *Banking Strategies*, BAI Online, <www.bai.org> (accessed 12 April 2007).

Mitchell, A. (2000) 'In one-to-one marketing, which one comes first?', *Interactive Marketing*, **1** (4), 354–67.

Möller, K. and Halinen, A. (2000) 'Relationship marketing theory: its roots and direction', *Journal of Marketing Management*, **16**, 29–54.

O'Malley, L. and Tynan, C. (2000) 'Relationship marketing in consumer markets: rhetoric or reality?', *European Journal of Marketing*, **34** (7), 797–815.

Palmatier, R.W., Dant, R.P., Grewal, D. and Evans, K.R. (2006) 'Factors influencing the effectiveness of relationship marketing: a meta-analysis', *Journal of Marketing*, **70** (October), 136–53.

Peppers, D. and Rogers, M. (2000) 'Build a one-to-one learning relationship with your customers', *Interactive Marketing*, **1** (3), 243–50.

Sheth, J.N. and Parvatiyar, A. (2000) 'Relationship marketing in consumer markets: antecedents and consequences', in Sheth, J.N. and Parvatiyar, A. (eds) *Handbook of Relationship Marketing*, Thousand Oaks, CA: Sage, pp. 171–207.

Sheth, J.N. and Sisodia, R.S. (1999) 'Revisiting marketing's lawlike generalizations', *Journal of the Academy of Marketing Sciences*, **17** (1), 71–87.

Uncles, M. (1994) 'Do you or your customer need a loyalty scheme?', *Journal of Targeting, Measurement and Analysis*, **2** (4), 335–50.

Woodall, P. (2000) 'Untangling e-conomics: a survey of the new economy (Part 1)', e-businessforum.com, *The Economist*, 27 September.

Zineldin, M. (2000) 'Beyond relationship marketing: technologicalship marketing', *Marketing Intelligence and Planning*, **18** (1), 9–23.

Notes

1 For example, in August 2010 Costa Coffee announced that more than 3 million customers had signed up to their loyalty card in the previous six months.

2 There is always debate about using terms such as Internet marketing or e-marketing when, in effect, they are new mediums for communication and interaction rather than new strategies *per se*.

3 Source: <www.internetworldstats.com>.

4 Mashable.com report that the number of US users doubled between 2007 and 2009.

5 Source: Social Media@Work.

6 <http://www.bellenden.net/srug/news/save-our-south-london-line-campaign>

13 Conceptual developments

Key issues

- The relationship marketing issue
- Customer relationship management
- Social marketing
- Service-dominant logic

Introduction

The first edition of this text concluded after Chapter 12. This additional chapter was added to the second edition (under the heading 'Back to the future') and was designed to bring the relationship marketing (RM) debate up to date with consideration of the influence of customer relationship marketing (CRM). In this edition these ideas are discussed and revisited. In addition, in the best part of a decade since the original publication, other distinct (but not wholly disconnected) concepts have developed which owe their existence, at least in part, to relationship marketing research. Two of these concepts, social marketing and service-dominant logic, are discussed.

RM research

The end of the twentieth century was a watershed for RM. Certainly the clarity (and to some extent the certainty) surrounding relational concepts in the 1990s was not as evident in the new millennium. Whereas there had always been differences in tactical emphasis and a lack of a precise definition (or definitions), researchers in the past appeared willing to accept, or at least acknowledge, a range of broad principles associated with relationship marketing. This 'broad church' approach was being challenged. A major rift developed between those who maintain a holistic view of diverse organisational relationships and those who wish to de-emphasise all relationships except that of the customer–supplier dyad.

From the earliest discussions on relationship marketing, a diversity of influences has led to a surfeit of academic perspectives from which RM theory (or more correctly theories) were to develop. With so many doubts concerning relationship marketing's origins and the development of regional schools of thought (see Chapter 2), it is no wonder that different perspectives were to appear. Relationship marketing in the new millennium covered a fragmented set of ideas and theoretical frameworks held together by a faith (largely untested) in the value of relationships within and without the organisation. This faith promoted the accusation that its discussion was characterised more by rhetoric than vigorous examination of what the concept actually means (Möller and Halinnen, 2000).

The new century also brought with it a push for greater marketing accountability led in the USA by the Marketing Science Institute[1] and in the UK by the Chartered Institute of Marketing.[2] This movement sought to justify, through measurement, marketing's place in the organisational framework. With 'marketing metrics' becoming more important on the mainstream marketing agenda, any theories built upon humanistic concepts (as opposed to process doctrine) was open to the charge that its processes were too subjective for the accountability that marketers believed they required.

Between the extremes ran a continuum along which most researchers travelled without being particularly argumentative about their views and accepting, in a reasonable manner, that there are diverse ways of thinking (Levy, 2002). Although broad variations created difficulties, this was accepted as part of RM's broad appeal. There was a problem with the diversity in operational approaches employed such that it was 'impossible to delimit the (RM) domain' as the boundaries were 'completely permeable and elastic' and this resulted in 'difficulties in identifying appropriate contexts for empirical research and exacerbated conceptual problems within the emerging discipline' (O'Malley and Tynan, 2000, p. 809). Despite this the broad 'school of RM' was holding together largely because the 'philosophy of relationships' was still a developing theme and RM research did appear to be extending the theoretical boundaries of marketing (e.g. through internal marketing).

To get an overview of the developing RM themes there is a need to track back. A feature of older definitions and writings on the subject of relationship marketing was that it focused wholly on the supplier–customer relationship (the 'supplier–customer dyad'). Later contributions to the relationship marketing debate, however, were seen to widen RM's scope (Buttle, 1996). According to Gummesson (1999, p. 20), marketing was more than just the dyadic relationship between the buyer and the seller; rather it represented the whole series of 'relationships, networks and interactions' that the company (or more strictly the company's employees or representatives) undertook as part of their commercial dealings. RM thinking, therefore, developed away from the strictly 'two-way dialogue' between the supplier and the customer towards the synonymous development of other company relationships.

At the beginning of the new millennium this largely agreed multi-relationship approach appeared to be under challenge. Although 'breadth of domain' had always been an issue, arguments appeared to be coalescing around two, perhaps irreconcilable, camps of researchers. A schism developed between those who conceive marketing from a broad and pluralistic orientation and those who take a narrower, functional marketing perspective. Ideas were polarising between those researchers who continue to support the holistic, multi-relationship definition of relationship marketing and those whose focus is solely concerned with the 'customer–supplier dyad' (Payne, 2000, p. 16). In effect, the schism was between a broad definition of RM with a narrow application (that could be termed 'focused') and a narrower viewpoint with a distinctly broader application (that might be called 'diffuse') (see Figure 13.1). Among this latter group the suggestion is that non-customer relationships are 'outside the domain of marketing' and that their inclusion in the marketing research agenda 'risks diluting the value and contribution of the marketing discipline in directing relationship marketing practice and research and theory development' (Parvatiyar and Sheth, 2000).

It would seem that the driving force behind the diffuse approach may be the belief that only by adapting RM in such a way that it can be embraced across the board can it have the potential to become the dominant paradigm and orientation of marketing (Parvatiyar and Sheth, 2000). A feature of this is the extension of the term 'relationships' to the non-personal, i.e. technology-driven contact associated with direct marketing and, latterly, customer relationship management.

Customer relationship management

Payne (2006, p. 4) defines customer relationship management as:

> a business approach that seeks to create, develop and enhance relationships with carefully targeted customers in order to improve customer value and corporate profitability and, therefore, maximize shareholder value.

It would be difficult, using this definition to separate RM and CRM so there is a need to look deeper than the rhetoric. Although frequently associated with RM, the term itself emerged from the IT supplier community rather than the marketing literature in the mid-1990s (Payne and Frow, 2005, p. 167). It was used to describe data collection and those activities surrounding the management of the customer–supplier interface (Boulding *et al.*, 2005, p. 156). CRM, according to Payne (2006) 'unites the potential of new technologies and new marketing thinking to deliver profitable, long-term relationships'. It has certainly caught the imagination of marketers. In 2008 the worldwide market revenue in CRM technology grew 12.5 per cent to $9.15 billion.[3]

As noted CRM is often associated with the use of IT in managing commercial relationships (Ryals, 2000, p. 259), where the database is regarded as 'an agent of surrogacy . . . enlisted to help marketers to recreate the operating styles of yesterday's merchants' (Sisodia and Wolfe, 2000, p. 526). Depending on your source of reference, a number of different aspects are associated with CRM. These include data

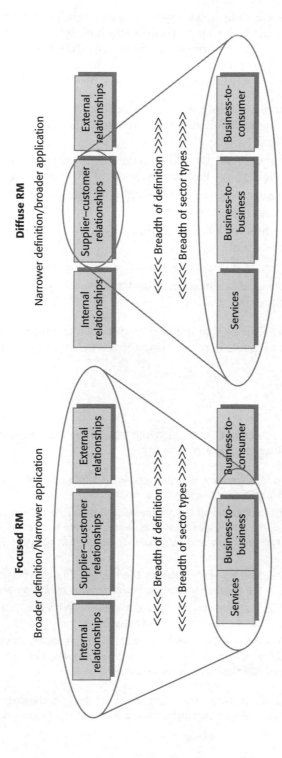

Figure 13.1 Focused and diffuse relationship marketing

warehousing, customer service systems, smart cards, call centres, e-commerce, point-of-sale terminals and web marketing together with operational and sales systems including analytical and predictive planning (McDonald, 2000, pp. 28–9; Little and Marandi, 2003, p. 199).

According to Kelly (2000, pp. 264–5), key analytical CRM applications include:

- *Sales analysis*: offering the organisation an integrated perspective on sales and enabling the sales function to understand the underlying trends and patterns in the sales data.
- *Customer profile analysis*: allowing the organisation to distinguish, from the mass of customer data, the individuals as well as the micro-segments.
- *Campaign analysis*: providing the ability to measure the effectiveness of individual campaigns and different media.
- *Loyalty analysis*: measuring customer loyalty with reference to the duration of the customer relationship.
- *Customer contact analysis*: analysis of the customer contact history of any individual.
- *Profitability analysis*: measuring and analysing the many different dimensions of profitability.

The suspicion remains that the largely unspoken assumption among senior managers that CRM is desirable may be misplaced as it is not the panacea (see Box 13.1) it is

Box 13.1 CRM myths

According to Little and Marandi (2003, pp. 205–6) there are a number of myths surrounding CRM that require correction, including:

- CRM means management of customers. *For management read manipulated. In reality it is often the customer who controls the relationship.*
- CRM software will solve all our problems. *Bringing information together in one place is useful but only if you know what to do with it. There is also the thorny problem of who 'owns' the system and who should have access to it. In reality this is where most systems fall down.*
- CRM applications will always pay for themselves. *The cost benefit is rarely convincing. Adding this to the number of total expensive failures makes a nonsense of this claim.*
- All customers love new technologies. *No they don't. Even those who are technically literate do not like being manipulated by systems.*
- Our organisation speaks to its customers with one voice. *Anyone with, for example, a credit card or a loan or a mortgage with a company will note how many times they are offered another one by the same company.*

As O'Malley (2003, p. 141) notes, companies are using 'technology that they don't understand very well in order to help implement a process they are unfamiliar with'.

often claimed to be (Stone *et al.*, 2001, p. 31). The problem is that the 'quick fix' offered by technology often fails to take account of customer care issues (O'Malley, 2003, p. 144). According to KPMG consultants (Sussex and Cox, 2002, p. 1), CRM is falling into disrepute because technology-led approaches fail to deliver real benefits.

RM and CRM are, therefore, as distinct as the terms 'sales' and 'marketing'. Despite their philosophical relationship they are different in three main regards:

■ RM recognises the complexity of the organizations relationships

■ RM looks to build relationships using technology where appropriate

■ RM is more appropriate to services and business-to-business

■ CRM concentrates on the customer–supplier relationship

■ CRM's concentration is on technology and what you can do with it

■ CRM is more appropriate to consumer goods and process services.

Social marketing

Social marketing is an area of marketing research that has developed alongside RM research. Its unique feature is that it takes lessons learnt from commercial marketing and applies them to helping resolve social and health problems (Stead *et al.*, 2007). According to Andreasen (2006, p. 91) it is:

> the application of commercial marketing technologies to the analysis, planning, execution and evaluation of programmes designed to influence the voluntary behaviour of target audiences in order to improve their personal welfare and that of society.

Social marketing, much like relationship marketing, is not a new concept. It has its roots in the earliest marketing literature but has really entered mainstream debate in and around the new millennium. Probably the first published mention of socially related marketing was by Cherington (1920) who, in the early part of the last century, pondered whether marketing performance and social welfare might be enhanced by focusing on the underlying functions of marketing. In the 1950s G. D. Wiebe, recognizing that marketing sold products, questioned 'Why can't you sell brotherhood and rational thinking like you sell soap?' (Wiebe, 1951). Kotler and Levy (1969, 1971) reintroduced the theme under the guise of 'de-marketing' and the phrase 'social marketing' itself was coined by Kotler and Zaltman (1971, p. 3). By the end of the first decade of the new millennium this field of study had produced numerous textbooks,[4] articles, its own academic journal (*Social Marketing Quarterly*) and a number of study centres. In 2008 the first World Social Marketing Conference was held in Brighton. Social marketing is now very highly regarded in marketing circles and is recognised and practised by numerous UN and government agencies, consulting and communication firms (Andreasen, 2006, p. 91).

Social marketing frequently deals with behaviours that require effort, over the long term, to change. As such this behaviour is 'more susceptible to strategic relationship marketing than traditional transactional thinking' (Hastings and Saren, 2003, p. 311). As with RM, social marketers have adopted the view that full engagement is the way to bring about behavioural change. However, strictly speaking, it is not a theory in itself. Rather, it is a 'framework or structure that draws from many bodies of knowledge such as psychology, sociology, anthropology and communications theory . . . to meet society's desire to improve its citizens' quality of life' (MacFadyen *et al.*, 1999, p. 1).

It differs from commercial marketing in that rather than exchanging goods and services for money social marketing usually involves the mutual transfer of psychological, social or other intangible exchanges (Hastings and Saren, 2003, p. 309). However, as the concept has developed discussion has started to take forms that may not be strictly non-commercial. The Chartered Institute of Marketing (CIM) have noted that although 'it's been accepted for years that social marketing can learn from commercial marketing, we're at a point when commercial marketing can learn from social marketing' (CIM, 2009, p. 46). In this they are relating to the importance for marketers to understand customer psychology and motivation in order to change behaviour. They are also perhaps pointing to commercial examples such as Dove's 'Campaign for Real Beauty', EDF Energy's 'Team Green Britain' and Sainsbury's 'Healthy Lifestyles' where the application of social marketing thinking uses the insights gained to develop successful marketing strategies. According to Drummond (2010, p. 1) the 'language of social marketing' is already used by Unilever, Proctor and Gamble and GSK.

This new '**corporate social marketing**', while evidently associated with commercial gain, fulfils the criterion of seemingly improving individual welfare and that of society albeit sometimes at a superficial level. According to Drummond (2010) corporate social marketing is:

> how companies use marketing principles and practices to motivate their customers to act on social issues in order to achieve short, medium and long-term commercial benefits.

Critics point to the Dove's campaign and draw attention to its Unilever stable mate Axe/Lynx and the seemingly conflicting messages of their campaigns! Whether social marketing and its commercial equivalent can co-exist theoretically will be an interesting talking point. Regardless social marketing is influencing, and no doubt will continue to influence, the broader marketing landscape.

Service-dominant logic

Service-dominant logic (S-DL) has, in a relatively few years, become one of the most discussed and debated theories in marketing. The ideas and conceptions around service-dominant logic (originally called 'new dominant logic') came to world attention in a *Journal of Marketing* article by Stephen Vargo and Robert Lusch (2004) which was greeted at the time of publication with considerable fanfare. Over the intervening period the original authors have published numerous follow-up papers (e.g. Vargo and Lusch, 2006a, 2006b, 2006c, 2008, Lusch and Vargo, 2006, Vargo, 2008) refining and consolidating the original ideas (see Box 13.3). Service-dominant logic has, over the period since its inception, stimulated journal special editions, conferences and workshops around the world and placed Vargo and Lusch high on conferences most-wanted lists. In 2009 alone there were S-DL conferences or workshops in Auckland, Cambridge, Capri, Hawaii, Leipzig, London, Tampere (Finland), Washington and no doubt other less formal sessions in venues around the world. According to Vargo and Lusch (2006c, p. 281) ever since evolving the new logic it has provided 'both impetus and ideas for enhancement as (they) continually strive to co-create a more marketing-grounded understanding of value exchange'.

As with most important marketing developments S-DL has grown out of earlier research. Indeed there is very little of service-dominant logic theory that is actually new. It is rather more a restatement or reordering of ideas from earlier research in areas such as services marketing, relationship marketing, marketing orientation, network perspectives, integrated marketing communications and the resource-based theory, than anything wholly novel (Aitken *et al.*, 2006). What is perhaps different and stimulating is the lens through which these developments are being interpreted. Its developers readily acknowledge that, in leading marketing toward a service-centred model, it is most likely to be achieved though reorientation rather than reinvention (Vargo and Lusch, 2004).

The transition from goods-dominated to service-dominated logic is seen as having passed through a transitional period which reflected many of the thoughts associated with relationship marketing (see Box 13.2). Thus S-DL is seen as the natural successor of RM.

Box 13.2   Goods-dominated to service-dominated logic

Goods-dominant logic		Transitional concepts		Service-dominant logic
Goods	→	Services	→	Service
Products	→	Offerings	→	Experiences
Features/Attributes	→	Benefits	→	Solutions
Value added	→	Co-production	→	Co-creation of value
Profit maximisation	→	Financial engineering	→	Financial feedback/learning
Price	→	Value delivery	→	Value proposition
Equilibrium systems	→	Dynamic systems	→	Complex adaptive systems
Supply chain	→	Value chain	→	Value-created network/constellation
Promotion	→	Integrated marketing communications	→	Dialogue
To market	→	Market to	→	Market with
Product orientation	→	Market orientation	→	Service orientation

(*Source*: Adapted from Lusch and Vargo, 2006, p. 286)

At the heart of Vargo and Lusch's (2004) original concept was the question whether, with so much fragmentation in marketing thought, the discipline was evolving towards a new, dominant service logic having been subjugated by a goods-dominant agenda for much of the proceeding century. The service-centred view was, according to the authors, concerned with the identification and development of core competences and other entities (potential customers) that could benefit from these competences. Goods, it was determined, should no longer be seen as the common denominator of exchange. Instead the value was seen to lie in the application of specialist knowledge, mental skills and physical skills. Goods were, in their conception, only the physical representation of the organisation's skills and techniques. Thus the purchase of a household good represents the acquisition of the skill, knowledge and other competences which go into manufacturing it in the first place rather than the object *per se*. Value meanwhile, long recognised by marketers as the outcome of marketing effort, was reconceived as something created and determined by the user in the consumption process and only then through actual use (so-called 'value-in-use') either directly or mediated by a good (Vargo, 2008). Consequently, in service-dominant logic thinking, it is not the enterprise that delivers value in the exchange. Rather the organisation makes value propositions to the customer/consumer who, it is speculated, is the one who actually creates this value.

S-DL is based upon a set of premises albeit not (yet) set in stone. The original ideas outlined in 2004 have, in some cases, been revised and added to over the decade (see Box 13.3). At the heart of the thinking is that service (as distinct from services) is the fundamental root of all exchanges and that this has been masked in the past by goods-dominant thinking. In this regard operant resourses (including competences and knowledge) are the source of competitive advantage and goods are simply distribution mechanisms for the service provision. Crucially it sees the role of the organisation as the provider of value propositions and the customer as co-creator of this value. Value is always determined, in service-dominant logic, by the beneficiary.

Whereas much of the recent literature appears to support the notion of S-DL (e.g. Baron and Harris, 2006, Ballantyne and Varey, 2006, Maglio and Spohrer, 2008, etc.) there is little evidence of how it would be implemented in practice (Tollin and Jones, 2009). The practical application of theory can only really be judged at the micro-marketing level. However well-fitting a theory might seem to be at the macro level, the devil is in the detail. Any concept that tries to generalise or is framed in universal terms runs the risk of blurring that detail, narrowing the agenda and curtailing rather than expanding the debate. As Stauss (2005, p. 222) notes 'a general definition of service that includes virtually everything defines virtually nothing'. In most FMCG companies, for example, the sheer number of disparate customers, the physical distances involved and real issues concerning efficiency and (above all) cost considerably inhibit attempts to integrate customers in to the production process (Stauss, 2005, p. 225). Even in services marketing (e.g. banking) in first-world markets the growing use of technology as mediator between the organisation and its customers has reduced considerably personal interaction. Is S-DL appropriate, therefore, for these production-line services? Despite the potential insights that the

Box 13.3   Foundation premises

	Original foundation premises	Revised foundation premises
FP1	The application of specialist skill(s) and knowledge is the fundamental unit of exchange	Service is the fundamental basis of exchange
FP2	Indirect exchange masks the fundamental unit of exchange	Indirect exchange masks the fundamental basis of exchange
FP3	Goods are distribution mechanisms for service provision	Goods are distribution mechanisms for service provision
FP4	Knowledge is the fundamental source of competitive advantage	Operant resources are the fundamental source of competitive advantage
FP5	All economies are service economies	All economies are service economies
FP6	The customer is always a co-producer	The customer is always a co-creator of value
FP7	The enterprise can only make value propositions	The enterprise cannot deliver value, but only offer value propositions
FP8	A service centred view is customer orientated and relational	A service centred view is customer orientated and relational
FP9	Organisations exist to integrate and transform microspecialised competences into complex services that are demanded in the marketplace	All economic and social actors are resource integrators
FP10		Value is always uniquely and phenomenologically determined by the beneficiary

(*Source*: Vargo and Lusch, 2004, Vargo, 2008)

service-dominant approach may bring, declaring victory and abandoning the notion of separate fields of research to accommodate a one-size-fits-all logic is not, in the judgement of some marketers, a satisfactory option (Lovelock and Gummesson, 2004).

As well as losing out on valuable research insights there is always a danger of becoming bound in a scholarly straitjacket over S-DL. By setting out Foundation Premises (FPs) the concept's supporters potentially lock marketers into a single-sighted viewpoint, particularly as there are a number of anomalies in these premises. That S-DL is predicated upon relationships has been noted. Relationship marketing research, however, has indicated that only customers can decide whether or not they want a relationship and/or whether a current relationship exists (Grönroos, 2006). That the customer is sometimes active and sometimes passive challenges the notion (FP6) that the customer is always the co-creator of value because customers are not always anything in particular (Schembri, 2006). In RM research a status of 'non-relationship' is acceptable and termination an option by either party. In S-DL it appears that a relationship is seen to exist whether it is wanted and required or not. Assuming a relationship exists in every exchange is potentially misleading and costly. Lessons from the past suggest that any definition of marketing must allow for both relationships and non-relationships (Grönroos, 2006, p. 329).

Co-creation of value (FP6), although logical to advocate, may also be questioned in other circumstances. Co-creation may be observable for many services (e.g. theatrical performances) but this does not necessarily prove the point. For example, it is easy to see that there are nearly always differences in value outcomes between two people on the same holiday dependent on how they personally responded to their experiences. However, some of the best experiences in life occur serendipitously. Where chance (as an external happening) is the motivator, can co-creation be said to have taken place if circumstances outside of the control of the consumer have determined the experience? If it is not easy to prove for services, it is extremely difficult for goods without reference to considerable poetic license. When considering physical goods the variability of value outcomes may be considerably reduced because of the known benefits (albeit a result of skills and competences) imbedded in them. Contrary to much marketing rhetoric the consumer of goods has limited control on the outcome of their choice (Shankar *et al.*, 2006) and, therefore, has limited power to create value other than what is offered to them. The concept of co-creating value has another theoretical flaw. If we take customer satisfaction as an indication of value creation (Anderson *et al.*, 2008, p. 366) then does dissatisfaction mean the destruction of value and what are the consequences of this for service-dominant logic? Simply broadening the understanding of co-creation (or co-production) to include everything would lead to the loss of many of those goods-specific and service-specific insights gained in earlier research (Stauss, 2005, p. 224).

Other insights that may be lost in the application of S-DL are those peculiar to the industrial or business-to-business (B2B) market, ironically an area that has had so much influence on service research in general and relationship marketing in particular. Under S-DL business-to-business appears to play a secondary role as a series of value propositions operating to and from supplier/customers seeking an equitable exchange (Ballantyne and Varey, 2006, p. 345). Reducing B2B to the provision of operand resources loses much of the insight and colour that prior research has uncovered. Trying to incorporate every aspect of the consumption process inside one service-based paradigm may be a journey too far.

There is also something inherently dangerous in the proposition that the organisation provides nothing other than value propositions (FP7). The implication of this is that any blame for an unsatisfactory outcome is (wholly or partly) the responsibility of the consumer. In abdicating the value creation process in favour of the customer and only accepting responsibility for suggesting what they might achieve as a result of the experience goes a long way to absolving marketers and businesses from any guilt, responsibility or negative consequence of their actions (Shankar *et al.*, 2006).

Another perceived flaw is the claim that the 'time logic of marketing becomes open-ended' with service-dominant logic (Ballantyne and Varey, 2006, p. 336). S-DL sees marketing as having a role at all stages of the consumption process including planning, selection, purchase consumption and disposal (Flint, 2006, p. 350).

Although this allows for environmental claims to be made on its behalf, in reality how many goods manufacturers are involved (or care) about those stages after purchase (beyond trying to sell over-priced warranty agreements)? Even where local legislation insists on recycling (and/or a price levy to pay for it) this rarely envisages it as the responsibility of the original supplier to look after his or her own product disposal. There are a number of products in use where the original company no longer exists (e.g. Rover Cars). Who then assumes this responsibility under S-DL? Some products may pass through several hands over a considerable number of years. Does a company still have an interest in its various exchanges or in its eventual demise?

S-DL, therefore, while being an exciting area for discussion, has a number of flaws which make its generalised application problematical. It does, however, open researchers' eyes to possible new insights.

Conclusions

Relationship marketing research has moved on. There is a place for customer relationship management, social marketing, service-dominant logic and more. However, in the same way that RM did not replace traditional marketing neither should these be seen to have superseded what went before.

Rather than abandon previous ideas (or exclude those that may come in the future) there is a cogent argument for adopting multiple, and sometimes contradictory, paradigms as part of marketing's theoretical armoury. Indeed research on marketing practices suggests most companies use a portfolio of strategies as they seek to differentiate themselves from the crowd. Research by Tollin and Jones (2009) concluded that there was no support for the idea of a single logic in marketing rather they provided evidence of several dominant logics operating at one time. This is what Lowe *et al.* (2004, p. 1062) called '**paradigm crossing**', a notion that involves recognising and working with multiple paradigms, accepting the co-existence of multiple truths and the expectation that these truths may be contradictory. This view would be regarded as dangerous in some quarters, especially those seeking one law-like generalisation for marketing. As Wilkie and Moore (2006, p. 226) have bemoaned 'virtually every research area is now a stream running its own course and there is coming to be no "mainstream" of academic marketing thought any longer'. This comment suggests marketing has lost its way. Rather is this not a reflection of the complexity of marketing and the need for a multiplicity of approaches? Progress in marketing comes from the sharpening of differences between viewpoints and not from abolishing those not currently in vogue (Stauss, 2005).

Summary

In this chapter the developments in relationship marketing research were discussed, in particular the perceived schism between the focused and diffuse thinking regarding relationships. It noted that the use of technology was driving much of this 'diffuse' thinking and that a feature of this is the extension of the term 'relationships' to the non-personal, i.e. technology-driven contact associated with direct marketing and, latterly, customer relationship management.

Customer relationship management was discussed as it is claimed to be philosophically related to RM. However the conclusion reached is that three main differences were evident regarding the complexity of relationships, the centrality of technology and the generalisability of application.

Social marketing was discussed as an important influence on current marketing thought and practice. It was noted that general marketing had potentially much to learn from understanding customer psychology and motivation. It also noted that corporate social marketing was evident where, despite the association with commercial gain, it still fulfils the criterion of improving individual welfare and that of society.

Service-dominant logic was also debated. At the heart of the concept is the understanding that marketing is evolving towards a new dominant service logic, having been subjugated by a goods-dominant agenda for so long. The concept views RM as being a transitional stage and S-DL is the logical conclusion of the transition from goods-dominated thinking. It was suggested, however, that the thinking behind the concept has a number of flaws. Despite this, however, it does offer a new lens with which to develop strategy.

In conclusion the chapter questioned whether rather than assuming one concept, theory or paradigm necessarily replaced another that the notion of 'paradigm crossing' should be recognized. This involves recognising and working with multiple paradigms, accepting the co-existence of multiple truths and the expectation of truths coming from apparently opposite positions.

Discussion questions
1 To what extent do you agree or disagree with Payne (2006, p. 4) that CRM 'unites the potential of new technologies and new marketing thinking to deliver profitable, long-term relationships'?
2 To what extent does social marketing theory contribute to marketing in general?
3 To what extent does service-dominant logic change our perception of value?

Case study   Feature: The perfect touch

Pub chain JD Wetherspoon has two tactics to turn occasional visitors into regulars. Cheap real ale, sourced from brewers endorsed by the Campaign for Real Ale. And clean lavs. It takes both very seriously. In addition to dozens of beer awards, it recently scooped Corporate Provider of the Year at the Loo of the Year Awards. Half of its pubs got a five-star rating, the rest meriting four stars.

'Over the years, we have tried to make our pubs appeal to women, since the presence of both sexes can have a beneficial effect on behaviour,' a spokesman said. 'We invested heavily in this area. Research shows that a high standard of loos, as well as helping the overall ambience of our pubs, is particularly important for women.' As if you need research to tell you that.

Sadly Wetherspoon is ploughing a lonely furrow. Marketers don't spend much time ruminating about latrines. The odour of trough lollies and the oomph of the blowdriers are overshadowed by more glamorous disciplines such as direct mail and database management.

But the modern marketer must be master of many trades. Every aspect of customer interaction must be scrutinised. Each moment of the customer experience must be dissected, analysed and improved. Traditional touchpoints, such as the cashier till, the helpline and staff are only part of the story. Every interface between the customer and the brand is important. If that means adding 'lavatory inspector' to the job description, then so be it.

Piped poetry

Sometimes the most significant touchpoints to consumers are invisible to marketers. It took a spike in demand at broadband supplier TalkTalk for its marketing team to realise how important hold music was for customers. Once they'd identified the touchpoint an improvement swiftly followed and the poet Roger McGough was commissioned to record a dozen readings. Instead of listening to Vivaldi's Four Seasons on loop callers are treated to McGough's greatest hits, such as Bill our Kid, Seagulls, Fame and Neighbourhood Watch.

In the minicab trade the crucial touchpoint is the back seat of the car. Which is why the minicab company formerly known as Blueback, now part of Addison Lee, built fridges into its cabs and offered free newspapers to customers.

At Vue Cinemas, founder Tim Richards believes every touchpoint should be multifaceted, so you can buy your ticket from the popcorn vendor. The benefits are also multifaceted, says Richards: 'It cuts the queues, you need fewer staff on the tills and it has increased our concession income. We now have higher concession sales per head than any other cinema.'

A full list of touchpoints would fill this magazine from cover to cover. Even external factors, such as neighbouring retail outlets and the availability of car parking are valid touchpoints in the minds of consumers. The only way to appreciate how these issues affect your brand is to track the path of the consumer from start to finish – so called 'customer journey mapping'.

In their shoes

You can't do customer journey mapping yourself. Fresh eyes are needed. Denise Pritchard, founder of Total Marketing Network, uses mystery shoppers to provide independent reports for companies interested in learning how the consumer really sees them. 'There are all sorts of hidden ways in which customers interact with brands,' she says. 'The only way to discover these is to live the experience. Mystery shoppers can tell you what the customer journey is really like.' Their testimony is then correlated with other sources of information. 'We gather feedback from focus groups. If you have a dozen people then you can have a good cross-section of opinions. They will give you an honest appraisal of the service you offer, and they will be able to tell you where you are going wrong.'

With reliable data you can start to alter your service to match your brand values. 'First Direct is a great example,' says Pritchard. 'Its brand values include chattiness and friendliness, so the company monitors its telephone operatives to ensure they are chatty and friendly on the phone. They don't leave an important issue like that to chance.'

First Great Western claims to have revolutionised the quality of its service by customer journey mapping. By examining the path customers take to buy a ticket, travel to the station and how they behave while on a train, First Great Western was able to implement improvements including faster ticket machines, at-seat powerpoints for laptops, free children's activity packs during school holidays, 1,700 more car parking spaces, clearer signage and staff with PDAs so they can instantly answer queries. The company even looked beyond the journey, analysing how it could improve integration with the next stage of passenger travel. Feedback is gathered online, on the trains, on the reverse of tickets and through customer representatives.

Nosiness helps

Customer journey mapping will open your eyes to new vistas of customer interaction. You'll start to notice areas of human activity that might never have occurred to you. Take Harrods and its dedication to a crucial touchpoint: nostrils.

With 300,000 customers a day, the store air is at risk of turning stale. So Harrods employs consultants to deliver the perfect smell at all times. The ladies shoe department is laced with the faint smell of vanilla and chocolate, garden living is pungent with freshly cut grass, luxury accessories is pomegranate, and entrances 3, 5 and 10 greet visitors with the musk of lime and basil.

Simon Harrop is the man behind the scents. He is the founder of The Aroma Company, the UK's best known corporate smell consultancy. He says marketers are barmy to overlook smell. 'We did research on marketing spend in the UK and found that 80 per cent was for the eyes alone. This leaves only 20 per cent for other senses. Yet our research shows which senses consumers use in creating a mental picture of brands, and although vision is number one, smell is very close behind at number two.'

He says marketers can use smell to manipulate the subconscious thoughts of consumers. 'The olfactory nerves are directly linked to the limbic system, which is the reptilian part of the brain. This drives the four "Fs" of food, flight, fight and, er, procreation. Sight and sound is processed by the cortex, a mammalian part of the brain. We can screen out and filter visual information. Smell is not filtered. Which is why it has the power to stop you in your tracks.'

Naturally you can't just waft any perfume through your store. 'The smells must be driven by your brand values. It is all too easy to be generic and just create muzak for the nose. We go to the heart of each brand and express its values and personality through an olfactory mood board. It's about perception mapping,' says Harrop.

This is more precise than it sounds. 'We know how fragrances are perceived by consumers. Citrus is universally fresh, alive, clean and bubbly. If one of the brand values a client wanted to express was cleanliness and energy we could use citrus to communicate that value.' Even abstract values can be articulated through smell. 'We had a bank that wanted to communicate courage. A woody note, like oak, will do that. Peppermint can suggest intelligence. If you want to be seen as green and environmentally friendly, you need a grass and ivy aroma.'

Using smell with other senses can magnify the impact. 'Superadditivity means that when you combine one sense with another, say touch with smell, one plus one equals three. There is a synergy.' But delivery of the smells is a science best left to experts. The Aroma Company uses a variety of delivery mechanisms, including squeeze and sniff boards, diffusing boxes and touch release. 'We don't say scratch and sniff, as you don't have to scratch anymore,' says Harrop.

The biggest pitfall is over-fragancing. 'You want a noticeable but light effect,' says Harrop. 'People have a varying degree of acceptance of smell and there are cultural factors to consider. In the Far East they have a high olfactory acuity. In the Middle East they like stronger smells. In the West we are between the two. Broadly, smell should be like a colour scheme – too strong and you'll put people off.'

Band aid

The goal for marketers is to harmonise all touchpoints. This means not just doing 'something' but doing the 'right thing'. Perhaps the biggest field of failure for marketers is music. The extraordinary power of music to influence consumers is well known, but is your tune-smithery producing a brand-aligned effect?

One man who is used to seeing marketers make a mess of it is Rob Wood. As a former editor of music magazine *Jockey Slut* and with 18 years as a professional DJ, Wood is the founder of corporate music consultancy Music Concierge. He says the vanity of marketers when it comes to music is a serious problem. 'It is so easy to get it wrong,' he warns. 'Many marketers think they understand music and put on loud, up-tempo chart hits. If you want to come across as mainstream, that's fine. But if you want your music to match your brand then you need to be more careful. Increasingly, marketers are realising that how you sound is as important as how you look. Being thoughtless will undermine your efforts.'

When the Connaught Hotel undertook a £70m refit it asked Wood to create a new audio identity. He researched the hotel's history, examined the age, origins and preferences of its clientele and talked to the staff.

'We came up with different playlists for different areas of the hotel. The Coburg Bar was redesigned to be a quiet, modern and chic place with its own distinct identity. They could hardly pipe through just any old music to achieve this. We created a playlist perfectly in keeping with the theme of the bar to create a relaxed atmosphere. We know we got it right because guests linger in the bar and 40 per cent of the reviews of the Coburg Bar mention the music.'

While some stores have a CD they use day after day, Wood derides this approach as medieval. 'We deliver our music to the client via broadband. This means we can control the playlist, changing and refreshing it when necessary.' He says that although the Internet might make it easy to deliver the music, it makes it no easier to select the right tunes. 'Our library has been painstakingly built. We have researchers in Berlin and Paris sending us the latest club tunes. And we have a classification that non-experts can't rival. We don't just have "jazz". We have a Swedish jazz category, prohibition jazz, African jazz. And then we handpick.'

This level of attention needs to be brought to every touchpoint. Leaving things to chance, or worse, ignoring touchpoints, will leave the consumer with a highly disjointed experience. This requires marketers to expand their horizons to include commercial factors way beyond the immediate.

'Culturally some marketers seem to have a problem understanding their remit,' says Denise Pritchard of Total Marketing Network. 'They want to focus on the immediate things. Things like how a store smells or whether staff are cheerful is outside their comfort zone. Even worse, other departments might not like marketers poking their nose in. HR think it is their job to manage staff, not marketers'. But that is outdated thinking. Marketers need to look at every area of the customer experience. Nothing is out of bounds.' Not even toilets.

Charles Orton-Jones *The Marketer* **February 2009**

Case study questions

1 What does the author mean by 'customer journey mapping' and why is it recommended that 'fresh eyes' are key to its success.
2 Using a service or product provider with whom you are familiar, analyse the customer 'touch points' and which are most crucial to customer satisfaction.

References

Aitken, R., Ballantyne, D., Osborne, P. and Williams, J. (2006) 'Introduction to the special issue on the service-dominant logic of marketing: insights from the Otago Forum', published proceedings, Otago University.

Anderson, S., Pearo, L.K. and Widener, S.K. (2008) 'Drivers of service satisfaction: linking customer satisfaction to the service concept and customer characteristics', *Journal of Service Research*, **10** (4), 365–81.

Andreasen, A. (2006) *Social Marketing in the 21st Century*. Thousand Oaks, CA: Sage Publications, Inc.

Ballantyne, D. and Varey, R.J. (2006) 'Creating value-in-use through marketing interaction: the exchange logic of relating, communicating and knowing', *Marketing Theory*, **6** (3), 335–48.

Baron, S. and Harris, K. (2006) 'A new dominant logic in marketing: pedagogical logic implications', *The Marketing Review*, 6, 289–300.

Boulding, W., Staelin, R., Ehret, M. and Johnson, W.J. (2005) 'A customer relationship management roadmap: what is known, potential pitfalls, and where to go', *Journal of Marketing*, **69** (October), 155–66.

Buttle, F.B. (1996) *Relationship Marketing Theory and Practice*, London: Paul Chapman Publishing.

Cherington, P.T. (1920) *The Elements of Marketing*. New York, Macmillan.

CIM (2009) 'Less smoke, more fire', *The Marketer*, Cookham, Chartered Institute of Marketing, 45–9.

Day, G.S. and Montgomery, D.B. (1999) 'Charting new directions for marketing', *Journal of Marketing*, **63**, 3–13.

Drummond, J. (2010) 'A brief introduction to corporate social marketing', *Corporate Culture*, <www.forceforgood.com> (accessed 21 July 2010).

Flint, D.J. (2006) 'Innovation, ymbolic interaction and customer valuing: thoughts stemming from a service-dominant logic of marketing', *Marketing Theory*, **6** (3), 349–62.

Grönroos, C. (2006) 'Adopting a service logic for marketing', *Marketing Theory*, **6** (3), 317–33.

Gummesson, E. (1999) *Total Relationship Marketing: Rethinking Marketing Management from 4Ps to 30Rs*, Oxford: Butterworth Heinemann.

Hastings, G. and Saren, M. (2003) 'The critical contribution of social marketing', *Marketing Theory*, **3**, 305–22.

Kelly, S. (2000) 'Analytical CRM: the fusion of data and intelligence', *Interactive Marketing*, **1** (3), 262–7.

Kotler, P. and Levy, S.J. (1969) 'Broadening the concept of marketing', *Journal of Marketing*, **33** (Jan), 10–15.

Kotler, P. and Levy, S.J. (1971) 'Demarketing, yes demarketing', *Harvard Business Review*, **49** (6), 74–80.

Kotler, P. and Zaltman, G. (1971) 'Social marketing: an approach to planned social change', *Journal of Marketing*, **35** (3, 2).

Levy, S.J. (2002) 'Revisiting the marketing domain', *European Journal of Marketing*, **36** (3), 299–304.

Little, E. and Marandi, E. (2003) *Relationship Marketing Management*, London: International Thomson Business Press.

Lovelock, C. and Gummesson, E. (2004) 'Wither services marketing? In search of a new paradigm and fresh perspectives', *Journal of Service Research*, **7** (1), 20–41.

Lowe, S., Carr, A.N. and Thomas, M. (2004) 'Paradigmapping marketing theory', *European Journal of Marketing*, **38** (9/10), 1057–64.

Lusch, R.F. and Vargo, S.L. (2006) 'Service-dominant logic: reactions, reflections and refinements', *Marketing Theory*, **6** (3), 281–8.

McDonald, M. (2000) 'On the right track', *Marketing Business*, April, 28–31.

MacFadyen, L., Stead, M. and Hastings, G. (1999) *A Synopsis of Social Marketing*, Stirling, Stirling University.

Maglio, P.P. and Spohrer, J. (2008) 'Fundamentals of service science', *Journal of the Academy of Marketing Science*, **36**, 18–20.

Möller, K. and Halinnen, A. (2000) 'Relationship marketing theory: its roots and directions', *Journal of Marketing Management*, **16**, 29–54.

O'Malley, L. (2003) 'Relationship marketing', in Hart, S. (ed.) *Marketing Changes*, London: International Thomson Business Press, pp. 125–45.

O'Malley, L. and Tynan, C. (2000) 'Relationship marketing in consumer markets: rhetoric or reality?', *European Journal of Marketing*, **34** (7), 797–815.

Parvatiyar, A. and Sheth, J.N. (2000) 'The domain and conceptual foundations of relationship marketing', in Sheth, J.N. and Parvatiyar, A. (eds) *Handbook of Relationship Marketing*, Thousand Oaks, CA: Sage, pp. 3–38.

Payne, A. (2000) 'Relationship marketing: the UK perspective', in Sheth, J.N. and Parvatiyar, A. (eds) *Handbook of Relationship Marketing*, Thousand Oaks, CA: Sage, pp. 39–67.

Payne, A. (2006) *Handbook of CRM*, Oxford, Butterworth-Heinemann.

Payne, A. and Frow, P. (2005) 'A strategic framework for customer relationship management', *Journal of Marketing*, **69** (October), 167–76.

Ryals, L. (2000) 'Organising for relationship marketing', in Cranfield School of Management, *Marketing Management: A Relationship Marketing Perspective*, Basingstoke: Macmillan, pp. 249–64.

Schembri, S. (2006) 'Rationalizing service logic, or understanding services as experience', *Marketing Theory*, **6** (3), 381–92.

Shankar, A., Whittaker, J. and Fitchett, A. (2006) 'Heaven knows I'm miserable now', *Marketing Theory*, **6**, 485–505.

Sisodia, R.S. and Wolfe, D.B. (2000) 'Information technology', in Sheth, J.N. and Parvatiyar, A. (eds) *Handbook of Relationship Marketing*, Thousand Oaks, CA: Sage, pp. 525–63.

Stauss, B. (2005) 'A pyrrhic victory: the implications of an unlimited broadening of the concept of services', *Managing Service Quality*, **15** (3), 219–29.

Stead, M., Hastings, G. and McDermott, L. (2007) 'The meaning, effectiveness and future of social marketing', *Obesity Reviews*, **8** (1), 189–93.

Stone, M., Woodcock, N. and Starkey, M. (2001) 'Assessing the quality of CRM', *Marketing Business*, July/August, 31–3.

Sussex, P. and Cox, J. (2002) 'Next generation customer relationship management: strategic CRM', Chartered Institute of Marketing Special Interest Group presentation, March.

Tollin, K. and Jones, R. (2009) 'Marketing logics for competitive advantage?', *European Journal of Marketing*, **43** (3/4), 523–50.

Vargo, S.L. (2008) Customer integration and value creation: paradigmatic traps and perspectives, *Journal of Service Research*, **11** (2), 211–15.

Vargo, S.L. and Lusch, R.F. (2004) 'Evolving to a new dominant logic for marketing' *Journal of Marketing*, **67** (1), 1–17.

Vargo, S.L. and Lusch, R.F. (2006a) 'Service-dominant logic: what is it, what it is not, what it might be', in Lusch, R.F. and Vargo, S.L. (eds) *The service-dominant logic of Marketing: Dialogue, Debate, and Directions*, Armonk, NY: M.E. Sharpe, pp. 43–56.

Vargo, S.L. and Lusch, R.F. (2006b) 'Service-dominant logic: continuing the evolution', *Journal of Marketing Science*, **36** (1), 1–10.

Vargo, S.L. and Lusch, R.F. (2006c) 'Service-dominant logic: reactions, reflections and refinements', *Marketing Theory*, **6**, 1–8.

Vargo, S.L. and Lusch, R.F. (2008) 'From goods to service(s): divergences and convergences of logics', *Industrial Marketing Management*, **37** (3), 254–9.

Wiebe, G.D. (1951) 'Merchandising commodities and citizenship on television', *Public Opinion Quarterly*, **15** (4), 679.

Wilkie, W.L. and Moore, E.S. (2006) 'Macromarketing as a pillar of marketing', *Journal of Macromarketing*, **26** (2), 224–32.

Notes

1 As one of the Institute's 1998–2000 research priorities (Day and Montgomery, 1999).
2 Under the heading of 'Campaign for marketing effectiveness'.
3 Source: Gartner.
4 Amazon list 18 titles on their Social Marketing book list.

Glossary

4Cs model of marketing A variation of the 4Ps model considered from the customer perspective thus price becomes cost to customer, place becomes convenience, product becomes customer wants and needs and promotion becomes communication.

4Ps model of marketing The marketing mix consisting of price, product, promotion and placement.

abductive research Reasoning for the purposes of discovery as opposed to the justification of scientific hypotheses or theories.

acquisition/retention cost ratios The ratio between the cost of acquiring a new customer and the cost of retaining one.

affinity partnering/packages A strategy in which the primary goal is to leverage the affinity, goodwill or brand name strength of a partner so as to enhance relational market behaviour. The programmes are known variously as affinity packages, cause-related marketing and other terms.

alliances Where a group or groups of competitors (as opposed to the whole industry) collaborate to achieve cost and efficiency objectives.

B2B marketing business-to-business or industrial marketing.

B2C marketing business-to-consumer marketing.

barriers to exit see *switching costs*.

BCG matrix The Boston Consulting Group Matrix based on market share and market growth.

bilateral relationships Bilateral relationships are those in which both parties are motivated highly enough to invest in a relationship.

bonds The (often invisible) constraints which hold individuals or groups together.

brand image A term used to describe the unique, emotional personality of a brand.

branding The act of differentiating products and services by a name, symbol, trade mark or other characteristic.

brand management model Marketing theory based on the management of the brand through the manipulation of the marketing mix.

business process reengineering (BPR) A management approach that aims at improvements through the increased efficiency and effectiveness of organisational processes.

buyer-maintained relationships Relationships maintained by the buyer who is usually dominant in a relationship.

campaign analysis The measurement of the effectiveness of individual campaigns and media.

cause-related marketing A partnership between an organisation and a charity or cause where the commercial organisation gains positive publicity and the partner gains usually monetarily (also see affinity partnering/packages).

client conversion rate The rate at which prospects are converted into customers.

co-branding A partnership between two distinct brands for mutual benefit.

collaborations The (usually formal) relationships between organisations that they are recognised externally as well as on a company-wide basis.

commitment The implicit or explicit pledge of continuity between relationship partners.

commodity approach An early 20th century school of thought that focused on those marketing actions involved in a particular product category.

communities of practice Networks linked by their behaviour e.g. Buzznet (music and culture).

conjoint analysis The determination of what combination of a limited number of attributes is most influential on respondent choice or decision-making.

cooptition Simultaneous competition and collaboration.

corporate social marketing When companies use marketing principals and practices to motivate their customers to act on social issues in order to achieve commercial benefits.

corporate social responsibility (CSR) A management concept where organisations consider the interests of society by taking responsibility for the impact of their activities on customers, employees, shareholders, communities and the environment in all aspects of their operations.

cost-per-thousand The cost of reaching 1000 target readers, viewers or listeners in a particular media.

critical episode An episode (or incident) that is of great importance to a relationship and upon which the continuation of that relationship is dependent.

cross-selling The encouragement to purchase additional products or services.

customer contact analysis The analysis of any individual customer's contact history.

customer exit When a customer severs the relationship with an organisation.

customer profile analysis An analysis which enables the organisation to distinguish, from the mass of customer data, the individuals as well as the micro-segments.

customer relationship management (CRM) A continuous performance initiative designed to increase a company's knowledge of its customers, to support access across all communications channels and to cut costs.

database marketing (DbM) The use of a database to hold and analyse customer information, thereby helping develop strategic information for marketing.

de-commodifying Differentiating your brand from the competition.

deductive research Argument from general principles to particular conclusions, thus analytical and certain. Deduced, or capable of being deduced, from premises. Deductive research is associated with a 'scientific' view of research.

demarketing Marketing designed to change behaviour (e.g. smoking) that is seen to be harmful either to the individual, the community or the environment.

demographic profiling The profiling of individuals on the basis of their demographic (e.g. age) profile.

digital marketing Marketing using the Internet, mobile telephony and other interactive channels.

direct marketing (DM) Direct marketing (DM) focuses on using a database to communicate (and sometimes distribute) directly to customers so as to attract a direct and measurable response.

discrete exchanges Individual exchanges (i.e. purchases) that are made without reference to any other exchange in the past or on any purchase in the future.

dissolution The termination of a relationship.

distribution management The function associated with distributing products directly or indirectly to the customer.

economic benefit The benefit, in financial terms, of an action or exchange.

economic value See *economic benefit*.

elasticity of demand The flexibility in supply or demand in response to variations in other factors.

empowerment The freedom to make decisions. It looks to the performer of the tasks for solutions to problems, and to these employees to suggest new services and products and to solve problems creatively and effectively.

episode configuration The episode types and number of each type that occur over time in the relationship between a provider and a customer.

FMCG Fast-moving consumer goods.

functional approach An approach to marketing that focuses on the marketing functions (e.g. communication) in isolation from other functions (e.g. human resources) rather than as an overarching organisational philosophy. See *functional silos*.

functional silos Where barriers exist between functions (e.g. marketing and HRM) and little if any coordination exists between them. See *functional approach*.

horizontal relationships The relationship between organisations that are at the same point in the channel of distribution (including competitors) who seek to cooperate and collaborate for mutual benefit.

inductive research Making empirical generalisations (i.e. founded on experience and observation and not theory) by observing particular instances. The conclusions go beyond the facts so they can never be more than strong possibilities. Inductive research is associated with qualitative research methods.

inertia The inclination to do nothing to change the *status quo* unless provoked.

inseparability Products may be produced in one location and sold in another. The production and consumption are, therefore, said to be separable. This is not the case for services, which are produced and consumed at one time and place. This inseparability occurs whether the producer is human (e.g. a doctor) or machine (e.g. an ATM machine).

institutional approach An early approach to marketing that focused on describing the operations of a specialised type of marketing agency, such as a wholesaler or a broker.

intangibility The intangible process characteristics that define services include such factors as reliability, personal care, attentiveness, friendliness etc. These can only be verified once a service has been purchased and 'consumed'.

interdependance The reliance of two companies upon each other.

internal marketing (IM) Any activity within an organisation that focuses staff attention on the internal activities that need to be changed in order to enhance the external marketplace performance and that improve internal communication and customer consciousness among employees.

internal partnerships/relationships The relationship between employees and the organisation.

issue-based communities Specific issues that band people together in a community even if only temporarily.

knowledge management The effective management of the sharing and retention of information in an organisation and the use of management techniques to optimise the acquisition, dissemination, and use of that knowledge.

lifestyle analysis The profiling of customers on the basis of their lifestyles.

lifetime value The value of customers' purchasing over the lifetime of a relationship.

loyalty A definition of loyalty in *behavioural* terms, is based on the number of purchases and measured by monitoring the frequency of such purchases and any brand switching. A definition of loyalty in *attitudinal* terms incorporates consumer preferences and disposition towards brands to determine levels of loyalty.

loyalty marketing A marketing strategy which seeks to encourage repeat behaviour and retain customers.

loyalty schemes A scheme designed to establish a higher level of customer retention in profitable segments by providing increased satisfaction and value to certain customers.

macromarketing school In the 1970s the macromarketing school examined the impact of marketing practices on society and society on marketing.

marketing Traditionally seen as that management process responsible for identifying, anticipating and satisfying customer's profitably. In philosophical terms a holistic approach by an organisation to the needs and wants of the customer and other stakeholders.

marketing orientation Where a business sees the needs of customers and consumers as vital and where they develop and market products or services to meet those demands.

market price The economic value of a product or service on the open market.

market segmentation Identifying specific markets and developing different products and/or services for each segment.

mass customisation Relates to the notion that, by leveraging certain technologies, companies can provide customised products while retaining the economic advantages of mass production.

mass-marketing The broadcasting of messages that will reach the largest number of people possible usually through mediums such as radio, television, newspapers, etc.

mission The attitudes and expectations within an organisation with regard to the business that the organisation is in.

monopoly A long-lasting situation where there is only one provider of a product or service in a particular market.

network-interaction marketing All activities undertaken by the firm to build, maintain and develop customer relationships.

network marketing Marketing through a network of contacts.

networks A series of formal or informal contacts.

non-price competition Competition based upon differential advantages and not price.

not-for-profit marketing Marketing in the not-for-profit (e.g. charities) sector.

oligopoly A market form in which a market or industry is dominated by a small number of suppliers.

one-to-one marketing One-to-one marketing (sometimes written as 1:1 marketing) is a strategy that emphasises personalised interactions with customers.

organisational climate The deep-seated, unwritten system of shared values and norms within an organisation.

organisational culture The policies and practices that characterise an organisation.

paradigm crossing Contrary to the notion of a single 'world-view' this suggests working with multiple paradigms, accepting the co-existence of multiple truths and the expectation that these truths may be contradictory.

partnering B2B partnerships with suppliers and/or customers.

part-time marketers (PTM) All of those employees (excluding full-time marketers) who, in any way, influence customer relations, customer satisfaction and customer perceived quality.

patronage concentration The share of a customer's cash-flow in a certain industry in which the customer chooses to concentrate on one provider.

perceived sacrifice Perceived sacrifices (e.g. price, physical effort etc.) across all service episodes in the relationship compared with some explicit or implicit comparison standard.

perceived service quality Customer's cognitive evaluation of the service across episodes compared with some explicit or implicit comparison standard.

perceived value Service quality compared with perceived sacrifice or cost.

perishability A characteristic of services are they are perishable (i.e. they cannot be stored for sale in the future).

permission marketing Where a marketer seeks permission from the customer to supply data (e.g. sales, updates, etc.), usually on a regular basis.

PEST(L) A pneumonic representing the analysis of political, economic, sociological, technological and sometimes legal factors influencing the organisation.

problem recovery The recovery from a critical situation or incident.

process management perspective (PMP) A PMP approach would see department boundaries broken down and the work-flow (including sales and marketing activities, productive, administrative and distributive activities and a host of 'part-time' marketing activities) organised and managed as a value-creation process.

processs services Where service output is standardised and/or service interaction is replaced by technology.

product life cycle The concept that products have a series of life-stages including the introduction, growth, maturity and decline (or reinvention).

production-led economies Economies dominated by product manufacturing (as opposed to services).

profitability analysis A key CRM application that involves measuring and analysing the many different dimensions of profitability.

prospects Potential customers.

psychological benefit A non-financial, personal benefit (e.g. status).

recency, frequency and monetary value (RFV) model A model used in the direct marketing industry to calculate the value of individual customers.

relationship costs The costs involved in setting up and maintaining relationships.

relationship drivers Those factors which suggest that relationship strategies would benefit the business.

relationship marketing (RM) May be defined as the means by which organisations can 'identify and establish, maintain and enhance and, when necessary, terminate relationships with customers and other stakeholders, at a profit so that the objectives of all parties involved are met; and this is done by mutual exchange and fulfilment of promises.' (Grönroos, 1994, p. 9).

relationship profitability The value outcome from the development of relationships.

relationship revenue The total revenue generated from a customer relationship during a fiscal year.

relationship strength The outcome measured using purchase behaviour and communication behaviour (word of mouth, complaints). The bonds between the customer and the service supplier also affect the behaviour.

resource dependence theory The theory that suggests that few organisations are self-sufficient in critical resources.

retention strategies Strategies that promote the retention of customers.

return on customer See *relationship profitability*.

return on investment (ROI) The percentage return on any investment.

return on relationships (ROR) See *relationship profitability*.

risk The perceived probability of making a loss as interpreted by the decision-maker.

sales analysis The analysis of sales for specific periods and across time.

salience The level of importance or prominence associated with an exchange (i.e. purchase).

scientific marketing management An early (1923) proposal which offered guidance to companies who wish to understand marketing. Used more recently to describe marketing's preoccupation with the manipulation of quantitative data.

scope Associated with an organisation's mission statement scope relates to the attitudes and expectations within the organisation, how the organisation rates against competition and how it fits into its environment.

search engine optimisation A term used to describe those processes and techniques utilised when preparing (or re-examining) a website in order to enhance its chances of being ranked highly by a search engine.

segmentation A group of brands or organisations sharing one or more characteristics that cause them to have similar needs.

seller-maintained relationships Relationships that rely on the seller to sustain them.

service bureaucrats A derogatory term for managers interested simply in systems maintenance and routine adherence to uniform operating guidelines and procedures.

service-dominant logic (S-DL) A theory of marketing developed originally by Vargo and Lusch (2004) that suggests the discipline has moved from a goods-dominant to a service-dominant phase. The ideas are framed in 10 premises upon which the perspective is based.

service encounters In the short-term they are the social occasion of economic exchange in which society allows strangers to interact. In the longer-term they provide the social occasions in which buyer and seller can negotiate and nurture their relationship.

service industries Those businesses where the greater part of the company's central offerings are intangible.

service-led economies Economies dominated by services (as opposed to manufacturing).

services marketing Strategies aimed at the specific needs of service markets.

SMART objectives A pneumonic which reminds us that objectives should be strategic, measurable, actionable, realistic and timely.

social marketing The application of marketing principals and practices with a view to influencing the behaviour of target audiences in order to improve their personal welfare and/or that of society.

social media Websites designed to stimulate personal relationships.

social networking Interaction using social media.

societal marketing Marketing that specifically acknowledges that organisations must respect the community and the environment.

STEP A variation of PEST (L) excluding legal aspects.

sticky demand curve An inelastic (i.e. low response to price change) demand curve.

strategic planning school In the 1970s the strategic planning school explored the relationship between environmental change and change within the organisation.

supplier–customer dyad The understanding that only the supplier/customer relationship is of value to marketers.

supplier withdrawal Where a supplier terminates the relationship with its customer.

switching costs Those costs involved in changing from one supplier or partner to another (e.g. search costs).

SWOT analysis The analysis of the strengths, weaknesses, opportunities and threats of and to an organisation.

toolbox approach The application (and perhaps the simplification) of marketing using models such as the 4Ps.

total quality management (TQM) A management strategy aimed at ensuring awareness of quality in all organisational processes.

transactional marketing (TM) A traditional viewpoint that sees marketing as a decision-making activity designed to satisfy the customer, at a profit, by targeting and making optimal decisions on the various elements of the marketing mix.

trust The confidence in the reliability and integrity of an individual or group.

value theory An area of economic and philosophical thought built upon by early marketers. Value theorists investigated how people value things (positively or negatively), the reasons why they make such evaluations and use consumer choice as evidence of intrinsic value.

values-based communities Neo-tribes where members share values, lifestyles or self images rather than demographic traits, e.g. Harley-Davidson (see Box 3.1).

variability In relation to services there are two dimensions to variability. The amount the production varies from the norm and the extent it needs to be varied to suit the individual customer's needs.

vertical relationships Vertical relationships represent those relationships that integrate all or part of the supply chain through component suppliers, manufacturers and intermediaries.

white and brown goods White goods are large kitchen appliances. Brown goods are typically small household electrical entertainment appliances such as DVD players and televisions.

zone of tolerance (ZOT) That range of service performance where small increases or decreases in performance quality do not lead to any (positive or negative) action.

Index